Across the Great Divide

Studies in Anthropology and History

Studies in Anthropology and History is a series which develops new theoretical perspectives, and combines comparative and ethnographic studies with historical research.

Edited by James Carrier, University of Durham, UK.

Associate editors: Nicholas Thomas, The Australian National University, Canberra and Emiko Ohnuki-Tierney, University of Wisconsin, USA.

VOLUME 1	Structure and Process in a Melanesian Society: Ponam's Progress in the Twentieth Century ACHSAH H. CARRIER AND JAMES G. CARRIER
VOLUME 2	Androgynous Objects: String Bags and Gender in Central New Guinea MAUREEN ANNE MACKENZIE
VOLUME 3	Time and the Work of Anthropology: Critical Essays 1971–1991 JOHANNES FABIAN
VOLUME 4	Colonial Space: Spatiality in the Discourse of German South West Africa, 1884–1915 JOHN NOYES
VOLUME 5	Catastrophe and Creation: The Transformation of an African Culture KAJSA EKHOLM FRIEDMAN
VOLUME 6	Before Social Anthropology: Essays on the History of British Anthropology JAMES URRY
VOLUME 7	The *Ghotul* in Muria Society SIMERAN MAN SINGH GELL
VOLUME 8	Global Culture, Island Identity: Continuity and Change in the Afro-Caribbean Community of Nevis KAREN FOG OLWIG
VOLUME 9	The Return of the Ainu: Cultural Mobilization and the Practice of Ethnicity in Japan KATARINA V. SJÖBERG
VOLUME 10	Tradition and Christianity: The Colonial Transformation of a Solomon Islands Society BEN BURT
VOLUME 11	Recovering the Orient: Artists, Scolars, Appropriations edited by ANTHONY MILNER AND ANDREW GERSTLE

Other titles in the Studies in Anthropology and History series:

VOLUME 12   Women of the Place: *Kastom*, Colonialism and Gender in Vanuatu
   MARGARET JOLLY
VOLUME 13   A History of Curiosity: The Theory of Travel, 1550–1800
   JUSTIN STAGL
VOLUME 14   Exploring Confrontation. Sri Lanka: Politics, Culture and History
   MICHAEL ROBERTS
VOLUME 15   Consumption and Identity
   edited by JONATHAN FRIEDMAN
VOLUME 16   Resplendent Sites, Discordant Voices: Sri Lankans and International Tourism
   MALCOLM CRICK
VOLUME 17   The Rationality of Rural Life: Economic and Cultural Change in Tuscany
   JEFF PRATT
VOLUME 18   The Textual Life of Savants: Ethnography, Iceland, and the Linguistic Turn
   GÍSLI PÁLSSON
VOLUME 19   Narratives of Nation in the South Pacific
   edited by TON OTTO AND NICHOLAS THOMAS
VOLUME 20   Nationalism and Ethnicity in a Hindu Kingdom: The Politics of Culture in Contemporary Nepal
   edited by DAVID GELLNER, JOANNA PFAFF-CZARNECKA AND JOHN WHELPTON
VOLUME 21   Savage Money: The Anthropology and Politics of Commodity Exchange
   C.A. GREGORY
VOLUME 22   A Politics of Presence: Contacts between Missionaries and Waluguru in Late Colonial Tanganyika
   PETER PELS
VOLUME 23   The Magical Body: Power, Fame and Meaning in a Melanesian Society
   RICHARD EVES
VOLUME 24   Across the Great Divide: Journeys in History and Anthropology
   BRONWEN DOUGLAS

This book is part of a series. The publisher will accept continuation orders which may be cancelled at any time and which provide for automatic billing and shipping of each title in the series upon publication. Please write for details.

Bronwen Douglas

Across the Great Divide

Journeys in History and Anthropology

LONDON AND NEW YORK

First published 1998 by OPA (Overseas Publishers Association) N.V.

2 Park Square, Milton Park, Abingdon, Oxon OX14 4RN
605 Third Avenue, New York, NY 10017

Routledge is an imprint of the Taylor & Francis Group, an informa business

First issued in paperback 2022

Copyright © 1998 Taylor & Francis

All rights reserved. No part of this book may be reprinted or reproduced or utilised in any form or by any electronic, mechanical, or other means, now known or hereafter invented, including photocopying and recording, or in any information storage or retrieval system, without permission in writing from the publishers.

Notice:
Product or corporate names may be trademarks or registered trademarks, and are used only for identification and explanation without intent to infringe

Publisher's Note

The publisher has gone to great lengths to ensure the quality of this reprint but points out that some imperfections in the original copies may be apparent.

British Library Cataloguing in Publication Data

Douglas, Bronwen
    Across the Great Divide : journeys in history and anthropology : selected essays, 1979–1994. – (Studies in anthropology and history ; v. 24)
    1. Oceania – History   2. Oceania – Civilization
    I. Title
    990

    ISBN: 978-9-057-02306-4 (hbk)
    ISBN: 978-1-03-234039-5 (pbk)
    DOI: 10.4324/9781315079233
    ISSN: 1055-2464

The illustration on the cover, entitled 'Nieuw Caledoniers', is an aquatint by Portman from a drawing by Kuyper published in Stuart's Dutch humanist treatise *De mensch* [*On man*] (1802–7, II: facing 68). The images were appropriated with considerable licence from Piron's neoclassical representations of Kanak engraved in Labillardière's account of his visit to New Caledonia in 1793. There is thus nothing empirical in the depiction of the woman and the man – though their accoutrements are shown with typical exemplary accuracy. Yet the picture inadvertently condenses ambiguities in ethnographic readings of indigenous gender relations and politics which this book seeks to convey: the woman kneeling in conventional deference beside the warrior may be meant to connote female subservience, but her extended arm tells another tale, of assault barred on an unseen third party. The image resonates with one of the book's theses: that Kanak women exercised significant restraint on male excess and aggression in fighting.

For
Charles, Kirsty and Allie

Contents

	List of Maps and Plates	xi
	List of Tables	xiii
	Acknowledgements	xv
PRELUDE	Now Into Then: Disciplined Encounters	1
PART ONE	**Leadership**	27
ONE	Rank, Power, Authority: A Reassessment of Traditional Leadership in South Pacific Societies	29
TWO	Ritual and Politics: The Inaugural Meeting of High Chiefs in New Caledonia	69
PART TWO	**Fighting**	
FOREWORD	Apologia on Gender	113
THREE	'Almost Constantly at War'? Ethnographic Perspectives on Indigenous Fighting in New Caledonia	123
FOUR	Reading Indigenous Pasts: The 'Wagap Affair' of 1862	159
FIVE	Winning and Losing? Reflections on the War of 1878–79 in New Caledonia	193

PART THREE	**Encountering Christianity**	223
SIX	Autonomous and Controlled Spirits: Indigenous Rituals and Encounters with Christianity in Melanesia	225
SEVEN	Dealing (With) Death in a Melanesian World: Indigenous Aetiologies and the 'Sickness of the Christians'	263
EIGHT	Power, Ritual and the Appropriation of God: Christianity and Subversion in Melanesia	285
FINALE	Whig in the Closet: Past Continuous, Future Perfect?	319
ABBREVIATIONS		323
BIBLIOGRAPHY		325
INDEX		351

List of Maps and Plates

FRONT COVER	'Nieuw Caledoniers' (Stuart 1803: facing 68)	
MAP 1	The South Pacific Ocean	36
MAP 2	New Caledonia, the Loyalty Islands and southern Vanuatu	71
MAP 3	Lifou: The road to Mou	84
MAP 4	Wagap, Touho and the *cèmuhî* language zone	166
PLATE 1	'Natives of the tribes of the chiefs Mango and Kahoua' (Garnier 1868: 41)	174
MAP 5	The Ouraïl district, 1878–79	196

List of Tables

TABLE 1	'Grand Meeting of High Chiefs, Mou–Lösi–Lifou; 17–18–19 December 1982': Timetable and Agenda, Day 1	83
TABLE 2	The play of alliances at Wagap in 1862 according to a contemporary colonial text and later ethnographic and indigenous texts	171
TABLE 3	Apengou/Apitéèngen in administrative and ethnographic texts	177
TABLE 4	Kahoua of Poyes in missionary and official texts, 1856–62, compared to modern ethnographic texts	180
TABLE 5	Kahoua of Poyes in a published, retrospective, non-official text	182

Acknowledgements

Since this book is a cumulative product of an academic life spanning nearly thirty years it is impossible to acknowledge all the persons and institutions whose contributions helped make it. Those not listed should know they are neither forgotten nor unappreciated.

Institutions are easier than people to recall and enumerate because they are relatively few. I am grateful to the Australian National University for providing a doctoral scholarship and funding for fieldwork and archival research. La Trobe University in Melbourne was my professional home for twenty-five years and generously supported my research and conference attendance. I received major research grants from the Australian Research Grants Scheme and the French Ministère DOM-TOM (Ministry of Overseas Departments and Territories) through the Centre national de la recherche scientifique. The staffs of the following libraries and archives gave cheerfully and unstintingly of their expertise, for which I remain enduringly grateful: the National Library of Australia, Mitchell Library, Australian National University and La Trobe University Libraries, Archivio dei Padri Maristi, Archives nationales de France, sections Outre-Mer and Marine, Société historique de la Marine, Archives de l'Archevêché, Archives territoriales de la Nouvelle-Calédonie.

During the 1990s I held three fellowships which provided priceless opportunities for unencumbered reflection, reading, writing and conversation with like spirits. Without them I should have had neither the space, the intellectual wherewithal nor the confidence to retrace the lengthy trajectory of my encounters with History and Anthropology. I am accordingly more grateful than I can say to the Australian National University and Professor Jim Fox of the Department of Anthropology, RSPAS, for the award of a visiting fellowship in the Comparative Austronesian Project in 1991; to the École des Hautes Études en Sciences Sociales in Paris and Alban Bensa for the award of a visiting professorship in 1995; to the Humanities Research Centre of the Australian National University and Professor Iain McCalman for the award of a visiting fellowship in 1996.

My personal debts, both private and professional, are manifold. Generations of undergraduate and graduate students shared my passion for knowing indigenous pasts and many gave as much as they received. Dorothy Shineberg supervised my PhD thesis and is a dear friend with unparalleled command of the historian's craft. Martha Macintyre shared with me and several marvellous groups of students the excitement and challenge of teaching and learning about Gender, Colonialism and Postcolonialism, while her writing brilliantly displays the value and virtue of combining anthropological and historical approaches. John Cashmere and Judith Richards are friends and colleagues to cherish. Greg Dening provides the ongoing inspiration of his writing and gave collegial encouragement and affection when it was needed most. Alban Bensa has long been a supportive friend and colleague, even when he found my English prose impenetrable, and he made me speak and write comprehensible French. Ranajit Guha confirmed that history is indispensable to the recuperation of colonised pasts and shows that passion and rigour can be two sides of a single academic coin. Nicholas Thomas, who amazes by his productivity and the quality of his ideas, suggested that I write this book and encouraged me to make the time to do so by giving up the dubious haven of a tenured teaching position for the exhilarating uncertainty of pure research. Klaus Neumann teased and troubled me to say what I mean and mean what I say. Shelley Mallett understands what I mean and thinks it is important to say it. Margaret Jolly shares my somewhat arcane obsessions, while her unstinting efforts on behalf of Gender and Pacific Studies and those who sail in them have helped keep them afloat.

My debts to friends in New Caledonia for their hospitality, patience and advice are too numerous to mention in detail, but the Bouarate family of Hienghène, Charles Haudra, Marie-Claire Beboko-Beccalossi, Winny Xenié, Helen Brinon, Bess Flores and Helen Fraser deserve particular thanks. In an effort to reciprocate something of what I received from Kanak people I set up the Melanesian Students' Language Program at La Trobe University, to provide English language scholarships for Melanesian students. The more than thirty persons who participated in the Program over thirteen years also gave much of themselves and kept me in contact with their homeland, for which I remain grateful. Those students included two of the three Kanak friends, martyred in the cause of Kanak independence, for whom I offer this volume as a memorial: Eloi Machoro, warrior and war leader; Jean-Marie Tjibaou, priest, orator, statesman; Yeiwéné Yeiwéné, his loyal and ironic deputy. They shall not grow old.

My greatest and most enduring debt is to my family. My mother, Jean Craig, slaved to give me an education and, if she never entirely grasped what I was doing, was nonetheless immensely proud. My husband Charles shared this journey from the beginning and we were joined along the way by our daughters Kirsty and Allie. I thank them for their love, patience, intelligent criticism and unfailing humour. This book is for them.

Most of the chapters contain some material which has been previously published in articles and book chapters.

Chapter One is an annotated revision of (1979) Rank, Power, Authority: A Reassessment of Traditional Leadership in South Pacific Societies, *Journal of Pacific History* 14: 2–27.

Chapter Two is an abridged, updated and annotated revision of (1985) Ritual and Politics in the Inaugural Meeting of High Chiefs from New Caledonia and the Loyalty Islands, *Social Analysis* 18: 60–84.

Chapter Three contains some material published in (1990) 'Almost Constantly at War'? An Ethnographic Perspective on Fighting in New Caledonia, *Journal of Pacific History* 25: 22–46.

Chapter Four contains material written originally in French and published in (1996) L'histoire face à l'anthropologie: le passé colonial indigène revisité, *Genèses* 23: 125–44.

Chapter Five is a revision of (1991) Winning and Losing? Reflections on the War of 1878–79 in New Caledonia, *Journal of Pacific History* 26: 213–33.

Chapter Six contains material published in (1989) Autonomous and Controlled Spirits: Traditional Ritual and Early Interpretations of Christianity on Tanna, Aneityum and the Isle of Pines in Comparative Perspective, *Journal of the Polynesian Society* 98: 7–48.

Chapter Seven is an abridged version of (1994) Discourses on Death in a Melanesian World, in D. Merwick (ed.), *Dangerous Liaisons: Essays in Honour of Greg Dening*, Melbourne University History Monographs 19, History Department, University of Melbourne, Parkville, Vic., 353–78.

Chapter Eight is an abridged version of (1995) Power, Discourse and the Appropriation of God: Christianity and Subversion in a Melanesian Context, *History and Anthropology* 9: 57–92.

I thank the following publishers for permission to reprint material to which they hold the copyright in the listed articles and chapters: the JOURNAL OF PACIFIC HISTORY INC.; the Department of Anthropology, University of Adelaide; Editions Belin; the Polynesian Society (Inc.); the Department of History, University of Melbourne; Harwood Academic Publishers.

I thank the National Library of Australia for permission to reproduce the plate on the front cover and the Cartography Unit of the Australian National University for preparing the maps.

Prelude

Now Into Then: Disciplined Encounters

For much of my academic life parenthood and teaching have induced staccato writing habits more apt to essay than monograph production. But my taste for the vignette is also a matter of preference in style and genre, while obsession for detail and a tendency to convolution make relatively small chunks of prose easier to produce and digest. Almost every article I wrote attained the size and complexity of a small book until confined to decent proportions through partition or ruthless pruning. The current publishing vogue for collected essays over monographs is something of a godsend, especially as I tend to produce clusters of related papers addressing particular themes.

This collection combines three such themes: indigenous Pacific leadership; fighting in New Caledonia; encounters with Christianity in Island Melanesia. The clusters are internally coherent but linked by recurrent theoretical and methodological concerns: to denaturalise conventional categorical boundaries, anchor abstractions and mediate oppositions; to explore ways of knowing indigenous pasts and identifying indigenous agency through critical readings of colonial texts.[1] In a mix of previously published, more or less radically reworked, and new pieces, the essays rehearse a changing intellectual praxis over more than two decades. They trace an historian's fruitful, often ambivalent engagements with History and Anthropology,[2] anticipating or paralleling experiments in each discipline with the other's concepts, methods or perspectives.

"ISLAND-CENTRED" EMPIRIC

My history is the idiosyncratic product of a radical egalitarian political commitment and an eclectic intellectual genealogy and formation. Antiracism only became a component of my radicalism in early adulthood, since I grew up in a generation of urban white Australians to whom Aborigines were all but invisible. Consciousness of racial prejudice and injustice as inseparable from colonialism dawned gradually in the context of the Aboriginal struggle for equal rights and citizenship in the 1960s and early scholarly encounters with colonialism in the Pacific.

As an undergraduate in Adelaide I must have been entertained by the anti-objectivism of Collingwood's *Idea of History*, since I heavily underlined passages insisting that history is a present process inseparable from the historian and "the here-and-now", that "the past"—since "it does not now exist"—is a creation of "the historical imagination", and that "all historical thinking" is reflective—"thinking about the act of thinking" (1961: 242, 248, 307). Such "idealism" did not go down well in Canberra, where I was subsequently trained in a severely empiricist, anti-imperialist school of Pacific history which had emerged at the Australian National University in the decolonising aftermath of World War II. Counterpart to indigenised African and Asian history, though with far less local professional involvement, it was one of those couplings of emancipatory politics and an entrenched ontological theory of knowledge that attained orthodox status in postwar social and colonial historiography. History was still positivist—conceived as a finite body of truth about the fixed real past contained transparently in documents and accessible via a tried and tested canon—but with subjects and audience democratised. The Canberra school was known for its signature "island-centred" method, which privileged Islanders' actions, experience and initiatives over the policies, doings and control of the colonisers, and claimed to know the Islanders' point of view (Davidson, 1966; Gunson, 1992a; Maude, 1971).

In some anticolonial, postcolonial and feminist demonology, such historians are variously charged with ethnocentrism, sexism, élitism, intellectual imperialism, and the hidden agenda of dissociating "us" from the sins of colonising ancestors while displacing blame to the victims of colonial oppression, "Westernisation", and their "fatal impact". The latter is an apt indictment of reactionary racists who hypocritically recolonise the idea of indigenous agency to serve an ideology of unfettered hyper-individualism. I prefer, though, to historicise my immediate disciplinary ancestors and earlier self as naïve empiricists writing in less ironic, seemingly more certain times than to repudiate us as closet colonial apologists. While our well-intentioned emancipatory projects did unreflectively universalise selective "Western" criteria of secular rationality, subjectivity, political propriety, and gender/class relations (Thomas, 1990b),[3] they also foregrounded Islanders and denounced a range of equally "Western" inequalities, inequities and iniquities. Traces of this early schooling persist in my adherence to an inductive logic and were later reconstituted as a hedged conception of indigenous and other subaltern agency.

ETHNOGRAPHIC ENCOUNTERS

"Island-centred" historians shared a utilitarian relationship with ethnographers of the then ahistoric structural–functionalist mainstream of Anglo-Australasian Anthropology. Scholars in both disciplines routinely prefaced their theses and monographs with first chapters based on information milked from the other, but rarely engaged with the other's perspectives or concepts. Historians wrote synopses of "their" Islanders' "traditional society" as base lines for narratives of "culture contacts" and "culture change", but systematically conceptualised neither "culture" nor "change"; anthropologists sketched the "historical background" seen to have culminated in the village "society" they invented in their timeless formal ethnographies, but otherwise elided the colonial encompassment of villagers which enabled and sustained their own fieldwork.[4]

At La Trobe University in the 1970s reflection on concepts and methods was taken for granted. It was mostly inspired by the resident "Melbourne Group" of ethnographic historians,[5] sometimes called "action-oriented" because they rooted their histories in contemporaneous descriptions of what past actors did (Philipp, 1983). Their Geertz-inspired semiotic notion of culture provided a dose of relativism and reflexivity to qualify the universalising secular humanism or radicalism with which well-meaning historians habitually efface difference (because to acknowledge it might be taken to imply belief in primitive irrationality). By so doing they ethnocentrically assimilate people in other places and times to their own liberal/radical, rationalist logic. The personal influence of the "Melbourne Group" endures in my conviction that traces of actions inscribed in contemporary[6] texts provide crucial, if often drastically distorted images of past indigenous worlds; in a partiality for thick historical narrative distilled from total textual immersion; in an allergy to hegemonic History's teleological conceptions of causation.

CHANGING AGENDAS

In the late 1970s I was provoked to a more systematic engagement with anthropology by a growing sense, shared with La Trobe colleagues trained in African and Pacific oral history (Spear, 1981; Stephen, 1977), that it was not enough to take for granted the "island-centred" empiricist canon of social change as internally motored rather than externally imposed; that we needed to theorise change as an inherent human and cultural potential. There was irony in this turn to anthropology for dynamic sociocultural models, given the timeless essentialism of the ethnographic present tense and the reification of systems in Anthropology's dominant structuralist and functionalist modes: they were, however, under serious attack from within the discipline. I was initially quite taken by Geertzian hermeneutics and seized for a while on his suggestion for a "more dynamic"—and historical—"functionalist approach" drawing on the argument that "some of the primary driving forces in change" were to be found in the "more or less radical discontinuities" between "culture" and "social system" (1975: 142–6). The sharp differentiation of ideas and action entailed in this formulation was conceptually neat, but hardly clarified their entanglement in the garbled textual residue of actual situations in the past.

Equally unhappy with a narrow idealism as with the utilitarian materialism of History's dominant empiricist and Marxist strains, I tried to imagine a theoretical dynamic located in the mutual implication of ideas, ideologies and practices in lived human experience.[7] I experimented with the varied practice-oriented dialectics of Barth, Bateson, Bourdieu, Jackson (1978), Meillassoux, Moore (1975), Sahlins (1976) and especially Turner (1967, 1974a, 1974b). Running through this theoretical and political smorgasbord was the theme of rejection or qualification of a rigid focus on formal structure, a resolve to make space for action as something more than the encompassed minor term in a binary opposition, without thereby merely swapping the tyranny of structure for the equally arbitrary anarchy of untrammelled freedom.

The relationship of structure and action, temporally situated, was an important, if untheorised thread in my 1979 synoptic article on south Pacific leadership—Chapter One of this collection. Its main drift was to dispute the *a priori* typification of indigenous Oceanic leadership as either "Polynesian" or "Melanesian" in favour of historically precise correlation of the ideology and practice of leadership in particular social settings. In line with the prevailing academic conceit of objectivity and distanced impartiality, I carefully camouflaged the antiracist, anti-evolutionist passion which fuelled my rejection of the Polynesia/Melanesia dichotomy by framing it as a detailed falsification of certain egregious deductive presumptions on which the classification rested—a not unworthy, but still objectivist enterprise. I was so allergic to racist agendas that I would neither impute them to anthropologists nor risk invoking them myself: I hardly mentioned the term "race" and rejected the opportunity to override the established racial/cultural divide by bracketing hereditary chieftainship with *Austronesian language*, rather than with Polynesian race/culture,[8] because to do so invited equally racist or evolutionist reifications, to the ongoing detriment of non-Austronesian speakers in Melanesia.

In gnawing intermittently at the problem over three decades, I have come to see it as *politically* and *methodologically* important to historicise and deconstruct longstanding "Western" (and Polynesian) assumptions that Polynesians are superior to Melanesians (and

Australian Aborigines) because they are aesthetically more pleasing to an ethnocentric or racist eye, and because their social organisation, customs and demeanour seem more familiar and "advanced" (Douglas, 1993, in press b).[9] Morally, such a critical strategy decentres and disavows repugnantly racist colonial tropes which would otherwise be left unchallenged or reinscribed through negation. Pragmatically, its systematic textual critique enables a more knowing, thorough and effective ethnohistorical colonisation and exploitation of texts which would otherwise be discarded as disgusting or resorted to piecemeal as unproblematic "sources" of "evidence". I used to tend to skip abhorrent physical descriptions and classifications of Melanesians in nineteenth century texts, while still citing decontextualised anecdotes and opinions culled from the same texts where they concurred with my own arguments. For instance, my ethnohistories of New Caledonia often invoked the ethnographic authority of the naval doctor Patouillet, a perceptive, relativist contemporary observer who set out to fill a "gap" in "Caledonian ethnography" by means of systematic fieldwork: "to break little by little with European customs and take on those of the natives" (1873: v).[10] In making detailed notes of this book in the late 1960s I all but elided a section entitled "Anthropology—size and colours" (1873: 66–72), because I could not stomach the casual racism of the physical discriminations—though they were hardly invidious for the era and genre of text, being limited to empirical description of "the external conformation of the *canaque* race" by an author who claimed "to do only ethnography" and "forego [physical] anthropology". Yet principled recourse to such texts for ethnohistorical purposes requires radical, integrated critique of the entire text in the light of both the author's idiosyncratic presumptions and the prevailing discourses on human similarities and differences which framed the questions, techniques, concepts and vocabulary he or she shared or disputed with an anticipated audience.

Learning how to read and exploit racially odious language and primitivist tropes in judicious critical fashion was hard enough, but it was even harder to learn to be reflexive about it: to acknowledge the personal political stake that part of my outrage at the hierarchical opposition Polynesia:Melanesia was at the misrepresentation and devaluation of "my" Melanesians (and indigenous Australians) in favour of more widely preferred natives. Like many radicals, I was romantically attracted to consensual aspects of Melanesian and Aboriginal social arrangements, to the extent at times, perhaps, of understating violence and inequalities of gender and status (Jolly, 1987; Thomas, 1989b). I maintain, however, that although this reverse prejudice was potentially essentialist and objectivist, it was neither racist nor hierarchical: framed in neither physical nor evolutionary terms, it subverted rather than inverted prevailing hierarchies of preference and value. Unrecognised bias is the bane of all analysis, but the positivist anodyne that bias can be banished by objectivity is a chimera. Reflexively acknowledged and problematised, the discursive conventions and epistemological/political/aesthetic partialities which shape our questions, readings and evaluations—like my leaning to reciprocities and mediation over hierarchies and polarities—are key elements in informed critique, as demonstrated in Chapter Four.

Even before 1979 I had taken oblique, purely substantive issue with the hoary but still potent ethnological trope that attributed innovation or putative evolutionary advance in "Melanesian" New Caledonia to "Polynesian" initiative (1970: 190–6). In Chapter One, muted criticism became an untheorised empirical refrain as I disputed the assumed homogeneity and discursive primacy of Polynesia in opposition to its devalued Melanesian reflex. Specifically, I displaced geographical proximity and discarded racial identity/difference/essence as *a priori* criteria for classification, in favour of contextually appropriate bracketing of reported practices. Theoretically the method implied interrogation and strategic fracturing of reified totalities, categorical boundaries and subject positions, with antennae alert to more fluid, pragmatic, contextual juxtapositions (Strathern, 1991: esp. 31–40, 51–5), but it remained empirical and inchoate for some time.[11] I eventually developed the technique in essays published in 1989 and 1993 (see also 1996b). The 1989 article—ancestor of Chapter Six—queried naturalised assumptions about the homogeneity and causal primacy of geographical/cultural regions with respect to indigenous aetiologies, and of denominational affiliations with respect to missionaries' personal demeanour and proselytising strategies. In 1993 I returned to the general theme of classifying Pacific Islanders, noting its ironic postcolonial complication in that "Melanesia" has joined "Polynesia" as a positive token in modern Islanders' regional identity politics (Lini, 1982; Narokobi, 1980). While granting the descriptive aptness of "Polynesia" in historical, linguistic and geographical terms, I took issue with "Melanesia" historically, as a semantically racist colonial device for negatively categorising hundreds of cultures with no more necessarily in common than they had with cultures elsewhere in Oceania.

DEDUCTIVE DETOURS

From the 1980s many anthropologists, sensitive to accusations of essentialism, primitivism and Orientalism, have embraced history evangelically, acknowledging that the discrete, pristine "traditional" societies of anthropological romance were always actually encompassed within colonial and other world systems. Simultaneously, social and cultural historians have borrowed conceptual repertoires from anthropology.[12] Yet their respective perspectives on the past continue to differ significantly. Anthropologists' classic analytic movement from ethnographic present to motivating past may be deplored by historians as unwitting presentism, in ostensible contrast to their own concentration on the past for its own sake and classic linear shift from prior cause to later effect. In practice, this seemingly innocent empiricism often belies historians' pre-identification of "effects" to fit the teleology of narrative closure and present interests (White, 1987: chs 1–2, 217). Both tend to universalise the present, but differently: anthropologists may anachronistically essentialise unbroken cultural continuity from precontact past to ethnographic present; historians may ethnocentrically project present morality or utilitarian, rationalist, notions of common sense as if they applied everywhere and always. Both, then, may be less than alert to the ways in which present concerns and positions can inflect evaluations of the past as cause of later designated outcomes.

Anthropology's quickening drift during the 1980s to action, process and real time nonetheless made it more, perhaps deceptively, familiar and congenial to an historian. My own methodological centre of gravity underwent a convergent shift, and for a while I jettisoned empirical historical rectitude for a brief flirtation with deductive reasoning. Again the problem was change, the goal to theorise an indigenous sociocultural dynamic equally applicable to both prehistoric and historical eras. It was a tall order, still not adequately filled, though its urgency has been deflected by the naturalisation of change as a given in much recent social thinking.

At the time, for a Pacific specialist already interested in the structure:action nexus, Sahlins' (1981a) intoxicating, historicised blend of Boas, Leslie White's cultural evolutionism, Saussurean structural linguistics and Bourdieu's *habitus* was the obvious theoretical resort. For a New Caledonian specialist, Leenhardt's Christian evolutionist phenomenology (1930, 1947), relational and cognitive in emphasis, was the obvious resource for a processual model of indigenous Kanak culture[13]—though his allergy to premature theoretical closure and his concrete, mediatory stance relative to classic dichotomies made his work an uneasy partner to Sahlins' structuralism (Clifford, 1982).[14] I brought them together in a 1982 article, not included here, which reinvented Leenhardt's speculation about changing conceptual modes in New Caledonia as Sahlins' cultural structure, and located it in broadly etched political settings as a case study in how a culture's logic might inform its transformation in novel action contexts, before as well as after European contact. The argument was somewhat stretched, partly because of overdependence on Leenhardt's sketchy symbolic and linguistic data and possibly dubious logic, but also because Sahlins' model promised more precision than it delivered: a tendency to self-fulfilling prophecy limited its value in teasing out the complexities and ambiguities of actual colonial encounters and their distorting but copious documentary traces. For Sahlins at this stage "action" was an abstract category, a system of relations, rather than the plural, contextualised performances of past actors which transfix historians. This was so of much modern anthropological theory, though not of the anthropology of experience and performance, to which I should turn shortly for inspiration, nor of the later Sahlins, who admitted some actors' interests and instrumental intentions to his structured conjunctures of culture and action—but only male aristocrats seen as causally potent personifications of a larger structure (1985, 1991).

Dissatisfied with the arbitrariness of this blend of grand theory and synoptic history and energised by a short return to the field in New Caledonia, where I attended the first general meeting of high chiefs in December 1982, I opted for a fairly trendy mix of anthropological theory and reflexive ethnography. The result, first published in 1985, is Chapter Two of this collection. Since it seemed critical to mediate the conceptual divorce of ideology and practice, I narrowed my focus from culture in general to ritual and its performative potential to transform by normalising innovations and defusing conflicts. The result was intellectually exhilarating, even if the theoretical concoction borrowed from Turner, Moore, Myerhoff, Kapferer and Langer was perhaps too strong a brew for the contrived ritualisation of the mundane in a modern political gathering. The paper was an early instance of scholarly attention to the "invention of tradition"—a recent hallmark of historical anthropology—though I only read Hobsbawm and Ranger's eponymous work (1983) and Keesing and Tonkinson's seminal collection on the politics of *kastom* in Melanesia (1982) while doing final revisions.

I had, though, read Boon's *Other Tribes, Other Scribes* (1982) and Clifford's iconoclastic "On Ethnographic Authority" (1983), as well as manuscript versions of two papers by Keesing (1985, 1987). They had introduced me to the paradigm-rattling notion that Anthropology's signature reification of culture as homogeneous, shared, systematic and enduring—a major stumbling block to theorising change, despite Sahlins—was the "hypercoherent", essentialist product of anthropologists playing at "cultural theologian", or of unadmitted collusion between ethnographic exoticism and a privileged, probably male indigenous perspective (Keesing, 1985: 202; Ortner, 1984: 144; Crick, 1982). "Cultural construction" and "invention of tradition" were conceptual corollaries of this discursive shift, as "culture" and "custom" were recuperated from a fixed, immemorial past to the status of labile tokens in all too present politics of identity (Jolly, 1992; Keesing, 1989a; Linnekin, 1992). Strategic implications of the shift included self-reflexivity and foregrounding the necessarily dialogic nature of ethnography. Concurrently antipositivist historians, notably Dening (1991) in Pacific historiography, were arguing, as Collingwood had, for the present embeddedness of histories, reconfigured as motivated re-*pres*entations of contested, plural pasts.

I remember losing a small editorial battle with an anthropology journal over my reluctance to include the required potted evocation of "the traditional society" in the original version of Chapter Two. The early pluralist encounters which inspired this anti-essentialist scrupulosity were sketched in a review article (1984)—the first of several papers in which, roaming the once lonely but increasingly legitimate spaces between History and Anthropology, I explored their emergent synergy (1992a, 1992b, 1996a, 1996b). This article was cast as friendly critique of the "Melbourne Group" of ethnographic historians and some of the anthropologists with whose ideas I had thus far engaged most. It was *conceptualising* concern about essentialism, rather than the concern itself, which was relatively novel in my work: even in earlier empirical mode (see Chapter One) I had deployed tenses deliberately, eschewing ethnographic and historical presents and strategically resorting to past tenses to signal the temporal locatedness both of anthropological and historical writings, and of the indigenous societies they described.

The review article bore substantively on New Caledonia, since I used a critical comparison of the works of Leenhardt and Bensa—past and present *doyens* of ethnographers of the Kanak—to ponder ironies, ambiguities and paradoxes in Anthropology's discursive shift to history, reflexivity and a pluralist, constructionist conception of culture. There are also national disciplinary differences to which I was then inadequately sensitive. Bensa acknowledges and has recently written reflectively about the need to be historical (1996). Yet unlike his more polemical pieces, his formal ethnographies lack that dimension (1990; Bensa and Rivierre, 1982, 1988; cf. Bensa, 1995). When he does write explicitly about the past it is often in essentialised, normative exegeses of indigenous oral histories, with little of the conventional discipline's chronological focus on particular past people, places and events, or of anthropological history's eye for the praxis of indigenous structural transformations. Like Leenhardt, Bensa stresses process over formal structure, but in markedly different fashion. Leenhardt's interest—evolutionist, rather than historical—was in the dialectics of the transformation of mythic, participatory patterns of indigenous thought and personhood in contexts of progressive individuation and the supposed emergence of a political sphere distinct from the affective domain of kinship (1930, 1947; Douglas, 1982). Bensa seeks to chart an internal dynamic in Kanak society, motored by the interplay of ideologically stable rank hierarchies with intensely competitive, fluid patterns of political practice. In so doing he has contributed important case studies to the anthropological literature on relationships between ideology and action, "action" here being an abstraction from ethnographic observation of indigenous behaviour.

Dialogue with indigenous interlocutors is a watchword in recent radical critique on the politics of ethnography, and in this respect Leenhardt and Bensa score well, since both privileged vernacular texts. But whereas Leenhardt repeatedly invoked the dialogic negotiations and translations of meanings on which his ethnographies rested, Bensa's authoritative, objective ethnographic voice—still the norm in French Anthropology—tends to mute those of the "Melanesian friends and informants" with whom he works (Bensa and Rivierre, 1982: 16). In this respect Bensa largely conforms to his discipline's pretensions to science and its strictures against authorial presence. In other respects he is an iconoclast, notably in espousing an anti-exoticism resonant with the burgeoning anglophone anthropological literature on the politics of indigenous identity and tradition—though his professed justification is rationalist, rather than the emancipatory commitment which fuels his practical politics. In these terms, Leenhardt was for Bensa a Christian primitivist, a politically myopic purveyor of a "fixed, traditionalist conception" of Kanak society (Bensa and Bourdieu, 1985: 76). Whereas Leenhardt reified culture as "lived myth" and sketched an idealised, normative model of social relations in which action, politics and violence hardly featured, Bensa reduces culture to politics by focussing on the strategic, instrumental use of oral texts in intense customary political competition. He thereby supplies an action dimension absent from Leenhardt's works, while tending still to homogenise and essentialise "the Kanak". Limitations notwithstanding—or perhaps partly because of them—Leenhardt's relatively early ethnography is invaluable, not only to anthropological historians of New Caledonia, but to Kanak seeking to define a distinctively indigenous identity and cultural style, and doing so, like people generally do, in unabashedly essentialist and oppositional terms (Tjibaou, 1976, 1981).

I ended the 1984 review article with Boon's plea for "a pluralistic system" (1982: 20–1). Differently appreciative of both Leenhardt and Bensa, I endorsed the historian's licence to be eclectic: "to ponder and plunder" all manner of texts, including ethnographies, providing they are systematically historicised and contextualised. These days, despite undiminished admiration for Bensa's anthropology, which I continue gratefully to plunder (see Chapter Four), I admit to a degree of exasperation with his residual essentialism and reluctance to be reflexive in print: to foreground the politics of his ethnographic knowing and representation, to relinquish the ontological safety net given by the separation of knowledge as object from knowing subject—to square his professional practice with his politics. But this complaint anticipates matters by several years. Then I had just begun to dabble in the risky waters of reflexivity and cultural construction, as when writing the ethnography reinscribed here as Chapter Two. But I was still some time from systematically interrogating my *historical* readings and representations, or from following through the narrative implications of a pluralist conception of cultures as contested, multiple and mutable: Chapters Three and Six retain strategic echoes of the holistic concept of culture deployed in their ancestral articles, both of which were infected by the trope of undifferentiated, enduring cultural essence when I tried to imagine present resonances of indigenous pasts. In any case, it is always easier to pontificate about such matters than to implement them. The violence which erupted over *l'indépendance kanak* while I was in the field in New Caledonia at the end of 1984 brought into brutal relief the present ambiguities of the past and the ludicrous inadequacy of theory or History's affectation of objectivity when real life involves the death and mutilation of friends and acquaintances. I exorcised some of the pain and professional frustration by writing a short, explicitly political piece on "Political Murder" for a Marxist journal (1985a). But ingrained habits were more tenacious when it came to writing about fighting for a conventional academic audience.

AUTHOR(IS)ING HISTORIES

I had been writing an ethnographic history of indigenous fighting in New Caledonia for some time, but the project went into recurrent abeyance while I indulged in theoretical and ethnographic experiment and became a peripheral observer of a civil war. All this convinced me of the historian's need to ensure that the confident authority of theory does not overburden the fleeting, often furtive textual traces of past actions it is intended to explicate. I gradually worked out that my epistemology, politics, personality and aesthetics require theory to be recast as method, apriority to be stringently interrogated, and the enigmas of continuity in change to be tackled via multifaceted working conceptions of indigenous agency and strategic appropriation of the novel, rather than high-level theoretical abstraction.

As I re-immersed myself in contemporary colonial texts—with a more discerning, ethnographic eye for intimate detail—I was increasingly exercised by the need to clarify the processes of textual inscription, reading and writing whereby the texted traces of past indigenous actions might be identified, deciphered in discursive, cultural and strategic contexts, and reworked into open-ended narratives which eschew outcome-driven causation and privilege agency over systems. In my purist "island-centred" phase I had unproblematically "sourced" my "evidence" in "documents" written by Europeans, yet had resisted as ethnocentric the blinding logic of Dening's early insight that "there *is* no history beyond the frontier, free of the contact that makes it" (1980: 42–3, orig. emphasis), that "natives" cannot be known outside their engagements with literate "strangers": because the recording, discovery and archiving of the debris of native pasts were artefacts of encounters with strangers for whom such collecting betokened identity, and because accessible indigenous histories, spoken or written, are always produced in post-encounter presents. I eventually admitted that doing ethnohistory presupposes doing a kind of decentred colonial history. The generic term does not position Europeans as pivotal in local conception, experience and action, but rather denotes that colonial texts are crucial resources to be exploited in writing histories about Islanders and their exotic encounters; to exploit such texts effectively and honestly one must know the authors and the discourses which partly shaped them. Decentring and problematising colonial texts makes space for identifying the imprint of indigenous agency and presence in their content and tropes (see Chapter Four). At another remove, decentring Europe with respect to its putative colonial peripheries sharpens sensitivity to the myriad, subtle ways in which colonial narratives, memories and precedents helped shape metropolitan discourses and imperial identities (Douglas in press b; Smith, 1960; Stoler, 1995).

From the mid 1980s I began publicly to endorse an antipositivist conception of knowledge as knowing—constructed, contingent, present and political—and argued as its ethnohistorical corollary that an historian's nearest access to the multiple realities of past indigenous actors is in the traces of their actions, what they did and said, inscribed in contemporary colonial texts. There was a defensive edge to this formulation, a defiant privileging of archival history—my particular bent, but under assault as oldfashioned and colonial—over oral, which I find intrusive and presumptuous in the absence of vernacular expertise. I allowed that the intimate cultural signatures of indigenous histories and the richer sociology of later ethnographies provide crucial keys to "read" and "translate" the sparse, texted traces of past indigenous actions, treated as cultural symbols with a public language of expression and communication, but that their salience to the past could not be taken for granted. Contemporary texts were thereby reconfigured from transparent repositories of a finite number of inert objects—"facts"—which can be slotted together to reveal the past as it really was, to idiosyncratic, discursive products of engaged human perception, conception and communication, which might serve as lenses on indigenous pasts (1989: 8; 1992a: 87, 91).

For several years I regularly used the metaphor of contemporary texts as "lenses" on past worlds—narrow and distorting, but often all there was. The tacit realism of this trope bespoke a blind spot in my professed antipositivism: an unwitting reluctance to problematise fully the ontological anchor of the "reality effect" (Barthes, 1967: 74), that presumption of an objective, fixed real past which is the bottom line of most of our history-making, existential, popular and academic. My struggle to reconcile empirical practice with anti-objectivist principle was evident in this oxymoronic aphorism in a 1989 seminar paper: "'the past' is a mental artefact, 'known' through the lens of a multitude of 'present' perspectives". I still wrote in quasi-objective empirical mode, if grudgingly, when compelled by editorial fiat, as in the ancestral version of Chapter Three (1990) and the 1991 original of Chapter Five. But my monograph on fighting bogged down in detail and eventually stalled on the paradox that if the believed-in real past is always a present construction, what is the point or propriety of historical narratives, which are purportedly "about" the past?

I began thinking through the paradox as a visiting fellow in Anthropology at the Australian National University in 1991, when I read widely about historical method, critique and philosophy, complementing the historically informed anthropological iconoclasms of Fabian, Rosaldo and Taussig, and Jackson's radical empiricism (1989). I re-read Collingwood, discovered Barthes, Chartier, Guha and White, and began to appreciate Foucault. It came to me in what I now recall as a blinding flash, after an uncomfortable seminar being grilled about relativism, reality and truth, that I agreed with Collingwood (1961: 243–5): that the believed-in real pasts of quotidian and scholarly experience are our own present mental templates—contextual, labile, but powerfully realistic—against which we test our histories for accuracy and authenticity. To argue thus is not to conflate history and fiction, which may share a narrative form but differ in content: fiction's content is imaginary, history's ought actually to have occurred (White, 1978: ch. 1; Greenblatt, 1991: 23). Nor is it to deny the multiple, contested, ephemeral realities of the human beings who lived and imagined them in the past. Rather it is to acknowledge that the past has gone and is present only as "relic", the "present sign of a dead thing" (Barthes, 1967: 74), in traces of past presents more or less randomly inscribed in "texts": written or spoken words, memories, gestures, dress, decorations, objects, buildings, landscapes, visual images.

Thus the deceptive, realist metaphor of contemporary texts as lenses on pasts is displaced by a metaphor of all texts as vehicles for representations. An epistemology which conceives knowledge as discursively constructed rather than ontologically given, renouncing History's claim to objectivity and mimetic realism, makes texts, and their politics of representation and reception, irreducible components in narrative construction. Such an epistemology is apparently deeply threatening to much conventional History, which holds tenaciously to the absurdities of the "'chastity of History'"—no apparent narrator—and the "referential illusion", the historian's claim to leave "the referent"—the unitary real past—"to speak for itself" (Barthes, 1967: 69, 74–5). Though frustrated by this politics and its policing, and long inclined to seek conceptual inspiration outside the discipline, I nonetheless retain strategic allegiance to some of the bread and butter of inductive historical method, refusing to exchange the ambiguities and paradoxes of a highly qualified, plural realism for the comfortable haven of pure textualism, in the sense of a focus on texts for their own sake. My project thus remains representational, in that I deploy texts to a quasi-realist narrative end: to tell stories by assembling images out of words which most appropriately describe, label and classify the past actions and worlds conceived through reading texts—see especially Chapter Five and Part Three. Narrative is thus a representational strategy, in the spirit of White's distinction between narration and narrativisation, between "a historical discourse that narrates and a discourse that narrativizes, between a discourse that openly adopts a perspective that looks out on the world and reports it and a discourse that feigns to make the world speak itself and speak itself as a story" (1987: 2).

Postcolonial positions

It remains easier to talk about antipositivism in the abstract than to practise consistently its pragmatic corollaries: reflexivity and explicit focus on the politics of representation and narrative construction. There are always tensions between the antithetical demands of narrative realism, textualisation and reflexivity, which exponentially complicate both the enunciation and the reading of historical narratives. Such narratives are rendered at once less accessible, because language and structure necessarily become more complex, and closer to the perils of solipsism and sententiousness. These stylistic hazards concern me more than the moral spectres of false histories and nihilistic relativism that antipositivism raises for opponents and sceptics. Philosophically, antipositivism does not inherently encourage or legitimate shoddy scholarship or obnoxious politics, though positivism's logical refusal of the need for self-critique may well do so. False histories and odious politics are best exposed via radical critique of the discourses and the criteria of selection and evaluation on which they rest, rather than reinscribed oppositionally by equally fundamentalist truth claims. Reflexivity—readiness to scrutinise one's own epistemology and morality as partial, perspectival and political, albeit conscientiously held—is the best defence against uncontrolled relativism, because to be reflexive requires more, rather than less, honesty and rigour. It does not mean that all positions are equally apt, scrupulous, ethical, or credible.

I returned to La Trobe University in 1992 to plan and teach courses on "Gender, Colonialism and Postcolonialism" with Martha Macintyre and on "The Politics of Indigenous Identity", during which I systematically encountered feminist anthropology and postcolonial histories and critiques.[15] They provided a metaphor—reading against the grain—for how to recognise, decode and explicit the specific and systemic prejudices, distortions, elisions, silences, ambivalences and incongruities of colonial texts. They confirmed my sense that rigorous critical histories are empowered, not vitiated, by reflexivity and renunication of History's objectivist fictions. They dared me to argue that between the moral absolutes of fundamentalism, the moral camouflage of objectivism and the moral abrogation of ultrarelativism there are ambiguous, existential middle grounds, negotiable pragmatically while picking a precarious way between assertion of personal and humanist values and allowance for contextual and cultural relativities.

I label—unemphatically—this congeries of sensibilities as "postcolonial", meaning not the absurdity that there are no more colonised people, but a mind-set appropriate to an era in which colonialism is widely invested with negative moral valence, so that it can no longer be taken for granted as inevitable and proper. "Postcoloniality" gave me courage to realign from a reactive antipositivism to a more optimistic pluralism: to listen to multiple voices, including muffled, discordant and uncomfortable ones; to recognise oral and other local representations of indigenous pasts as partial, like all representations, rather than dissemble or be defensive about my own partial positions; to celebrate honest partiality as difference—potentially useful, interesting or exciting—rather than deplore it as error or contradiction, requiring objective refutation or resolution.

From my academic infancy a libertarian commitment fuelled outrage at the pervasive, dehumanising "Western" representations of "primitive" worlds as fragile, hermetic culture machines, doomed to destruction, along with their helpless native cogs, before the advance of inexorable colonialism/modernity. Not only are these self-confirming images anathema to the "island-centred" creed I had absorbed so readily, but they did no justice to the pragmatic resilience and vitality of village communities in New Caledonia, where colonisation was on-going and hardly benign. In pre-*Orientalism* days, I was scarcely aware of the embedded, discursive quality of the ethnocentrism and racism informing "civilised" primitivisms, whether well-meaning or malevolent, and their shared, core trope of the "fatal impact"; but it seemed wrong to depict human beings as passive, vacuous objects of abstract or external causal forces—historical, structural, psychological, material, economic, ecological, divine, or whatever.

I avoided causal questions—there are none in my doctoral thesis—long before thinking through a sense of unease at the extent to which the social sciences are in thrall to outcomes: to the urge to reinvent the past as cause of a later present, teleologically designated as effect, and to telescope backwards in time later assumed outcomes taken as inevitable, such as "colonial conquest", "cultural destruction", "underdevelopment". Teleology looks like a widespread human propensity and is intrinsic to all Judaeo-Christian and Whig varieties of history. It is an occupational hazard for historically-minded anthropologists, given the compelling immediacy of the ethnographic present it is their purpose to explain. Causal thinking may be a human given, but it does not have to be unwitting or anachronistic; to reflect on it is to disarm teleology by restoring to past presents a modest approximation of their myriad latent contemporary possibilities. Rejecting outcome-driven history is one index of my philosophical inclination to see actors, including women, as intending subjects, rather than mired or subsumed in the abstract causality of much conventional historiography, radical as well as conservative. I do not intend thereby to argue for unrestrained individual subjectivity, but to challenge the academic hegemony of hierarchical oppositions—structure : action, society : individual, determinism : freedom—in which the human terms in the binary pairs are encompassed as mindless effects of their reified antitheses.

The intellectual, political and aesthetic "journey" sketched in this Prelude begins with a naïvely libertarian "island-centred" image of Islander initiatives and endogenous social change, partly detached from colonial existential and textual trappings (1970, 1972, 1979, 1980a). I pause briefly with the abstract notion of "action" as the systemic reflex of structure, and their dialectic as the site for a sociocultural dynamic (Chapter One, 1982). I tarry longer over the idea that past "actions" performed strategically by "actors" are symbolic artefacts which may leave decipherable traces in colonial and other texts (Chapters Two, Three, Five, Six, 1994b). I am still moving towards a systematically theorised, politically and textually embedded concept of indigenous, including female, "agency" and "appropriation" (Part Two—Foreword, Chapters Four, Seven, Eight, in press a, in press b). The intent to depict actors as exercising circumscribed agency is scarcely unproblematic, but here is not the place to tackle the thorny, contested questions about personhood and subjectivity which loom large in recent anthropological, postcolonial and feminist literature (e.g., Spivak, 1988 cf. Ram, 1993; Mohanty, 1992; Moore, 1994; Scott, 1991; Strathern, 1988).[16] In my formulation "agency" embraces and transcends "action" to include actors' desires and volition. It does not imply a bounded, autonomous, modernist subject, but refers to a general human capacity for action, choice, self-representation and deployment of strategies, always historicised in terms of circumstantial and structural possibilities and constraints.

Exploring varieties of indigenous agency—located culturally, situationally and with reference to the uneven domination of particular colonial régimes—can illuminate the multiple, unstable ways in which "Western" ideas and institutions are reconfigured in the process of appropriation and naturalisation. Just as "agency" is not code for untrammelled individual subjectivity—an oppositional reflex of the Eurocentric trope of the passive native victim—so "appropriation" is not invoked in simple inversion of the usual ethnocentric equation of linear imposition by colonisers on colonised. I certainly do celebrate creative indigenous reception, but argue further that colonial impact—even hegemony, in the Gramscian sense of internalisation by the dominated of dominant evaluations and structures—is inescapably inflected in indigenous practice and experience by contested local logics, values and relationships, which crucially impinge even when the colonised seek most earnestly to reinvent themselves in the supposedly desired image: "the game", remarked Chartier, "was always two way" (1989: 172).

Chapter Four expounds and exemplifies a method—critical reading and juxtaposition of contemporary texts, indigenous histories and ethnographies—through which past indigenous agency might be identified and narrated. Part Three applies the method to construct narratives of strategic indigenous engagements with and appropriations of Christianity. These chapters creatively dislodge and take advantage of the unwitting, ethnocentric presumptions of nineteenth century missionaries; they also call into tacit question the unthinking ethnocentrism of modern Western secularism, including that of academics, including myself.

EPILOGUE

I have always been pedantic about selection and deployment of words, tenses, grammar and syntax, but lately, influenced by Barthes and Guha, I have been gripped by the critical, if subliminal importance of the politics of language in the wider politics of representation, as explored in Chapter Four, the most recent of these essays. My own linguistic rules of thumb are metonyms for some of the major themes traced in this Prelude: an interest in precisely situated human strategies, choices and actions over monolithic structures and forces; in change and variety over enduring, homogeneous essences. I pluralise on principle, prefer indefinite to definite articles, use tenses strategically and choose active grammatical forms, like gerunds and continuous tenses, instead of abstract substantives and the passive voice. Linguistic choices, both deliberate and inadvertent, intimate an entire epistemology, a sociology, an ethics, an aesthetics, a politics. Consider the world of difference between "experiencing", the gerund—implying something one does or is contextually—and "experience", the noun—implying an autonomous, external something that happens to one or that one has. Little words do speak to whole semantics, just as minutiae of human actions and experiencing in unimportant places, remote in time and space, may speak to matters of far wider, even universal moment.

Irreducible though its use is, language can at best reductively approximate the subtleties and ambiguities of experiencing. Mobilised synoptically with a view to closure, words obliterate even the counterfeit complexity achieved in discourse—it is hard to conclude without banality. My banal conclusion is that in the fitful personal trajectory I have imagined, from unreflective empiricism to empirically grounded pluralism, there are two major crosscurrents. There is an undertow of political consistency in the shifts from "island-centred" history/internal change, to action, to actions and actors, to agency/appropriation. There is a sea-change in narrative strategy, from mimetic realism and objective falsification to qualified realisms, reflexivity and the politics of representation, from the historian's pretence that the past is speaking for itself to a threatened glut of authoring. At a metalevel, these things are what the stories in this book are about.

NOTES

[1] "Texts"—written, made, performed, spoken, remembered—are vehicles for representations. "Colonial text" is shorthand for all kinds of "texts" produced about indigenous people by Europeans and their affiliates from first contacts until decolonisation, though in practice I discriminate finely between eras, genres and media. Most such texts were ideologically "colonial", in that their authors sought to "possess"—symbolically and intellectually, if not actually—exploit, transform or control indigenous people. In practice, "colonial" intentions, both informal and formal, were variously and ambiguously realised, if at all.

[2] I capitalise these terms when referring to the formal academic disciplines of History and Anthropology.

[3] In a generally sympathetic critique of "the historical literature" on Polynesian chiefs, the anthropologist Marcus deemed it "still history from the European point of view", despite "focusing on indigenous actions and interests", because it "is not sufficiently sensitive to the distinctively indigenous worlds inhabited by these chiefly personalities" (1989: 197).

[4] For example, the first chapter of my doctoral thesis on culture contact in New Caledonia is entitled "The Society", by which I meant "pre-contact". It summarises information culled from twentieth century professional ethnographies, correlated *post hoc* with references to earlier ethnographies by missionaries and naval medical personnel (1972: 1–38). Of a dozen modern Pacific ethnographies selected at random from my library, ten start with brief summaries of historical (=colonial) background.

[5] So called by Geertz (1990). The leading figures are Clendinnen, Dening and Isaac. Dening (1980, 1992, 1995) has been a particular inspiration.

[6] "Contemporary" means contemporaneous to the actions described.

[7] A key moment in this journey was a conference paper (1980b: 4–5) in which I defined "culture" à la Geertz as "shared patterns of meanings,... syntheses produced by the dialectical interaction of ideas and of ideas and social practice, external and environmental factors", but continued: "On the level of ideas... there operates an internal dynamic which can encompass outside influences.... Through the processes of interpreting and explaining new things, new practices and new concepts, both existing and newly introduced ideas are modified, resulting ultimately in fresh synthesis". These days I'd bridle at both the holism of the culture concept professed and the idealism which divided ideas from practice while privileging the former—as, indeed, did several historian colleagues at the time. The passage is interesting for its foretaste of Sahlins' theoretically far more sophisticated explorations of the dynamics of the conjunction of cultural structure and action (1981a, 1981b, 1985).

[8] At some stage while preparing the article I annotated the map of "Places, Peoples, Cults and Languages" in my copy of the *Papua New Guinea Resource Atlas* (Ford, 1974: 55) with a colour-coded correlation of "hereditary chieftainship" with AN (Austronesian) and NAN (non-Austronesian) languages, but in the published version I refused to specify an AN/chiefs connection. The linguist Pawley (1982: 46-7) and the anthropologist Scaglion had no such scruples, the latter arguing bluntly that "hierarchy, and consequently 'chiefs,' are primarily Austronesian characteristics and concerns" (1996: 2; cf. Standish, 1978; Young, 1994: 274). In a concern parallel to mine, Abramson (1989) noted that "in contrast to a now expanded and—supposedly—uniform 'Polynesia'... the old region of Melanesia has shrunk [to Papua New Guinea]..., but its structurally irreducible diffuseness remains conceptually crucial".

[9] The insidious, *a priori* logic of racial (and class) differentiation was evident in a passage in one of my favourite early ethnographies of New Caledonia, by the naval surgeon Rochas. The "regularity" or "nobility" he perceived in the facial features of some "aristocratic" indigenous men "would be reckoned handsome in every country of Europe" and indicated "foreign blood" specifically the presence of "two very distinct races", "Polynesian" and "Melanesian". Their "mixture" had produced a hybrid populace much more "beautiful" than its "Melanesian" neighbours, but less so than "the yellow race". Rochas yoked prejudice to local traditions of "Polynesian emigrations" to confirm his rhetorical sequence and the imaginative reconfiguration of these legendary Polynesians into a "conquering race" who had "imposed their laws and language" on the "primitive" Melanesian population (1862: 114-15, 123-5).

[10] Throughout this book all translations of texts originally written in French are mine, except where otherwise indicated.

[11] In this vein I called in 1980 for a "multifaceted approach" to the study of violent conflict in colonial societies; it should be acutely sensitive to change, variety, place and period, and, by abandoning the conventional Eurocentric dichotomisation of "resistance" and "collaboration", enable indigenous and anticolonial clashes "to be integrated within a common interpretive framework" (1980: 25, 51).

[12] On intersections of anthropology and history in the Pacific see Barker and Jorgensen, 1996; Biersack, 1991; Carrier, 1992; Douglas, 1984, 1992b, 1996b; Gewertz and Schieffelin, 1985; Jolly and Mosko, 1994.

[13] I use the term "Kanak" (invariable in person and number) out of respect for the majority of the indigenous people of "New Caledonia" who now so style themselves.

[14] From the late 1970s there was a sharp revival of anglophone scholarly interest in the work of the Protestant missionary turned ethnologist Leenhardt (e.g., Douglas, 1984; Dubinskas and Traweek, 1984; Young, 1983a), evinced by the

publication of an English translation of *Do kamo* (1979) and by Clifford's biography (1982), which celebrated anticipations of postmodernity—or at least antistructuralism—in his work.

15 I was especially attracted to the postcolonial positions of Chakrabarty, Diaz, Guha, Mani, Mohanty, Prakash, Said, Stoler and Thomas, as propounded in works listed in the bibliography.

16 I address this theme in a forthcoming book entitled *Postcolonial Histories: Narrating Colonial Encounters in Oceania*.

Part One

Leadership

Like many of my generation, I enacted libertarian politics mainly in the arena of anti-war activism. Yet from the outset my intellectual interests looked at odds with these existential commitments. I wrote my Honours thesis on military leadership in World War II, a topic which might be seen to have yoked the Historical truism of great men to great power politics by other means: but it was the human face of war which moved and appalled me and many of my best "sources" were novels. My shift to the Pacific and "culture contact" was respectably radical, given the strongly anticolonial stance of "island-centred" history, but old concerns insidiously resurfaced: indigenous "leadership" and "war" were for years my main thematic foci. It was, however, great man history and military history tarred with a very social and demotic brush. My enduring concern with respect to leadership is popular constraints on constituted authority and strategies for containing or evading power. The heroes of my histories were opponents or manipulators of colonialism. Restraint, reciprocity and peacemaking are as salient in my histories of fighting as are violence and aggression.

CHAPTER ONE

Rank, Power, Authority: A Reassessment of Traditional Leadership in South Pacific Societies[1]

FOREWORD

This chapter was first published in 1979 in a special issue of the Journal of Pacific History *(14: 2–27), which I initiated after convening a colloquium on the theme of south Pacific Islands leadership. The article first brought my work to anthropological attention by interrogating key elements of received wisdom about Oceanic societies: their a priori distribution into "Polynesian" and "Melanesian" cultural/racial types, differentially located in a social evolutionary hierarchy and characterised by the opposed leadership modes of hereditary chieftainship and achieved bigmanship. That it could do so while hardly mentioning race, evolution or gender—failing to historicise the racialisation of human difference in the Pacific and innocently reinscribing the profoundly gendered standpoints of most colonial, academic and indigenous discourses—now seems remarkable, but was in keeping with contemporary criteria of scholarly objectivity and gender neutrality (cf. Clark and Terrell, 1978: 294–300; Douglas, in press b; Hau'ofa, 1975: 285; Jolly, 1987; Thomas, 1989b). While it is apt to historicise the article and signal certain shortcomings, it is also fair to emphasise its strengths, especially its anticipation—pragmatic and empirical, without explicit reflective or theoretical design—of positions which would become canonical in "post-Orientalist" anthropology from the mid 1980s: anti-essentialism; factoring in history, colonialism and change; mediating oppositions via an optic on similarities as well as differences; problematising reified categories and categorical boundaries.*

That the argument struck sensitive anthropological nerves showed in the responses it evoked and in the numerous congruent surveys and critiques which appeared at about that time and since, of which I list only a small sample (Allen, 1984; Chowning, 1979; Godelier, 1982: 253–90; Hau'ofa, 1981: 291–3; Jolly, 1987; Jolly and Mosko, 1994; Marcus, 1989; Pawley, 1982; Scaglion, 1996; Standish, 1978; Thomas, 1989b). These days the positivist urge to reconstruct "traditional" indigenous systems as a kind of stable, uniform, hermetic departure point for changes wrought by colonialism and modernity has thankfully faded, an unlamented casualty of Anthropology's paradigmatic shift away from structure, determinism, essence and stasis to action, agency, cultural construction and process, and of Islanders' strategic, present concerns to repossess and re-identify themselves and their pasts. It is perhaps unsurprising that a recent collection of essays on Pacific leadership focusses on "chiefs"—that is, "customary" leaders—"today", and that its contributors make little or no systematic differentiation of "Melanesian" leadership from other Pacific "types", except as historical tokens of past discourses (White and Lindstrom, 1997).

In the two decades since I wrote the article academic interest in Pacific Islands leadership has persisted, becoming in general theoretically more sophisticated, and ethnographically better grounded in Polynesia. Scholarly visions of Oceania still cleave along de facto regional lines, but boundaries are significantly altered and more fluid. Few professional anthropologists would these days insist on the primacy or integrity of the Melanesia/Polynesia divide, though amateur anthropology and some general histories are another matter (Campbell, 1989: 24–7; Luders, 1996: 292–5). What has long been archaeological and linguistic orthodoxy—that "Melanesia" and "Micronesia" are "outdated", "largely unhelpful" categories, while "Polynesia" is only salient to relatively recent prehistory (Green, 1989: 35; Clark and Terrel, 1978; Pawley, 1982 Spriggs, 1984)—has permeated anthropological consciousness to the extent that the Melanesian : Polynesian dichotomy is largely discredited as an evolutionary trajectory and categorical opposition of racial or cultural types. In its place as a basis for classification and comparison, decided mostly by the pragmatics of anthropological interest, ethnographic accessibility and regional geopolitics, is a loose cultural/linguistic/ political/circumstantial differentiation of Austronesian societies—with a Polynesia +Fiji "core"—from Papua New Guinea— with a Highlands "core" (e.g., Mosko, 1992: 697; Thomas, 1992c: 925). In these schemata island Melanesia, coastal and insular Papua New Guinea and Irian Jaya generally remain marginal.

Concerning leadership specifically, there have been related but partly divergent emphases (Marcus, 1989: 178): one ethnographic and tending to flatten or correlate significant regional differences; the other historically reconstructive and explicitly theoretical in regionally distinctive fashion, but with a bridging common interest in indigenous conceptions of personhood and gender (Strathern, 1988; White and Kirkpatrick, 1985). It is now widely acknowledged that effective political leadership everywhere was and is likely to involve specific blends of genealogy, kinship, force(fulness), competition and success (Otto, 1994: 223, 234–5). Though highlands ethnography often retains an oddly archaic, essentialist focus on classic anthropological themes like kinship and exchange (but cf. Warry, 1987), recent ethnographic perspectives on Oceania commonly invoke or imply broad similarities in leadership exercised in small-scale agricultural communities grappling with dilemmas of identity, custom and modernity—either as disadvantaged indigenous minorities in postcapitalist former settler colonies, or at the grassroots of new states politically and economically marginal to global systems. In the former, indigenous affairs bureaucracies and in the latter, national/provincial politics and bureaucracies supply novel leadership contexts articulating significant global commonalities with local idiosyncrasies. Notable are the continued, if altered salience of chieftainship in Fiji, Tonga and Samoa and its (re)invention as tradition in Vanuatu and the Solomon Islands (Feinberg and Watson-Gegeo, 1996; Linnekin, 1985; Marcus, 1978; van Meijl, 1994; Warry, 1987; White and Lindstrom, 1997).

Historical reconstruction of ancient Polynesian polities has retained its intellectual allure, but profited from a productive interplay of history and anthropology. Historians such as Dening (1980, 1995) and Thomas (1986, 1990a) complemented the empirical precision of predecessors like Newbury, Gilson and Gunson with theoretically informed sensitivity to indigenous cultures and concepts. Sahlins, who had earlier historicised functionalism by recasting social structure in evolutionist terms (1958, 1963), revolutionised historical anthropology by reconfiguring cultural structures as history, enacted and transformed in culturally specific variations on a common Polynesian/Fijian theory of kingship (1981a, 1985, 1991; Hooper and Huntsman, 1985). Gunson, who had pioneered painstaking empirical identification of significant elements of charismatic and female power in ancient Tahitian polity (1962, 1964; see also Rogers, 1977), did further important comparative work along these lines (1979, 1987, 1992b), in the process contesting hegemonic official versions of Polynesian histories. Such official histories derived from partial complexes of genealogy and myth which had been normalised as immemorial, proper and real by winners' coalitions of mostly male chiefs with European missionaries, administrators and anthropologists, all variously intent on marginalising and controlling disorderly rival, demotic and female elements. Thomas brought a more systematically theoretical and reflective gaze to bear on shamanism (1990a, 1992b, 1994b), thereby instancing a growing scholarly interest in the dialectics of what Marcus (1989: 176–81) called "the kingly side and the populist side" of Polynesian chieftainship; such a focus, Marcus thought, had the potential to mediate reconstructionist and ethnographic perspectives, while effectively collapsing Sahlins' categorical distinction of chief and big man and the conventional polarity of Melanesia and Polynesia.

  Since 1980 theoretical and ethnographic studies of leadership in Papua New Guinea and island Melanesia have alike been dominated by the trope of inequality (Helliwell, 1994; Jolly, 1987), a far cry from the naïve conception of egalitarianism which informed cruder versions of the big man stereotype. Scholarship on inequality in the highlands, though, was typically hermetic, as anthropologists (from the perspective of "their" particular societies) hypothesised likely transformational trajectories which might account for perceived varieties of leadership in terms largely internal to the region. Exchange, gender and personhood were the conceptual axes of a rich ethnographic and ethnological literature, increasingly focussed on Godelier's "great men", how they might have become "big men", and whether they were best conceived not as autonomous, bounded, rugged individuals, but as Marilyn Strathern's "*partible persons*"—*shifting relational composites*, "*more than atomistic individuals but less than subscribers to a holistic community of shared meanings*" (1991: 53; Feil, 1987; Godelier, 1982; Godelier and M. Strathern, 1991; A. Strathern, 1982; M. Strathern, 1988). There was some reflection that the complexity of highlands and other Melanesian exchange systems might match that of the elaborate rank and political hierarchies in Polynesia (Douglas, 1993: 18; Green, 1989).

By contrast, the recent anthropology of leadership in coastal and insular Papua New Guinea and island Melanesia has generally been framed in terms of hierarchy, variously enabled, contested and constrained, and increasingly in terms of the politics of tradition (Allen 1984; Feinberg and Watson-Gegeo, 1996; Jolly and Mosko, 1994; Lindstrom and White, 1997). Some imported Sahlins' "divine king", or at least his heroic, socially-encompassing "social-historical individual" (Lutkehaus, 1990; Sahlins, 1985, 1991); others characterised the big man as a "relational" (= "partible") person, rather than an individual (Clay, 1992). Mosko (1992) explored the salience of both divine king and partible person to a coastal Papuan hereditary hierarchy and decided that Strathern's concept, de-essentialised from its highlands parochialism, was not only more apt to the Mekeo, but might also better elucidate Polynesia than did Sahlins'. My sense, predictably, is that a bit of both is in order: that incorporation and decomposition are culturally—and historically—configured human propensities, that the partible person may be a culturally and historically resonant analogue of decentred, relational poststructuralist and feminist conceptions of the person, which are themselves culturally and historically specific, and to which, as Moore points out, anthropology has been surprisingly resistant (1994: 28–70; Davies, 1991; Scott, 1991).

Since the article from which this chapter derives is itself a discursively embedded historical artefact, I resisted the at times compelling temptation to make more than cosmetic changes, though I have modernised geopolitical nomenclature and added internal headings to aid conformity across the collection. I have updated some references, though not systematically, and in the interests of economy and readability have sharply abridged the ultradetailed original documentation, which now has a somewhat archaic flavour. Anyone interested in the *compulsive breadth of my reading and the contemporary incidence of the theme of leadership in anthropological literature on the Pacific Islands may consult the original article. Throughout this book I have pared references to a minimum in every chapter for which detailed documentation is available in an earlier version. In this and the next chapter, both of which are to some extent period pieces, I footnote a few "editorial" comments and clarifications.*

PROLOGUE

Although leadership has been an important focus of sociopolitical investigation in particular Pacific societies and in Polynesia generally, there have been few attempts to produce general or theoretical analyses on a Pacific-wide basis. Those few depicted two stereotypes: one Polynesian and based on hereditary rank (ascribed status) in a context of social hierarchy; the other Melanesian and based on achieved status in a context of egalitarianism and competition. The most influential was that of Sahlins (1963) whose two "abstracted sociological types" of political leadership, each characteristic of one of "two contrasting cultural provinces" into which he divided the southern and eastern Pacific, represented "the extremes of... [a] continuum, the western Melanesian underdevelopment against the greater Polynesian chiefdoms" (1963: 285–6; Valentine, 1963).

Methodological objections to this approach are obvious. Prescriptive regional generalisations have been made on the basis of individual cases considered, *a priori*, to be typical of either "Polynesia" or "Melanesia". Generalisations so formed tend to be parochial and too dependent on the specific case. Thus Sahlins' typification of the Melanesian big man was overly reliant on Oliver's (1955) examination of Siwai (Bougainville) leadership. A more serious weakness stems from the *a priori* categorisation of south Pacific leadership systems as either Polynesian or Melanesian. Accordingly, hereditary leadership in New Caledonia and Fiji became "political approximations of the Polynesian condition", "aboriginally transitional between Melanesia and Polynesia" (Sahlins, 1963: 286; Valentine, 1963: 27). One might as aptly so designate Maori leadership, which in many respects resembled the Fijian and New Caledonian systems more than those of the "greater Polynesian chiefdoms" (Hawai'i, Tonga and Tahiti), on which Sahlins based his Polynesian political type. In terms of the Polynesian/Melanesian dichotomy, however, the leadership systems of New Caledonia and Fiji were annoying exceptions. To preserve the classification one had either to attribute their "peculiarities" to Polynesian influence, or even subsume them within Polynesia (Sahlins, 1963: 286;

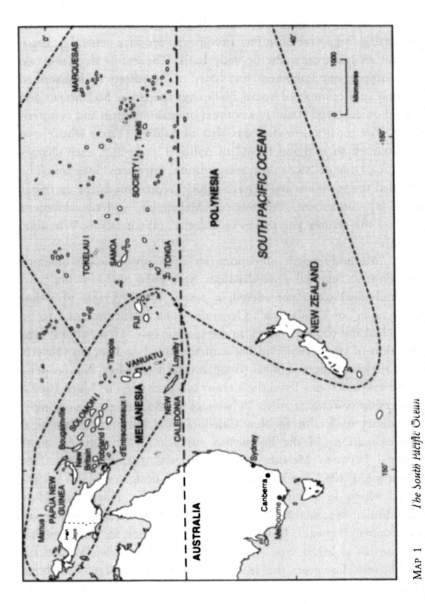

MAP 1   The South Pacific Ocean

Valentine, 1963: 9, 10, 27, 46, 47–50). The less stratified forms of hereditary leadership commonly found in coastal areas elsewhere in Melanesia were still more embarrassing and were either ignored or excused as "clearly exceptional" "bumps in the geographical gradient" (Sahlins, 1963: 286, 294; Valentine, 1963: 8–9, 26, 47).*

There are two other major weaknesses in the conventional approach:# though explicitly evolutionist, it is effectively a static model which telescopes particular histories into outcomes preordained as

---

* *I think now that I let Sahlins off lightly (cf. Hau'ofa, 1975; Thomas, 1989b). While he admitted an element of caricature, his partialities were manifest and invidious: "Melanesian societies broke off [political] advance...at more rudimentary levels", were "constrained", "truncated" and "underdeveloped", in contrast to the larger scale, more "advanced" political structure, "historical performance", "native...political genius", "political accomplishments" and "quality of leadership" of Polynesians. Sahlins opposed the "bourgeois", "self-interested cunning and economic calculation" of "the" self-made "Melanesian big-man" (who "have been styled 'harangue-utans'") with the "regal" bearing, "refinements of breeding" and "true pedigree" of "the Polynesian chief" (1963: 286–90). The oddity of an evolutionary schema in which bourgeois capitalism preceded aristocracy was not entirely lost on me, but I merely recoiled in egalitarian outrage from Sahlins' positive : negative valency of aristocrat : bourgeois, while missing its irony in terms of Marxist demonology, in which "bourgeois" was the dirtiest of words. I failed to see that the enabling thread in this congeries of tropes was the contemporary discursive primacy of the concept of racial difference, the reality of which even antiracists like Sahlins and myself took for granted. When first writing this paper I was relatively insensitive to the lengthy historiography of the racial classification of Pacific Islanders, from its scientific genesis in the early nineteenth century to its perduring naturalisation in academic and popular discourses, including indigenous ones. Postcolonial displacement of the conceptual primacy of race is a recent, equivocal and fragile phenomenon.*

\# *Jolly (1987: 171; 1994: 383) drew attention to a further glaring anomaly in the classic stereotypes: the parallel conflation of personally achieved leadership with egalitarian social systems, and of collectively ascribed leadership with hereditary rank and social hierarchy. Disavowal of these nexuses was a recurrent strand in my argument, which I made explicit in passing (see esp. n. 9). Yet I completely ignored the most striking negative instances: the elaborate hierarchies of north Vanuatu, in which political status depended on rank achieved in graded societies according to a "competitive egalitarian ethic commonly associated with big-man polities" (Allen, 1981: 24–9).*

"phase[s] in the progress of primitive culture" (Sahlins, 1963: 285); it ignores entirely the interrelationship of ideology and practice in particular social settings. As an alternative I propose to examine the relationship, both ideological and actual, between ascribed and achieved aspects of leadership recruitment and roles in a variety of south Pacific societies. Two related perspectives emerge: the overlap or distinction between kin group and local or territorial group leadership; and descent (rank) and force (power) as related or alternative bases of social interaction, status and authority.[2]

In 1970 Goldman published a study of the evolution of Polynesian status systems in which he suggested that "an abstract model can readily distinguish ascribed from achieved status, but historical reality is ambiguous" (1970: 5). He provided a valuable examination of the range of interplay between ascription and achievement in status acquisition, improvement and loss in particular Polynesian societies. The societies considered here, which of course are not limited to Polynesia, similarly exhibited a wide range of interrelationship between ascribed and achieved elements in the recruitment and roles of leaders. Thus it is clear that ascription and achievement were not polar opposites, but a matter of emphasis in particular contexts.

It is in just this area that the "abstracted sociological types" of Sahlins and Valentine are most inflexible and least appropriate. They relegated the numerous examples within Melanesia of hereditary chieftainship of varying degrees of complexity to the position of exceptions and/or the results of Polynesian or Micronesian influence. They obscured similarities between particular leadership systems separated by the geographical boundary between Polynesia and Melanesia. They played down the considerable variety in the nature and degree of social stratification within Polynesia. Finally, they ignored the importance of force in the achievement and exercise of political power in some Polynesian societies. Thus Valentine maintained without qualification that in Polynesia "status is ascribed through descent as validated by genealogies and mythologies", while Sahlins claimed: "Polynesian chiefs did not make their positions in society—they were installed in societal positions... The chiefly lineage ruled by virtue of its genealogical connections with divinity, and ... people of high rank and office *ipso facto* were leaders" (Valentine, 1963: 4; Sahlins, 1963: 295). The generalisations made in this chapter are more tentative but also less arbitrary and less prescriptive. They are both more specific, because they involve studies of particular leadership systems rather than regional stereotypes, and more general, in that the framework adopted is dynamic, and the patterns examined are not confined within artificial geographical boundaries.

ACHIEVEMENT AND ASCRIPTION IN WESTERN OCEANIA
Colonised contexts

To make a categorical distinction between big man systems and small-scale chiefly systems in Melanesia is tempting but misleading. Problems arise because it seems likely that hereditary rank and chieftainship were more widespread, especially in coastal areas, at the onset of European contacts than they are today (Codrington, 1891: ch. 3; Seligmann, 1910; Williams, 1940: 88–92). Such factors as mission influence, government policy, pacification and the introduction of new avenues for achieving status probably operated in some cases to democratise more rigid forms of social stratification which had once reflected the monopoly by privileged groups of resources, wealth objects or particular status positions. Hence the current incidence of heredity as an important factor in leadership in coastal societies and the present-day "mix" of ascription and achievement in societies generally will often differ more or less radically from the past.* Leadership in societies in New Guinea[3] and

---

* *Despite the prevalence of chieftainship in early anthropological reports on coastal Papua, the first colonial administrators consistently denied the presence of chiefs on whom they might hang a system of indirect rule along Fijian lines. MacGregor, Lieutenant-Governor of British New Guinea, who had previously served in Fiji, complained in 1889: "the great trouble, no chiefs to take responsibility. I of course am trying to give certain authority to certain men, but that is a slow process" (MacGregor to Gordon, 6 Feb. 1889, in Joyce, 1971: 159).*

surrounding islands, the Solomon Islands and Vanuatu, formerly the New Hebrides, (henceforth labelled "western and central Melanesia"), is best differentiated in terms of relative emphasis on ascribed status and/or ranking of descent groups or their segments rather than on the basis of discrete structural categories, while the past should where possible be distinguished from the "ethnographic present". From this viewpoint it appears that achievement-oriented societies of the region often also demonstrated the operation of ascriptive principles in some social contexts and at some levels of segmentation; while in coastal areas there were many societies with a bias towards ascription.

"Mixed" systems

Throughout this region political units generally ranged in size from very small in some coastal areas to several thousand in some New Guinea highland societies, although settlement tended to be more dispersed in parts of the highlands. Larger political formations were often established by mobilisation of kinship and affinal ties and exchange partnerships, and in support of particular leaders, but they were relatively short-lived and unstable. Kinship

---

Murray, Lieutenant-Governor of Australian Papua, wrote in 1935: "in.. Papua ... there are practically no Chiefs worth talking about, no existing administration ... there is in fact no one to rule through and nothing to serve as a foundation" (cited in Jinks, Biskup and Nelson, 1973: 126). Faced by communities which looked to them like small savage isolates, undifferentiated by rank or permanent offices and statuses, MacGregor and Murray appointed village constables to serve as administration agents. There was no significant devolution of colonial authority, but such roles, and their equivalents in German, later Australian New Guinea, were attributed local meanings and contested or appropriated for local ends. Compounding these ironies, some anthropologists in the era after World War II thought they had detected instances of local opportunists manipulating the novel possibilities and statuses of an introduced colonial hierarchy to establish petty local tyrannies in place of earlier "anarchy" (Brown, 1963; Hogbin, 1946: 41–8; 1963). Hogbin found "the story ... so fantastic in some of its aspects as to be almost incredible" (1963: 189). Today it is the anthropologist's disbelief in indigenous agency which seems fantastic.

terminology generally provided the idiom for relationships within local groups, but there was a wide variety of kinship and descent criteria, and norms were usually flexibly applied in actual recruitment to local groups, which were mainly autonomous. There was relatively little social stratification, no hierarchical ranking of neighbouring groups and no centralised political organisation.

Within this context the "big-man" has been accepted as the "normal" type of leader (Meggitt, 1971: 194):

> An historically particular type of leader-figure, the "big-man" as he is often locally styled, appears in the underdeveloped settings of Melanesia. ... the indicative quality of big-man authority is everywhere the same: it is *personal* power. Big-men do not come to office; they do not succeed to, nor are they installed in, existing positions of leadership over political groups. The attainment of big-man status is rather the outcome of a series of acts which elevate a person above the common herd and attract about him a coterie of loyal, lesser men.... Within his faction a Melanesian leader has true command ability, outside of it only fame and indirect influence (Sahlins, 1963: 288–90, orig. emphasis)

Sahlins' portrait of the "big-man" was not just a model for achieved, informal leadership, but a model for *Melanesian* leadership, and as such was widely adopted as a convenient anthropological shorthand.

The emergence of big men in one form or another, through various avenues and capacities, was a potential in most western and central Melanesian societies, though it was often not realised, and there were societies apparently so egalitarian in ethos that leadership was scarcely possible at all, especially in the West Sepik and the Great Papuan Plateau (Mitchell, 1978; Schieffelin, 1980: 505). The potential for big men was least where formal age-grades or a strong ideology of descent confined candidature for leadership to qualified persons, cohorts or descent groups, or where the structural importance of the agnatic descent group limited the ability of an aspiring leader to recruit outsiders in his support.[4] Everywhere in combinations above the basic segmentary or local group level, leadership was exercised by individuals demonstrating an approved combination of qualities, abilities and achievements. Thus major big men who controlled solidary groups can be seen as territorial rather than kin-group leaders, though their following would normally have included a large component of kindred; they were "autonomous men", able to "transcend the system" (Young, 1971: 113) and achieve authority despite the often conflicting values of their societies, such as the widespread tension described by Read between the ideals of "strength" and "equivalence" (1959: 430–6).

A range of possibilities is suggested by Oliver's material on southern Bougainville. The classic case of the *mumi* (big man) Songi—a basis of Sahlins' Melanesian political type—appeared as an extreme amongst the Siwai and neighbouring peoples in 1938–39. Throughout the region "a clearly marked range in emphasis from maternal to paternal ties and descent... [was] paralleled by a shift in the bases of the status hierarchy, from kinship and age (northwest) to greater stress on renown and a system of inherited class status" (1971: 276, 281–96; 1955: ch. 12). This was reflected in differences in leadership. Songi was essentially a territorial group leader whose authority had spread from a basis in his own and his father's matrilineages to incorporate a whole region. By successful competitive feast-giving he had humiliated rival *mumi* and forced them to withdraw from the quest for renown. But there was only one Songi and it was confidently expected that he would shortly be without peer in the region. At the other extreme, smaller neighbouring communities which at that time lacked the cohesive influence of a successful *mumi* held together on the basis of kinship ideology alone.

In hamlet activities everywhere authority was generally shared by hamlet "Old ones" ("the older members, male and female, of the kin segment which possesses... title to the land on which the most hamlet residents live and garden") and/or matrilineage seniors ("First-born"). Age and kinship rank were crucial qualifications for these roles, which were therefore at least partly ascribed (Oliver, 1971: 281; 1955: 238–9, 283). In Buin, in the southeast of the region, there was a system of hereditary rank, though positions of influence were not (or were no longer) limited to members of aristocratic families, since non-aristocrats had begun to rival them in renown acquired through feast giving. This process had apparently begun before European contact, but been accelerated by it (Thurnwald,

1934: 125–41). Oliver stressed the fluidity of this range of political alternatives, and the need to see each case as the present outcome of cumulative changes over time and as a stage in a cyclical process related to the presence or absence of notable big men (1971: 286–96).[5]

Valentine classified the Manus people as having a "mixed system of hereditary rank and egalitarian competitiveness", and implied that this was a type intermediate between the "characteristic [big man] patterns [which] take their most typical form in western Melanesia" and the chieftainships which only begin to emerge in "the more easterly reaches of Melanesia" (1963: 8) as one mounts Sahlins' "upward west to east slope in political development" (1963: 286) towards Polynesia. Valentine cited Mead: "In times of peaceful economic functioning, actual wealth and economic leadership overshadowed ... status relationships based on kinship ... In times of crisis clan and rank would come to the fore".[6] It seems likely, supported by Oliver's example, that societies throughout western and central Melanesia (and, as will be seen, throughout the south Pacific) were in one way or another "mixed". Where there were big men, leaders at basic levels of segmentation—localised clan, clan segment or lineage—tended to owe their positions to biological and/or genealogical seniority. These leaders were often more prominent in the absence of successful big men, though in such cases the operative political unit would be notably smaller. There were societies in the ethnographic literature, such as the Fore and the Bena Bena of the Eastern Highlands and the Dani and the Star Mountains peoples of Irian Jaya, in which descent groups were politically irrelevant, ties of co-residence and co-operation prevailed and all leadership was of local groups or ego-centred networks. There were others, such as the Melpa of the Western Highlands, where descent was important in social organisation, but in which by the time Andrew Strathern wrote (1966) leadership seemingly owed nothing to descent criteria. Even here age was generally a factor in the status of leaders, if only because it took years to acquire a reputation, organise a following and discharge obligations to sponsors. In many societies, moreover, especially where big men represented solidary kin-based groups, age was a specific prerequisite for leadership, and only elders had authority, though effective leaders needed also to be able, energetic and successful. Ethnographic examples include the Lakalai of New Britain, the Abelam of the Sepik and the Orokaiva of northern Papua.

In most big man systems, though no formal mechanism existed to ensure transmission of achieved social position to a nominated successor, and though hereditary rank was of little political importance, it could nonetheless be an advantage to be the son of a big man. Some people, moreover, professed an ideal of agnatic primogeniture in the succession of leaders, although in practice leadership could be achieved by any group member who was able to demonstrate the requisite qualities and ability. Three fifths of the Melpa big men studied by Strathern (three quarters of the major big men) were sons and often grandsons of big men (1971: 209–10); Siwai told Oliver that "'a mumi is simply a man who is the *peki* [offspring] of former mumis'" (1955: xix, 82–3). Similar patterns were reported on Choiseul, in the Solomons, and on Goodenough, in the d'Entrecasteaux (Schleffler, 1965: 179–91; Young, 1971: 108–9). Even amongst the Dani, where leadership was described as entirely territorial and almost entirely achieved, Heider (1970: 93–4) thought that "several factors... make it more likely that a leader will be the son of a leader... the important man will be able to give his sons pigs, and... they will have easier access to wealth for the marriage exchange than the son of a poor man". In general advantage was gained, not by direct inheritance of office or property, because a big man did not hold office and his wealth was often distributed on his death, but through example, connexions and aid, especially in obtaining wives and pigs or learning important ritual formulae and techniques during the life of the father/sponsor. In particular, transmission of achieved social status to a chosen successor seems to have been likely in societies in which knowledge of ritual secrets and a reputation as a priest or shaman were essential to leadership, as was described for the Madang people of Papua New Guinea and the Tannese of Vanuatu. It is clear, however, that everywhere a nominated successor had to demonstrate the qualities his society esteemed in leaders or he would fall by the wayside.

Heredity, therefore, could play a role in the succession of big men; furthermore, age was generally a concomitant of leadership, and genealogical seniority was an important principle at certain levels and in certain situations in many societies which otherwise stressed achievement in the recruitment and status of leaders; finally, more rigid social stratification seems to have existed in the past in at least some societies. For instance, according to Strathern, discussing the Mount Hagen area in the early years of European contact:

> the first-hand account by Vicedom & Tischner [1943–48] ... suggests that the power of big-men was then greater. Big-men are described as chiefs, belonging to rich lineages and ruling over clans. The chiefly lineages monopolised the pearl shell valuables and circulated these in *moka* transactions only among themselves. Pigs could be reared by all, but only the pearl shells carried prestige.

Elsewhere he elaborated: "Rich men ensure that their sons are endowed with wives, land, pigs and valuables, so that they inherit their father's status, although they may not all become as eminent leaders as their fathers" (1966: 362; 1971: 205). Although sceptical about the rigidity of the model proposed in this early account, Strathern gave it some credence, especially the suggestion that a degree of *de facto* social ascription resulted from the monopoly by big men of the *moka* exchange system and the prestige associated with success in it. Thurnwald also detailed the operation and the initial stages of the loosening of a system of social stratification in Buin in southern Bougainville, apparently similar to the one described by Vicedom. It involved a fairly rigid class distinction, and hereditary chieftainship in the hands of an aristocracy which monopolised the traditional valuables, pigs and shell money. Oliver hypothesised that this system "may be viewed as an extreme but logical variation on the prestige-ranking theme, a crystallisation in dynastic form of beliefs and practices present, incipiently, elsewhere" (1971: 284–6; Thurnwald, 1934: 125–41).

Hereditary offices

This example and Oliver's suggestive comment lead logically to consideration of another group of societies. For in addition to varied manifestations of ascription where leadership was basically achieved, there were also many reports of societies in western and central Melanesia, particularly along the southern Papuan coast and in the Massim, which emphasised ascription in one form or another and demonstrated hereditary succession to leadership office. The variable quality, unreliability and ambiguity of the data available make it difficult to chart the past nature and extent of such societies, but certain people or places were persistently so designated.[7] In southeastern and southern Papua they included much of the Massim—notably the northern Trobriands—plus the Koita, Motu, Mekeo, Roro, Toaripi, Elema, Koriki and western Trans-Fly. North of the New Guinea mainland they included Manam and Wogeo Islands. On Bougainville they included the area around Buka Passage, in the north, and the Buin, in the south. In the Solomon Islands hereditary leadership was reported on Nissan, in the Lau and Langalanga lagoons on Malaita, and at Sa'a, in south Malaita. In Vanuatu, heredity was associated with the title systems of the central islands and the small scale chieftainships of Aneityum, in the south. Most of the "Polynesian outliers", Polynesian language communities on islands located within Melanesia, had hereditary chieftainship. There were certainly others.

Except for the Buin people, the Koita, and the Toaripi, Elema, Koriki and Trans-Fly peoples of the Gulf and Western Provinces of Papua New Guinea, all those cited are Austronesian-speaking. Despite some correlation between Austronesian language and a tendency to hereditary office, it is of doubtful validity to invoke specific relationships between particular cultural traits and linguistic or racial affiliations, since several thousand years of migration, interaction and flux in western Melanesia have produced a complex mixture of cultures (cf. Scaglion, 1996).

The presence of hereditary offices in western and central Melanesia, apart from in the Polynesian outliers, was commonly ignored or, in the case of the northern Trobriands, which Malinowski made too famous to ignore, regarded as highly exceptional (e.g. Brunton, 1975: 544; Sahlins, 1963: 286; Valentine, 1963: 8, 47) Ironically, in the context of the societies listed the version of ascribed leadership described in the Trobriands does appear unusual in that there was ranking of descent groups rather than hereditary chieftainship as such. In the 1950s leadership within the sub-clan (*dala*) was seen as basically achieved:

> In practice at least primogeniture seems to be of little significance in determining succession... The sub-clan leader is in effect selected on the basis of his achievements in comparison with those of others eligible by sub-clan membership, age and so on, and the more ambitious or dominating personalities tend in effect to compete with each other for selection (Powell, 1960: 127-8).

The principle of rank, however, meant that leadership of local groups—villages and village clusters—was ascribed, in the sense that it was limited to members of the highest ranking sub-clan associated with a particular locality (Powell, 1960: 125-6).

In some respects this system resembled stratification amongst the Melpa and in Buin as described by Vicedom and Thurnwald.[8] There were similarities also to the Samoan title system, in the sense that ascription in the Trobriands provided a pool of genealogically qualified candidates, from amongst whom leaders emerged as a result of their own efforts. Leadership office existed, especially at the sub-clan and village levels, but power was a personal creation of particular leaders rather than inherent in offices, especially at the wider political level of the village cluster (Powell, 1960: 118, 132). As will be seen, in south Pacific societies generally political power tended to be created by the incumbent of an office.

In all the societies listed above the size of the political unit remained small and social stratification was generally limited to a distinction between office holders and non office holders. There were, however, notable variations in relative emphasis on ascription and achievement in the recruitment of leaders and in the nature and extent of their authority.[9] All these societies professed an ideological commitment to some form of hereditary succession and a varying degree of actual deviation from the norm. In hereditary systems throughout the Pacific, in fact, ideals were tempered in practice by the requirement that both incumbent and heir demonstrate a basic fitness for the office. The extent to which practice could differ from ideology is suggested by the village of Kalauna, on Goodenough

Island, where "the 'bossman' of a hamlet is ideally the senior male member of the genealogically senior patrilineage". In sixteen hamlets surveyed by Young in the late 1960s, only nine conformed to the norm. The rule of male primogeniture operated principally to differentiate candidates for leadership when all other factors were equal. He saw Kalauna leadership as essentially achieved, and as a limited form of big-manship (1971: 77–8, ch. 5).[10]

Among the Polynesian-speaking Tikopia serially described by Firth over five decades, leadership of dispersed clans (*kainanga*), the foci of ritual activity, was ideally and to a large extent actually based on agnatic primogeniture; yet the clan chief priest (*ariki*), "the most senior person in his lineage", "had to be created chief by a specific act of elevation, and accepted by popular will—at least nominally; he was an elected leader with responsibilities to the people, and not simply a god-given monarch with divine mandate to rule as he wished". At the local group level the village chief was normally the senior member of the highest ranking resident descent group segment. Tikopia was genealogically stratified but otherwise relatively egalitarian (1970: 35, 40; 1936: chs 3, 9, 10). Amongst the Mekeo in the 1960s leadership of the localised clan segment was said to depend almost entirely on hereditary rank and allow little scope for achievement. Mekeo succession norms, however, were fairly flexible, since a chief could nominate his successor from among his sons, or in the absence of sons nominate a daughter or adopt a male heir (Hau'ofa, 1971: 164). In the western Trans-Fly in the 1930s hereditary village headmen of vaguely-defined status were reported to operate in an essentially egalitarian setting and share influence with others who owed their status to personal attributes, popularity and the ability to impress and dominate (Williams, 1936: 242). At about the same time on Ontong Java, another Polynesian outlier, age looked like the only qualification for chieftainship, apart from competence. These Polynesians seemed to have no commitment to genealogical seniority (Hogbin, 1931: 408, 410, 422–5), and their succession principles and practice bore less resemblance to Sahlins' "Polynesian type", even in its rudimentary form, than did, for instance, those described for the Mekeo and Roro.

The authority attributed to leaders in these societies also varied considerably, from instances of quite powerful chieftainships whose incumbents exercised generalised authority over members of their groups and had at their command imposing sanctions (e.g., Mekeo, Manam, Sa'a), to weak systems of hereditary headmanship in which the extent of leaders' authority depended on personality, and in which they merely expressed a general consensus rather than made binding decisions (Trans-Fly). Nowhere do groups and their leaders seem to have been hierarchically ranked on the basis of genealogical seniority (not even, apparently, the Tikopia *kainanga*), although a hierarchy of leaders was sometimes reported within groups (Mekeo, Koroki). The scope of ascribed leadership was generally limited, and wider territorial combinations usually arose as a result of competition between the chiefs or headmen of localised kin-group segments, who were qualified by rank to compete for political leadership. Thus amongst the Motu, while leadership of the localised clan fragment (*iduhu*) was ascribed by agnatic primogeniture, status at the village level was achieved and decisions were the result of informal negotiations (Groves, 1963: 17–18, 30).

ASCRIPTION AND ACHIEVEMENT IN CENTRAL AND EASTERN OCEANIA

Sacred chieftainship

As noted above, inheritance of sacred objects and ritual knowledge could provide an appearance of hereditary succession in societies in which leadership was mainly achieved. The link between ritual potency and leadership was marked where there was actual hereditary chieftainship, which usually had a strong ritual component. Whether or not a chief specifically fulfilled the role of priest or shaman, his putative position as senior member of a descent group usually made him the direct descendant of gods, or at least the closest living link with deified ancestors, and provided extrahuman sanctions for his authority. Chiefly office holders were often sacred to a greater or lesser extent, and were the object of more or less elaborate forms of respect, restriction and avoidance. The most extreme patterns of sanctity and deference were reported in the more highly stratified societies of Polynesia, where the highest ranking titleholders were often themselves regarded as gods. If reinforced by sanctions provided by control of resources and force, the ritual authority of hereditary chiefs could be complemented by real power; the highest ranking chiefs, however, were not always also secular and political leaders, in which case their role tended to be that of religious figurehead.

All southern Oceanian societies outside western and central Melanesia—New Caledonia, Fiji and all of Polynesia—had a strong though not identical bias towards hereditary chieftainship. Except in some very small atoll societies, political units were generally larger than in western and central Melanesia. More or less complex hierarchies existed in many societies, often based on force and on either the progressive integration, at least in theory, of lower order descent group segments into higher, or on the ranking of titles on a territorial basis, as in Samoa.

It is neither possible nor necessary to attempt here a general survey of leadership patterns in these societies.[11] Several points emerge clearly, however. Because the nature and degree of social stratification varied so much between Polynesian societies, it is misleading to typify Polynesian leadership in terms of the most highly stratified examples. And because leadership in small atoll societies, such as the Tokalaus (Huntsman, 1971: 322–5), functionally if not ideologically most resembled that in some of the small-scale hereditary chieftainships in western and central Melanesia, it is inappropriate to maintain a crude dichotomy between Melanesian and Polynesian types. Furthermore, the leadership systems of New Caledonia and eastern and coastal Fiji may usefully be grouped for analytic purposes together with those of some of the less stratified Polynesian systems, such as the Maori, but they should not simply be subsumed as instances of Polynesian influence. Finally, achievement, in particular through the political exercise of force, was a major determinant of status in many places.

Leadership in New Caledonia

It is relevant here to discuss New Caledonian leadership in some detail.* Traditional New Caledonian socio-political organisation centred on localised, patrilineal and patri-virilocal clans, and on tribes, aggregates of clans paying allegiance to the chief of one of their number. A descent idiom defined relationships between clan and tribal members and validated chiefly status: clan members claimed common descent and owed allegiance to an hereditary chief, in theory the genealogically senior man of the senior lineage; a tribe was regarded as a group of related clans with a common founding ancestor, which paid allegiance to the senior male member of the senior lineage of the original clan. The chief was a clan's "great (firstborn) son", the deeply respected "elder brother" of its members (Leenhardt, 1930: 88–98; 1935: 131; Tjibaou, 1976: 282). An idiom of brotherhood was extended into the tribal context, where, however, it served as a symbol for unity *vis-à-vis* other groups rather than as a formula for recruitment. It denoted a complex set of spirit-sanctioned reciprocal rights and obligations which patterned relationships within clan and tribe.

Neither the ideology of common descent nor that of chiefly seniority was necessarily borne out in practice, however. As might be expected, divergence was greatest in the case of the tribe, which was a territorial political unit rather than a descent group. Both clans and tribes commonly absorbed unrelated individuals and groups, and

---

* *I have left unaltered the following reconstruction of "traditional" New Caledonian social organisation, despite its conceptual and methodological limitations (cf. Bensa and Rivierre, 1982; Bensa, 1986; Bensa and Goromido, in press; Douglas, 1994b). It is usefully mnemonic of a phase when my ethnohistorical starting point was modern anthropological authority and my rhetoric was in uneasy flux between realism and reflexivity. My shift from ethnographic essence to contemporary action descriptions, from authority to critique, and attendant recoil from the unwitting teleology of an historical perspective which reconfigured the past as antecedent of later ethnographic presents, were apparent by Chapter Two. They become axiomatic in Parts Two and Three, and in a recent detailed historical ethnography of "chieftainship" in New Caledonia (1994b).*

rationalised the process in kinship terms. Ideology was thus satisfied, but common residence was in practice a key factor in group cohesion. A newcomer was sometimes installed as tribal chief by earlier inhabitants, who nonetheless continued to exercise covert authority through their control of land. Such recent exterior origin of a chiefly clan was generally concealed in myth, but its occurrence illustrates that the principle of seniority of descent could be evaded at the highest political level. None of the great tribal chieftainships appeared to be able to trace its pedigree beyond eight generations, and genealogy was not an important validation of political status (Guiart, 1963: 641, 643–5).

A clan or tribal chief was paid great deference by his "brothers".[12] He enjoyed many prerogatives and possessed authority because of his role as intermediary between the group and its ancestral spirits and totem, but he was no autocrat: abuse of his role or poor performance denoted bad relations with the ancestors and could cause them to withdraw their support, threatening the security and socio-economic welfare of the group. Should the affairs of the group not prosper, should the chief be a poor orator, lack generosity in redistribution and gift exchange or abuse his "brothers'" rights, he might be replaced by a close kinsman or abandoned. In such instances he normally retained the trappings of rank to which his birth entitled him, but none of the substance of authority. The office of chief would in general ultimately revert to his direct descendants (Leconte, 1847: 851; Leenhardt, 1930: 78–9, 89–90, 98; Rochas, 1862: 178, 225, 243–7). Again, rank and authority were repeatedly separated by the operation of a succession principle whereby the chief ceded ritual and ceremonial precedence to his son at birth, but only relinquished secular authority by degrees until the youth reached maturity.[13]

The chief was neither the sole office holder nor the only decision maker in a group. He shared authority with such dignitaries as the war leader, masters of the soil,[14] priests and powerful sorcerers, who with respected elders formed an advisory council which assisted the chief to reach the consensus on which group action was usually based. In secular affairs the chief was mainly a spokesman, an administrator and a diplomat (Guiart, 1963: 38–41; Leenhardt, 1930: 38–46, 89–90). At the clan level the role of chief was firmly anchored in the ideal of brotherhood, but at the tribal level it was essentially political. Relations between a tribal chief and the chiefs of member clans were mainly a matter of compromise and negotiation between relative equals and realisation of the potential of the position of tribal chief depended on the ability and character of the individual incumbent.

Thus New Caledonian socio-political units demonstrated a complex interaction between the principles of ascription and achievement in recruitment to local and descent groups and in succession to and retention of chiefly office. Power was relatively diffused. It appeared to reside mainly in the office of tribal chief, which was theoretically but often not actually a function of genealogical seniority. In many instances, however, those who were attributed precedence—original settler clans, masters of the soil—exercised power covertly, together with the priests who communicated directly with the spirits. The sanctity of New Caledonian chiefs and the deference to which they were entitled rested on their implied genealogical connexions with deified ancestors. However, any suggestion in ideal terms of segmentary lineage organisation was not borne out in practice, especially at the tribal level. Tribes were not fixed political entities, but expanded and contracted in size and influence according to the vicissitudes of the political and military situation, and the success or otherwise of their chiefs (Douglas, 1979; Rochas, 1862: 242–3).

Maori leadership

This model of New Caledonian leadership shows most correlation in emphasis and many details with reconstructed traditional leadership systems in coastal and eastern Fiji (Nayacakalou, 1975: 31–43; Reid, 1977; Scarr, 1970: 95–105), and in what might be called "mid-range" Polynesian societies (neither the least nor the most stratified). For analytic purposes, therefore, they may usefully be grouped together, as a brief comparison of New Caledonian leadership with Maori will illustrate. In degree of political fragmentation and size of major socio-political units Maori society seems to have been roughly comparable with New Caledonian, though in ideological commitment to genealogical principles and degree of correlation between kinship and territorial groups it was rather different.

Demonstrable genealogical seniority seems to have been a primary qualification for Maori leadership within each more or less inclusive segment of the ramified descent group model in terms of which Maori conceptualised their social relationships (Bowden, 1979; van Meijl, 1994: 281-5; Winiata, 1956). However the genealogical system itself provided avenues which offset the rigid status divisions inherent in the application of this principle and gave those with ability but junior rank some possibility of acquiring rank to suit their aspirations. The principle of "optation" (the right to trace descent through either male or female line by affiliation—claiming rights of residence and to land—with the highest-ranking group in which such claims could be sustained, though descent in the male line was preferred) and the process of fission (segmentation of the lineage group to create a new ranking) provided structural means to minimise junior rank (Firth, 1968: 209-12; Oppenheim, 1973: 104 Winiata, 1956: 221).

Ascribed status through descent seems therefore to have been a more fundamental qualification for leadership amongst the Maori than in New Caledonia, though the descent ideology itself was probably more flexible. In addition, however, achievement was a crucial component of effective political leadership. This is made explicit in the Maori concept of *mana*, spiritually-sanctioned power/efficacy. *Mana* seems to have been inherent in a descent group and been differentially inherited by all members on the basis of seniority, but it was subject to increase or decrease, especially as a result of a chief's success or failure (Oppenheim, 1973: 15-15, 104-5; Smith, 1974: 25-7). A chief who sought an effective political role beyond his own descent/residential group (*hapuu*) had to demonstrate a wide range of qualities and abilities: he had to be able, skilful and lucky, brave and victorious in warfare, astute in diplomacy with chiefs of allied *hapuu*, able to gain and keep the support of his close kinsmen, to attract new adherents from among more distant kin, and be successful economically.[15] The existence of structural avenues to bypass junior rank and the requirement of ability and success in chiefs at the political level suggest that "achievement rather than ascription was the operative factor in establishing the power position of very influential chiefs, though of course these chiefs had to have at least acceptable descent" (Oppenheim, 1973: 104). Smith illustrated the way in which ascription and achievement provided alternative avenues to status, symbolised in the conflict between the conservative, ascription-oriented elder brother, secure in the possession of his *tapu*, "sacredness", and concerned to defend established values, and his ambitious, achievement-oriented younger brother, aggressive, shrewd and only able to succeed despite the disadvantages of birth (1974: 8, 61–9).

In both New Zealand and New Caledonia, then, rank was ascribed by birth and could not normally be lost, although in the case of defeat in war and capture a Maori was apparently reduced to the non-person status of slave. For rank to be translated into effective political and economic action, however, a chief had to be able, lucky and successful. At the level of clan and *hapuu* kinship ties were of primary importance in administration, social control and social relations generally, and the sanctions at the disposal of the chief, as the group's senior member, were predominantly extrahuman. Beyond this level ties of co-residence and cooperation came to the fore, though kinship still provided an idiom for social relations and an ideal for group unity. Amongst the Maori, moreover, a close correlation seems to have existed between their segmentary descent model and territorial affiliations, though the upper levels of the model did not normally operate as integrated political units (Winiata, 1956: 212–21). In both societies the highest-ranking chief, while retaining ritual precedence and authority, frequently relinquished secular control to a more capable leader. The latter was generally a close kinsman who in Maori terms had compensated for relative deficiency in inherited *mana* by the quality of his achievements (Oppenheim, 1973: 105; Smith, 1974: 65–9; Winiata, 1956: 226–7). Sometimes, however, rank/ritual authority and political power diverged to the extent that they became prerogatives of distinct lineages. Instances include the New Caledonian tendency to install a newcomer into a tribal chieftainship and the separation in Bau, Fiji, between the sacred god-chief, the Roko Tui Bau, and the Vunivalu, or executive chief (Scarr, 1970: 96; see also Reid, 1977: 5, 8–9).

Effectively, however, no great power resided in chiefly office at any level in either New Caledonia or New Zealand. Consultation and consensus were respected principles both within the kin group, where elders and experts combined to advise the chief, and in the wider political sphere, where "the chief... did not stand at the apex of a hierarchy of command but rather in the position of *primus inter pares*. He was supported because he achieved victories" (Oppenheim, 1973: 105). The implications of divergence of social rank and political authority/power were blurred by the relatively small scale of the political arena and by particular emphases in either context. In New Caledonia the potential power of tribal chieftainships was restrained by the continuing though obscure role of the masters of the soil, whose control over land stemmed from their relationship with the ancestral spirits residing there. In New Zealand genealogy remained too important for power to become the dominant basis of status, as happened in Samoa, while the existence of genealogical avenues for enhancing rank meant that class barriers were not erected between the upper and lower ranks, as occurred in the Society Islands and Hawai'i.[16]

Thus in most respects New Caledonian and Maori leadership patterns were more alike than either resembled the leadership stereotype for the culture area to which they were assigned. This difficulty has hitherto been simply resolved by including New Caledonia and Fiji within Polynesia and/or by attributing their leadership patterns to Polynesian influence or conquest (Bourgarel, 1862: 253; Dumont d'Urville, 1832: 12–15; Garnier, 1870: 432; Routledge, 1985: 27). The latter thesis rests on plentiful evidence for prehistoric contacts between Polynesia and New Caledonia and Fiji, especially Tonga and Fiji. It should be noted, though, that before the nineteenth century Fijian influences on Tonga may have been at least as important as the reverse (d'Entrecasteaux, 1808, I: 312–13, 341–3; Martin, 1827, I: 78–9). In New Caledonia most chiefly lineages were not originally Polynesian, though in the north-east, especially, affinal links were common with Polynesian-speaking settlers on the Loyalty island of Ouvéa (Bensa and Rivierre, 1982; Douglas, 1970). There is, moreover, no necessary reason why Melanesians should require tutelage from Polynesians in order to develop the institution of chieftainship, and nor does the presence of Polynesian-speaking populations within Melanesia necessarily mean that the existence of this form of leadership elsewhere in the region must be attributed to Polynesian influence.

At least as plausible an hypothesis is suggested by the likelihood that New Caledonians, Fijians and Tongans shared ancestral origins. Recent linguistic and archaeological research has implied strong formative links between eastern Melanesia and western Polynesia. The earliest settlers in both Fiji and Tonga, apparently coast dwellers, seem to have possessed the so-called Lapita pottery, and to have been "a closely related cultural community, the perfect candidate for (in linguistic terms) the pre-Polynesian... speech community" (Groube, 1971: 306, 278–316; Grace, 1968: 66–74; Green, 1967: 228–36). Lapita potters also settled in New Caledonia, though they may not have been the earliest inhabitants. Cultural differences between western Polynesia on the one hand and New Caledonia and Fiji on the other would by this reasoning have resulted from separate internal development and subsequent immigration and external contacts in the latter groups, which modified Lapita culture and ultimately produced more heterogeneous societies (Green, 1967: 234; cf. Spriggs, 1984).

Rank and power

As suggested above, some splitting of religious and secular leadership (sacred rank and political power)[17] was likely at the tribal level once co-residence began to outweigh kinship as the main basis of intragroup cohesion, though the implications of such a divergence were fully worked out in neither New Caledonia nor New Zealand. It is necessary, however, conceptually to separate rank and power, kinship system and political system, in two groups of societies. In the first, instanced in different ways by Samoa and the Marquesas, the rules of succession to title and/or office were ambiguous: Samoa lacked a prescriptive rule of title succession, although all titles themselves were strictly ranked according to putative seniority and were the prerogatives of particular descent groups, whose male (mostly) members competed for election to the most prestigious; in the Marquesas all first-born were sacred more or less irrespective of relative seniority, and were thus potential leaders of their descent groups or tribes, although all may not have enjoyed equal opportunity. As a result, in both groups the main practical determinant of status, in contexts of intense and fairly equal competition, was achievement. In each case an aristocracy monopolised positions of power and authority, but the élites were to an extent self-created. At the higher levels force or the threat of force determined political alignments, while the politically successful exercised considerable power within a limited geographical span (Goldman, 1970: chs 8, 11; Gilson, 1970: chs 1, 2, esp. 47–64; Robarts, 1974: 20–6, 326–35).*

The second group comprises those societies in which there was a high degree of stratification and tendencies to centralisation: Hawai'i, Tonga and the Society Islands. Here stress on and energetic furtherance of lateral ties between the highest ranking members of descent groups ultimately resulted in societies characterised by the emergence of class divisions, which cut across lineal descent and territorial groups and differentiated all chiefs from non-chiefs. Strict class endogamy, especially at the highest level, preserved exclusiveness, and members of the upper class monopolised sanctity, controlled resources and exercised extremely onerous sanctions. Rank and power were intricately interrelated. Oliver's monumental three volume work, *Ancient Tahitian Society* (1974),

---

* *I have resisted the temptation to fiddle with these remarks on the Marquesas— which relied heavily on Goldman's inadequately informed secondary synthesis (1970)—despite their limitations in the light of the more recent scholarship of Dening (1980) and Thomas (1990a). Thomas described indigenous Marquesan hierarchy as unstable, fractured and contested. Chieftainship was highly localised and atomistic, there being no encompassing hierarchy or general dependence on the ritual efficacy of chiefs, since fertility was attributed to shamans: "What distinguished the chief... had no enabling element: it related above all to a state [tapu], rather than special or unique capacities. In the more typical form of chieftainship, the state (of sanctity) and the capacities (for ritual efficacy) went together; in the Marquesan case the latter were associated rather with the shamans" (1990a: 13, 26–37; 1994b: 117, orig. emphasis).*

demonstrated a wide range of interaction of descent and force as bases for status in the Society Islands.

It had been generally assumed that there was total correlation in these societies between the highest social rank and the greatest amount of political power: "smaller units are integrated into larger through a system of intergroup ranking, and the network of representative chiefs of the subdivisions amounts to a coordinating political structure" (Sahlins, 1963: 287). While there is an element of truth in this statement, it ignored the shifts and role differentiation which could occur at the highest levels. Oliver argued in great detail that in Tahiti kin-group leadership and tribal political leadership need to be analysed separately. They may well have overlapped in particular cases, but did not necessarily do so, because they involved different contexts or dimensions. Furthermore, they rested on different bases: the highest social rank stemmed—in theory at least—from purity of genealogical descent. The authority of the kin-group chief was mainly exercised through extrahuman sanctions and according to an ideology which stressed values such as deference, respect, benevolence and generosity (1974, II: 627–46). Tribal leadership, however, stemmed from the exercise or at least the threat of force, and was held by capable leaders who were not necessarily the highest ranking. In this sense tribal leadership was open to achievement, though the range of possible candidates in any particular case would almost certainly have been limited to the upper echelons of the *ari'i* class, and probably though not necessarily to near kinsmen of the sacred chief (1974, II: chs 23, 24). There was a dialectical relationship between rank and power, mediated in practice by the process of alliance formation. Political success tended to be enhanced and validated through marriage or the forging of friendship pacts with holders or transmitters (in the case of first-born women) of the highest ranking titles; conversely those of high rank sought to translate their ritual potency into effective political action by alliance with the strong. The idea seems to have been authority over a tribe in the hands of its highest ranking member, but the flexibility of the descent ideology and the frequency of rivalry and ambition meant that the ideal was often unrealised, and conflict and warfare were endemic.

The complex interaction of rank and power, religious and secular leadership, is illustrated by events and relationships in the Society Islands in the mid to late eighteenth and early nineteenth centuries. The emergence of rigid class divisions seems to have been relatively recent, linked to the spread of the cult of the war god 'Oro and the ritual and social pre-eminence of the kin-group whose family *marae* (temple) at Opoa, Ra'iatea, was the centre of the 'Oro cult and the source of the highest ranking and most sacred associations in the whole group (Oliver, 1974, II: 660–85, 1121–32). Centripetal tendencies generated by the alliances, ambitions and achievements of the chiefly lineage of Pare-Arue (the Pomares) were opposed by the leaders of other tribes who, while acknowledging the ceremonial and ritual paramountcy of the Pomares, denied their political, territorial and economic aspirations (Gunson, 1964 Newbury, 1967; Oliver, 1974, III). Within both tribes and kin groups rank and authority were periodically separated by the principle of early succession to titles. As in New Caledonia chiefs yielded rank and title to, usually, their first-born sons, and thus both ensured stable succession and freed themselves as administrators of group affairs from the more onerous burdens of sanctity (Oliver, 1974, II: 642–4). In Pare-Arue before 1773 Tutaha, a younger brother but a brave warrior and forceful leader, acted as tribal chief while the tribe's highest titleholder was successively his older brother and the latter's son and grandson. In Pa'ea in the 1770s and 1780s tribal political leadership and the highest social rank seem to have been divided between separate lineages: Te To'ofa was clearly the effective tribal chief despite the superior rank of the holder of the title Tevahitua i Patea. In Fa'a'a before 1773 rank and power were fused in the person of Te Pau i Ahurai, but after his death in battle his titular successor was overshadowed in the tribal sphere, probably by Te To'ofa of Pa'ea (Oliver, 1974, III, ch. 25).

Further variations on the rank/power interrelationship are suggested by Tonga. Although by about the sixteenth century rank and power were divided between a sacred chief, the Tu'i Tonga, and the *hau*, or temporal ruler, a prescription of marriage between the Tu'i Tonga and the first-born daughter of the *hau* provided a continuing link between religious and secular leadership. It also ensured the dominance of the sacred ritual head in terms of kinship (*kainga*) rank, because a sister's children outranked their mother's brother and his offspring and enjoyed rights over the latter's property and services. The *hau* was not chosen strictly according to descent seniority, but was selected from amongst those eligible on the basis of capacity, ability and power. During the eighteenth century, however, the legendary symbiosis of religious and secular leadership came under serious strain. The Tu'i Tonga retained nominal ritual and ceremonial precedence throughout the archipelago, but with contenders for the position of *hau* engaged in lethal competition, local chiefs successfully disputed the *hau*'s authority over their islands or districts, resulting in political fragmentation. This was an apparent reversal of immediate pre-contact tendencies towards increased political centralisation in Tahiti and Hawai'i (Bott, 1981; Cummins, 1977: 64–7, 69, 77; Gunson, 1979; Rogers, 1977: 165–80; Ve'ehala and Tupou Posesi Fanua, 1977: 35–8).

EPILOGUE

It appears that the greater the stress on kinship and descent as elements in group formation and cohesion, the more likely seniority and heredity were to be important leadership principles, not only in societies which emphasised ascription but also as aspects of the recruitment and status of leaders in societies where leadership was mainly achieved. Conversely, where ties of co-residence and local/territorial group membership provided the main social cement, descent was either unimportant in determining leaders or was complemented or superseded by requirements of competence, capability and success. Genealogical or descent criteria commonly delineated a pool of candidates for leadership, and where force was a final arbiter genealogy or a common descent idiom were often used to validate a new order: ideology and practice were thus intimately entangled. Throughout the south Pacific there was a much greater interplay and overlap between ascription and achievement than has usually been allowed. In western and central Melanesia heredity was often a factor of some importance in succession to leadership, genealogical and biological seniority were frequently stressed, and more rigid social stratification may sometimes have existed in the past. In the more stratified societies ability and success were generally essential components of secular and political authority, and in some cases force had supplemented or even superseded rank as a dominant basis of hierarchy.

Ideal typification of leadership in terms of Polynesian and Melanesian extremes is here replaced by reference to a number of related criteria, on the basis of which certain south Pacific societies may be analytically grouped: social and political scale; degree of complexity (that is, nature and extent of stratification); and especially the relationship between ascription and achievement as emphases in the recruitment, roles and status of leaders, variously phrased as the interaction between rank and power, sacred and secular leadership, descent and locality, kinship and political system, ideology and practice. Careful examination of the dynamic interplay between ideology and practice in particular settings and comparisons of specific interrelationships are essential, for it is here that older models are least useful. Anthropologists, concerned to elucidate institutionalised social relations, have tended to stress normative systems to the detriment of actual practice. Thus in regard to Polynesia, especially, observers and analysts have often been unduly preoccupied with ideology, with the logical fit of local or analytic models for the relationship between leadership and descent groups, with the awe-inspiring presence of chiefs whose pedigrees linked them directly with divinity and who might themselves be gods. Sahlins, for example, compared Polynesian ideology with Melanesian practice, and devalued Melanesians in consequence.*

---

* *This aphorism partly missed its mark. My ideology : Polynesia :: practice : Melanesia formula for Oceanic anthropology was largely a reflex of regional differences in the history of anthropological practice: before the 1970s anthropology on "acculturated" Polynesia tended to ethnological historical synthesis, in "pristine" Melanesia to highly focussed fieldwork-based ethnography. Ethnology is almost by default normative, since filtering out the extravagant idiosyncrasies and inconsistencies of human actions is an obvious information management strategy for a broadly comparative project. A similar, but inverted ideological artifice may be posited for the western Pacific: that the ubiquitous ideological*

I have not entirely abandoned conventional categories: for instance, although hereditary leadership systems in central and western Melanesia are not categorically distinguished from big man systems, they are nonetheless separated conceptually as differing in important ways. These differences may well be more apparent than real, a reflection of the difficulties of correlating data culled from disparate sources with wide variations in time of writing, presuppositions, perspectives and categories. How such problems are resolved determines, for example, whether one regards Vicedom's model of pre-contact social stratification in the Mount Hagen area as wrong, an aberration in a basically achieved leadership system, or an instance of hereditary rank, if not chieftainship, to be considered in similar terms to descent group ranking in the Trobriands, stratification in southern Bougainville, or even the territorial ranking of titles on the basis of seniority of descent in Samoa.

Oliver provided a key when he proposed that social stratification in a part of southern Bougainville "may be viewed as an extreme but logical variation on the prestige-ranking theme, a crystallisation in dynastic form of beliefs and practices present, incipiently, elsewhere" (1971: 285–6). His stress on the dynamic element in the variety of political forms found in this small area, and on a model which correlated rather than opposed achieved and ascribed

---

egalitarianism (between men) reported in many societies in Melanesia served to camouflage structural asymmetries as well as practical inequalities of status, whether achieved, inherited or otherwise ascribed (Jolly, 1987: 172). Salisbury, for example, remarked of the New Guinea highlands: "Although the indigenous ideology was one of democratic equality and competition, the empirical situation ... was one of serial despotism by powerful leaders" (1964: 225; Allen, 1981: 24). Given the insistent ethnohistorical subtext of the varied manifestation of populist antihierarchical principles and practices in hierarchical Pacific polities (e.g., New Caledonia [Douglas, 1994b]; Polynesia [Marcus, 1989]; Maori [van Meijl, 1994]; Fiji [Sahlins, 1981b]), it might be concluded that "inversion" is better reformulated as difference, in textual and contextual emphases and rhetoric.

leadership,* illustrates in microcosm the kind of common interpretive framework best applied to leadership in societies throughout the south Pacific.

---

* *Pluralist critiques of all kinds of oppositional reasoning were gaining impetus at the time, both within and beyond anthropology (e.g., Bernstein, 1983; Booz, 1982; Jackson, 1989). So were practical repudiations: Bott (1981: 9), from the other extreme of the conventional Pacific leadership continuum, argued: "Sahlins thinks of the 'big men' of Melanesia as a contrast to the established chiefs of Polynesia. The Tongan case suggests that both established chiefs and 'big men' were integral to the system"; Marcus (1989: 180), from a culturalist perspective, extended the same point: "chiefs who share much in common with Melanesian big men are to be found in Polynesia, but... big men who share much in common with chiefs, and in fact are chiefs, are to be found in Melanesia".*

NOTES

[1] Though my concern is partly with the structural analysis of a social institution, a diachronic perspective is always implicit. In relation to Papua New Guinea the term "traditional" (by which I mean pre-European contact) must be qualified, since my main sources are modern ethnographies, mostly based on fieldwork undertaken well after the establishment of administrative control and pacification. Elsewhere I imply reconstruction of traditional leadership patterns, while acknowledging the problems inherent in "historical ethnography". The term "south Pacific" here includes Hawai'i.

[2] The following are my working definitions for the most important terms used: "status"—relative social position; "ascribed status"—social position gained from innate qualifications over which an individual has no control, such as age, genealogical rank, membership by birth of a particular group, category or social class; "ascribed leadership" implies formal office; "achieved status"—social position gained in competition with others through the exercise of personal qualities such as ability, skill, character, personality; "rank"—status ascribed by seniority of descent in a genealogically-based society; "power"—the ability to determine the destinies and actions of others, primarily through control of scarce or valued resources, and often by exercise of threat or force; "authority"—acknowledged right to lead.

[3] That is, the island of New Guinea, now split between the independent nation of Papua New Guinea, formerly an Australian colony/Territory, and the Indonesian province of Irian Jaya (West Papua).

[4] Sahlins proposed, to explain the apparently limited political role and authority of New Guinea highlands leaders in comparison with the Siwai *mumi*, that "the greater the self-regulation of the political process through a lineage system, the less function that remains to big-men, and the less significant their political authority" (1963: 289). Yet studies of "despotism" provided ample evidence that individual highlands leaders could achieve long-term positions of considerable power and authority (Salisbury, 1964: 225–8; Watson, 1971), and Strathern demonstrated that Melpa big men were not unduly restricted by "enclavement...within a segmented lineage organisation" (1971: 2). However, because they apparently did not create solidary factions, but operated mainly through dispersed networks of exchange partners, they do seem to have had only limited political authority.

While inappropriate generally to highlands polities, Sahlins' proposition seems nonetheless to have broad applicability (Young, 1971: 111). Allen, moreover, argued that "in pre-state societies matriliny...is much more likely to stimulate evolutionary development". He attributed the emergence of "rudimentary forms of hereditary social stratification" in Melanesia to the "inflexibility" of matriliny as a basis for political institutions, compared with "the sheer effectiveness of the agnatic model and hence the absence of any major stimulus for the freeing of politics from the restraints of kinship" (1981: 13–32; 1984).

5   Terrell (1978) revisited a debate between Oliver and Thurnwald over social stratification in Buin in the light of then recent theories about cultural evolution and his own Bougainville archaeological surveys. He concluded that immediate social structural differences between Buin and the Siwai might have been overdrawn, and that the grand metahistorical question of the origins of social stratification is probably futile, better recast in pragmatic, functional terms.

6   Mead, 1956: 60, cited in Valentine, 1963: 8. Meggitt (1971: 193–5, 204) also depicted the Mae Enga of the New Guinea highlands as a society "in which systems of achievement and ascription of power co-exist", and invoked the bodily metaphor of "alternating systole and diastole" to represent a similar political rhythm of "compression" and expansiveness. Otto (1994: 232) saw the mix of ascription and achievement in one Manus society in synchronic terms: "The relative ranking of leaders of high [inherited] rank was determined by their success in warfare and feast-giving".

7   Detailed historical and ethnographic documentation of hereditary office amongst the people and in the places mentioned in this paragraph was provided in the original of this chapter; see also Chowning, 1979: 69–70.

8   Brunton proposed in relation to the Trobriands that "where conditions are such that men can act to limit strategic exchange items and pre-empt others from gaining access to them, then the stage is set for the development of rank and chieftainship" (1975: 556). Although he specifically contrasted this situation with the openness of trade and exchange systems in the highlands, Vicedom's model of pre-contact social stratification in the Mt Hagen area correlates well with his analysis (Strathern, 1971: 204–8), as does the Bougainville example described by Thurnwald (1934: 125–41). Macintyre, historicising variants of hereditary leadership reported in the Massim in terms of the constraints and opportunities provided by colonial interventions, argued that heredity was an "inherent yet contestable" principle that "emerges as a *claim* in competitive systems of leadership that attain stability" (1994: 242, orig. emphasis). She thought that colonial presence supported (and Malinowski reified) a particular chiefly hierarchy in the Trobriands while subverting chiefly power elsewhere in the Massim.

9   Just as "ascription" is not used solely as a synonym for "hereditary chieftainship", so "achievement" not only implies "big men" but may refer to a more general requirement that leaders demonstrate skills, ability and effectiveness.

10 In later works Young explored more fully the modalities of hierarchy on Goodenough; he argued that "some notion of rank is woven into the egalitarian fabric of Massim societies" and given expression in formal public exchanges (1983b: 7; 1994).

[11] There are several synoptic studies of Polynesian status systems, especially Goldman, 1970.
[12] Lambert, 1900: 112–14; Leenhardt, 1930: 63–5, 97–8; Rochas, 1862: 237, 258. Leenhardt saw chiefly ritual as "nothing but [an extension of] the marks of ritual respect due to the elder brother. There are no rites which specifically concern the chief" (1930: 98).
[13] Patouillet, 1873: 132; Vieillard and Deplanche, 1863: 69. Should an heir be too young to succeed his father in secular affairs, a near kinsman acted as his "regent". The regent usually retained his authority until his own death, when the chief or his descendant, who had continued to receive ritual deference, assumed full control of the affairs of the group (Montrouzier, 1860: 48; Vincent, 1895: 23).
[14] "Masters of the soil" were clans which claimed and exercised the rights of earliest inhabitants of a particular area. They were generally not tribal chiefs, but exercised authority through control of the land and command of the rites associated with it (Leenhardt, 1930: 45; 1935: 140; Guiart, 1963: 35, 41).
[15] Oppenheim, 1973: 15–16, 104–5; Smith, 1974: 65. Cf. Lepervanche's image of a New Guinea highlands big man engaged in building up and maintaining his group and his prestige (1967–8: 176–85).
[16] Most Maori, it was said, could make plausible claim to aristocratic status (Bowden, 1979: 52; Winiata, 1956: 229). Van Meijl attributed the absence of "autocratic chiefdoms" in New Zealand to "the contradiction between hierarchical and antihierarchical ideologies", which substantiated the "claims to autonomy" of basic kinship units (*hapuu*) hierarchically encompassed within "tribal confederations", and of the chiefs of lower ranking *hapuu* (1994: 281–5).
[17] My analytic distinction of religious authority/social rank from secular leadership/political power implies differences in contexts and emphases, rather than normative distinctions. It must be taken with the caveat that it refers to societies in which most natural and social occurrences and relative human efficacy had ritual, spiritual dimensions.

CHAPTER TWO

Ritual and Politics: The Inaugural Meeting of High Chiefs in New Caledonia

FOREWORD

*T*he *article (1985b) from which this chapter is abridged and updated had serendipitous beginnings. I was the only Western scholar present at most of the meeting described, and enjoyed privileged, if partial, access unavailable to a French anthropologist who briefly attended. Theoretically I was turning from Geertz' and Sahlins' too idealist, too monolithic conceptions of culture to Turner's more sociological brand of symbolic anthropology, with its focus on the dynamics and pragmatics of ritual performances. I had also begun to read antipositivist critiques of the culture concept and of the politics and practice of ethnography. The result is an experiment in reflexive, dialogic, anti-essentialist ethnography and a partly unwitting case study of custom as enacted, negotiated presence.*

I thought afterwards that the theoretical apparatus tends to overburden the fleeting traces of ephemeral, mundane actions it is meant to elucidate. But the chapter is theoretically significant in its extended demonstration of the entanglement of "conditioning and creativity" (Bourdieu, 1977: 95) in the contrivance, workings and efficacy of a secular "nonce" ritual. "Ritual", with its dual quality of received immemoriality and performative reinvention, is an apt metonym for an engaged, constructionist, action-oriented notion of culture and tradition. As an index of my growing discontent with classic binaries, this chapter goes beyond simple opposition, or encompassment, or even mediation, to a strategy of synthesising polarities and exploring their practical ambiguities and inversions.

PROLOGUE

In the late afternoon of 16 December 1982, and early the next morning, an unusual number of Melanesians,* mostly mature men, took flights from Nouméa for Lifou, largest of the Loyalty group, about 100 kilometres east of the large island of New Caledonia. The occasion was the first meeting of New Caledonian and Loyalty Island high chiefs to be convened by one of their number, Henri Boula Wahemuneme of Mou, high chief of the district of Lösi.[1] I was invited to attend the meeting, which ran from 17 to 19 December, as a specialist on indigenous cultural history in New Caledonia, with a particular interest in traditional and customary authority.[2]

My interpretation of what went on, created in dialogue with others present, derives from a pluralist position that social realities are experienced and construed in cultural terms. I am interested in culture for the meanings with which it imbues actions for protagonists, rather than as an autonomous system of symbols and meanings (Schneider, 1976). I refer also to "ideology", meaning more than simply "patterns for action", since it conjoins instrumental, evaluative and interpretive dimensions. Ideology provides alternative strategies to be implemented selectively in action contexts and in the manipulation, negotiation and creation of social reality. Ideological statements, often mutually contradictory, indicate things which

---

* *Selecting terms of reference for the original inhabitants of the island Cook called New Caledonia is problematic, since they had no general labels for themselves or their island. When I wrote this paper Mélanésien was still in wide indigenous use in New Caledonia and the Loyalty Islands, while in the independent Pacific "Melanesian" denotes shared regional political interests, a lingua franca and reified national cultures (Anova-Ataba, 1984: 27; Tjibaou, 1981, 1996b: 119–20) But Mélanésien was a legacy of a racist colonial discourse, of Europeans' evolutionary discriminations on the basis of skin colour. Like canaque and indigène it was discarded by pro-independence activists in the 1980s in favour of the ironic phonetically rendered "Kanak", from which they derive "Kanaky" to name their prospective nation. Here, nonetheless, I retain "Melanesian" as a term of general reference in order to preserve the contemporary flavour of the chapter, reserving "Kanak" for those who so identified themselves politically at the time.*

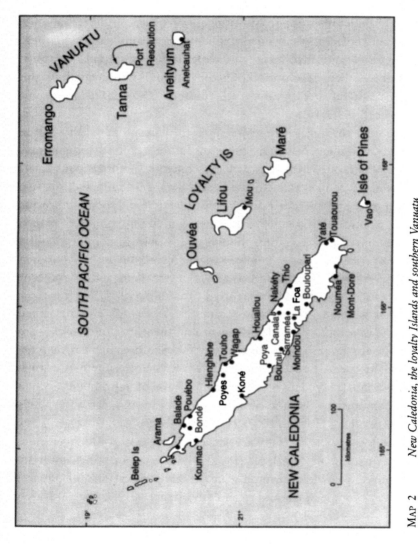

MAP 2   New Caledonia, the Loyalty Islands and southern Vanuatu

are particularly valued, and "tend to stress the harmonious and cohesive aspect of social relationships". Thus, "any major ritual that stresses the importance of a single principle of social organisation only does so by blocking the expression of other [conflicting or contradictory] important principles" (Turner, 1967: 33, 40). Alternatively, a ritual may explicitly confront contradictions, ambiguities and inconsistencies experienced in mundane reality and force their resolution, transformed and transcended in the other reality created by the ritual (Kapferer, 1979: 5,11; Moore and Myerhoff, 1977: 16).*

In actors' exegeses, major rituals often express widely-shared, integrative values, belonging more to Turner's collective dimension of *communitas*, society regarded as a concrete "homogeneous totality" of real people, than to the abstract, norm-dominated, divisive and often conflict-ridden dimension of structure, "society regarded as a structure of segmentarily or hierarchically opposed parts". *Communitas* and structure, though, are related in complex, subtle and not necessarily contradictory ways (Turner, 1974a: 100, chs 3, 4 1974b: 44–56). "Communitas", said Turner, "can and does occur both in structured and unstructured situation" (1977: 51); it is typically a breeding-ground of structure (1975: 15–33). In ritual aspects of structure—order, convention, formality, conformity—are commonly harnessed to the creation and reinforcement of *communitas*. In the stylised, emotionally-charged atmosphere of ritual, *communitas* may derive a compelling aura of inevitability which compensates for its lack of social power and may carry over into other contexts (Turner, 1967: 29–30; 1974b: 53–6).

My objects of study are social actions, observed in particular situations and in terms of actors as subjects, enacting culturally conceived roles and manipulating ritual, political and ideological elements for personal and group advantage.# I describe the Lifcu

---

* *This argument for ideology as strategic and reality-constituting was a significant theoretical advance on the simple, unmediated opposition of ideology and practice in the previous chapter.*

The image of actors as culturally constructed subjects, implementing strategies, was an improvement on "island-centred" historians' ethnocentrically universalist

meeting as a processual whole with a distinct phase structure, in line with Myerhoff's observation:

> in extended rituals there is a tendency for fixed segments to alternate with open or variable segments. Often the former are associated with sacred... elements, the latter with secular, regional or highly particular elements... [T]he fixed pieces... usually precede, follow and regularly punctuate the improvised or localized sections (Moore and Myerhoff, 1977: 18–19; Myerhoff, 1977: 200–2).

In these terms, the meeting was a "secular ritual", with a "work" phase framed by extended ritual phases and interspersed with performances of customary songs and dances. I locate it in wider cultural, historical, political and administrative contexts, but emphasise its internal dynamics, focussing on the ritual phases, seen as "key scenarios"[3] which evoked and dramatised *communitas* while suppressing conflicting ideological complexes. Ritual and work were mutually complementary rather than exclusive, dialectically related in the overall phase structure of the meeting.

BACKGROUND

Unlike the peoples of the independent nations of the southwest Pacific, in 1982 the Kanak of New Caledonia shared broadly similar cultures and social systems and agreed generally as to what constituted *la coutume*, "custom" (cf. Keesing and Tonkinson, 1982). It was the shared experience of customary life and the persistence of certain traditional values, as well as common subjection to the separate legal system of customary law under the French colonial régime, which distinguished them from all other ethnic groups.[4] Nonetheless, the Melanesian community was sharply differentiated by linguistic diversity, indigenous political fragmentation and varied colonial experience. There was general consensus about "the existence

---

trope of autonomous individuals acting on the basis of rationally assessed interests (e.g., Douglas, 1979; 1980a: 50). It was not yet an adequately theorised conception of agency.

of regions having linguistic and cultural homogeneity" and linked by traditional "circuits" and "gateways", along and through which inter-regional relationships were channelled (Union calédonienne, 1980: 13–14), but some disagreement as to detail on the main island.

Apart from the regional pattern, there was also a broad distinction between the large island (*la Grande Terre*) and the Loyalty Islands. I call the former the "mainland": I used to regard it as centre to the other islands' periphery, reflecting my research interest in certain mainland clans and tendency to adopt mainland Kanak perspectives. This was inappropriate, since traditionally mainland and island clans and chiefdoms were structurally equivalent and mainland groups played no metropolitan role; some of the largest and most complex traditional polities were located in the Loyalties. Administratively, the Loyalties were dependencies of the French colony of New Caledonia from the 1860s, but their colonial histories were very different from those of the mainland. There was no enforced European settlement or loss of traditional lands, unlike on the mainland, where only a small proportion of land was retained by Melanesians. There was also much less official interference in local structures of authority in the Loyalties (Howe, 1977: 81). Islanders had enjoyed far better educational opportunities for far longer than most mainlanders, partly because of the work of Protestant missionaries, local as well as European, in societies less affected by colonialism. As a result, until recently a disproportionate number of Melanesians who were successful and politically active on a Territorial[5] scale were Loyalty Islanders, especially Lifouans.

Relatively few Lifouans, however, played leading roles in the Front indépendantiste (FI), a coalition of mainly Kanak political parties whose slogan and goal were *l'indépendance kanake* et socialiste*. The FI easily won the commune of Lifou in 1983 municipal elections, which evinced a high degree of popular support for independence in Lifou, but customary authorities there were unanimously

---

* *In 1982 the Kanak independence movement was yet to break politically with French grammatical practice by declaring the term "kanak" to be invariable, though it sometimes takes the plural "s" as a noun.*

opposed, and before the 1983 elections the commune was controlled by an anti-independence mayor, a customary dignitary of the district of Lösi. Elsewhere in the Territory, chiefs and customary dignitaries tended to be more evenly divided on the issue, though a greater proportion was ambivalent or committed to the continuation of French rule than amongst the indigenous population generally, about 80% of whom were said to support the FI. There was mutual suspicion between mainlanders and islanders, especially Lifouans, that the others would gain a dominant role in a future Kanak state and use it to impose parochial interests (Union calédonienne, 1980: 1; Luc Bouarate, Letter to the Editor, Nouvelles, 29 Aug. 1983; Lino-Lepeu, Letter to the Editor, ibid., 27 Nov. 1984).

Loyalty Island societies, especially on Lifou, were far more "traditional" than those of the mainland. Lifouans, most of whom were devout Christians, two-thirds Protestant, regarded their societies as reservoirs of authentic custom—a dynamic blend of reworked tradition with localised Christian and modern technological elements. Mainland Melanesians, also mostly Christian, but two-thirds Catholic, acknowledged the strength of custom in Lifou, but there was some resentment of the flamboyant self-confidence of Lifouans in matters customary, especially given mainlanders' often painful efforts to re-authenticate or re-discover practices and symbols which had been neglected or abandoned in the face of far more onerous and oppressive colonialism than in the Loyalties. There was no perceived antithesis between Christianity and custom, unlike in parts of Vanuatu and the Solomon Islands (Brunton, 1981; Keesing and Tonkinson, 1982; Tonkinson, 1981). Lifouans and mainlanders were also in competition for control of the public presentation of indigenous festivals, especially the 4th Festival of Pacific Arts, scheduled for Nouméa in 1984. Among the main protagonists were senior Melanesian bureaucrats and politicians, who had become prominent through involvement in festival organisation and were also customary dignitaries.[6] They were convinced of the political efficacy of customary symbols and their public expression in generating cultural awareness and pride, and community solidarity, though a few leading Melanesians were sceptical about this, especially some radical elements of the independence movement

(Tjibaou, 1996a; Trolue and Caihe, 1995). Lifouans, befitting their reputation as customary performers, had been very prominent in earlier festivals, but were less conspicuous in the planning and organising phases of the 1984 Festival, a source of considerable chagrin to some.

The Lifou meeting stemmed indirectly from an earlier gathering of high chiefs convoked at Sarraméa, on the mainland, in 1980 by the then conservative French administration and the Commission pour la promotion mélanésienne, an official body headed by Frank Wahuzue. This gathering was widely seen, especially by independentists, as a government front, called specifically to formalise and strengthen the authority of high chiefs at the expense of less formal, more traditional relationships, institutions and values, which, especially after World War II, had again become prominent in indigenous communities (e.g., Similien Nahiet, Letter to the Editor, *Presse calédonienne*, 2 Dec. 1980). These included the dispersal of authority amongst customary dignitaries, of whom chiefs were by no means necessarily the most influential, and a stress on customary decision-making processes through discussion and consensus by "councils of elders", rather than chiefly fiat.

At issue were profoundly different modes of conceiving human interaction, which have been in dialectical relationship ever since French colonial authorities sought, after annexation in 1853, to control Melanesians and incorporate them in a formal administrative hierarchy: one, official, emphasised structure and entity; the other, indigenous, emphasised movement and relation. The French defined authority in terms of a uniform, Territory-wide structure, legally vested in formal officeholders (*de grands chefs*, "high chiefs", and *de petits chefs*, "petty chiefs"), who controlled people and resources in clearly-delineated territories ("districts" comprising "reserves", each occupied by *une tribu*, "tribe") and were responsible to their immediate superiors (white officials until recently) in the colonial hierarchy. Melanesians conceived authority in fluid social relational rather than structured territorial terms, expressed in language and values derived from consanguineal kinship and the convention that "chiefs" ("eldest sons and brothers"), even in the most complex traditional chiefdoms, were installed by their "subjects", "junior kinsmen", and might be replaced or abandoned should they prove unsatisfactory.

Indigenous political systems in New Caledonia[7] are best represented in terms of localised patterns of allegiance to clan segments of "chiefly" rank or to organised chieftaincies. Rank was phrased genealogically, but derived from the putative order of emergence of clan segments in the space of origin and itineraries with which a clan identified and from the relative length of residence of clan segments in an actual place. There were wide variations in the nature, extent and degree of political integration and hence in the contexts and scope of political authority. The basic political units, residential agglomerations of ranked, localised clan segments, were sometimes quasi-autonomous, sometimes embedded in wider hierarchies. The latter ranged from small, independent chiefdoms comprising local groups of varied origin, each of which fulfilled a specific ritual and political function *vis-a-vis* the senior "chiefly" clan segment, to complex chiefdoms embodying hierarchies of smaller chieftaincies and local groups. Whatever the contexts, authority was everywhere dispersed amongst complementary dignitaries linked by overlapping patterns of reciprocal rights and obligations. The structural basis of indigenous societies, in localised descent group segments linked to others in various ways, was effectively stable, while political ideologies stressed permanence and equilibrium, but actual groups, their composition and interrelationships were unstable as a result of constant flux and competition. Links with places to which a clan segment could sustain a relationship, actual or past, were of profound emotional and, potentially, political significance, but were not conceived in terms of discrete territorial units controlled by office-holders. The enforced disjunction of people from places with which they identified and in which their ancestors resided, an experience suffered by most mainland clans during the colonial period, meant great hardship, while the elevation of tribal chiefs to positions as group managers and controllers of reserve land could distort complex patterns of social relationships (Douglas, 1982).

The distinction between European and indigenous concepts of authority and social relations was in no sense permanent or rigid, but was contingent over time and in space and context. Colonial roles and entities became part of indigenous lived reality (custom), blended with traditional aspects, and were undoubtedly experienced and exploited by local people differently from the colonisers' intentions. By the second half of the twentieth century, most Melanesians had a triple status, with often discordant ideologies, rights and constraints. In practice this could mean overlap and confusion in local authority, decision-making and administration, but it also provided opportunities for individuals and groups to manipulate contexts and statuses to their own advantage. Indigenous people are members of a dispersed, patrilineal clan and are "subjects", "junior kinspeople", of its "chief" and of the "chiefs" of any residential agglomeration or chiefdom in which their localised clan segment is integrated: this is the primary domain of custom as locally practised and currently conceived. They and their clan segment (*un clan* in colonial administrative parlance) also belong to a "tribe" occupying a reserve, and are under its chief and a district high chief, whose authority might or might not be acknowledged as "customary": this is the primary domain of formal customary law (*le droit coutumier*), to which most Melanesians are subject in accordance with their particular status (*leur statut particulier*), differentiated from members of all other ethnic groups and those indigenous people who are under the common law (*le droit commun*). Melanesians are also French citizens, entitled to participate in municipal, Territorial and French national elections and subject to French law in areas outside their particular status. The first two contexts are neither fixed nor discrete, but overlap in structure, personnel and routine, and are now equally "indigenous".

The French tried at times to embody in legislation something of what they took to be the ethos of indigenous social relations. For example, the concepts of "clan", "clan property", "clan council" and "council of clan chiefs" were recently incorporated into customary law.[8] This legislation, however, did little to resolve ambiguity between the fluid, experiential domain of custom and the formal structure of customary law, since "clan" and "clan chief" were reduced to segment and role, respectively, within the administrative framework of the "tribe". Melanesians have increasingly confronted such ambiguity as they sought to define authentic custom and translate it into a formal institutional basis for an independent state. There was, and will continue to be, tension between lived custom and customary law, because the latter was a colonial and (will be ultimately) a postcolonial artefact, a collection of formal rules and principles abstracted from the kaleidoscope of collective lived experience and reified.

The overlap of different concepts of authority and criteria for the selection of chiefs meant that high chiefs, especially on the mainland, were a mixed lot. Formerly local autocrats in colonial theory, recently they shared authority with councils. Some were universally acknowledged in traditional terms, especially where their districts corresponded to places occupied by clan segments which accepted their ancestors as "chiefs", as was generally the case in the Loyalties. On the mainland, especially where there was colonial interference in "chiefly" succession and where people of diverse origins occupied reserves bearing little relationship to their ancestral places, high chiefs—the so-called "administrative chiefs"—might be regarded as colonial appointees, though actually chosen by district councils. The distinction was by no means clear; few admitted to being "administrative chiefs" and some were descendants of men deliberately pushed to the forefront in order to deflect official attention, or because they possessed appropriate skills. The question was further complicated from the mid-1970s as the state accorded greater autonomy and financial competence to communes, in an attempt to defuse the movement for national independence. A majority of communes outside Nouméa and its immediate environs was controlled by mayors and councils committed to *l'indépendance kanake et socialiste* (Dornoy, 1984: 240–3; *Nouvelles*, 7, 12 Mar. 1983); ambiguity in differentiating tribal, district and municipal responsibility could cause serious tensions, especially for Melanesian mayors in relation to tribal or high chiefs (e.g., Luc Bouarate, Letter to the Editor, *Nouvelles*, 29 Aug. 1983).

Following the Sarraméa meeting in 1980, Henri Boula, high chief of Lösi, and the dignitaries of the chiefdom, especially the chief of protocol and master of ceremonies, Noël Wahuzue, and the latter's brother Franck, decided that the high chiefs should be convoked for the first time on the initiative of one of their number. The gathering would be modelled partly on a traditional meeting of chiefs and couched as a modern customary festival. There were close links between several Lösi dignitaries, including Franck Wahuzue, and the Rassemblement pour la Calédonie dans la République (RPCR), the main conservative, anti-independence political party. One motive for the meeting was no doubt the goal of enhancing Wahuzue's prestige in Territorial political and administrative hierarchies. By late 1982 this was fairly urgent, for in June Wahuzue had lost his position on the Council of Government with the emergence of a pro-independence majority, while his previously pivotal bureaucratic status in Melanesian cultural and customary affairs had declined since the election a year earlier of a Socialist government in France. Boula's decision, however, was phrased in customary terms. This was consistent with the centrality of custom in the modern structure of authority in Loyalty Islands societies. Contradiction between European and indigenous concepts and loci of authority was not such a problem in the Loyalties, at least for chiefs and dignitaries, since colonial and customary systems largely overlapped. However, the control of custom in the lives of ordinary people could be stifling, especially in respect to personal access to communal lands and resources (Similien Nahiet, Letter to the Editor, *Presse calédonienne*, 2 Dec. 1980). The three Loyalty Islands consistently returned pro-independence majorities in all elections after 1977 (Dornoy, 1984: 237–70; *Nouvelles*, 20 Nov. 1984).

PRELIMINARIES

The intention formulated, customary channels were used to effect it. The messenger of the Lösi chiefdom was responsible for invitations, which on the mainland were mainly channelled through Boula's councillors who worked in Nouméa, especially the brothers Wahuzue. Each high chief was sent a letter of invitation to the meeting and official invitations were also sent to the High Commissioner (the French head of the Territorial government), to the Vice-President of the Council of Government, a Kanak, and to the organising committee of the Pacific Arts Festival. About 30 of a total of 54 high chiefs from all parts of the Territory eventually came, many accompanied by spokesmen, while others sent representatives; in all there were more than 150 visitors, including many of the 350 odd petty chiefs. It was said to be the first time that the High Commissioner had attended a customary gathering as representative of France, rather than as head of the Territory, and implications for the question of sovereignty were noted. The Vice-President, who was also mayor of his local commune, came as a customary representative and spokesman, rather than in his official capacity, though the latter was relevant during the work phase of the meeting. It was said that the Festival organisers did not respond according to customary protocol, and neither the chairman nor the director (see above, n. 4) formally attended, though the chairman was nearby during the later stages of the meeting; a team sent to film the dances and ceremonies was seriously hampered as a result.

I first heard there was to be an important meeting of high chiefs in Lifou about a fortnight beforehand and conceived an instant passion to attend. A semi-formal invitation was arranged by a personal friend, a Lifouan, not from Lösi. He was president of a cultural association which for years worked to promote indigenous culture and custom, but was particularly identified with the Lifouan community in Nouméa. He and his association had been very active in earlier festivals, but he was seriously estranged from the organisers of the 1984 Festival. Noël Wahuzue was a member of this association. My friend and I therefore joined the second party of mainland high chiefs to fly to Lifou and accompanied them from the airport along the traditional route of entry to the seat of the Lösi high chieftainship at Mou. At the gateway to Mou my friend made custom on my behalf to Wahuzue, the master of ceremonies, and asked if I could be received *à côté de* ("beside") the visiting delegation. Wahuzue replied that I should be received *dedans* ("within") the delegation and encouraged me to witness the private ceremony where the visitors prepared their customary gift to the hosts. The chiefs seemed a little nonplussed at my presence, but politely agreed and accepted a contribution to the offering on my behalf. I then joined the formal ceremonies of admittance and welcome of the invited guests and was presented to Boula by Wahuzue as part of the visiting delegation, as a specialist on Melanesian history and a friend of the cultural association. I observed, listened, talked, ate and slept as a member of the delegation, fortunate that the main language used publicly, and often privately, was French, due to the gathering's inclusive nature.

The link with the cultural association was clearly crucial in my acceptance by the hosts, but my own research background and previous field experience meant that I identified with the mainlanders amongst the visitors. Sponsorship by the cultural association entailed the informal reciprocal obligation on my part to "write a history" of the meeting, but my friend the president insisted that my interpretation should be my own. The interpretation presented here is mine, but it owes much to a dialogical process, and without his and others' advice I should have remained oblivious to much of the significance of the action observed, especially from a Lifouan viewpoint. Acknowledging this perspective was an important corrective to my tendency to identify with the mainland delegation and to construct reality in mainland terms.

At the airport in Nouméa I was given a copy of the program a roneoed, typed, double-sided, A4 sheet, in French, presenting a formidably timetabled agenda. It was headed "Grand Meeting of High Chiefs, Mou—Lösi—Lifou, 17–18–19 December 1982" and at top and bottom right-hand corners bore the Boula coat of arms—a crossed spear and club encompassed by a sling in warlike mode, as if wrapped about the head for ready access. The first day's timetable and agenda are in Table 1.

The program was a typical amalgam of "Western" format and indigenous content, as Melanesians appropriate the formal conventions of meeting procedure and enact them within indigenous schemata. In retrospect I saw the program as a polyvalent ideological statement: in its seeming encompassment of *travail*, "work", by ceremony and commensality; in its expression of the value attributed to order and system—a recurrent motif in indigenous social and political ideologies in New Caledonia (Bensa and Rivierre, 1982; Douglas, 1982). The vagaries of practice did not seem to matter, since ideology was as much an interpretive model and strategic framework as an ideal: the program thus conjoined a blueprint for action, a set of alternative strategies and an image of action. Neither timetable nor agenda was strictly followed: each item eventuated with little

TABLE 1	"GRAND MEETING OF HIGH CHIEFS, MOU—LÖSI—LIFOU, 17–18–19 DECEMBER 1982": TIMETABLE AND AGENDA, DAY 1
	Friday 17 December 1982
7 H 30	— Welcome to Hnassé—By Petty Chief HLUPA and his tribe — Breakfast
9 H	— Welcome to the High Chiefdom of Mou by the High Chief and his district council — Song: Tribe of Jozip — Dance: Tribe of Kéjeny
11 H 30	— Lunch — Song: Tribe of Wiwatul
13 H 30	— Work Session
15 H	— Dance: Tribe of Hmélek (Féhoa: Haïtr) — Dance: Tribe of Hnaéu (Féhoa: Ekehnej)
17 H 30	— Tea — Dance: Clan Itra Eötr — Cigarettes + Coffee: Clan Ange Hnalapa
19 H 30	— Dinner — Song: Tribe of Thuahaïck
20 H 30	— Animation: Group of young people of Lösi

concern for sequence or duration and each day ended three to four hours later than planned. The relative significance attributed to the various items was a matter for evaluation and negotiation on the basis of personal and group interests. This would become apparent gradually. At that stage I had little idea what it all might mean.

RITUAL PHASES

Welcome

On arrival at the Lifou airport the visitors began a ritual progress of steadily increasing intensity, lasting several hours, designed from the Lifouan perspective to transform them from outsiders into temporary "subjects", who could be admitted into the high chief's domain and welcomed. At each stage there were exchanges of gifts and oration, ever more elaborate as the visitors drew closer to Mou, and the hosts performed customary songs and dances. From the airport the visitors proceeded by bus to Hnathalo,

84 ACROSS THE GREAT DIVIDE

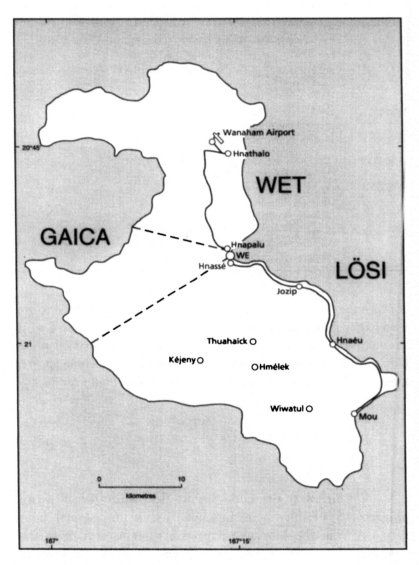

MAP 3   *Lifou: the road to Mou*

seat of the high chief of the district of Wet, where the airport is located, to pay their respects and be welcomed. From Hnathalo they went to Hnapalu, on the northern outskirts of the administrative centre of Wé, but still in the district of Wet. The chief of this quarter, a subject of the high chief of Wet, is keeper of the keys to the three districts of Lifou, and had to authorise entry. Duly authorised, they entered Lösi and stopped again on the southern outskirts of Wé at Hnassé, the first tribe encountered in Lösi when coming from the exterior, the last tribe in Lösi from the customary, high chiefly, perspective of Mou. Its chief is sentinel of the district and his representative has to accompany all visitors to Mou. Thus accompanied they retook the buses to the outskirts of Mou and disembarked at the house of a chief of Api Co, clan of the keepers of the key to the high chief's domain, without whose permission no further progress was possible.

By this stage several themes had become apparent. From a Lifouan perspective, the route, the sequence and the general form of speech and gesture comprised a key scenario prescribed by custom (cf. Tjibaou, 1996a: 43). Only the number of visitors and the scale of the enterprise were unusual. The visitors had no shared precedents for action and had to adapt and improvise from their local variants of custom as they went along, while the very role of visitor implied reactive conformity to the hosts' dictates. There had obviously been much informal discussion amongst individuals and groups as to suitable procedures, together with ritual preparation and amassing of items for customary gifts at district and regional levels, as well as in Nouméa the day before their departure (*Nouvelles*, 17 Dec. 1982). It was my impression that decisions as to who should act as spokesmen and what would comprise appropriate custom were quickly made after brief discussion, usually focussed on Jean-Marie Tjibaou, Vice-President of the Council of Government, a leader of the FI and an acknowledged expert on indigenous culture (Tjibaou, 1976). According to Lifouan protocol, high chiefs ought not to speak for themselves and two prominent petty chiefs quickly emerged as principal spokesmen for the visitors, both members of mainland clans with traditional links with Lösi. One was a pastor's son raised in Lifou, who spoke *drehu*, the Lifouan language.

I took his choice as both a gesture of respect to the hosts and a minor prestation through which to exercise some control over proceedings.

The Lifouan ritual theme of transformation and encapsulation of outsiders was quickly matched by visiting spokesman. They reiterated more global themes, of particular concern to mainland chiefs, that the gathering aimed to reinforce or recreate custom, which had been degraded, and to re-forge links between all the regions of the mainland and the islands. This could imply reverse encapsulation, of the islands by the mainland. At Hnassé a spokesman introduced the metaphor of a cord linking mainland and islands, which had deteriorated over time (as a result of colonialism, which forbade casual voyaging beyond tribal boundaries until after World War II, and Christianity, the missions having discouraged continuation of traditional links, especially with pagans or supporters of the rival faith).

At the Api Co house on the outskirts of Mou, Noël Wahuzue appeared for the first time, speaking as Boula, to request permission from the keeper of the key for the guests to prepare their major customary offering. This solemn private ceremony, *la préparation du travail*, was performed in a traditional round house and begun by general consensus by Tjibaou, acting as spokesman for the district of Hienghène. The gift, amassed with care and deliberation, included numerous large *manou* (lengths of brightly coloured cloth), a considerable quantity of cigarettes, tobacco sticks, matches and currency, and, most significant, several packets of traditional shell money, including a quantity of "black" money, the most valued and "weighty" form. This was a matter of pride for mainlanders because it is no longer made in the islands. Lifouans compensate by attaching high denomination notes to elaborate bouquets of flowers and leaves, said to be a Christian symbol incorporated in the customary discourse of reception. Formerly, specialist clans in all regions fabricated shell money, but only a few mainland clans retain the knowledge. It is presented on significant traditional occasions, such as marriage. Shell money was the key "summarizing symbol"[9] in all socially important transactions; without it, social relations could not be established or endure. Here it was undoubtedly a prestation.

The shell money was placed on top of the other items, flanked by a folded sling and two sling stones. A mainland high chief later explained to me pointedly that a folded sling meant peace and an end to war, conflict and suspicion, especially when separated from its stones by traditional money, symbol of peace and solidarity—in contrast to the warlike mode of the sling in the Boula coat of arms on the program. The gesture symbolised a communion of all Melanesians, underlined when a spokesman reintroduced the image of the broken cord by knotting the end of a large *manou* and suggesting it be presented to Wahuzue/Boula. The contrasting themes of ritual encapsulation and indigenous unity, representing the reversible asymmetric opposition Lifou : visitors, reached their climax in the next stage of the ritual.

After Wahuzue/Boula presented custom on the guests' behalf to the keeper of the key, the latter led them to the large courtyard of the high chief's compound, where the main body of hosts waited. To the fore, enthroned in strict conventional silence on a red vinyl armchair, sat Boula, a tall, impressive middle-aged figure with a constantly replenished glass of whisky, flanked by his family, customary dignitaries and official guests, including, on his right, the High Commissioner. The visitors assembled opposite, leaving an open space in which the climax of the welcome ceremony was enacted. In drenching rain, the ceremony of presentation of the key to the high chieftainship was performed by members of Api Co. An old man declaimed: "... here on this soil, no one may come here without authorisation. He who would come here must walk in the footsteps of his fathers, because he who comes here without these footsteps, well, he will die at once". He meant that only people with ancestral ties to the place could walk or speak there, and that the visitors had to become "subjects", "junior kinspeople", of the "chief" of Api Co, keeper of the key, in order to be accepted by "my high chief Wahuzue [Boula]".

The keeper of the key himself now spoke, presenting five large keys roughly cut from plywood to representatives of the various regions of the Territory. He announced that the high chieftainship was open to the guests, but only for this occasion; he intended to change the locks, as he did not trust mainland chiefs like his own brother-in-law (a joke). As a result of this ceremony, the objects exchanged and the words spoken, dialogue and ordinary life could proceed. Noël Wahuzue (Boula) could occupy centre stage, where he remained until the dying moments of the meeting. Following exchange of formal speeches, the guests' customary offering was displayed with great tenderness and care. A spokesman for the visitors presented a knotted *manou* to Wahuzue with several 1,000 franc notes enclosed in the knot, symbolising ancient, now broken links between mainland and islands. Wahuzue, forewarned by my friend, acknowledged the gesture by untying the knot, then retying it to symbolise recreation of the links at this meeting. The initial ritual phase concluded with a reception line, along which the guests shuffled to be formally presented by Wahuzue to high chief and dignitaries. Boula did not speak, but gestured graciously to acknowledge the presence of his temporary "subjects".

Customary performances

The next two days were devoted to commensality and "work", accompanied by or interspersed with the performance of Lifouan dances and songs, some specially composed. They included an elaborate dramatic re-enactment of the reception of the first Protestant missionary teacher at Mou, involving dozens of actors. The most important and stirring performances were two *féhoa*, genealogical dances and citations of clans, presented on the first evening. Traditional orations in which the most valued customary knowledge available to a community, the relative positioning of groups, is publicly displayed, these *féhoa* are reserved for profoundly significant occasions and had last been performed in the 1950s. Their presentation here was an index of the importance attached to the meeting by the customary authorities of Lösi.

Such performances depend for effect more on the participants' vigour, rhythm and exuberance than on brilliance of costume. In a typical, highly choreographed Lifouan dance, males wear a uniform of patterned *manou*, with sometimes a calf-length skirt and necklace of coconut leaves. Fibre leggings are always worn and sometimes armbands, while head decorations comprise either garlands of flowers or leaves, or cloth bandanas or turbans, often matching the *manou*. They brandish clubs or long bunches of stiff grass. Women, whose engagement is much more sedate and mainly choral and instrumental, wear "mission dresses", usually of similarly patterned fabric to the men's *manou*. Wooden drums, rattles and whistles provide rhythmic accompaniment to the chanting, songs and stamping of the performers. Music and songs are mostly of Christian inspiration.*

It is impossible to convey in print the sensory impact, visual, aural and gustatory, of Lifouan custom in ceremonial mode, the so-called "Lifou cinema": but it was profound and incessant. At first, as in the program, the ritual phases and other customary performances seemed to submerge the work (*le travail*) planned for the meeting, but ultimately I saw ritual and work as structurally equivalent, dialectically interrelated phases, in both of which song, dance and drama were significant elements. Their relationship recalled that discerned by Turner between the "two clearly distinguishable poles of meaning" of Ndembu dominant ritual symbols, the sensory or emotional and the ideological or normative (1967: 28; 1974b: 55–6): ritual "is precisely a mechanism that periodically converts the obligatory into the desirable", while simultaneously ennobling emotions through contact with social norms and values (1967: 30; Geertz, 1975: 90–141). Thus in the ritual phases, an "interchange of qualities" between norms and emotional stimuli was symbolically

---

* *Critics moved by a romantic politics of authenticity may deplore such eclecticism as the degenerate, derivative debris of the "fatal impact" of Christianity and Westernisation (e.g., Babadzan, 1988). Tjibaou, himself the main organiser of the remarkable 1975 festival Mélanésia 2000, landmark in the Kanak struggle for national identity (Anon. 1995; Tjibaou et al. 1976), put a pragmatic, antiessentialist view with respect to the trappings of custom:*

> *the manner of dancing of people today, the material they use, are what they live culturally, and we do not have the right, in the name of an authenticity the blueprint of which is located 50 or 150 years ago, to criticise what they are today; they dance with manous, with whistles, with watches, rings ... [sic], it is their actual mode of expression, which corresponds to their actual authenticity. Authenticity is tied to time, and it is always tied to history, to a certain existentiality of being (1996a: 42).*

effected in the juxtaposition of solemn invocation, exhortation and exchange with the ardour and excitement of dance and song. The latter were part of a highly formalised, integrated process of symbolic interaction between hosts and visitors. From the hosts' perspective, the initial ritual phase achieved the temporary creation of a single meta-community, which incorporated the visitors in a capacity at once structurally junior and privileged.

Farewell

A further ritual phase occurred on the Sunday, a ritual farewell which symbolically dismantled the meta-community created by the initial phase and restored equivalences through exchanges. It began with the formal exchange between hosts and guests of their main customary offerings: the hosts' included an impressive quantity of *manou* and yams, staple vegetable, coded male, of profound symbolic significance to clans throughout New Caledonia; the visitors' was that which had been prepared and displayed during the welcome. Separation of the ritual meta-community into its constituent parts occurred with a shift of focus to the hosts as a group for their ceremony of redistribution of the visitors' gift. The guests as a body then performed the final ritual act by planting a commemorative coconut palm in a prominent position near the entrance to the high chief's compound; each visiting chief threw a handful of soil into the hole. The contrast, as in the ritual of welcome, between the formal, prescribed quality of Lifouan actions and the *ad hoc* pragmatism of the visitors, was again apparent during the final phase. The hosts' redistribution was integrated into the farewell ritual, conducted before the assembled gathering by the appropriate dignitaries, and followed a traditional "road". The visitors' redistribution of all items which had been received as gifts during the meeting took place informally, after completion of the farewell; the terms on which it was based and the shares were negotiated on the spot, without fuss or obvious disagreement. In style and dramatic content the visitors' redistribution could scarcely have differed more from the hosts', but culturally it was no less traditional or significant.

WORK PHASE

Dramatised and validated in the ritual phases, an ethos of harmony, unity and common purpose, variously construed but compelling, was translated to the intervening work phase. This was enlivened by regular presentations of dance, song and staged drama, which recalled the ritual experience while, reciprocally, work provided a respectable context for performance (Geertz, 1975: 90, 449; Moore and Myerhoff, 1977: 18–19). Two sessions totalling five and a half hours were buried in the program under the rubric *réunion de travail*, "work session", but there was uncertainty beforehand about what they might involve (e.g., *Nouvelles*, 17 Dec. 1982). Tjibaou told me at the Lifou airport that he would only stay if the meeting was "serious". Late on the first afternoon the participants divided into two work groups, one including Tjibaou, to which I attached myself, the other including Franck Wahuzue, for discussions which, it became clear, were to address the formation of a Council of High Chiefs.

The question of what roles high chiefs collectively might play in the national administrative and political systems was of general concern. Following the Sarraméa meeting in 1980, and at the instigation of the Commission pour la promotion mélanésienne, formal moves had been initiated by the then conservative administration to create a Council of High Chiefs (*Presse calédonienne*, 2 Dec. 1980). On the other side of Territorial politics,[10] at the 1980 Congress of the Union calédonienne (UC) it was proposed that parliamentary institutions in an independent New Caledonia should consist of "a National Assembly with Executive power, and... a Senate, or grand Council of Chiefs, with Consultative power"; this was afterwards incorporated into the UC's platform (Union calédonienne, 1980: 6, 1; *Pacific Islands Monthly*, Jan. 1983: 15). Late in 1981, with a new Socialist administration in France professing a changed attitude to Kanak aspirations, the Territorial Assembly passed a resolution creating a formal framework for a Council of High Chiefs as the official channel for consultation between the Territorial administration and customary institutions (Délibération no. 352, 10 Dec. 1981, *JO* 1981: 1728–9). The process of giving content to the framework was to be decided by the high chiefs themselves. There matters stood until the Lifou meeting, when the politically unlikely coalition of Tjibaou and Franck Wahuzue combined to force the issue.

Apparent similarities in the positions taken on this question by Melanesians of pro- and anti-independence stance stemmed partly from the fact that national political differences between indigenous people are not always relevant where custom is concerned. Most share pride in their culture and institutions and a real sense of difference in world view, attitudes, experience, goals and opportunity from members of other ethnic groups. Nonetheless, there were clearly divergent political perspectives. Those opposed to *l'indépendance kanake et socialiste,* both European and Melanesian, undoubtedly believed that the proposed Council would be a conservative, pro-French body, the institutional authority of which would counteract the influence of Kanak radicals and enhance the capacity of individual high chiefs to contain the spread of pro-independence activities in their districts. For their part, the UC and the Front indépendantiste as a whole were ambivalent about chiefs, especially those called "administrative chiefs", regarded as colonial appointees and opponents of independence. There was justified apprehension that a Council of High Chiefs would be politically conservative and opposed to *l'indépendance kanake et socialiste.* Conversely, most independentists on the mainland regarded clearer definition and bolstering of customary authority, especially in the clan context, and its integration into party and ultimately state structures at local, regional and national levels to be essential if indigenous values and institutions were be relevant, especially for the young, and be viable bases for a future independent Kanak state (Union calédonienne, 1980; "Réunion des chefs du district nord à Pouébo", *Nouvelles,* 18 Dec. 1981).

In the work sessions I attended the high chiefs took little public part, because important chiefs customarily do not speak publicly, but also because they were perceived, as a group, as needing to be convinced that a Council of High Chiefs should be established. The key was the initial session, appropriately held in the impressive gloom of a traditional round house. Participants sat or lounged on mats around the hearth flanking the massive central column, traditional symbol for a "chief", overarched by radiating beams which comprised the structure of the building and symbolised the dignitaries whose authority complemented and limited the "chief's". Tjibaou, from an unobtrusive position in the shadows well away from the door, manipulated roles skilfully to produce an acceptable consensus. He entered the discussion quite late, befitting an experienced orator who sought to gauge the temper of the meeting before committing himself. Another visiting spokesman, a petty chief, had painted a dire picture of the fate of chiefly authority and custom should high chiefs not re-establish their relevance in the rapidly changing modern world: if chiefs went, the central pillar of the house would have collapsed and with it the whole edifice of custom. In response to an expression of disquiet by a Lifouan about the future status of the islands in an independent state, he referred provocatively to the land problem on the mainland, a divisive issue because it is irrelevant in the islands.

Initially Tjibaou spoke as customary representative and expert on indigenous culture, invoking summarising symbols to recall the meeting's ethos of harmony and unity and to reconcile divergent perspectives; his symbols included a distinction between European concepts of land "ownership" and the indigenous concept of "patrimony", never sold, but within which the stranger prepared to respect the hosts' place and word might be welcomed and installed. He stressed the common indigenous tradition of welcome, despite historical differences between the mainland and the islands in relation to land. He then altered role, to speak as an elected local government official—mayor of his commune—alluding to the need for Melanesian mayors and councillors to work within the framework of custom and cooperate with chiefs in customary matters where they had authority. He noted that the absence of formal channels for consultation with high chiefs meant that white administrators by-passed their authority. Later he used irony to great effect, pointing to the humiliating expedients forced on chiefs—meeting at the bandstand in Nouméa's central square—because they lacked corporate identity. When the work groups reconvened the next day, outdoors, Tjibaou again spoke at length, pragmatically, with firm and rather remote authority as senior representative of the Territorial government, no longer in the restrained and diffident style of a customary orator seeking to persuade. He now stressed the need for administrative efficiency, for high chiefs to have their own representative body within the national administrative system, through which they might be formally consulted on issues relating to customary law, and which would "carry their word". He pointed out that the planned institution was new, not customary, and that many would suspect conservative political motives, in which context he mentioned Wahuzue.

There was general acceptance of Tjibaou's proposal that they choose a provisional committee of high chiefs, with regional representation, to decide on implementation of the Assembly's 1981 resolution. Yet it took hours of discussion and negotiation, in public and privately in Boula's house, to work out a basis for representation. With the satisfactory resolution of the work phase, the rest of the meeting was devoted to commensality, song, dance, Christian worship and customary ritual, reiterating and confirming the spirit in which the decision was made. The provisional committee subsequently did its job. In March 1983 a Council of High Chiefs was installed, with Henri Boula as secretary and Franck Wahuzue as administrative secretary-general. This new institution, an outcome of the Lifou meeting, was significant to the wider socio-political contexts in which the meeting was located. For instance, the Council was represented, by Wahuzue, at important Round Table discussions in France in July 1983 to consider the future of the Territory. But wider transformations shaped by the meeting are not at issue here. The meeting itself as performance and aspects of its processual and transformational dynamics have been my focus so far, and require further systematic reflection.

DISCUSSION

Goals and intentions

The goals and intentions which produced the meeting can be subdivided into general social and personal/group goals. The explicit, public goal was that the high chiefs should meet for the first time on their own initiative: meeting was an end in itself. It was also to be an instrument, a means to achieve discussion and decision on the formation of a Council of High Chiefs. Most participants were aware of the latter goal, but only those actively involved in Territorial administration and politics at relatively senior levels, none of whom was a high chief, understood its wider implications. For them, whatever their political affiliation, specific intentions and status in the context of the meeting, the latter goal was the meeting's *raison d'être*. Both goals, to meet and to engage in directed discussion, were widely conceived as contributing in an imprecise but tangible way to an axiomatic good, reinforcement of custom. This was construed, not without qualification and ambiguity, as likely to enhance the well-being of indigenous society and of Melanesians within wider New Caledonian society.

Idiosyncratic goals were more varied, ambiguous or contradictory. Those publicly announced by individuals and groups coincided with the general social goals, but the latter were cover and context for competition, through which persons and groups might enhance their prestige and advantage in customary or wider political spheres, and diminish rivals. My evidence for personal and sectional goals is speculative: motives guessed from comparison of actions, including symbolic actions, and words, including speculation, comment and gossip by participants about their own and others' intentions. These specific, impressionistic data are correlated with details of personal biography and placed in relevant socio-political context.

The main impression I formed about personal and sectional goals during the actual meeting, as an outsider introduced by the hosts, placed structurally in the category of visitor and tending to identify with the numerically dominant segment amongst the guests, was of attempted manipulation and point-scoring by Lifouans, and by Lösi dignitaries and the Wahuzue in particular. The latter, inevitably, were highly visible as sponsors of the meeting and controllers of its major ritual roles, significant prizes in the competitive contexts in which the meeting was set. My immediate impression of one-sided manipulation was reinforced by certain situational aspects: the sensually battering process of ritual transformation and encompassment of the visitors; the omnipresent "Lifou cinema", enthralling in detail but overwhelming in total; the elaborate protocol and restrictions of Lifouan social hierarchy, and the pressure exerted by customary authority on ordinary Lifouans; the (to me) appalling ceremonial persona of Boula, kept in a state of near stupor, publicly tonguetied, his identity conventionally subsumed in his ceremonial mouthpiece; the experience of members of the Festival cinematographic team, whom I knew personally and who were inadvertently placed in contempt of Lifouan protocol as a result of a squabble between senior officials for control of artistic direction of the Festival.

The mainland societies I knew well were less frenetic and less rigidly hierarchical. I could not see why my acquaintances among the mainland chiefs seemed so relaxed. One, a UC member and high chief of a district seriously affected by dispersion and expropriation of clans after defeat in the 1878–9 colonial war, provided clues: while the meeting did involve an attempt by Lösi dignitaries and the islands to regain control of the independence movement, for mainland chiefs the goal of strengthening custom was crucial; young people no longer listened to the elders, unlike in the Loyalties, where customary authority was respected. There were blatant political motives at work, he agreed, but it was irrelevant because everyone knew it; what mattered was that the chiefs had met, reached a decision and taken steps to implement it. He thus phrased the goals of mainland chiefs in terms of the axiomatic good underlying the meeting's general social goals. My immediate reaction was to juxtapose what seemed like the selfish motives of the meeting's Lifouan organisers with the disinterested goals of mainlanders.

On reflection, though, I realised that the idea of one-sided manipulation was my own partial, engaged perspective under the emotional impact of the episode. I came to see the meeting as a processual whole and to locate it in the wider socio-political contexts of which it was a significant small element. The question of relative self-interest and disinterest in goals is always complex; neither actions nor words can be taken at face-value. For instance, to further the axiomatic good of strengthening custom could be of strategic importance to mainland chiefs in their own social contexts, which included colonial authority roles and local interpretations of colonial notions of authority as part of lived reality (custom). The mainlander's exegesis was a chiefly perspective, not necessarily those of complementary clan dignitaries, elected Melanesian officials or ordinary clanspeople. If "reinforcing custom" meant "reinforcing chiefly authority" it could imply "at the expense of other dignitaries and consultative bodies, both customary and introduced". Interested chiefly exploitation of colonial presence and policies was certainly not unknown in the past, either on the mainland or in the islands (Douglas, 1982: 403–7). Similarly, the impression of unanimous, enthusiastic participation by Lifouans was carefully contrived and obscured internal differences and dissension over political goals and status.

My initial interpretation of the ritual progress of the opening day as an aggressive Lifouan attempt to subsume and control the visitors had also to be modified, as I came to see it as parallel processes of attempted encapsulation, cloaked in the conventional courtesy appropriate between host and visitor. Their interaction was mediated by a ritual mode which suppressed or transcended differences by collapsing them within a common symbolic idiom. The main ideological theme put by both hosts and visitors was harmony, unity and common purpose. The ritual and symbolic action at once sustained and inspired by this ethos created social reality for the duration of the meeting, "including in society both structure and communitas". As Turner acknowledged, structure and *communitas* are best seen not as polar opposites, but as "contrasting social experiences", archmodalities in social realities and processes, "intrinsically related, perhaps even... not contradictory in the ultimate, nondualistic sense" (1974b: 56, 46, 44). At the Lifou meeting they were reversible: what was experienced as *communitas* by one side could mean structure (hierarchy, subordination, division) to the other, because the key concept "unity", implying "communion", had different, even contradictory, meanings.

The goal of the Lifouan ritual was to transform strangers into "kinspeople", "subjects" of the host chief. This was necessary in customary terms to protect the hosts from the threat posed by the incursion of strangers and to insulate the visitors against the dangerous potency of local spirits, inseparable from the land itself. (Recall the old man's speech during the ceremony of presentation of the key to the high chieftainship.) The status of "subject" in a ritual setting should not imply subordination or inferiority. In traditional ethos, if not always in colonial practice, "chiefs" and their "subjects" are reciprocally, as well as hierarchically, complementary (Douglas, 1994b; Jolly, 1994). Furthermore, the apparently aggressive self-confidence of Lifouan ritual actors masked a widespread unease and defensiveness, articulated during the work phase, in an evolving national political scene in which Lifouans were no longer the most influential indigenous category, and the potential outcome of which was feared by many.

Conversely, the mainland chiefs adopted the notion of unity partly in response to the inherently reactive role of guest, especially in the compulsive ambiance of a Lifouan ritual occasion. Ideologically the notion implied advance of common indigenous interests against those of other ethnies, but in practice it meant precisely that subsumption of islanders and their interests within the general body of Melanesians which Lifouans, especially, mistrusted. The mainlanders' theme was symbolised by the folded sling divided from its stones by shell money and by the knotted *manou*; Noël Wahuzue's acceptance of the latter and response to the gesture implied acknowledgement of the theme. But to Wahuzue and other islanders it recalled traditional reciprocal relationships, exchange links and equivalence between members of autonomous groups whose island or mainland location was incidental. That the mainland concept of unity did not mean reforging tradition became clear when a spokesman for the visitors referred to Lifou as "an island which is part of *la grande terre*". The Lifouan who expressed doubts during the work phase about the likely position of the islands in an independent state was reminded of the land problem on the mainland, a response neither intended nor received as reassurance. Tjibaou's role as mediator and conciliator in this context has been mentioned. The mediate status of non-Lifouan islanders, as both islanders and guests, was also noticeable and was symbolised during the hosts' redistribution ceremony when a gesture of inclusion was made to a clan from Maré which was part of the traditional exchange "road" of Lösi. The opposition Lifou : visitors was enacted during the ritual phases; during the work phase and informally the opposition islands : mainland was more salient.

Scrutiny of goals and intentions shows clearly that, even within a common cultural system, perceived reality is heterogeneous, influenced by divergent historical experience, context, and varying subject positions, such as centre/periphery, "chief"/"subject", senior/junior, man/woman (Keesing, 1987). An axiomatic good like strengthening custom will be widely compelling while it remains imprecise, but may become divisive if imbued with overly specific content (cf. Keesing, 1982: 299; Tonkinson, 1982: 304–5). Tjibaou's anxiety to stress that "the meaning of custom is everywhere the same", that "the meaning of exchange is the same, from the north to the south of the country", despite regionally variant customary practice, was clearly expressed during the work phase of the meeting (Union calédonienne, 1980: 13; Tjibaou, 1996b: 122).

Form and performance

Consideration of goals and intentions requires reference to the form of the meeting and to actual performance. Form and performance are dialectically linked. In this case, because of the manufactured aspect of the meeting (cf. Moore, 1977: 166), its unprecedented, improvised quality, form itself became a deliberate instrument of strategy to a far greater extent than with a prescribed traditional ritual. Yet the distinction is only one of degree, since the most seemingly immutable of social forms is subject to the contingency of the actual event and to interpretation and manipulation by actors in the translation of form into discrete performances, while it is in performance that a ritual achieves its effects (Kapferer, 1979: 6; Moore, 1975). Such meetings belong to a genre of secular ritual labelled "nonce rituals" by Myerhoff: "rituals among strangers and acquaintances gathered together on an *ad hoc* basis for the nonce, once only bringing with them diverse experience and personal histories" (1977: 201). This meeting's "nonce" quality was more salient for visitors than Lifouans, for whom the ritual phases were customary key scenarios. Nonce rituals invoke traditional values and practices to legitimate and traditionalise a transient historical performance, typically via the juxtaposition in structured sequence of fixed traditional segments and open segments specific to the particular occasion.

A traditionalising effect was initially derived from the overall form given to the Lifou meeting, and was reinforced by internal sequencing. Its form was a modern customary festival, an established convention which embraced useful novelties like published programs and agenda, and in some cases—as with the Boula coat of arms—represented them as customary symbols. The festival metaphor was not only appropriate to the axiomatic good which the meeting was meant to advance, but gave it a ready-made order and legitimacy and was a key strategy for the Lösi dignitaries, both within Lifou and beyond. Lifouans revel in customary ceremony. The opportunity for public cultural expressivity on a grand scale, showing the Arts Festival organisers that Lifouan expertise could not be ignored, helped mobilise most of Lösi and much of Lifou to contribute to the massive cost and effort of staging the affair. The festival metaphor and, during the actual meeting, recurrent intense involvement in song, dance and staged drama temporarily masked serious internal divisions within the Lifou commune over the question of independence and what many local independentists saw as abuse of customary authority for political ends and of political office for personal gain. The mask of unanimity was not entirely convincing, for during the first night someone pulled down all the French flags with which Mou had been liberally adorned, felling flagpoles in the process to prevent replacement.

For the Territory generally, the festival metaphor established the successful fiction that the meeting was not primarily political and administrative in intent, an important gloss given the notorious uneasiness of high chiefs about national politics and administration. The metaphor was sufficiently compelling to render non-attendance difficult for custom-minded chiefs (and they nearly all are), but, reciprocally, meant that attendance need not imply conformity with the hosts' well-known political goals. There had apparently been much discussion about the implications of Boula's invitation and whether to accept. I was told that one independentist high chief, also a mayor, advised fellow UC members amongst the high chiefs in his region not to go, and only one did so. Independentists from other regions were reasonably well-represented, and the overall level of attendance was a triumph for the organisers.

Through the symbolism of the initial ritual phase the axiomatic good of reinforcing custom and its corollary, the festival metaphor, were translated into a generally experienced *communitas*. But it was vulnerable and ambiguous, because variously construed at different stages and by different sets of participants. The relationships involved may be conceived in terms of a hierarchy of successively more inclusive manifestations of *communitas*, each intensely experienced but embedded in a wider structure: thus, the Boula chieftainship < Mou < Lösi < Lifou < the Loyalty Islands < the mainland < Melanesian society. Inherent in these relationships were incipient, mainly structural contradictions which threatened the *communitas* on which the meeting depended: for example, there was contradiction between the overall form of the meeting and aspects of its internal sequencing, which in other respects were mutually reinforcing. The metaphor "festival" presupposed sequential performance of customary dances and songs, the main attraction for many Lifouans because it was an opportunity to display and celebrate Lifouan custom and actively involved them as performers and audience. But it was also, consciously or not, a prestation in an implicitly competitive context, in which the impending Arts Festival loomed large, and it distanced and partly excluded the visitors, especially mainlanders, as passive, non-reciprocating audience. Similarly, the shell money presented by the guests encapsulated the ethos of the meeting as a symbol of peace, solidarity and harmony, but was also a prestation by mainlanders, celebrating a key symbolic field in which mainland custom excelled over island.

Hosts and visitors, locked in symbiotic relationship within the role structure ascribed by the form of the meeting, attempted to maximise advantages and minimise the disadvantages of their respective positions. Outnumbered and relatively insignificant in wider Territorial settings, the hosts exploited formal elements and fixed segments over which they had most say. They determined the meeting's form and sequence and controlled its formal ritual and performative roles, dominating the ritual phases. The visitors introduced powerful independent summarising symbols to modify the ritually-created Lifouan vision of *communitas* along lines more congenial and meaningful to themselves. These symbols, shell money separating folded sling and stones, and the knotted *manou*, used traditional symbols to express meanings specific to the occasion appropriately. Less constrained than the hosts were by their festival metaphor and ritual mode, the visitors dominated the work phase. They did so, however, within an overall context shaped by the customary festival/ritual conventions which they, too, had endorsed.

Outcome and efficacy

The remaining theme for discussion is the outcome of the meeting and the efficacy of its form, phase structure and performative modes. The organisers' personal and group goals were satisfactorily realised through the fact that the meeting took place, was well attended and ran smoothly, with no serious public disagreements or organisational hitches, apart from the discomfiture of the Festival team, which upset the brothers Wahuzue not at all. In pragmatic, institutional terms, the main outcome was to effect a transformation of considerable potential significance for the Territorial administrative structure and the hierarchy of indigenous social institutions, though that potential has not to date been actualised. The general social goals, that the high chiefs should meet and discuss and decide the question of forming of a Council of High Chiefs, were successfully achieved. The pragmatic outcome was also a personal triumph for Franck Wahuzue, subsequently appointed to a key administrative position on the new Council. So far as the Festival was concerned, the meeting was clearly a Lifouan cultural and political success: they gave dazzling demonstrations of expertise in customary performances; the Festival film team was only allowed to function on terms dictated by Mou authorities; the Festival organisers were given a sharp lesson in protocol and a reminder that their bureaucratic status in Nouméa did not necessarily count in customary contexts. Ultimately, it was all for nothing: at the last moment, amid political confrontation and widespread civil violence in late

1984, the Festival was postponed indefinitely and was eventually held in French Polynesia (Fraser, 1984; *Pacific Islands Monthly*, Jan. 1985: 16; Carell, 1985 cf. Danielsson, 1985).

Of more interest here are the transformational dynamics of the meeting itself. In summary, through the unifying and condensing power of ritual symbols and ritual action, the structural differentiae of region, national politics and relative status were not so much suppressed as transcended for the moment in *communitas*. Despite vulnerability to structural factors and experiential ambiguity, *communitas* persisted through discussion and decision-making during the work phase and through symbolic dismantling in the final ritual phase. It was transformed and subsequently incorporated, as is usually the fate of *communitas*, within the constraints of social structure (Moore, 1975; Turner, 1974a: 120; 1977: 46–8), as an emergent ideology of chiefly solidarity, with chiefs alerted to areas of mutual interest, sharing a broader sense of common purpose and newly possessed of institutional means for their pursuit and expression.

The meeting derived legitimacy mainly from its form and internal sequencing. The festival metaphor enabled fusion, under the authority of an accepted modern customary convention, of elements drawn from disparate contexts of experience and meaning: traditional ritual, lived custom and European procedure (cf. Myerhoff, 1977: 214, 219). The sequence juxtaposed and alternated fixed and open segments, ritual and work, and the mainly presentational symbolism of song, dance and dramatic re-enactment with more discursive modes. The sequencing owed its effectiveness in the performative context mainly to the conjunction of powerful emotional stimuli and ideological imperatives, mutually confirmed and reinforced through a transfer of qualities, the former ennobled, the latter rendered desirable.

The experience of *communitas* which emerged in and through the ritual phases was vivid and real because of the capacity of ritual action and symbols to transcend difference, ambiguity and contradiction and to persuade those present that for the moment the reality created was more "real" than others which hovered behind the scenes of the ritual and pressed their claims insistently during informal moments and in the open segments of the work phase. Like most key ritual symbols, the meeting's ethos of harmony and unity owed its efficacy to its multivocality, its capacity to "resonate among many meanings at once like a chord in music" (Turner, 1974b: 51), to condense and unify disparate referents and intentions and to transform contexts in its own image. However, a reflex of multivocality is ambiguity and this is part of the characteristic paradox of ritual: it is a traditionalised and traditionalising medium which is often creative and transformative; it is an eminently man-made contrivance which reifies as given and immutable the man-made, contingent and socially constructed (Moore and Myerhoff, 1977: 10, 18; Moore, 1977: 166, Myerhoff, 1977: 199); it employs a symbolic mode which may require variant or contradictory meanings and goals to be condensed within a single symbol, while simultaneously the possibility of contradiction or significant variation is explicitly denied (Turner, 1967: 276); its ordered formalism and regular cadences typically provide the means and the context for the emergence of *communitas*, that most spontaneous and unbounded of experiences. Given this characteristic ambiguity, the question of *how* ritual achieves its effects is particularly vexed (e.g., Geertz, 1975: 90; Kapferer, 1979: 5).

Kapferer stressed the need to differentiate the several modes of performance in any ritual, since their transformational potential could vary (1979: 8–9, 16). The media of performance during the Lifou meeting, within the broad division into ritual and work phases, included oration and formal discourse, impromptu speechmaking, formal and informal dialogue, symbolic gesture, *féhoa* (genealogical dance), *bua* (war dance) and other representational dances, choral singing, mostly with a Christian devotional theme, historical re-enactment and Christian service. I have inadequate detail for a finegrained analysis, but these performative modes and phases can be grossly differentiated and their relationships and efficacy evaluated in terms of Langer's distinction between presentational and discursive symbolism (e.g., Kapferer, 1977: 111–20).

For Langer, symbolisation achieves the meaningful transformation of experiences perceived through the senses. Words are the most important, but by no means the only instruments of human symbolic expression (1957: ch. 2). "Language", she said, "has permanent units of meaning which are combinable into larger units". Its meanings:

> are successively understood, and gathered into a whole by the process called discourse; the meanings of all other symbolic elements that compose a larger, articulate symbol are understood only through the meaning of the whole, through their relations within the total structure.... This kind of semantic may be called "presentational symbolism," to characterize its essential distinction from discursive symbolism, or "language" proper (1957: 96–7).

The holistic, synthetic quality of presentational symbolism is a key to its power and persuasiveness, together with its capacity to bombard the mind with endless simultaneous sense impressions (Langer, 1957: 93). Thus in ritual it fixes and confines meanings within an integrated, internally validated, emotionally compelling system. Kapferer suggested that presentational symbols, the reality they create and the behaviour they induce may be less contingent, less amenable to subversion than discursive symbols, because the latter are separable into component meanings which can be attacked in detail (1977: 112).

The ritual phases of the Lifou meeting mainly, though not exclusively, involved presentational symbolism. Verbal symbolism, when it occurred as oration, incantation or harangue, was usually monologic and effectively presentational, rather than dialogic and discursive (Kapferer, 1977: 119). An important qualification was the mediatory significance of humour and hyperbole in the meeting's major transformative processes. A feature of both initial and farewell rituals was several outrageous impromptu speeches by the aged patriarch of Api Co, whose status as both oldest member and representative of the most junior branch (guardians of clan ritual) of this influential clan gave him the rare and socially important right to speak freely where and when he liked. On several occasions this man seemed deliberately to threaten the *communitas* created in the ritual of welcome, with caustic remarks about pro-independence chiefs, to whom he is opposed politically. This apparently discordant note had the paradoxical effect of reinforcing *communitas* because, by exposing differences over Territorial politics to good-humoured, in-group ridicule, which most of those present seemingly appreciated, he effectively negated their disruptive potential for the duration of the meeting. The underlying tension between islands and mainland was similarly defused by the keeper of the key of the Boula chiefdom through the gross symbolism of the plywood keys and his joking threat to change the locks after the meeting. In a ritual context, then, otherwise unmentionable aspects of alternative, threatening realities were disarmed and distanced by a symbolic mode combining presentational and discursive qualities.

In the ritual phases, the presentational symbolic forms of dance and song were integral, irreducible elements of a total system. In the ritual of welcome they helped create a compelling reality, an experience of *communitas* powerful enough to transcend its own inherent ambiguity and the undoubted instrumental intentions of those who invoked it. The meeting as a whole, the festival metaphor and the ritual phases were means to varied ends, but they were also valued ends in themselves, in the emotional intensity of ritual and *communitas* and the sheer expressive exuberance of dance and song. During the mainly discursive work phase presentational symbolism—dance, song, dramatic re-enactment and Christian service—recalled the experience of *communitas*, threatened by release from the confines of ritual; it also restrained, though it could not ultimately repel, the disintegrative potential of discursive symbolism. During this phase, presentational forms could also differentiate: they involved an element of competition between groups of Lifouan performers, an overt Protestant/Catholic distinction and a distancing of hosts as performers from visitors as audience. In ritual contexts, differentiating aspects were submerged within an encompassing presentational whole.[11]

The survival of *communitas* during the work phase, despite exposure to conflicting mundane realities and their powerful structural differentiae, stemmed partly from the intensity and persuasiveness of the ritually-invoked experience, but also owed much to Tjibaou, who stage-managed a result, reasonably satisfactory to most, through skilful manipulation of structural roles and by invoking compelling summarising symbols, irony, the common interests of chiefs and his own administrative authority. The integration of *communitas* and structure in the work phase was confirmed and re-enacted symbolically in the ritual of farewell, in which the meta-community created in the initial ritual phase was dismantled. This did not mean reversion to the *status quo ante*, since relationships and attitudes were potentially changed, given the transformative implications for wider social and political structures of the prag-matic outcome of the meeting, institutionalisation of chiefly author-ity in the Council of High Chiefs. Altered dialectically in discursive, analytic contexts of discussion and decision-making during the work phase, a transformed *communitas* re-entered social structure in the restricted form of a nascent national chiefly ideology, portent of the incipient superimposition of national class differentials across customary social hierarchies, which had continued thus far to be defined primarily in terms of residential and kinship seniority.

EPILOGUE

The Council of High Chiefs offered chiefs a forum to express shared interests as members of a social category, to the possible detriment of their customary roles and relationships. In the short term, this threat was overtaken by events. Heightened political tension, violence and confrontation after November 1984 strained customary values which stressed compromise, negotiation and consensus, while highlighting the supra-local roles of national independence leaders and young militant activists. Chiefs and the values they defended seemed irrelevant to some as the indepen-dence struggle moved to a more intense and dangerous plane. In Lifou, popular militancy induced a political reorientation by the three high chiefs to at least covert support for *l'indépendance kanak et socialiste*. Several customary dignitaries who persisted in active commitment to the RPCR were publicly repudiated, including the President of the Territorial Government, a local tribal chief (*Bwenando*, 11 July 1985).

There was about the final stages of the meeting no air of nos-talgia or regret, but rather a general impression of a job well done, of having had a rewarding experience. From the schematic orderliness of the program through the experiential kaleidoscope of action to the representation here devised, the episode exhibited a high degree of symmetry, coherence and completeness, derived primarily, no doubt, from the fact that the meeting worked. It invoked, created and transformed tradition, and might in theory have "become" tradition—retrospectively losing its "nonce" aspect—as a model for subsequent similar gatherings (cf. Hobsbawm, 1983). To my knowledge, however, no such tradition has been forged in New Caledonia.

AFTERWORD

The Council of High Chiefs established in March 1983 was shortlived, but each revision of the constitutional statute for New Caledonia promulgated during the 1980s provided for an advisory body on custom: in effect for a council of chiefs. None was given substance until after the Matignon Accords of 1988, in which Tjibaou, always equivocal about chiefs, was the major Kanak player. Under the Accords a decision on independence was postponed for a decade, while custom, seemingly subsumed or displaced by development as a priority of indigenous leaders, was devolved from the territorial arena to become a responsibility of the three Provincial Assemblies, two of which have been consistently controlled by the FI's successor, the FLNKS (Kanak Socialist National Liberation Front). Each of the eight custom areas (les aires coutumières, major language zones) has its own Custom Council (le Conseil coutumier) and sends two representatives to the Territorial Advisory Council on Custom (le Conseil consultatif coutumier du Territoire)—the linear descendant of this chapter's Council of High Chiefs, but of far less actual moment than some had envisaged for that body. The Advisory Council must be consulted on all draft resolutions of the Provincial Assemblies relating to customary law and land law, but has no role or competency in provincial or territorial decision-making: its marginality is patent in "the lack of any customary representation at the heart of organisations whose action is of major importance for the tribal milieu", notably the Agency for Rural Development and Land Management (ADRAF). This complaint was made in a glossy publication issued by the Council late in 1996, seeking a wider role in "the social, cultural and economic development of the tribal populations from which it issues and of which it is the most authentic representation" (Kawa, 1996; "Les grands chefs montent au créneau", Nouvelles, 16 Nov. 1996).[12] In July 1997, after considerable uncertainty and delay, a "Grand Palabre" of the eight Custom Councils was held in Nouméa, all but ignored by the local press. The muted calls for custom and customary authorities to be accorded wider relevance may fall on deaf ears, given the prejudice amongst politicians of all persuasions that custom is a positive obstacle to the holy grail of development.

NOTES

[1] After 1946, when Melanesians were granted full rights as French citizens, district high chiefs, together with representatives of the two Melanesian political parties and Melanesian veterans' and employees' associations, met on several occasions as a Council of Notables (*conseil des notables*), which advised the colonial government on indigenous issues (Kurtovitch [1997]: 84–92).

[2] I distinguish "custom" and "tradition", though the concepts clearly overlap and in common usage in Melanesia they are synonymous. I use "custom" fairly synchronically to describe what Melanesians actually did and do in indigenous action contexts. "Tradition" relates more to culture and is used diachronically: though it is imbued experientially with an aura of permanence and timelessness, I do not limit it to pre-contact patterns, but imply a dialectic between continuity and creativity in indigenous ways of perceiving, constructing and acting in the world. For example, "making custom" (reciprocal offerings of respect) is a customary practice and items exchanged customarily include *manou* (cloth), money (French Pacific francs) and cigarettes. None of these objects is traditional (though *manou* and money are surrogates for bark cloth and traditional shell money), but the gesture, in terms of its meaning and emotion for those participating, is certainly traditional. My distinction recalls one made at the 1980 congress of the Union calédonienne (see n. 10) between regionally variant customary practice and generally shared customary meaning ("tradition" in my sense); "customary institutions" were defined as "institutions such as they are currently lived" (Union calédonienne, 1980: 13; cf. Hobsbawm, 1983: 2–3).

[3] "Key scenarios" are key symbols which "both formulate appropriate goals and suggest effective action for achieving them" (Ortner, 1973: 1341).

[4] The population of New Caledonia in 1982 was approximately 43% Melanesian, 36% European and 21% "other", mainly Polynesians from Wallis Island and Tahiti.

[5] The terms "Territorial" and "national" refer to New Caledonia as a whole, the former to the actual colonial dispensation, the latter implying the eventual existence of an independent state.

[6] They included Jean-Marie Tjibaou from Hienghene, on the mainland east coast, pro-independence Vice-President of the Council of Government and member of the organising committee for the Arts Festival; Rock Wamytan, independentist from St Louis, near Nouméa. director of ODIL (Office du développement des îles et de l'intérieur) and chairman of the Festival organising committee; Jacques Iékawé, independentist from the small island of Tiga, near Lifou, assistant Secretary-General of the Territory and Festival director; Franck Wahuzue, anti-independentist from Lifou, former director of the Commission pour la promotion mélanésienne, former conservative

member of the Council of Government, and member of the Festival organising committee, but alienated from most of his colleagues, especially Wamytan.

[7] The following summary owes much to Bensa's excellent ethnography of the cèmuhî language zone (Bensa and Rivierre, 1982: 19–116). See also Chapter One; Douglas, 1994b.

[8] Délibération no. 116, 14 May 1980, *JO* 1980: 627; Délibération no. 351, 10 Dec. 1981, *JO* 1981: 1728; Ward, 1982: 50.

[9] "Summarizing symbols" are that class of key symbols which "operate to compound and synthesize a complex system of ideas, to 'summarize' them under a unitary [and emotionally compelling] form which ... 'stands for' the system as a whole"; they "speak primarily to attitudes, to a crystallization of commitment" (Ortner, 1973: 1340, 1342).

[10] The political spectrum in New Caledonia in 1982, as since, was divided along ethnic lines. Almost all non-Melanesians—Europeans, Polynesians and Asians—and some Melanesians supported the conservative, anti-independence parties, of which the RPCR was the most important. Most Melanesians and a few European socialists supported the FI, a coalition of parties demanding *l'indépendance kanake et socialiste*, of which the Union calédonienne (UC) was the largest and most moderate, though it embraced a range of political and tactical opinion. At each political extreme were radical, non-parliamentary factions which condoned the use of violence and advocated confrontation. Until June 1982 the conservatives, in coalition with several centrist parties, formed a majority in the Territorial Assembly and controlled the Council of Government. At that time the majority was defeated in the Assembly on a censure motion and the centrist parties, which had voted for the motion, subsequently entered into coalition with the FI to form a new majority. Tjibaou, a moderate member of the UC, became Vice-President of the Council of Government, while Franck Wahuzue, who had recently resigned from the RPCR and become an independent, lost his position on the Council.

[11] Kapferer posited a close correlation between religious ritual and presentational symbolism on the one hand, and secular ritual and discursive symbolism on the other (1977: 117–20). My case suggests a congruent distinction between ritual and secular phases of a secular ritual in terms of dominant symbolic mode. Given a close association between presentational symbolism and sacred contexts, the Lifou meeting supports Moore and Myerhoff's contention that "the sacred is a wider category than the religious" (1977: 3).

[12] I thank Stephen Henningham for kindly supplying information on the *Conseils coutumiers*.

PART TWO

Fighting

FOREWORD: APOLOGIA ON GENDER

If the idea had even occurred to me at the time, which it did not, I should no doubt have considered Chapter Two to be gender neutral. I now see that not only did I gender the world in ethnocentrically universalising male terms, but also unwittingly inscribed traces of Kanak men's gendered understandings; the result was a double perpetuation of profoundly male visions and versions of reality. Women were ubiquitous at that Lifou meeting of high chiefs I attended in 1982, though they made no obvious contribution to public discussion and debate. They were spectators during the work phases, decorous participants in dance and choral performances, and caterers and organisers of accommodation—roles critical to the very occurrence of the meeting, let alone its smooth and successful running. Yet I took all this for granted and was largely oblivious to the muted interventions and expressions of opinion by women which must have taken place. I do not recall speaking to a single woman about my professional interests or about their understandings of what was happening or about their aspirations, problems and strategies; nor are there traces that I did so in my notes, photographs and cassettes. This unconscious bias does not invalidate the chapter—indeed, the experience of a later female anthropologist in Lifou suggests that as a woman I was fortunate not to have been confined by local male authorities to a female domain they (or some of them) considered to be non-public (Paini 1996: 46–7)—but it certainly, unfortunately, did render my perspective a great deal more partial than I then suspected.

Fifteen years later—formally engaged in a research project on indigenous women and with feminist antennae finely tuned to gender relations and inequalities—I sat in on sessions of the 1997

"Grand Palabre" of Custom Councils held in Nouméa. That earlier obliviousness to the importance of women's behind-the-scenes activities at the Lifou meeting was ironically—and in retrospect uncomfortably—displaced by indignation that the major contribution by women to the event should still be as cooks: a meeting I had arranged with a Catholic women's group was cancelled because, said the husband of its president, the members would be too busy catering. Two Kanak women prominent in women's affairs were invited to address the "Grand Palabre", a first acclaimed as a breakthrough. I was disappointed when they spoke only to individual workshops and not at the plenary sessions to which the presidents of the various commissions, all male, made their reports. When I mentioned this dissatisfaction to one of the two women she remarked that small steps were the wisest strategy, so as to lull men's apprehensions. I was reminded that while reflexivity may disclose ethnocentrism, it is not easily eradicated; perhaps it is chimerical to try.

My writing on fighting in New Caledonia was also blinkered to gender differences, with women—I now acknowledge—inappropriately conspicuous by their absence. Here the distortions were exponential: not only were the limitations in my own vision doubly compounded by the implicit gendering of colonial authors whose texts bore the cryptic stamp of the partial perspectives of their male indigenous interlocutors, but both were further refracted through the profound ethnocentrism, if not racism of colonial discourses (Stoler, 1995; Torgovnick, 1990). Traces of indigenous female agency in such texts may be so embedded that their recuperation challenges the most imaginative and reflexive textual archaeology. To redress my own sins of omission, I opt here for a separate segment highlighting the meagre sherds of my textual excavations on gendered engagements in fighting, rather than interpolate them as surreptitious corrective and condiment to what is already written.

The indigenous role of warrior in New Caledonia was evidently gendered male. Contemporary European observers typically represented fighting as a quintessential male activity in which women were peripheral, passive objects of men's actions: as *casus belli*, whose bodies men competed to own and control; as millstones needing warrior protection during combats, along with old people, children and valuables; as victors' victims or spoils. The doctor-ethnographer Patouillet, a participant in colonial campaigns in 1868–9, compiled every one of these tropes, including the assertions that women were the main motive for war—"'*Cherchez-moi la femme*'"—and that "out of ten canaque quarrels, nine are caused by the rape or seizure of a woman" (1873: 155–64). Expanding the nexus to novel contexts, the first Catholic missionary bishop, Douarre, gave a visiting American trader to understand "that murders committed" by Islanders on visiting Europeans "were usually in consequence of women" (Wallis, 1994: 112). The Polynesian Ta'unga, a Christian evangelist in New Caledonia at the very outset of regular foreign contacts, came from a society in which women sometimes did fight. Shortly after quitting Melanesia he wrote accounts of "all the customs of the islands" for "my missionary in Rarotonga". Infused with a convert's eye for pagan excess—"their hunger for human flesh" and "their vindictiveness"—his texts nonetheless purveyed a more pragmatic, activist image of women's involvement in fighting (1968: 86):

> All the women accompany them to the battle but do not actually take part in the fight. They remain at a distance and when each side meets to fight each party of women stays behind its own side. They take baskets on carrying poles to fetch the slain. Even when one of their own side is killed they rush forward to carry the body away from the battlefield. They scramble for it, cutting it up with a knife called tuatava. Then they place the pieces into their baskets, shouting with glee because their wants have been satisfied. And when they see that another has been killed they rush in and grab him. That is how they behave with the dead. The women from the other side do likewise with the dead on their side.... When an enemy is taken, they grab him and chop him up in pieces and give him to the womenfolk who carry him back to their houses (1968: 87, 90).

Ta'unga's pragmatic detail was partly confirmed, minus gore, by a contemporary naval sojourner with the Catholic missionaries in the far north: "In these great [inter-tribal] wars, as in the smallest..., the women accompany the combatants in order to clean out the enemy's gardens, and return loaded with yams, taro and bunches of sugar cane" (Leconte, 1847: 835). Another naval officer in 1878 allowed women an active supporting role during a Kanak attack on a French stockade: "A beam of the action, not a great distance away, in the bush, the women stirred up the warriors" (Rivière, 1881: 211).

The prime text for the early ethnohistory of New Caledonia is the official Catholic mission journal written by Douarre (1843–53). At an early stage of my research on fighting, already convinced that "vengeance" was its prime mover, I prepared a detailed inventory of "motives for vengeance" imputed or implied in this text. While hardly as categorical as Patouillet's nine out of ten quarrels caused by women, "Women" nonetheless constituted by far the largest class of motive in my list: more than three pages out of about ten, with seventeen entries spread over nearly five years, eight of which were clustered in two fragmented narrative episodes. The episodes are suggestive blends of an orthodox missionary plot, gendered male, with a subversive sub-text. The plots featured male protagonists, generally rival local "chiefs", "making war to avenge outrages received in the person of their [actual] or future wives" (Douarre, 1843–53: 8 Mar. 1846). The wives were represented as the shadowy, passive objects of men's desires, competition or mutual antagonism. The sub-texts told a contrasting, covert story of circumscribed female agency, clothed in the standard missionary trope of sexual misdemeanour and sometimes qualified by a dose of class prejudice.

The first episode occurred late in 1845. Douarre met "a chief who had been offended in the person of one of his wives and is preparing to make war on the party who injured him, as well as on the latter's friends". The bishop anticipated only "a few skirmishes, [with] little blood spilled", but enjoined the "chief" to "punish [only] the culprit or the two culprits, for his wife is not worth much money"—this I take as a misogynist allusion to the obligation to pay compensation in shell money in the aftermath of a fight to those who suffered loss or injury. In a subsequent entry Douarre reported that "war" had duly broken out, but gave a different twist to the origins of the affair: it was over "a chief's wife, who behaved badly with a *hiambouète* [*yabwec*, 'junior', 'subject']". I read this subtle shift in emphasis, from an image of the woman as a pawn in male politics to a qualified concession of her agency as adulterer, as registering the injection of class presumptions into a gendered equation (Douarre, 1843–53: 21, 22 Dec. 1845).

The second episode was a drawn out, convoluted story of husband-swapping, "infidelities" and theft of valuables involving two women and a trio of high-ranking men, and of fights the women's actions purportedly provoked. The tale is enigmatic to the point of incomprehensibility, but its common denominator is the women "Tialo" or "Thiaola" of Pouébo, who over a period of several months in 1852 made regular appearances in the mission journal, and her "sister" "Nandia". Tialo was depicted as moving back and forth between three very prominent men—Bouarate of Hienghène, Pouan of Pouébo and Tiangoun of Balade—in the process helping herself, or her latest favourite, to her previous partner's wealth items. The first and last of these men were "friends", allies, while Pouan might have been an affine of both and was certainly their enemy. The story began when Tialo returned to her "former husband" Pouan, and colluded with him to steal a bracelet from her present husband Bouarate. Subsequently she wanted to return to Tiangoun, also a former "husband", when he married her sister, who subsequently left him. None of Tiangoun's family, remarked Douarre wryly, "is lucky in marriage". Later still, Tialo again left Tiangoun, without his knowledge, taking with her a bracelet to replace that which she had stolen from Bouarate, "her husband before last", to whom she now returned (Douarre, 1843–53: 9, 13 May, 22 July, 22 Aug., 4 Sep. 1852). Douarre annexed the story as a morality tale in a wider narrative linking cannibalism, festivals, uncontrolled passions, sexual immorality, cupidity, revenge and war as functional correlates of heathenism: the women's actions were simply sexual transgressions, presumably satanically induced, which served to incite wars between powerful men and their supporters. For me their traces in the mission texts provide cryptic hints of female agency and strategies, problematising the dominant colonial tropes that indigenous women in New Caledonia—especially wives—lived "a harsh and long servitude", were "condemned to hard labour and often bad treatment", were "regarded almost as beasts of burden and treated as such", and were held "in contempt and slavery" by men (Lambert, 1855–75: 22; Leconte, 1847: 839–40;

Pénard, 1857: 16; Rivière, 1881: 20; Rochas, 1862: 116; Vieillard and Deplanche, 1863: 74).[1]

During the colonial wars of 1878–9 some missionary authors were preoccupied with the matter of captured Kanak women, especially when their converts were in direct competition for women with pagan allies of the government. The mission texts left little space for female agency on this issue, though they are infused with strong intimations of the agency of indigenous men. These texts hovered hypocritically in tone between prurient disapproval of official policy when the women went to pagans—in accordance with the governor's undertaking to allied "chiefs" to hand over "the wives of the rebels so they might be married to their warriors" (Servan to Antonio, 1 Aug. 1878, AAN, 16.1)—and unsavoury gloating when Christians got them. Thus the missionary at Thio complained bitterly when eleven women and children who wanted to settle there with Christian relatives were forced to go to the pagans of Canala, but when thirty-seven captured women and children were assigned to his Christians, he exulted: "the Thio mission will increase very quickly, for our people are going to fight to extinction some rebels whose women and children they will keep, by order of the Governor". He asked his superior's permission to marry these women to Christians while their pagan husbands were waiting in the bush to be exterminated by the Christians, and regretted its denial (Moris to Fraysse, 26 July, 6 Nov. 1878, 1 Jan. 1879, AAN, 16.1, 16.2).

By contrast, inadvertent traces of female agency in fighting, including that of prisoners, were patchily inscribed in official campaign reports, defying colonial authors' presumptions about gendered proprieties and the passivity of women. In Chapter Three I argue that restraint was a key value and practice in indigenous fighting in New Caledonia. Scattered references to women in reports from the later stages of the wars of 1878–9 suggest that the exercise of restraint in fighting owed a lot to women's initiatives and readiness to take extreme action—even "betrayal"—to thwart men's intransigence, especially that of "chiefs". By late September 1878, after three months of dour French repression, captured Kanak women were recounting the rising toll taken on the warriors by wounds and sickness, apart from those killed outright. Notably, the wife of the Kanak leader Naïna told her captors that her husband was becoming "desperate" and that she had "twice prevented him from hanging himself". A few days after being taken prisoner, in what I see as a deliberate strategy to end this debilitating war, she "indicated to our troops the points where the *canaques* might be found" (Hilléreau to ?, 24 Sep. 1878, APM; *N-C*, 2 Oct. 1878). This was by no means an isolated occurrence: towards the end of the war anecdotal traces of such actions by female prisoners—not just revealing the whereabouts of Kanak refuges, but actively guiding French detachments to them—became almost a refrain in official and some missionary texts. I can think of no more appropriate way to construe them than as systematic efforts by women to broker peace.[2]

Most such textual instances of putative "betrayal" of their men by Kanak women elicited no commentary from the colonial authors. One newspaper report, though, did note as "an excessively curious detail about native women" the just mentioned action of Naïna's wife, and the puzzling demeanour of female captives who, "immediately married to *canaque* auxiliaries", crossed "from one tribe to another without the least indication even of disquiet". The item concluded with the sanctimonious reflection that the treatment of women by native men was "sufficiently disagreeable that they find themselves as badly off on one side as on the other". Governor Olry, making a virtue of expediency, thought that "the women...granted to the allied tribes...always appeared delighted by this solution"—as well they might, given the alternatives on offer, the drawn-out agony of a continued fugitive existence, or a brutal death (*N-C*, 2 Oct. 1878; Olry to Min., 28 Sep. 1878, ANOM, Carton 43; Rivière, 1881: 226). "Surrender" of captured women was a key element in the deal struck by the French with their major allies at the outset of the war (Olry to the warriors of Canala, 11 July 1878, MS copy, AAN, 16.1; see Chapter Five), but enhancing group strength via appropriation of refugees, especially women and children, was evidently a standard practice in indigenous fighting, and very likely an impetus to its outbreak.[3] Patouillet, on the basis of experience a decade before 1878, couched it in more positive, reciprocal terms. He allowed that "in the ardour of attack, the blacks have massacred women and children", but added: "when the first fire of their fury has passed, if the *Canaques* find a woman, they spare her and take her as a companion, forgetting, as does she, the animosities which put their tribes at odds" (1873: 164).

These murky, fragmentary traces of gendered engagements in indigenous fighting unearthed in more or less sexist, usually racist, colonial texts hardly lend themselves to an historical ethnography or ethnohistory of gender relations in New Caledonia, though a more systematic, focussed textual archaeology might well do so (e.g., Mani, 1991; Ralston, 1989; Thomas, 1989a). I am inclined to read them as intimations of gender complementarity and human emotions, but particularly female agency, initiatives, strategies and choices, rather than the unmitigated, brutal male domination of colonial convention. My intent is avowedly political, but has the virtue of being wittingly so, unlike most standard readings of indigenous gender relations, which are just as political but unreflexive: this applies as much to demeaning colonial objectifications of indigenous women as pathetic, passive, disgusting victims of savage men as to its equally objectifying reflex, the tendency of some Western feminists and indigenous nationalists to romanticise "traditional" gender relations as pastoral, egalitarian, or even matriarchal.

NOTES

[1] Patouillet, whose cultural relativism distinguished him from most missionaries and whose ethnographic experience far exceeded that of most colonial observers—he had had "the opportunity to observe closely and at length the domestic life of the *Canaques*"—provided a pragmatic, if still essentialist and condescending, caveat on conventional depictions of indigenous women as brutalised and degraded: "the woman is not an object of scorn or aversion for the man. Less wretched than she has insistently been represented in the accounts of voyagers, who perhaps relied too much on appearances, she is generally considered the servant, not the slave of her husband" (1873: 82, 87–8). Rochas, too, qualified his general depiction of the "legal condition" of indigenous women as deplorable by acknowledging individual exceptions. These he attributed, ethnocentrically, to the "generosity" of a husband moved by sentimental attachment to his wife, or to "the tact natural to the weak sex", which enabled her "here as everywhere, to triumph over brutality and acquire a certain empire over force" (1862: 226–8). For a further discussion of discordant missionary representations of indigenous wives as at once passive victims of their husbands' brutality and faithless libertines "constantly deserting their husbands" (Geddie, 1852: 19–21)—this time by Presbyterians in Aneityum—see Douglas, forthcoming.

[2] The motif of women as peacemakers featured in a story about indigenous fighting in Vanuatu told with ironic relish by Tepahae, the foremost expert on custom in Aneityum and a reflexive, critical historian. He recounted how a Malakulan field worker at a Vanuatu Cultural Centre workshop insisted that women were "rubbish", but when asked who had the right to stop fights answered "Only women" (Tepahae, 1997: 15 Aug. 1997).

[3] The benefits from adding women were exponential: wives meant affines, who were potential allies and as maternal uncles were the source of life to the next generation; wives were mothers of potential offspring who would become warriors or women to exchange with affines for more wives, and might ultimately, as ancestors, be a source of assistance and protection for the group; appropriating women meant, reciprocally, depriving enemies of wives, affines, uncles, offspring and ultimately ancestors (Bensa and Goromido, in press).

CHAPTER THREE

"Almost Constantly at War"?[1]
Ethnographic Perspectives on Indigenous Fighting in New Caledonia

FOREWORD

*I*n *1990 I published an article in the* Journal of Pacific History *with a title similar to the above. It derived ultimately from my major work then in progress: an ethnographic history of fighting in New Caledonia. More immediately, the article was excised from the original manuscript of a reflective, rather didactic contribution to Carrier's edited collection on anthropology and history in Melanesia (1992a), and rewritten along lines appropriate for a journal notorious (or celebrated!) for empiricist rectitude and allergy to authorial presence. The present chapter is effectively new. Its content and import differ significantly from those of the article, with greater emphasis on the ethnographic recuperation and transcription of traces of indigenous fighting inscribed in early colonial texts, and relatively less on colonial encounters, which are the particular focus of Chapter Five. It is also more explicitly reflective than the article, but remains representational in intent and execution: that is, it is an ethnographic distillation of a complex of actions and meanings in a past indigenous world, strategically larded with scraps of realist narrative. In Chapter Four I spell out the epistemological politics of my reading and deconstruction of colonial texts, and illustrate strategies and method for their ethnohistorical exploitation. That chapter might usefully be read before the present one, which is, however, antecedent to it in structural, historical and chronological terms.*

DOING HISTORICAL ETHNOGRAPHY

Fighting occurred regularly in New Caledonia before 1880, intermittently until 1917 and was renewed in 1984 and 1988. This chapter distils traces of the activity of fighting lodged in the texted residue of interaction between Kanak[2] and Europeans after the onset of regular contacts in about 1840. My interest is the existential one of what people did and what it meant, rather than the teleology of causes or wider functional relationships. My representation is constructed mainly from traces of indigenous actions inscribed in firsthand and other contemporary narratives, read critically against the grain and correlated with the reworked reflections of more formal contemporary texts, mainly ethnographies written by missionaries and French naval medical officers. Like most ethnographers, these men authoritatively transmuted intense, but narrowly localised personal experience into generalised renditions of essential social and cultural entities. Twentieth century anthropologists mentioned fighting rarely, in mainly normative terms, while references in indigenous oral histories published so far are also sparse, often sanitised and heavily allegorical, as if, commented Bensa and Rivierre, "the memory of wars is cast back into the shadows of the pagan world" (1982: 209).

Histories—including historical ethnographies—are always present, text-dependent acts of reimagining pasts. The authoring, language, politics and aesthetics of "texts" are thus of the very fabric of "histories" and the pasts they re-present. Colonial texts on New Caledonia were mostly written by French men, always ethnocentric and variously blinkered by gender, race, religious and class prejudices. Their biases were not just personal but systemic and discursive, embedded in particular national versions of the nineteenth century Christian, civilised sense of mission, destiny and superiority to "savages". Identified, deciphered and critically compared, such prejudices can aid, rather than debar the ethnohistorical exploitation of colonial texts.

Some of the most significant early descriptions of Melanesian actions in New Caledonia referred to part of the northern region called Hoot ma Waap and focussed on the place known as Balade, site of earliest known European contacts and most French naval and missionary activity until after annexation in September 1853. A cluster of texts written after the settlement of French Marist missionaries amongst the Puma of Balade in December 1843 is invaluable in relation to indigenous fighting, which provoked few first-hand descriptions after about 1860.[3] Like all texts, these offer very partial perspectives: views from a weak, divided, therefore vulnerable and inconsequential chiefdom, written by persons with quite alien notions of instrumentality and morality, whose main local sources of information were male "chiefs" and young converts. An ethnography derived from such texts is very specific as to time, place and context, but so are most ethnographies. Like all ethnographies, that specificity is here partly disguised by a generalising idiom.

VIEWS FROM BALADE: "PERPETUAL WARS"?[4]

Like Cook seventy years earlier, the French naval officers who helped install the Catholic mission depicted the Puma as a sober people, currently at peace. In 1774 the prevalence of arms had suggested this was not always so, and the narratives of d'Entrecasteaux's 1793 voyage told a tale of treachery, violence and cannibalism.[5] D'Entrecasteaux himself gave an early glimpse of indigenous offensive tactics in describing the attack on a French shore party of a disciplined body of 2–300 warriors. They were "armed and in good order", "the first rank with spears raised; and those of the last hurling stones, which struck several of our men". They withdrew in the face of musket fire and gunfire from one of the ships with two or three warriors wounded (1808, I: 334–5). During the missionaries' first 16 months at Balade, the mission journal made no mention of fighting. This absence challenges later conventional wisdom that "all these diverse tribes are almost constantly at war, for mutual plunder and devastation", that "peace is only a suspension of regular combat on the field of battle", that male Kanak were "men of war above all else" (Leconte, 1847: 822; Rougeyron, 1846–9: 21; Pénard, 1857: 15). The sharp variations in early European eye-witness estimations of Kanak "character" are partly covert registrations of indigenous actions and self-presentations in the content and fashioning of colonial texts (Douglas, in press b).

The potential for fighting was evidently ubiquitous, but contemporary action descriptions implied something of a rhythm in indigenous politics, alternating relatively relaxed, peaceful periods and more tense, violent times. When fighting did occur, its dramatic impact on outside observers, filtered through stereotypes of savagery, was often so compelling as to shape their representations of the normal. The Polynesian LMS teacher Ta'unga, based on the southeast coast from 1842–5, mentioned no fights in the diary of the first three months of his stay, announced that "we found no great evil in the land, war was abandoned", and recorded the desire of two "chiefs" that "there be no war". Subsequently the people with whom he lived were involved in numerous fights, culminating in their defeat and dispersal. The general image of New Caledonians afterwards contrived by Ta'unga, and telescoped retrospectively to span the whole of his stay, was of people who "never stop fighting". In an ethnographic text written decades later, recalling their way of life, he described the gruesome slaughter and eating of men in a war attributed to the third day after his arrival. Yet his trope of the insatiable cannibal confounded that of incessant fighting: "the reason for man-stealing was that it was a long time since there had been a war and there had been no human flesh to eat" (1968: 31–40, 55–76, 86–95, 108–13).

The first fight mentioned in the Catholic mission journal—an intra-Puma exchange of spears and slingstones "between the men of our chief and [those] of a neighbouring chief"—occurred during a "chiefly" circumcision ceremony in April 1845. Having rhetorically escalated the episode from "brawl" to "combat" to "war", Bishop Douarre appropriated it to a narrative of missionary agency, claiming responsibility for averting "more fatal results" thanks to a shot fired in the air by one of the priests (1843–53: 12 Apr. 1845). From this time traces of fighting, including some extended episodes, punctuated the Balade mission texts: up to September 1853, their culturally and spatially circumscribed perspective on an area comprising less than one-quarter of the total land mass of New

Caledonia tallied at least 24 local fights, plus four between Kanak and foreigners, five occasions on which foreigners were successfully ambushed and killed, and three retaliatory expeditions by French naval forces. The status of the references varied—from unconfirmed rumour, to more or less reliable hearsay, to first-hand witness—as did the seriousness of the clashes.

"SAVAGE WAR" IN THEORY AND TROPE

Some modern ethnographers of "traditional war" in New Guinea categorised types and intensity of permissible violence in segmentary terms, according to relative social and political distance (Berndt, 1964; Heider, 1979: 84–112; Meggitt, 1977: 16–43; cf. Hallpike, 1977: 202–11). Though plausible in relation to New Caledonian *norms*, such a model casts uncertain light on actual fighting described in early colonial texts. Nine of the 24 fights involving only Islanders were intra-Puma, one was within the neighbouring Mwelebeng chiefdom of Pouébo, while the rest involved two or more autonomous political groups. Casualty figures were wildly unreliable, but their drift was predictable: fewer than eight per cent of reported deaths and more than 85% of reported injuries occurred in internal fights. Puma did place normative limits on behaviour deemed proper in clashes between co-members of a political group: they gave Douarre to understand that certain actions were "unusual in encounters between villages of the same tribe", and distinguished such engagements from "war as waged by enemy tribes, consequently war to the death". Some—I surmise that they were "chiefs"—told Douarre that attacks by ordinary warriors on "chiefs" were "unheard of in wars between individuals of the same tribe", though several such attacks were reported in the mission journal during 1852. By the same token, local political ideology and fighting rhetoric gave no quarter to "indhiou iaré", translated by the missionaries as "other men", "strangers", "enemies" (Douarre, 1843–53: 1 May 1845, 29 Apr., 16 May, 18 July, 28 Nov. 1852; Rougeyron to S-G, 3 Sep. 1846, APM; Wallis 1994: 146–7).

In more formal texts, contemporary Europeans seized on such normative distinctions to articulate a hierarchy of "wars":

"between neighbours of the same village", "between villages [of the same tribe]" and "between tribes". The latter were "terrible", "wars of extermination", "horrible butchery", culminating in cannibalism and widespread devastation (Leconte, 1847: 834–5; Montrouzier, 1860: 42–4; Rochas, 1862: 242; Rougeyron to S-G, 3 Sep. 1846, APM). The trope of butchery was clearly hyperbolic: colonial texts seldom mentioned the actual occurrence of mass killings, other than as the rare, heat-of-battle sequel to a successful surprise assault.[6] Massacres were routinely avoidable with caution or flight by a weaker or vanquished party. "Butchery", then, was a conventional reflex of "savagery" for Europeans, ratified in Puma stories about their periodic sacking by the Mwelebeng before the missionaries' arrival at Balade, though Ta'unga forged a similar image from personal experience in the far south.[7] The Catholic missionaries, more familiar with intra- and inter-"village" fights because of their frequency at Balade, categorised them as "less deadly", though materially destructive. However dubious the stereotype of butchery, there was no doubt about the appalling material impact of fighting: charred remnants of settlements, ruined gardens and coconut groves littered the landscapes evoked in the early texts, though accidents and mourning rituals would have contributed a proportion. The naval surgeon-ethnographer Rochas said that the devastation inseparable from "foreign" wars regularly led to famine, called "result of war" (Douarre, 1843–53: 10 Dec. 1845, 6 July 1852; La Billardière, 1800, II: 228, 229, 232; Leconte, 1847: 843–4; Rochas, 1862: 242, 267–70).

Formal European representations of indigenous politics and fighting in New Caledonia invoked a neat segmentary structure: "divided into an infinite number of tribes, subdivided... into villages,... [it is the] general rule that each tribe is the enemy of those adjacent to it" (Montravel to Min., 27 Apr. 1854, ANOM, Carton 40). This model may have echoed local exegeses, but political and military practice, as adventitiously inscribed in colonial texts and reconstituted in modern ethnographies, was more complicated: movement and relation were keynotes rather than structure and entity (Douglas, in press a). Contemporary Europeans thought terms like "Puma" and "Mwelebeng" were the names of permanent, homogeneous "tribes" occupying discrete "territories". More likely they betokened indigenous tendencies to extend the name of a high "chiefly" clan to all who acknowledged its authority,[8] and to experience political ties as unstable, negotiable relationships of allegiance and reciprocity with localised clan segments of "chiefly" rank. There was evidently a wide range of political integration: from quasi-independent residential clusters, to small, autonomous chiefdoms, such as the Puma, to complex chiefdoms, such as at Canala, on the Isle of Pines and in the Loyalty Islands (Bensa and Rivierre, 1982; Guiart, 1963; Guiart and Bensa, 1981).

LOCAL TENSIONS, LATERAL TIES

Intra-Puma clashes seemed virulent during the 1840s and 1850s,[9] but only their intensity was remarkable: the span of secure relationships in New Caledonia looked narrowly local, with rivalry and mundane grievances between close kinspeople and neighbours often flaring into brawls and fights, into which outsiders were sometimes drawn thanks to personal ties that constituted part of the fabric of relationships between different places. A corollary of domestic insecurity was the reported high incidence of small-scale migrations and relations over considerable space with a wide variety of "strangers"[10]—affines, allies, enemies. The mission journal made numerous references to resident strangers and to regular visits between particular "tribes". I take these contemporary textual traces to have been prognostic of an insistent motif in later ethnographies and oral histories, which depicted persons and groups in New Caledonia as enmeshed in overlapping webs of enduring relationships and known itineraries across whole regions and beyond (Bensa and Rivierre, 1982, 1988; Guiart, 1957, 1963, 1966). Lateral ties belied formal European segmentation of the political landscape into discrete solidary corporate entities and ensured a potential for alliance formation over wide areas, in both indigenous and colonial contexts. "These sorts of alliances", noted another ethnography written by naval doctors, "often result in a very wide span of country becoming engaged in a war of long duration over a simple quarrel, the cause of which is usually [a matter] of indifference to the majority of the allies" (Vieillard and Deplanche, 1863: 21).

In just this way the Hoot ma Waap region was patterned, chequerboard fashion, by a spatially stable political and ritual opposition between places identified as Hoot and Waap respectively, providing contexts for incessant small-scale movement and far-flung, lasting ties of alliance and enmity, marriage and exchange (Douglas, in press a). The mission journal bore the imprint of this opposition in Douarre's differentiation of guests at a Balade ceremony into "strangers" (enemies) and "strangers friends of the tribe" (allies) (1843–53: 16 May 1852), while Wallis gave it a name: "The inhabitants of the islands are divided into two classes, one is called the *whawhap* [Waap] and the other the *ot* [Hoot]. The towns of these two classes are intermixed" (1994: 146). The opposition would be of marked, though not invariable, salience in alliances forged against and with the French during colonial wars.

COLONIAL REPRESENTATIONS: ACTIONS

Virtually everything Melanesians did or did not do when fighting was damned by missionaries and most other European commentators as contemptible, disgusting or foolish. Their convention of extravagant verbal aggression and bravado, combined with tactical preferences for avoiding open confrontation with a strong opponent and attacking individuals by stealth, usually kept casualties low, but seemed to Europeans at once bombastic, hypocritical, cowardly and bestial: "their courage", sneered Douarre, "is not always in perfect accord with their cries" (1843–53: 11 Feb. 1852). Yet another of the naval surgeon-ethnographers called on a menagerie of tropes to deny the humanity of elusive and athletic foes:

> agile as the squirrel, supple as the snake, these savages slip, without being seen, through even quite low bushes and grass, awaiting the moment when their enemy's back is turned, then, swift as the tiger launching himself at his prey, they spring forth brandishing their club or their axe, and with it strike a blow at their victim's skull (Bourgarel, 1860: 286).

The mutilation, dismemberment and eating of the corpses of fallen foes in the aftermath of battle and the triumphant display of enemy relics seemed unspeakably cruel and barbaric to Europeans: "no one is spared [and] what is more revolting, these unfortunate souls are not left alone in death; great care is taken to carry them off in order to cook and eat them; their bones are then suspended from the doors of the houses" (Rougeyron to S-G, 3 Sep. 1846, APM).[11] European missionaries derided as a "crowd of superstitious practices" the ritual consultation and invocation of appropriate spirits through prayer and sacrifice, and the close attention paid to omens, yet in indigenous aetiology rituals and omens were indispensable to any military enterprise ([Gagnière], 1905: 46–9; Lambert, 1900: 174–7, 180–2; Montrouzier, 1860: 43). By contrast Ta'unga, who was both a devout and knowledgeable Christian convert and the scion of a Polynesian priestly line, was more attuned to an instrumental view of ritual, which he made the centrepiece of his account of "warfare" in New Caledonia: "how do they begin their battles? First they unwrap their war gods and, when their incantations to those gods are over, they fight. They take their gods to the battlefield. They do not leave them at home lest they be killed... As they take the proper ritual precautions, they do not fear the enemy spears" (1968: 87; Patouillet, 1873: 156–7; Wallis, 1994: 146).

The tone of Douarre's descriptions oscillated between a dismissive impression that particular fights were limited and not entirely serious, much ado about relatively little, and an appalled sense of the cumulative desolation, tension and uncertainty which resulted from recurrent violence. I take this ambivalence as a textual imprint of a rhythm in indigenous fighting, escalating repeatedly from injuries or insults inflicted by individuals and abating with the temporary re-establishment of equivalences, by force or diplomacy. In such a military setting particular clashes were usually limited in scale, duration and loss of human life, victory turned on omens and small gains and the vanquished normally survived to fight another day; but single clashes were also episodes in on-going exchanges between individuals and groups and might be embedded in enduring patterns of enmity and alliance, like those which criss-crossed the Hoot ma Waap region.

COLONIAL REPRESENTATIONS: VALUES

As Christian moralists and conventional subscribers to the revived Roman military values of their era,[12] Douarre and his colleagues contemptuously rejected most of what they—and I—read as the basic premises of indigenous political interaction and fighting. They inferred those premises, appropriated and transformed to suit their own discursive ends, from actions seen and rumoured. I do likewise from the traces of such actions registered, distorted and amplified in early colonial texts, but do so reflexively, via radical textual critique, with relativising ethnographic intent.

It was evidently a prime axiom in New Caledonia that maintenance of relative equivalences and prestige demanded revenge for insults and injury. A missionary who in 1847 witnessed the triumphant parade of parts of a human body, before their presentation to the father of a girl said to have been killed and eaten by associates of the victim, was revolted by the act, the method and the motivation, but sought no further rationale: "It is not in war that they killed this man, it is by treachery ... vengeance is eternal amongst these savages; they do not know what it is to pardon" (Rougeyron, 1846–9: 21). Ta'unga also lamented that "these islands have no equal when it comes to vengeance", and deemed "vindictiveness" to be "what causes wars and cannibalism, and fights" (1968: 108–10). Related principles, equally abhorrent to European Christians, were that kinspeople, friends and allies might be held responsible for the actions of individuals, and that morality was relative to relationship. In 1845, Douarre exhorted a "chief", preparing to attack the "friends" of his wife's paramour, to punish only "the guilty party", though he believed that the others, "according to the customs of the country, are obliged to support their friends good or bad, innocent or guilty", and by that token were presumably liable to retaliation (1843–53: 21, 22 December 1845).[13]

Enacted in indigenous contexts these principles had several pragmatic corollaries: that an unsuspecting or defenceless enemy was the best possible victim—"they hardly ever kill each other except by surprise and take vengeance on the first arrival from the enemy tribe, provided they can do it without danger" (Douarre, 1843–53: 15 July 1845); that victory was more important than the manner in which it was achieved; that death or injury to oneself and one's kinsfolk and friends were to be avoided in order to protect group integrity and prevent triggering a cycle of vengeance and counter-vengeance, with all its escalatory and destructive potential. Thus ambush, surprise raid and destruction of gardens, trees, buildings and canoes were favoured, because least risky, tactics; ruse and deception were honoured principles; the weak were always vulnerable and unwary individual enemies, especially women and children, were fair game; withdrawal was a preferred defensive mode against a stronger assailant, while avenues of retreat and places of refuge were always kept open in case of a rout.[14] Open battles were probably fairly rare—"because tactics in war consist of surprises and ambushes"—and normally occurred only "when feelings have long been excited and follow outbursts of a growing anger" (Rochas, 1862: 205; Leenhardt, 1930: 44). The texts contain few authentic accounts of pitched battles,[15] since they presupposed the concurrence of both parties, equally confident of success, and were also unusual in European experience of New Caledonia: they would have been shunned by the Puma because of their weakness relative to more powerful neighbouring chiefdoms, while prestige gained from the installation of the mission at Balade enabled them to avoid such engagements entirely in the 1840s and 1850s; the tactic, moreover, was rarely used by Kanak against Europeans, relative firepower being what what it was.

Rochas the naval surgeon, writing on "War", revealed a more sensitive, relativist grasp of indigenous priorities than did Douarre.[16] He stressed that their concepts of courage and honour were very different from Europeans'. It was not cowardice which led one side to disengage after the loss of two or three warriors, but the critical necessity to secure the dead and wounded from the enemy. A "chief" did not lead his warriors into battle because his life was deemed too precious to risk and his death or, worse, the capture and consumption of his body, would be unbearably shameful (see also Bensa and Goromido, in press).[17] In strategic terms, "to engage in equal combat with an alert enemy, is an error... For them honour depends exclusively on success, and temerity which costs life is idiocy, and which is worse, a disgrace". Warriors hid scars rather than display them with pride, for they evidenced clumsiness in dodging blows, while death in battle was a blot on a person's memory (Rochas, 1862: 206–7; Vigors, 1850: 138, 251).[18] In so many ways indigenous values in relation to fighting look like a mirror-image of European, though French colonial practice was to prove at least as expedient and ruthless, and more relentless. Ironically, the bishop, putative man of peace, complacently collapsed the entire martial performance of another culture into his own summarising metaphor of savagery, implicitly contrasted with a "civilised" chivalric ideal, while the quasi-professional military commentator endeavoured to explore the alien pragmatic values informing the others' actions.

RESTRAINT, RECIPROCITY AND RHETORIC

Few contemporary authors credited the deliberate exercise of restraint in indigenous fighting in New Caledonia, presumably because it was at odds with the double edge of the prevailing trope of savagery: unbridled violence and cringing cowardice. The restraint implicit in many of the actions traced in Douarre's journal went unremarked by the bishop, subsumed as a brutish reflex triggered by fear: "if they do not destroy each other with still more fury, it is because they reciprocally fear each other" (1843–53: 1 May 1845). Yet Melanesian actors clearly did seek to limit the duration and deadliness of their conflicts, external as well as internal, as the occasional more dispassionate commentator acknowledged. The missionary-ethnographer Lambert noted that "their combats ... are not very deadly, they have the decency to stop after having secured a few victims" (1900: 177). Wallis, who talked ethnography at length with one of the Catholic missionaries but had a mind of her own, opined that "if they go to fight a hostile tribe, their motto seems to be 'victory or run away'. When a tribe fights with their own people, their motto is more like 'victory or cripple'. They do not appear to desire to kill, only to wound and maim" (1994: 146–7).

Surveying ethnographies of warfare in Melanesia, Knauft argued that nineteenth century missionaries shared with early ethnologists and later functionalist anthropologists an interest and intent "to minimize and downplay the extent of violence in 'traditional' Melanesian society while emphasizing the violence visited upon Melanesians by traders and blackbirders" (1990: 253-4, 258-65). The assumption and condemnation of trader violence certainly were frequent themes in missionary discourse, but they were set beside twin, ambivalent images of Islanders, mapped roughly on to a Christian/pagan divide: the helpless, passive native victim, and the unbridled savage. Thus early missionaries, including the Catholics in New Caledonia, deplored what they took to be the limitless violence of paganism. My identification of restraint as a pragmatic indigenous strategy, deployed to minimise and deflect the actual and potential violence which plagued them, is at odds with both, equally objectivist, motifs in European representations of the ferocious, craven savage. In making a case for restraint as a kind of culturally nuanced, situational agency, I do not underwrite what Knauft condemned as romantic or "rationalist defense of the primitive", or a functionalist image of Melanesian war as "rational and purposeful, limited in its disruption and actually therapeutic in the...integration of society" (1990: 261). Rather, the theme of restraint in fighting in the following ethnographic overview is distilled from its persistent, if camouflaged residue in mostly unfriendly colonial accounts.

Though Melanesians might harbour grievances for generations and warriors' ferocity in the heat of battle was a by-word, their actions were normally less violent than their rhetoric: "They fight without shedding much blood", said Wallis, "as they run as much as they fight" (1994: 124). Leenhardt maintained that "without heat, without ardour, no war [was] possible", so that warriors and their weapons had to be rendered hot for combat, through fiery oratory, dance, magic and favourable omens (1930: 39; Rochas, 1862: 256-7, 274). Particular engagements and the anger fuelling them were usually short-lived: one missionary described the duration of an 18 day war in 1856 as "quite extraordinary. Habitually their wars are limited to one or two encounters, and each party says: It's enough" (Villard to S-G, 30 Mar. 1856, APM). Confrontation was commonly avoided by temporary self-exile or emigration of a weaker party, leaving the aggressors to discharge their anger in destruction and plunder. As the contrived passions of combat subsided the "chiefs" of the opposing parties normally made overtures for peace, negotiated exchange of compensation for casualties and authorised the return of the vanquished or their incorporation by the victors. Though whole groups were occasionally all but obliterated in successful surprise attacks, conquest of places and expulsion of residents were seemingly fairly unusual. "Masters of the soil" were normally left undisturbed by a conqueror, so as not to offend the spirits to which they controlled ritual access. All men might at times be warriors, but none was exclusively so, and the demands of subsistence provided a ubiquitous incentive to limit and contain fighting.

While the need to restrain violence was pragmatically compelling, restraint in actions, though not in rhetoric, also looks like a widespread cultural preference. It was a correlate of a commitment to reciprocity and equivalence which pervaded relationships of all kinds, friendly, neutral and unfriendly (Douglas, 1994b). There was a hint of ways in which these values informed indigenous notions of "proper proportion" (Schieffelin, 1980: 505) in social relations in a tantalising snippet in the journal of Douarre's colleague Rougeyron. During a deadly epidemic of previously unknown sickness, which had devastated all the places known to the missionaries during 1846, the Mwelebeng "chief" Goa ordered the missionaries to go to Pouébo on the morrow "in order to make peace". When Rougeyron protested that they were not at war, the messenger replied: "You are,... since you make everyone die" and added that the missionaries should therefore forget about all the thefts they had suffered (1846–9: 6). The episode also provided a glimpse of how notions of reciprocity could integrate dimensions and sequences of experience which a Western system of ethnographic classification might subsume in discrete analytic categories: sorcery, war, theft, compensation, peace-making. To Rougeyron, the whole affair was "curious, or better deplorable". Predictably, given their distaste for most things pagan, missionaries tended to reduce reciprocity to negative manifestations—vengeance and coercion—or trace a functional relationship between the obligation to share and all they abhorred in local practices. Squabbles observed during a distribution of valuables provoked Douarre to contemptuous dismissal: "sharing is only a custom which compels them, because they fear war or vengeance; if they did not have that to fear, one could only compare them to dogs, which wrangle over their prey" (1843–53: 15 Mar. 1846). Another missionary adopted a radically functionalist line, drawing explicit causal links between "communism" (the obligation to share), "improvidence", "feasts", "famine" and "these murderous wars which they have in order to eat each other" (Verguet, 1854: 62–3).

Norms and values are best considered not as compulsory patterns for action but as part of flexible repertoires of alternative strategies for action, evaluation and interpretation which cultures make available to those who conceive and negotiate them. In this sense, reciprocity and equivalence were not binding obligations imposed by a nebulous abstract force, such as "society" or "custom", but general dispositions, for aesthetic as well as instrumental reasons. In relation to fighting, negative and positive dimensions of reciprocity were intimately related, so that the same action might display elements of both, depending on perspective. Vengeance, in the sense of hurt, harm or punishment inflicted in return for wrong or injury experienced, was one manifestation of a pragmatic and emotional partiality for equivalence; it was almost always an element, if not the dominant motive, in particular fights and especially in their replication in sequences of related clashes. Vengeance was cited or strongly implied as a major motive in 21 of the 24 fights mentioned in the mission journal between 1843–53, with none suggested for the remaining three. Reported escalation of fighting invariably derived from collective decisions taken to honour reciprocal obligations to support kinsfolk and "friends" (allies). There was escalation in at least 15 of the 24 fights, often through counter-vengeance. Seven of these, all within chiefdoms, began unequivocally with the action of an individual, as apparently most fights did, including those between autonomous political groups, while the same principle of reciprocity contributed to the escalation of both internal and external fights.

Though persuasive, this norm of collective reciprocal support for "friends" was not necessarily prescriptive. Like norms generally, it was subject to manipulation and interpretation in particular contexts, depending on the status and situation of protagonists. Escalation of external conflicts was often deliberately promoted through mobilisation of reciprocities. "Chiefs" anticipating vengeance would attempt to divide responsibility amongst their own allies or neutralise their opponents' by distributing parts of a dead enemy's body: sharing a human corpse meant to "embrace, by that very fact, the quarrel of the donor" and assume an obligation to help meet ultimate vengeance (Rochas, 1862: 206; Goujon, 1848–54: 15 July 1849; Ta'unga, 1968: 92). Douarre recounted how the "chief" of Koumac—which was Waap—sought to erect a defensive alliance and dodge eventual retaliation for the killing of three Hoot enemies by distributing a cooked body to his Waap allies and to other Hoot groups. The bishop acknowledged the norm of reciprocity which informed this action: every "chief" who accepted a portion of the body was "obliged to run the risk of war, in the event that the wronged tribe wanted to exact vengeance for the murder; which cannot fail [to happen] sooner or later". Yet neither the certainty nor the enthusiasm of support could be guaranteed: assistance to an ally was never automatic, but a matter for discussion, negotiation and decision. In 1852 Puma warriors who went to Koumac to help avenge persons killed by common Hoot enemies limited their intervention to a "military march"—"very probably", sneered Douarre, "to their great satisfaction" (1843–53: 1 May 1845, 11 Feb. 1852). Later that year Wallis reported that the Mwelebeng "chief" had refused a Hoot ally's request to join an attack on Waap enemies, on the grounds that "'Our gods say that we must not fight'" (1994: 142). Later still, "war" was said to have been imminent between Koumac and a Hoot coalition: "our Canaks [the Puma]", Douarre thought, "will be obliged to respond" to a call to support their Waap allies. The obligation was apparently equivocal, since the Puma warriors reneged when the bishop refused to give them ammunition (1843–53: 5 Dec. 1852).

The most potent assistance provided by an ally was not necessarily physical. Lambert described how a threatened party might also invoke ritual support by sending an ally a larger quantity of shell "money". He and Leenhardt explained the "language" of symbols, knotted lengths of bark cloth and bunches of grasses and leaves, always accompanied and confirmed by lengths of shell "money", by means of which Melanesians communicated military messages: inciting assassination or attack, requesting alliance, declaring war, authorising repatriation, negotiating peace, offering compensation (Lambert, 1900: 173-4; Leenhardt, 1930: 43-6, 51-2). In colonial contexts this quite simple repertoire of symbols supplied a local code whereby messages could be exchanged and action organised unbeknown to most Europeans.[19]

An action sequence outlined by Douarre displayed several common elements in indigenous fighting (1843-53: 3 Dec. 1851). A party of Puma, seeking pots, paid a visit by canoe to a settlement of the neighbouring Mwelebeng of Pouébo, normally their enemies. Several Paak of Bondé, allies of the Mwelebeng, claimed that the canoe belonged to a stranger from Ouvéa, who had resided with them since its seizure; they would have killed its occupants but for the intervention of mountain people from Pouala, allies of the Puma. The occupants sounded the alarm at Balade and at once the Puma warriors set out for Pouébo. They quickly returned, however, since peace had been made; three mountain dwellers had been killed by the Paak and jointly eaten by Paak and Mwelebeng. The matter seemed settled, when the Pouala people realised that one of the dead belonged to them and at once sought vengeance by wounding two Mwelebeng. The rumour that they had been killed spread at Balade, and during the night all the Puma warriors gathered about the mission house, in anticipation of imminent Mwelebeng vengeance. They took the precaution of loading their valuables on canoes. Presumably the affair was peacefully resolved, since it received no further mention.

Inconclusiveness aside, the episode illustrates the sequential build-up and release of tension which I take to have comprised much of the rhythm of indigenous politics. The potential for rapid escalation of violence was plain, as individual actions were translated into group responses through enactment of norms of collective responsibility and mutual support for "friends". The self-perpetuating cadence of reciprocal vengeance and counter-vengeance, fuelled by actions committed in anger and difficult to circumvent, was starkly in evidence, as were precautions available to a weaker party anticipating flight in the event of reprisals for their own or, in this case, their allies' actions. The potential for limiting escalation through peace-making and, presumably, non-violent restoration of equivalences was less obvious, but always implicit. Mention of resident strangers and small-scale visiting for exchange purposes hints at the extent of individual mobility and suggests that the category "enemy" did not preclude a whole range of other kinds of relationships between members of normally hostile groups.

TARGETING EUROPEANS

Eight of the nine attacks on foreigners mentioned in the early mission texts deployed the favoured tactics of ruse, surprise or ambush, and in five cases all or most of the victims were killed instantly, without loss to the assailants. They included a surprise attack in 1850 by Nenema Islanders on 14 well-armed sailors manning a boat from the French warship *Alcmène*: 11 died at once, while the others were adopted by local people until rescued (Bérard, 1854: 103, 119–37). Later oral testimony recorded by Lambert depicted the attack as materially and politically motivated: the strangers were killed "'so their valuables might become our valuables and so they do not take them, together with their arms, amongst our Koumac enemies'". He detailed preparatory rituals performed to seek favourable omens and render the warriors invulnerable, the victims unsuspecting and their arms ineffective. He outlined the stratagem adopted: the leader, a powerful priest and sorcerer, approached the French party with an innocent and indifferent air, as if intending to trade, while his followers each stood beside a chosen target. As the leader struck, so did they, giving the unsuspecting victims no chance to use their arms.[20] The Nenema shared the bodies with their closest allies and the actual attackers sacrificed the heart of the presumed French leader (1900: 32–5).

In the other three cases, those beset fled or defended themselves and few lives were lost. A cluster of texts recounted how in

1847 the Puma used deception in an assault on the Balade mission, luring the occupants from their house to face a sudden onslaught by a dozen armed warriors. Though a lay brother was mortally wounded, a random gunshot saw the attackers withdraw, allowing the Europeans to regain the house. The next day a large party of warriors—"two hundred cannibals"—launched a tactical facsimile of an artillery bombardment, hurling large stones long and hard enough to splinter a wall of the house. Since the attackers remained under cover, "it was impossible for us to hit them, they, however, dared not invade the yard" (Verguet, 1854: 239, 240). The stalemate ended when the warriors fired the house, but they concentrated on plunder and allowed the mission party to flee to Pouébo: "I passed amid this furious horde", one recalled, "without anyone doing me harm" (Collomb, 1847: 28). Despite their respect for firearms and for the esoteric powers of the Catholic priests, the Puma must surely have taken the house by frontal assault had they seriously tried, since of a mere five defenders, two—a bishop and a priest—refused to fire on the assailants. Only after ransacking the storehouse did they finally despatch the wounded brother, who had been abandoned by his fleeing friends (Collomb, 1847; Rougeyron, 1846–9: 18–36; Verguet, 1854: 238–46).

Such actions and the demeanour attributed to the warriors— "daubed with charcoal and making ferocious cries" (Verguet, 1854: 240)—suggest that they aimed not to kill but to intimidate the Europeans in order to gain access to the mission storehouse. Rougeyron signalled as much—"these avid savages had thought more of stealing than of killing the missionaries" (1846–9: 24)— though his rhetoric of cupidity and excess cloaked what I take to be the textual imprint of pragmatic and relatively restrained indigenous behaviour: at a time of severe local famine, the storehouse was stashed with food and goods, which the missionaries, violating local norms of reciprocity and generosity, had refused to share with their needy Puma hosts. In Wallis' ironic retelling of the story she heard from the priests five years later, indigenous restraint and missionary transgression were important sub-texts:

> [The missionaries] planted a garden, got themselves comfortable and had been there something over a year when the natives

began to cast anxious looks towards their property. They did not appear to wish to destroy the lives of the missionaries, but told them to depart. The warnings were neglected, and the establishment was attacked, set fire to, and robbed—or rather, robbed first (1994: 125).

Three weeks later a French warship evacuated the demoralised mission party from Pouébo. Though the missionaries were convinced that the Mwelebeng also plotted their destruction, the "chiefs" expressed consternation when the Europeans showed they intended to leave with most of their remaining property. Committed to going, the latter dismissed this as "crafty words" (Verguet, 1854: 257–8), an opinion confirmed when an attack took place during their retreat to the ship. But it makes better and more consistent sense of Mwelebeng actions to interpret the last-minute assault as a furious response to abandonment perceived as betrayal and to the disappearance of valuables, a share of which they claimed in return for admitting the missionaries into their community. Rougeyron heard Bonou, the high "chief", say "that I was very wicked since I was going", and he refused to be mollified with gifts (1846–9: 35). After a thwarted attempt to ambush the party as it retreated to the beach under heavy naval escort, Mwelebeng warriors engaged in persistent skirmishing on the flanks and rear of the French column, during which one died and five seamen suffered spear wounds, two seriously. An anonymous officer described the deadlock resulting from a combination of indigenous refusal to confront the disciplined firepower of trained troops and the latter's inability to inflict significant damage on an agile and elusive foe:

the Caledonians did not dare [stage] a frontal attack, made a rush at the rearguard. They stayed hidden in thick scrub, it was impossible to see them, but arrows[21] and spears which rained like hail gave an indication of their number. Several times headlong charges were made [by the French] on the edges of the route, without being able to hit anyone, a single Canaque ... paid for his rashness with his life (Anon. 1847: 6–7).

The attacks on the mission and its relief party and the *Alcmène* affair provoked French punitive expeditions. In 1847 buildings, canoes, trees and gardens belonging to Mwelebeng and

Puma were destroyed, but there were no reported human casualties as the people took to the nearby hills; thwarted, the French behaved, wrote the anonymous officer, like "true devastating demons" (Anon. 1847: 10; Rougeyron, 1846–9: 35–6). In 1850, in a nine-day orgy of vengeance, the crew of the *Alcmène* claimed to have killed 20–30 people and ravaged several islands; but most of the alleged casualties occurred on the first day and the Nenema, who had previously met few Europeans, then hid or fled, abandoning their houses and gardens to a stronger enemy—they were "more adept at fleeing us than fighting us", sneered Patouillet in retrospect (1873: 27; Bérard, 1854: 140–50). During both episodes some local people fought against others. In 1847 a handful of children, mostly baptised Christians, served the missionaries as spies and guides, while the "chiefs" of two Puma settlements vigorously condemned the assault on the mission and fought with the high "chief". In 1850 six Puma warriors accompanied the *Alcmène*'s expedition against the Nenema, who were Hoot and their feared enemies, while Waap people came from several places to harass and plunder any Nenema refugees.

These early texts provide only a sample of confrontations between Kanak and Europeans in one region of New Caledonia during the first decade of intensive contacts, before the formal installation of a colonial régime. The traces of actions inscribed therein predictably rehearsed indigenous patterns of fighting, but also anticipated the "singular compositions of system" (Rochas, 1862: 207–8)—adapted, transformed indigenous methods, and innovations—which Kanak adopted in colonial encounters. They included an ongoing preference in offence for ruse and ambush of isolated, preferably unwary individuals and small groups; a refusal to front armed, alert Europeans in open battle unless with marked advantage in surprise or numbers; a tactical reliance against French columns on harassment by spear, slingshot and occasionally gunshot from heavy cover, or skirmishing on the flanks and at the rear; a tendency to prefer plunder to killing except in the heat of anger. The stalemate which ordinarily ensued from such tactics saw the frustrated French respond with devastation, a corollary of fighting all too familiar to Melanesians. Some local people also showed readiness to fight with, or parallel to Europeans, as Christians or when their own enemies or interests were engaged.

COLONIAL FIGHTING

Even so, there were a few reported instances of frontal assault by Kanak on European positions, as in 1868 when a party of Tea Janu, said to be several hundred strong, came to the coast near Pouébo and launched two attacks on a large settler establishment reinforced by a detachment of 20 soldiers. After battles timed at five hours and one hour respectively the assailants were repulsed without loss to the defenders, but on the second occasion 50 warriors were officially claimed as victims of the latter's "well-sustained, intelligently-directed fire" (*Moniteur*, 22 Nov. 1868). The figure is ludicrous, since no indigenous assault party would have stayed in range long enough to suffer such losses, and dead and wounded were always carried off the battlefield, making a reliable estimate of casualties impossible. Numerical legerdemain aside, the episodes showed the problems Kanak faced against well-armed troops holding a sound defensive position and practising good fire discipline. Throughout the colonial period Kanak never possessed artillery, usually had few effective firearms, and mainly relied on clubs—increasingly replaced by the lethal steel axe—and on slings and spears. Despite indigenous skill and accuracy with these weapons, they were inadequate in offence against disciplined use of firearms, even the inefficient muzzle-loaders with which French forces were armed before their re-equipment in 1869 with the *chassepot* rifle. Rochas commented:

> New Caledonians are of great bravery, and despite the inferiority of their armament, for they have almost no guns in good condition, they are able to offer us a courageous and sometimes intelligent resistance. If these people were provided with firearms, and especially good ones, they would be redoutable adversaries, for they quickly learn to handle a gun, and make skilful marksmen (1862: 208-9).

Accordingly, early French military governors sometimes armed Christians with firearms in response to specific crises, and in the

1860s established two small companies of "native fusiliers". Equipped with musket and bayonet—the latter having no pre-contact equivalent—they were acknowledged as effective in offence against Kanak (Patouillet, 1873: 50, 143).

In one rare instance during the colonial wars of 1878-9 Kanak did manage to capture significant quantities of firearms and ammunition. They then adapted an indigenous model to incorporate the new armament, implementing in isolation a defensive tactic not unlike that used systematically by New Zealand Maori in their wars against the British in the 1840s and 1860s.[22] Leenhardt commented that Kanak traditionally closed valleys for defensive purposes using barriers of banyan groves or hedges, or walls made of piled stones (1930: 34-5). On this occasion warriors from Poya and Bourail combined to construct a fortified position at Cap Goulvain, which the French governor described admiringly:

> the valley of Mouéara ... is enclosed between two ridges and takes the form of an elongated oval, moreover it is full of high rocks ... and covered with trees and bushes which make it inextricably jumbled. On the edges, the *Canaques* had built a series of small walls out of large stones, disposed in a very intelligent fashion and which allowed them to see and to fire quite comfortably, while remaining under cover (Olry, "Récit détaillé des événements de l'insurrection canaque", 22 Dec. 1878-16 Jan. 1879, ANOM, Carton 43).

A French frontal attack was repulsed with two dead and five wounded, all to gunshots. A subsequent expedition found the position entirely evacuated, having presumably fulfilled its purpose or proved to be no longer tenable; a similar experience often befell British forces assaulting Maori *paa*—fortified hilltop settlements—since abandonment at need was integral to Maori strategy (Belich, 1986: 63-4, 106-7).[23]

According to Leenhardt (1930: 38), "each village group has a refuge hidden in the mountains for times of danger". Fortified bush settlements were described in 1878, while weathered limestone formations, riddled with caves, were prized as natural strongholds; several were reported during colonial wars, particularly in 1878-9, and most recently in 1988 in Ouvéa. In November 1878, after strenuous efforts, two French columns and several hundred indigenous allies managed to take a natural citadel at Adio, but found most of the defenders gone. Like the second expedition to Cap Goulvain, this was lauded officially as a notable French victory, but the Catholic chaplain at Bourail, with a sounder grasp of Kanak tactics and intentions, acknowledged that the place, "which was to be the rebels' tomb[,] was in white hands only a cage without a bird" (Lecouteur to Fraysse, 28 Nov. 1878, AAN, 16.2; Olry to Min., 2 Dec. 1878, ANOM, Carton 43). Withdrawal thus remained the favoured indigenous defensive tactic. It was effective when permanent conquest of territory was not an issue, as in most local conflicts in the Hoot ma Waap region and with isolated French punitive expeditions. When expeditions were followed by expropriation of Kanak and permanent installation of settlers under military protection, withdrawal tended to preserve lives but seriously disrupt livelihood.

Plunder of European property seems to have been a more important end for Kanak than killing, though killing could be a means to achieve it. Plunder of known Europeans was presumably often a way to restore equivalence or enforce reciprocity: retaliation or forced redress for perceived insult, expropriation, broken promises, depredations by livestock, miserliness, or failure to meet on-going exchange obligations incurred in return for occupation and use rights. Stinginess at a time of local stringency and unmet exchange obligations look like major Puma grievances against the Balade missionaries in 1847. The ambush and killing of two gendarmes near Pouébo in 1867 were probably in retaliation for the punishment of "chiefs" and the actuality or threat of expropriation. Most secular colonial authors, even the even handed Rochas, joined missionaries in condemning the "lively" and "tenacious" passion for vengeance as a Kanak moral failing (1862: 158). It was commonly agreed that they were "capable of nurturing vengeance for years at a time" (Montravel to Min., 27 Apr. 1854) and of concerting long-term plans for war with substantial coalitions: most striking was the lengthy diplomatic groundwork for the wars of 1878, intimations of which percolated into some colonial awareness (see Chapter Five).

Nonetheless, most actual attacks on Europeans, like those on other Islanders, were sudden, delivered in heat, and fairly short-lived, presumably concluded once vengeance had been taken, immediate grievances redressed or losses suffered. The same could be said of many isolated French expeditions, when logistical difficulties imposed constraints analogous to those under which warrior-gardeners always laboured. Kanak might have expected the French to act with similar circumspection, restraint and humanity during the three major nineteenth century colonial wars—1856–9 in the south, 1868–9 in the north and 1878–9 in the west. If so, they would be disillusioned: French military leaders, given an assured line of supply and sufficient political will in Paris, were culturally and professionally attuned to dreary, drawn-out campaigns conducted to the bitter end. It was a proclivity predicated on ruthlessly hierarchical class and racial values: a readiness to exploit the troops' disciplined subservience to those "Roman military ideas" of "unquestioning obedience" and "self-abnegation" identified by Keegan (1976: 64); a denial of the human equivalence of "enemies", especially when they were "savages".

Endorsement/justification of a strategy of attrition was a refrain in colonial texts, as in 1863 when the official newspaper proclaimed: "Experience proves that the sole means of repression to use against the natives is occupation of a territory from which one expels them and whence one can effect unexpected forays on their points of refuge, until, weary of war and dying of hunger, they make their submission" (*Moniteur*, 27 Sep. 1863). Similar experience taught the same lesson during an inland expedition in 1868, when the French and their indigenous allies managed only to destroy the settlements and gardens of a slippery enemy, who evaded face-to-face encounters and was impossible to catch in wild and inaccessible terrain: "The duty to pursue the task begun by France", intoned the *Moniteur* (14 Feb. 1869), had led the colonial government to "adopt against savage tribes the sole system of repression which could achieve the desired end... [O]nly by dispersing and expelling these ferocious mountain people from their territory... [and] by creating several forward posts... can we manage, step by step, and in time, to pacify and occupy New Caledonia completely". Despite spasmodic metropolitan nervousness about cost, morality and likely political backlash, such a strategy was implemented by the military government in Nouméa in each nineteenth century war. It had the acknowledged bonus potential to free large areas of land for colonisation through dispersal of Kanak opponents (Forget to Min., 15 June 1860, CM; Rivière, 1881: 259).

The same 1869 report allowed that most of the interior of the northern third of the main island was still hostile and uncontrolled territory—after nearly 16 years of colonial rule, including seven years of strenuous efforts to bring the natives to heel. Moreover, within two years of this campaign, inland groups in the north had regained much of their autonomy, as war in Europe drained resources from the colony and forced the virtual withdrawal of French military forces to the south (see Chapter Five). After annexation in 1853, the French never doubted their own centrality in New Caledonian affairs, to the extent that Kanak violence of all kinds was usually categorised in official rhetoric as "revolt" or "rebellion" against legitimate sovereign authority, as indeed it was in colonial logic—but that is no excuse for historians unthinkingly to reinscribe the labels, as did Saussol (1979: 106–18) and Dousset-Leenhardt (1976: 37–8). Islanders doubtless interacted in ways which did not necessarily involve the French and brought local political agenda to clashes with Europeans (Douglas, 1980a, 1992). The French are best seen as only one element—albeit often a significant one—in the unstable, contested politics of New Caledonia to 1880. Only after the wars of 1878–9 could they impose permanent authority on substantial areas outside the south, which had been effectively pacified by 1859, but even after 1880 French control was patchy in the north, and remained so into the twentieth century. Like most colonial occupations, that of New Caledonia by France was erratic, at times regressive, and far more onerous, lengthy and expensive than its initiators had anticipated.

The colonial strategy of attrition was fully developed during 1878, accomplished by mobile patrols of troops and flying columns of irregulars, radiating from a network of hastily constructed fortified posts, guided and accompanied by indigenous allies. The latter—persons and groups choosing active alliance with the French—were numerically and strategically critical in every colonial war. Their motives are obscure and were no doubt varied, but probably often owed more to indigenous political considerations than to subservience or commitment "to the cause of civilisation, that is to French sovereignty", as the colonisers publicly proclaimed (*Moniteur*, 6 Sep. 1868). The label "collaborator", implying "co-operation with the enemy", is hardly apt for such autonomous groups, since "the enemy" was always contextual and might as well be indigenous as foreign.[24] In 1878 the Canala leader Nondo at times led 3–500 warriors into the field against Kanak opponents of the French. The Australian journalist Stanley James had no doubt about the allies' significance in that war, an opinion inflated by cynicism as to French performance:

> Almost everything which has been done, except the destruction of plantations, in which the French soldiers excel, has been by the Canaque auxiliaries. The great chief Atai [instigator of the war] and his son were their victims. Indeed, in the bush fighting in the thick scrub around La Foa, it is, as I have witnessed, almost impossible for regular troops to operate (*SMH*, 15 Oct. 1878).

Though French campaign reports usually downgraded allies to a purely auxiliary role under European direction, there are textual indications that allied contingents often operated autonomously under their own priest and war leader and for their own purposes. One officer deplored their tendency "to regard themselves as indispensable to our security" (Olry, "Récit détaillé", 16 Jan.–5 Feb. 1879, ANOM, Carton 43), but it was a well-founded opinion. "The blacks", complained a missionary, "see that the whites cannot pursue and kill them in the mountains,... they see and they *say* that the whites need blacks to destroy blacks" (Moris to Fraysse, 1 Jan. 1879, AAN, 16.1, orig. emphasis). Allies received bounties and loot and seized opportunities to balance accounts with their enemies, colonise remote areas and absorb refugees, especially women and children—a major impulse to fighting. French reliance on allies forced them to ignore otherwise proscribed actions, even cannibalism according to one experienced observer in the 1860s: "it would have been both useless and impolitic to thwart the customs of these always faithful allies, and we closed our eyes on deeds which we despaired, alas! of being able to prevent" (Patouillet 1873: 50).[25]

COLONIAL BILE AND THE IMPRINT OF INDIGENOUS AGENCY

The generally negative tone of early European descriptions of indigenous fighting was echoed in most accounts of their military action in colonial contexts, though there were a few generous evaluations: the perceptive Rochas noted that "their audacity is often admirable having regard to the inferiority of their armament" (1862: 208) and a participant in the repression of 1878 praised their "boldness" as "astonishing, coming up as they do to 50 or 60 yards of the camps, and showing a front to our bullets and rifles" (*SMH*, 17 Aug. 1878). The argument of inferior arms cut no ice with James, who was unimpressed with French soldiery and weapons. Patronisingly sympathetic, he belittled the tactical sense of Kanak and attributed to cowardice their refusal to confront armed bodies of troops and preference for surprise attack on defenceless opponents: "the natives had no knowledge even of savage warfare", he asserted puzzlingly, "and were afraid of the military" (Thomas, 1886: 58–60, 72, 76).

The ubiquitous colonial trope of the mindless, craven, savage horde rests on racist denial of indigenous agency compounded by shaky (fearful?) arithmetic. Injection of a concept of agency recasts "fear" as strategic prudence, on the premise that human choices and actions always entail an entanglement of emotion and reason, rather than their *a priori* polarisation, whether on general conceptual or cultural/racial grounds. A major constraint on agency and an important condition of prudence was the marked numerical inferiority of Kanak warriors to French troops and their allies in most colonial encounters. By this reading, traces of Kanak tactics sedimented in colonial texts bespeak two sides of a single, pragmatic coin, appropriate to outnumbered, outgunned, (probably frightened!) part-time warriors: belief in the psychological value of short, sharp explosions of extreme violence, coupled with a readiness to exercise restraint. The killings which initiated every major colonial conflict, notably in 1878, were probably intended to be decisive, not preliminary to drawn-out campaigns for which Kanak were logistically ill-equipped. In outline and ethos the indigenous tactical repertoire was not markedly different during the colonial era from what it seems to have been earlier, but their demonstrated flexibility and adaptability argue that Melanesians were not locked into culturally preordained patterns: they eagerly sought firearms, handled them expertly and made significant defensive tactical innovations to accommodate their use in fortified positions; in 1878 they did their best to disrupt French communications by cutting telegraph wires.

What to me is culturally informed, strategically constrained choice has been interpreted by some historians—projecting unreflective, ethnocentric assumptions about inevitable outcomes on to other people's pasts—as a blind, savage conservatism which doomed from the outset indigenous resistance to French intrusion (Latham, 1978). Even Saussol, who wrote a meticulous history of land matters in New Caledonia, attributed the Kanak defeat in 1878–9 to poor co-ordination and inefficient decision-making resulting from the commitment to "precolonial methods" of a people incapable of envisaging more than a return to the old order. At best they managed the odd technical imitation; their only asset was mobility, which enabled them to escape capture but could not ensure victory; while their "finest feats of arms" were mere "defensive reflexes" at the Adio rocks and Cap Goulvain. Thus, he argued, "as much technically, through lack of firearms, as tactically, Melanesians were badly adapted to this new war", initial successes gained through surprise were not repeated and they became "bogged down in a hopeless guerrilla" conflict (1979: 189, 228, 240). But inadequate armament is scarcely an index of failure to adapt: on the contrary, one aim of the initial attacks in each theatre of the war was to obtain firearms and ammunition, as even Saussol allowed (1979: 216). "Defensive reflex" is a harsh judgement on Kanak efforts at Cap Goulvain and Pic Adio, since they won the former engagement and mostly escaped from the second; these carefully constructed positions formed part of a co-ordinated strategy in the northern theatres which cost the French and their allies inordinate effort, gave the defenders a lengthy breathing-space and enabled most of them permanently to avoid capture, though at the price of abandoning much territory (Lecouteur to Fraysse, 28 Sep., 7, 22 Oct., 19, 24, 28 Nov., 11 Dec. 1878, AAN, 16.2).

Though ultimately Kanak lost every colonial war, it is clear, even from colonial campaign reports, that they were usually not defeated militarily, but chose or were forced to negotiate when the costs of continued fighting became unacceptable. A subsistence economy could not sustain armed mobilisation indefinitely, especially in the face of an effective strategy of attrition. Textual residues of Kanak actions imply that they scorned political martyrdom and saw no virtue in fighting to the bitter end against daunting odds. Yet intimations of the effectiveness of Kanak military action percolated colonial texts, even the most racist and demeaning. It showed in the length of time and amount of French effort necessary before Kanak decided that endurance of inequities and oppression was less destructive of their interests than violence; in the arduousness for Europeans and the inconclusiveness of particular campaigns; in the generally heavy French reliance on allied support; in the extent to which Melanesians forced the French to adopt their methods. James commented in 1878 that "this war of repression on the Canaques had to be made *à la Canaque* ... [The French] appreciated this to a certain extent, and native manners had been adopted in the burning of villages and tabus, and the destruction of cocoanut trees and vegetation" (Thomas, 1886: 64). The *Sydney Morning* Herald's resident correspondent made much the same point, in overtly racist terms, to justify the slow progress of repression: "the tedious process of starvation, and of black against black, are the means which must be depended upon for the reduction of this handful of agile devils, who leap from rock to rock, dive into the friendly covering of thick tangled bush by paths known to themselves only, or disappear in the numerous ravines" (*SMH*, 3 Aug. 1878).

RESONANCES IN LATER PRESENTS

Some aspects of renewed Kanak fighting against French colonialism in 1984—of which I was a peripheral spectator (Douglas 1985a)—and 1988 look strikingly familiar in terms of my historical ethnography of indigenous fighting. As Leenhardt remarked from personal observation in 1917, "today Kanak war is modern" (1930: 41–2): in the 1980s they used firearms, radio, roadblocks and propaganda in a guerrilla conflict which everyone knew could not be won militarily, only politically. But modernity had intimations of older patterns. Tactically, Kanak again where possible avoided open confrontation with opponents who had an overwhelming monopoly of force; they emphasised negotiation and withdrawal; ambush and surprise were their chosen offensive modes when direct action was seen to be unavoidable. They preferred compromise to martyrdom and emphasised selective, controlled, intensely psychological violence, often verbal rather than physical and aimed at property rather than persons. At times this was so convincing, confirming entrenched European (and Polynesian) stereotypes of Melanesian savagery, as to provoke extreme responses from their opponents: the murder after ambush of ten Kanak by settlers in 1984, the shooting of the Kanak leader Eloi Machoro and his deputy by élite sharpshooters in 1985, and the storming of a Kanak-held cave in Ouvéa by anti-terrorist forces in 1988, at a cost of 19 Kanak and two French lives. On each occasion the Kanak independence movement (FLNKS) subsequently displayed awesome restraint and discipline in the face of extreme provocation.

Essentialist evaluation of "national character" is rightly anathema in postcolonial studies, but it is most people's quotidian vice. It is my impression, historically and existentially, that Melanesians in New Caledonia are usually slow to anger, passionate and sometimes extremely violent in expressing anger, but quick to seek negotiation and restoration of equivalences in its aftermath.[26] Their indigenous political ideologies permitted, indeed demanded, extremes of violence towards "other men", "strangers/enemies", while such values were expressed in the extravagant threats and hyperbole of their political rhetoric. Yet in action a variety of pragmatic considerations—informed by widely endorsed dispositions for reciprocity, equivalence and restraint—tended and tend to contain violence and encourage conflict resolution by other means, except in the heat of actual fighting. Something of this paradoxical amalgam of ardour and discipline was enacted personally by Machoro in 1984: his widely-publicised image, smashing a ballot box with an axe, appalled Europeans, but this most passionate of Kanak leaders was also quite coldly clinical about the political efficacy of symbolic violence, as well as remarkably restrained in his own military practice.

Again and again during the colonial period in New Caledonia, the cost of military solutions decided indigenous people to try strategies other than open violence. So too, the killings and traumas of the 1980s convinced the most influential leaders of the FLNKS to eschew direct confrontation with the overwhelming French military presence. They opted instead to enter into uneasy partnership with the French state and local European powerbrokers, with the still largely-unrealised aim of obtaining sufficient local political muscle and metropolitan subsidies to advance the economic interests of the Kanak people ahead of the political. What has happened in New Caledonia in the 1980s and 1990s attests to the inadequacy of binary anticolonial models of indigenous fighting and colonised reactions. Such models cast violence and non-violence as polar opposites—as in excess:restraint, resistance:collaboration—and privilege violent resistance in colonial contexts as more courageous and romantic. Violence and non-violence are more aptly identified as reiterated, ambiguous, intertwined, partly interchangeable motifs in Kanak agency and colonial experience. Magic, for instance, must often have been deployed tactically by Kanak against Europeans, though its textual traces are predictably exiguous. In cultural intent magic can be a very violent weapon indeed, as detailed in Part Three, but a routine utilitarian anticolonialism is likely to deplore or elide it, as irrational, "primitive", despairing and the very reverse of activist.

NOTES

[1] Leconte, 1847: 822.
[2] Historically I apply the term "Kanak" particularly to opponents of the French. With reference to the colonial past, "Kanak" does not imply a shared sense of indigenous national identity or national unity, since until after World War II identities were framed in shifting local or regional terms. It does have a certain ironic appropriateness, since Europeans often used *canaques/canacks/kanaks* to mean "pagans" or "enemies", in opposition to "Christians" or "friendly natives". I use "ally" to refer to people fighting parallel to the French and "neutral" to mean currently "uninvolved". The denominations "Kanak", "ally" and "neutral" are neither generic nor immutable, since personal and group allegiances were labile, regularly contested and renegotiated on the basis of interest and experience. These terms imply positive differentiation between categories of indigenous choice and action, and refusal to take Europeans for granted as the touchstone for native *re*action, as, say, do "anti-French" and "pro-French". In the remaining chapters "New Caledonia" means the large island thus named by Cook and the small islands within its fringing reef; it does not include the Loyalty Islands.
[3] These texts include an official journal by the head of the mission (Douarre, 1843-53; Rougeyron, 1846-9); mission correspondence and publications; naval officers' accounts; the journal of Mary Wallis (1994), a Protestant American who spent three months at or near Balade in 1852 with her trader husband and talked ethnography with the English-speaking Catholic missionary Forestier. Her "great interest" in "savage customs" (Douarre, 1843-53: 5 July 1852) was relativised by lengthy experience in Fiji, and her narrative is an important departure from the heavily male, missionary, Catholic, French bias of colonial texts on New Caledonia.
[4] Rochas, 1862: 242.
[5] Cook, 1961: 528-46; d'Entrecasteaux, 1808, I: 330-62; La Billardière, 1800, II: 183-249; La Ferrière, 1845: 63-111; Pigeard, 1846: 83-129.
[6] Wallis, who had been warned in advance that the New Caledonians "are exceedingly treacherous", was later told by a resident European that they "are not as treacherous among themselves as the Fijians are, although treacherous acts are sometimes performed by them". She relayed his hearsay account of an episode in which a "chief" feigned hospitality in order to trap and kill the numerous killers of his brother: "This affair is spoken of among the natives as a great and uncommon event" (1994: 113, 136).
[7] Montravel, senior officer on the local French naval detachment during 1854, cautioned against too literal an interpretation of "the tall tales of these great [Puma/Mwelebeng] wars which...end in a day" in mutual withdrawal, though he did acknowledge that a vast tract between Balade and Pouébo remained uninhabited and strewn with the blackened débris of former wars (Montravel to Min., 25 Dec. 1854, ANOM, Carton 40).

8. Leenhardt, 1930: 105. George Forster, naturalist on Cook's *Resolution*, remarked: "they called... the district beyond the hills on the S. W. coast, Teabooma; which being also the name of the chief, occasioned several conjectures" (1777, II: 406).
9. European texts from this period depicted the Puma chiefdom as riven by recurrent, long-standing competition for the high "chiefly" title—often flaring into open violence—between its two most highly ranked clan segments.
10. Leconte, a shipwrecked naval captain who published a treatise on native "customs" after spending two months at Balade near the mission, explained: "Natives who come from other parts of the island to visit this district have a denomination analogous to strangers" (1847: 822).
11. Bensa and Goromido (in press) put a strong case that the indigenous rationale for consuming captured enemy bodies was to deprive enemies of relics which were the key to attracting ancestors, who might be propitiated for help and protection.
12. Keegan noted that "from the seventeenth century onwards, it is Roman military practices—drill, discipline, uniformity of dress—and Roman military ideas—of intellectual leadership, automatic valour, unquestioning obedience, self-abnegation, loyalty to unit—which are dominant in the European soldier's world" (1976: 64). Such values underpinned the contempt in which French soldiers generally held indigenous military priorities and performance, as in the following extreme example of denigration and misrepresentation by the head of the colonial engineering service: "As a fighting man, the Caledonian today would be a sorry auxiliary; he knows how to creep and surprise, he dares not wait for danger. His battles are rapid incursions rather than combats, the first resistance halts them; sometimes the two sides flee at the same time, and the battlefield remains open to whoever takes courage first" (Chef du Génie et du Service des Ponts et Chaussées, "Mémoire militaire...", 20 Apr. 1863, ANOM, DFC, Carton 1). These slurs were not only defamatory, but hypocritical, given heavy French reliance on indigenous allies in colonial wars before and subsequently (see also Chapter Five).
13. Years later Douarre had so absorbed the local idiom of collective guilt that he wrote of "making war on the guilty village" of an individual delinquent (1843–53: 28 Nov. 1852).
14. Traces of indigenous actions from which this ethnographic digest was distilled are located in Douarre, 1843-53: 1 May, 15 July, 10, 22, 25 Dec. 1845, 9 Jan., 20 Feb., 8 Mar. 1846, 17, 29 Nov., 3 Dec. 1851, 29 Apr., 9, 13 May, 19, 22 July 1852; Montravel to Min., 27 Apr. 1854; Leconte, 1847:835–6; Rochas, 1862: 156, 202–7; Wallis, 1994: 124.
15. For plausible first-hand descriptions of battles, see Garnier, 1868: 8–11; Montrouzier, 1860: 42–3; Patouillet, 1873: 161; Rochas, 1862: 205; Vigors, 1850: 249–51.

[16] Rochas evidently tailored tone to topic. In the first part of his chapter on indigenous "moral physiognomy", "character", "intelligence", "qualities and faults" and "passions", he characterised Kanak by a conventional compendium of demeaning primitivist tropes: "cruel"; "perfidious"; "anthropophagous"; like "the child who knows no curb, because lacking in moral sense and education"; "proud like an ignoramus"; "lazy"; notable for "capriciousness"; "fecklessness", "vengeance", "jealousy". Evenhanded, he qualified this negative conspectus with an equally essentialist list of positive qualities: "brave" in war; showing "courage and often audacity", "shrewdness", "prodigious facility for elocution", "patience"; "endowed with an excellent memory" (1862: 155-68).

[17] Wallis elaborated behavioural implications of this norm, alluding to a structural dimension: "The eldest son of a chief of high rank is Tea... The Tea never goes to war. The second son of the Tea is called Muaiau [*mweau*]. He is the warrior who avenges insults, and fights for the family. He *leads behind* in their wars" (1994: 147, orig. emphasis).

[18] That these were widespread Oceanic values rather than peculiar to New Caledonia was evident from the early contact literature on parts of Polynesia. The *Bounty* mutineer, Morrison, remarked of Tahitians that "a man never obtains the Name of a Warrior tho he kills his Man, should he receive any wound himself, as they think that a Man Who suffers himself to be wounded does not know how to defend himself, and tis more Honour to return with whole bones then broken ones" (1935: 174). Mariner's amanuensis, John Martin, recorded that Tongan nobles deplored the action of a man who "ventured his life to throw his spear at the muzzle of Mr Mariner's carronade" as "rash ... and unworthy a great and brave mind, that never risks any danger but with a moral certainty, or at least reasonable expectation, of doing some service to his cause. In these respects they accuse Europeans of a great deal of vanity and selfishness" (1827, I: 199).

[19] Occasions when the exchange of such messages did come to colonial attention were mentioned in *SMH*, 9 Oct. 1878; Lamadon and Merle, "Renseignements sur un combat canaque... ", 20 Feb. 1897, ANOM, Carton 5.

[20] A virtually identical tactic was reported in successful attacks on a trading brig at the Isle of Pines in 1842 and on settlers at Mont-Dore in 1857 (Ta'unga, 1968: 52; [Foucher] 1890: 28–36; see Chapter Five). It recalls certain classic, if probably fairly rare stratagems which recur in the texts: enticing potential targets to attend a ceremony where they might be killed; surrounding enemy dwellings at night in order to strike down unsuspecting individual occupants as they emerged, sometimes precipitated by the firing of their houses (Douarre, 1843-53: 20 Feb. 1846; Goujon, 1848-54: 9 Nov. 1849; Wallis, 1994: 136). Europeans, often incautious and complacent, might well have been more susceptible to such a ruse than local people.

[21] Bows and arrows were reported as sometimes used for sport and fishing, but not in fighting (Montrouzier, 1860: 44; Rochas, 1860: 402).

[22] Belich (1986) described how radical Maori engineering and tactical innovations transformed an indigenous fortification model into the modern *pa* system, reduction of which demanded disproportionate expenditure of British military resources.

[23] Olry later placed a better face on this episode, reporting, as information received from a Kanak prisoner, that "the last shots fired by the rebels in this affair were like a despairing blow: the rebels, she added, left the same evening of the attack..., without taking care to bury the bodies of those killed, and in fleeing they carried a great number of wounded on improvised litters" ("Récit détaillé", 16 Jan–5 Feb. 1979, ANOM, Carton 43). In 1866 allies of the war leader Gondou were described as entrenched on rocky outcrops forming a "sort of natural fortress", which they used as a base for offensive operations against allies of the French. A war party, in concert with a French detachment, invested the position, but was unable to take it by assault. Eventually, after the French had withdrawn, shortage of provisions apparently induced the defenders to abandon the strongpoint (*Moniteur*, 24 Feb. 1867).

[24] I have elsewhere sketched anatomies of indigenous alliances with the French and argued for the inappropriateness of a simple "resistance: collaboration" model (1980a, 1992: 96–104; cf. Dousset-Leenhardt, 1976: 143).

[25] After recounting a particularly gruesome instance of "the barbarity of our savage allies", this author disavowed sensationalist motives: "I am only the historian of what I have seen and of what many others have been condemned to see like me, without being able to prevent it" (Patouillet, 1873: 163–4).

[26] Modern anthropologists have reasoned similarly (Leenhardt, 1930: 38; Bensa and Bourdieu, 1985: 82–3). So, embarrassingly to a radical like myself, did the leader of the squad of élite gendarmes who stormed the Kanak-held cave in Ouvéa in 1988: he described "Melanesians" as being "of a fundamentally pacific temperament even if he [sic] is subject to accesses of fever" (Legorjus, 1990: 289).

Chapter Four

Reading Indigenous Pasts: The "Wagap Affair" of 1862

FOREWORD

This new chapter derives from a paper delivered to an Anthropology seminar at the Ecole des Hautes Etudes en Sciences Sociales in Paris in 1995, subsequent to which I wrote an article in French for the interdisciplinary journal Genèses *(1996a). My brief for both performances was twofold: to provide French scholars and graduate students in Anthropology with an introduction to recent critical trends in Anglophone postcolonial and feminist writings; to outline and illustrate my ethnohistorical method, particularly techniques for against-the-grain critique and exploitation of colonial texts. The chapter tackles the second of these tasks, elaborating and applying general epistemological and methodological concerns, the genealogy of which was sketched in the Prelude. Though the chapter might sit a little awkwardly between two exemplars of earlier, less reflective, more realist modes of historical enunciation and narration, nonetheless its politics and strategies were already implicit in the assumptions and convictions underpinning Chapters Three and Five. In politics, theory and method, this chapter is the pivot on which the whole book turns.*

The main technique adopted is extended critical dissection and comparison of the structure, components and rhetorical ordering of different genres of texts, using tabular juxtaposition of parallel extracts. Though highly selective and with clear potential for distortion, since the extracts are wrenched from their textual and discursive contexts, the technique has the advantage of packaging and systematising a far wider range of representations in relatively digestible fashion than would otherwise be possible. As with historians' routine recourse to exemplary quotations, readers have to trust that my selections and contextualisations are as representative and scrupulous as I know how to make them. In reading this chapter they will need also to decide how far to credit the reflexive moves by which I seek to make clear the principles of choice used.

PROLOGUE

I identify myself as antipositivist and pluralist. This potentially ultrarelativist epistemology is anchored morally and politically by a postcolonial, emancipatory commitment to radical critique. I am impatient with the analytic primacy usually accorded system and structure in the social sciences, and demand discursive space for the concepts of agency and appropriation. I see agency as at once enabled and constrained—systemically by culture, discourse, power, gender, race, class and age; contingently by context, circumstance and personality. To be alert to indigenous agency is to decentre colonialism and humanise and animate representations of the colonised. Appropriation/domestication of the novel is variously a knowing indigenous strategy and a necessary cultural/contextual reflex. Chartier argued, following Bourdieu:

> the notion of appropriation makes it possible to appreciate the differences in cultural apportionment, in the creative invention that lies at the very heart of the reception process.... The practices of appropriation always create uses or representations that are hardly reducible to the wills or intentions of those who produce discourse and norms (1989: 171–4; see Chapter Eight).

Both agency and appropriation were unstable but ubiquitous elements in colonial encounters; both were randomly but insistently inscribed in colonial texts.

Such an epistemological politics discredits essentialist notions of "traditional" societies as timeless, homogeneous and inert. In postcolonial reckoning, rupture, flux, multiplicity and creative invention displace continuity, uniformity and passive inheritance as key motifs. Narratives of indigenous naturalisation of the novel do logically presume that meanings made of past alien encounters are knowable through the prism of their texted debris. We cannot, though, take for granted that the later lived present of indigenous historians or the ethnographic present of anthropologists are unproblematically linked to indigenous pasts, given the creeping encompassment of world systems, and the varied, ambivalent, often traumatic local engagements with external contacts, colonialism, decolonisation and modernity. Indigenous histories, whether oral or written, and ethnographies do not mimetically register indigenous pasts by virtue of inherited or sympathetic indigeneity. Like all texts they are subject to multiple imperatives of context, discourse, author and audience. Historically and politically, indigenous histories are privileged by their relative scarcity, and the cultural and spatial intimacy of their local, usually subaltern optics. Culturally and sociologically, together with ethnographies, they provide crucial clues for identifying and systematising ethnohistorical inscriptions in contemporary colonial texts—the inadvertent, partial, shadowy traces of local agency, relationships and settings. Such textual traces are keys to exploring the preliterate worlds and colonial engagements with which they were contemporaneous: colonial tropes and classifications at once "invented" *and were partly shaped by* particular indigenous actions, desires and contexts which, filtered through screens of colonial prejudices, fantasies and phobias, dialectically helped constitute the very images in which they were themselves constituted historically.[1]

This is not to discount the ethnocentrism, racism, sexism, paternalism and other biases which render such texts uncongenial to the point of repulsion for most present-day readers. The partialities, absences and distortions of colonial texts bear the idiosyncratic fingerprint of particular authors, but they are also systemic and discursive, able to be deciphered, deconstructed, compared, and exploited in narrative construction. Colonial discourse was neither monolithic nor stable: critical deconstruction of colonial texts and exemplary juxtaposition of components of different genres can reveal dissonance within and between colonial texts and discourses,[2] throwing light on ethnohistorical inscriptions in such texts, as this chapter illustrates. Colonial texts need creative, not literal reading, across their grain, with precise attention to discourses, tropes, nuances, inflections, single instances, asides, trifles, silences, ambivalences, and discrepancies between authors' expectations and perverse experience. Their representations of past indigenous worlds are always narrow and deformed, but in some cases—such as early indigenous-European contacts in parts of the Americas and in southeastern Australia—they are virtually all there is.

That is certainly not the case with my exemplar: the so-called "Wagap affair" of 1862 in the *cèmuhî* language zone on the central east coast of New Caledonia. Three vernacular histories—a *ténô*, "poem", a prose "narrative" and a written text, all collected by Bensa and Rivierre during the 1970s and translated and annotated by them—embed the episode thickly in indigenous contexts and perspectives.[3] The pro-missionary, Catholic viewpoint of the written text is at odds with that of the two oral histories, signalling ancient rivalries between local groups. Internal differences notwithstanding, these indigenous histories recorded in the twentieth century all differ sharply from contemporary French representations, which were lodged in texts of varying degrees of immediacy—firsthand, to non-participant, to retrospective—and belong to three, often discordant genres of colonial discourse—missionary, official and secular non-official. Modern anthropologists also provide a detailed, if not entirely congruent, ethnographic corpus on the region (Bensa, 1981; Bensa and Rivierre, 1982, 1988; Guiart, 1963: ch. 3). In this chapter the "Wagap affair" serves as a vehicle to display how the distinctive, but complementary discursive and temporal perspectives offered on the past by the disciplines of history and anthropology and by people's histories might be selectively blended or juxtaposed to fashion multi-layered, reflexive narratives out of disparate, contested stories written in and about shared, if very different pasts.[4] Since a full-scale narrative is here neither fitting nor feasible, I offer snippets to convey something of the mechanics and potency of the proposed method: they speak, successively, to the themes of Contexts; Identifications; Poetics and Rhetorical Strategies.

CONTEXTS

In this section, for scene-setting purposes, I resort to the first step in the classic strategy of objectivist causal history writing—what Guha calls *"context-event-perspective* ranged along a historical continuum": "The representation of ... [an event] ends up thus by having its moment intercalated between its past ["context"] and future ["perspective"] so that the particular values of one and the other are rubbed into the event to give it the meaning specific to it" (1983b: 30, 22, orig. emphasis). My intentions are (relatively conscious and pragmatic, not causal—there is no reference to outcomes, and thus no "perspective" imposed. But it would be disingenuous to maintain the neutrality of chronological ordering or sequence, any more than of my prose, which, belying the veneer of a disinterested "balance of tense [mainly pluperfect] and person [third]" (Guha, 1983b: 19), is, of course, loaded with choices, meaning and values.

In January 1862 French Catholic missionaries had maintained a limited presence in northern New Caledonia for much of two decades, but only since 1852—a year before French annexation—had they managed to ensconce themselves at Pouébo and Belep, in the far north, and on the centre-north coast at Touho and the place Europeans called "Wagap", amongst people they knew as the "Wagap tribe". They represented that "tribe" as powerful, turbulent, divided and a frequent source of missionary grief, despite the favourable disposition of the so-called "high chief"[5] known to Europeans as "Emmanuel Apengou" and locally as Apitéèngen.[6] In early 1862 nearly ten years of French "rule" had had minimal local impact in most of the northern two-thirds of New Caledonia, apart from sporadic punitive expeditions, materially devastating, but usually not so to human life.[7] However exiguous their actual presence and import, from 1855 the French saw the colony as assailed by successive "northern coalitions", the *raison d'être* of which was imagined to be resistance to mission influence and, by extension, colonial rule (du Bouzet to Min., 27 Feb. 1858, ANOM, Carton 42; Saisset to Min., 1 Feb. 1860, ANM, BB4 723; *Moniteur*, 26 Feb. 1860). Administrators and missionaries alike, relentlessly ethno- and egocentric, saw fighting between Melanesians in terms of explicit support for or opposition to France and civilisation/ Christianity, and usually attributed the local status of their leading opponents to rejection of colonial and/or mission authority. Twice Apengou of Wagap was credited with saving or helping to save another mission station purportedly assailed by a pagan horde assumed to be intent on its destruction. Late in 1861, though, Apengou died. Scarcely two months after, a new coalition, attributed in colonial texts primarily to the "criminal designs" of the "family of the high chief" (*Moniteur*, 23 Feb. 1862), had destroyed the Touho mission and invested Wagap's: these were the first acts of the "Wagap affair of 1862".

IDENTIFICATIONS

Bensa and Rivierre (1982, n.d.) described *cèmuhî* oral traditions of whatever genre as histories in a specific cultural register, strategically deployed in local political competition, where power is at once unstable and depends "on the accumulation of symbolic [rather than material] capital". Players in such a politics, in which words count more than things, seek to weave about themselves the thickest and most varied web of personal relationships, manipulating the mythic ingredients of toponyms, itineraries, names and symbols in order "to establish between two persons totally unknown to each other social relationships at every level necessary for their coexistence within a single local group" (Bensa and Rivierre, n.d.). Histories of this nature share neither the hagiographic or demonising concern for great men and great villains of dominant Western historiographies, both sacred and secular, nor classical Anthropology's fetish for systematic depersonalisation and detemporalisation. Rather than decry such differences as contradictions to be resolved objectively on a truth/falsity basis, a pluralist strategy, prepared to forego total solutions and narrative closure, can leave space for all three representational modes, in their own right, juxtaposed and blended.

This section displays a spectrum of representations of two Kanak protagonists in the colonial and indigenous pasts and seeks to locate them socially and spatially; the next considers the poetics and politics of representations of these men and some of the events in which they figured. They are Apengou, already mentioned, and "Kahoua of Poyes". Both could equally serve as hero or villain in a nationalist narrative, but only Apitéèngen (Apengou) features significantly in the local histories collected by Bensa and Rivierre—the official history of his Waka Amô lineage published by Rivierre took him to have been still alive and a key political player in the Wagap

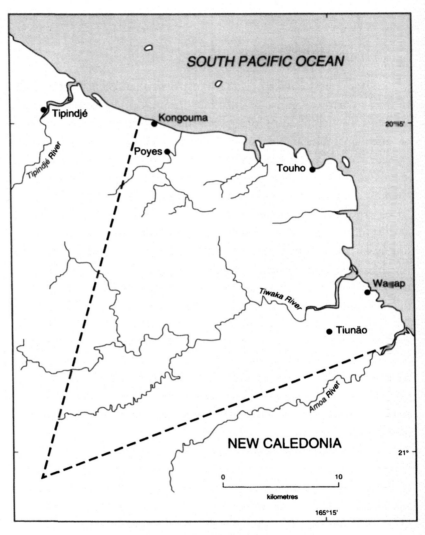

MAP 4   *Wagap, Touho and the* cèmuhî *language zone*

affair (1994: 53–4). The person and actions of this recently deceased "chief" also cast a long shadow over colonial apprehensions of the affair. A few years previously the Marist priest Vigouroux provided an early missionary reading of the local politics and the man, in the course of which he casually claimed responsibility for establishing the Wagap mission:

> The Uaka [Waka] tribe is the strongest in the vicinity and the sworn enemy of that of Tuo. On our arrival in the latter post, we sought to flatter the strong to enable the weak to live; and these measures... determined us also to attempt the bastion of the strong. The chief is regarded as absolute although quite a young man... [He] is without nose and lips, a frightful canker has eaten everything and was threatening to go further when we undertook to cure him on the advice and prescriptions of the surgeon of the steam corvette Prony which came to visit us at Tuo. The canker finally succumbed and the chief seems to be grateful to me for the care I gave him over several months. He does all he can for religion; but his subjects take a lot of coaxing (Vigouroux to his brother, 4 Dec. 1854, APM).

By contrast, the lineage history placed the initiative for bringing a missionary to Wagap firmly with the *daame*, "chief", who was said to have identified the missionaries with the ghost of his light-skinned son and, discerning a special affinity between himself and Vigouroux, to have adopted the French priest "as his son". According to the standard Kanak political technique for admitting strangers, this would mean relinquishing the chieftainship to the newcomer: "Now one of the Fathers is lefthanded... and it happens that Apitéèngen is himself lefthanded. At once the latter calls on him: 'Eh! I adopt you as my son..., since you are lefthanded like me'. The missionary answers him: 'Good, I shall come to your place tomorrow'" (Rivierre, 1994: 41–3).

An anti-objectivist, postcolonial reading would see nothing contradictory in the two stories, however different they are in emphasis and detail. I can think of no basis on which to privilege either as historically more "true" or more "accurate", other than *a priori* theoretical or political interest of the kind fundamentalists camouflage as objectivity. There are two significant differences between the narratives: in the attribution of agency, each author represented himself or his hero as the motor of the action and the other main participant as its object; aetiologically, the texts invoked different orders of causation, medical/scientific in the missionary case, esoteric in the indigenous case. But the differences are not neutral, since the missionary account borrows the universalist hegemonic authority of colonial discourse, while the Kanak story has purely local—indeed factional—resonance, and is susceptible to dismissal by a rationalist historiography as partial, mythic and superstitious. Yet in Kanak terms there is nothing inappropriate in the bundling of political, personal and esoteric motivations. For me, the particular interest of the indigenous text is in its clear demonstration that the colonised do not share the colonisers' invariable assumption of their own pivotal status in native conception and action. For its part, the missionary text not only invokes the colonial trope of routine savage subordination to absolute chiefly authority, but displays its vulnerability to subversion by traces of autonomous popular action registered in the same text: "his subjects take a lot of coaxing". This unwitting ethnohistorical inscription in a colonial text foreshadows Bensa's later ethnographic image of the relationship between Kanak "chiefs" and "their subjects" as a "reversible hierarchy", in no sense authoritarian, articulating complex sets of reciprocal rights, obligations and dependence (Bensa and Rivierre, 1982: 91; Bensa, 1986; Douglas, 1994b).

In November 1861 Lieutenant-Colonel Durand, commandant of the colony, briefly visited Wagap a few days after Apengu's death and received from the resident missionary a highly partisan but informative briefing on local history (see Table 3a). Scarcely two months later the commandant received news that on 16 January 1862 "the Wagap tribes, leagued together in concert with the chief Kahoua, had attacked the Touo Mission and burned it... [T]he Wagap Mission was from one moment to the next in fear of the same fate" (Durand to Min., 25 Feb. 1862, ANM, BB3 730). Kahoua is an enigmatic figure, presumably a war leader who attained political prominence in turbulent times, since he was described as personally leading warriors into battle, whereas the *daame*, "chief", did not participate in actual fighting (see Chapter Three, n. 17). Between

1856 and 1862 at least twenty references in French administrative and missionary texts depicted him as the most ferocious and dangerous enemy of colonialism and Christianity. Yet this demonic role contrasts oddly with his virtual absence from the oral histories as heard and recorded by Bensa and Rivierre, and from recent ethnographies on the Pwèi chiefdom, which modern anthropologists imagine he once led (see Table 4).

On receipt of the news of the attack on Touho and the threat to the Wagap mission, Durand went in person to Wagap with an improvised force of more than 150 men, including some artillery. He was quickly convinced—he said by Barriol, the local missionary—that a punitive expedition was "indispensable", "to strike terror into every heart", "to protect religion and its Ministers" and "to avenge the disaster of Touo ... by burning and ransacking everything ... [so as] to drive the hostile Natives back into the upper reaches of the [Tiwaka] valley". The expedition—in which Durand was accompanied by Barriol "who wanted to follow me and serve as interpreter"—took place from 5–7 February and was horribly destructive in intent and execution, though it claimed few lives. Durand's final balance sheet of the campaign, dry in tone and statistically quite unreliable—military arithmetic is dubious at best, but never more so than when counting so-called "savage" opponents—nonetheless conveys a chilling image of devastation inflicted:

> we burned thirty-seven villages established in an area of about fifteen square leagues [approximately 240 square kilometres], a great part of the gardens have been ravaged; the three thousand Natives who constantly, and with rare energy opposed the convergent march of our two columns, were beaten in every encounter and driven far from their territory. The enemy's losses must have been considerable; we are ignorant of them so far.... On our side, we have no accident to deplore, there were only a few light bruises and two minor wounds. The country, henceforth, belongs to us by right of conquest and not a single Wagap native will ever think of reclaiming possession of it [!] (Durand to Min., 25 Feb. 1862, BB3 730).

In the wake of the expedition a military post was established close to the Wagap mission—again, Durand claimed, at Barriol's urgent request.[8] Four "chiefs" who sought to make peace with the commandant of the post were summarily judged by a military tribunal—with Barriol as interpreter—condemned to death and executed. The main colonial narrative of the affair is an official report written by Durand on his return to the colony's headquarters (Durand to Min., 25 Feb. 1862, ANM, BB3 730). The text cited Barriol, "very much *au fait* with the language and customs of the country", as his informant on the region, the people, and "the causes of the Touo disaster": these "go back", so the story ran, to "the death of the last high Chief, Emmanuel Appengou" (see Table 2a).

The colonial narrative (Table 2a), complacently assured of European centrality in indigenous actions, ranged in focus between the personally particular—named individuals—and the regionally geopolitical, thereby exemplifying a general colonial tendency to conceive native politics in terms of authoritative rulers ("chiefs") controlling discrete territorial units ("tribes") (Douglas, in press a). By contrast, Bensa and Rivierre's commentary on the political implications of their *cèmuhî* texts, like the texts themselves (Table 2b, c), privileged indigenous agency and meanings. In keeping with anthropological convention, these authors pitched their remarks between the personal/regional extremes, in the generalised intimacy of the ethnographic voice. Their entire commentary remarked only two personal names apart from Apitéèngen, thought to be still living in 1862. The ethnographers echoed the stories they had heard, recorded and reconstituted as "texts", evoking the domestic interests of contending local factions and placing the missionaries firmly in the context of Kanak strategies and political culture, notably the manipulation of social reality through myth, and "the oft-noted opposition between strangers and masters of the soil". By this reading, the coming of Europeans offered "a supplementary strategic possibility... for clans in conflict" (Bensa and Rivierre, n.d.). The extract from the Waka Amô lineage history (Table 2c) mentioned one person apart from Apitéèngen: the man called Pwodaalu—Durand's "Pondaouiou". This was a cryptic but approving reference to the execution of the four "chiefs", of whom Pwodaalu was one; it differed sharply in tone from the elegiac quality of the other indigenous histories (see below). Pro-missionary, Catholic stance notwithstanding, the

| TABLE 2 | THE PLAY OF ALLIANCES AT WAGAP IN 1862 ACCORDING TO A CONTEMPORARY COLONIAL TEXT AND LATER ETHNOGRAPHIC AND INDIGENOUS TEXTS |

(2a) Contemporary colonial representation	(2b) Ethnographic representation	(2c) Indigenous representation
"Four brothers [by blood or adoption] of Emmanuel Appengou, named Pondaoulou..., Aoûtindan..., Thiéou... and Ounin Damoa, all influential and feared chiefs, secretly incited by their uncles, Pouandata and Attinda, resolved to get rid of the Missions. Initially concealing their project, they sought everywhere for adherents, who joined them in great numbers... Kahoua, the terrible chief of Pouaye, had been beaten by them... in October 1861; knowing his audacity, his resolution and his influence over certain small tribes, they managed to make him forget their recent victory and attach himself indissolubly to them. Kahoua became their powerful ally and brought the cooperation of the weak tribes of Ounoy, Ouma, Wali, Poatim, Nendi and Congoouma. The way thus prepared, they determined on a great blow... Kahoua gave the signal to strike" Durand to Min., 25 Feb. 1862, ANM, BB3 730	"The Apacé-Pwöcâbin occupied the Tiunäo plain...Their opposition to the Amô was very sharp at the time. In fact the latter had just installed some of their subjects at Tiunäo.... the Galaahî. We therefore have in this zone two mwo-daame ['container-of-chiefs'] in conflict for the chieftainship [of the Waka clan]. Moreover, within the local groups in which they hold power (and the land) the Waka Pwöcâbin and the Waka Amô have problems with their subjects. The Pwöcâbin are challenged by 'strangers' who received wives and lands from the Waka, [and] are trying to reverse the political situation. Since their chief...is in conflict with Apitéègèn Amô they will support him and therefore join him on the side of the missionaries. The same process will be repeated within the local group of the Amô of Tiunäo: here the Galaahî are opposing their chief. They will thus find themselves in the group hostile simultaneously to Apitéègèn and the Wagap mission" Bensa and Rivierre, n.d.	"Another time, later, when Apitéègen has become old, he shows great solicitude for the one he has taken under his protection [the missionary], for he fears things will turn bad when he is no longer there. One day he seizes Uéé-hê-éémwa, **Pwodaalu**. They lure him to Pwèéo [Wagap] into a cloth enclosure [a tent], the soldiers fire on him and hit him. He manages to get out of the enclosure. Then a bird, a magpie, leaves his body and he dies" Rivierre, 1994: 53–4

lineage history inverted the usual ethnocentric colonial oppositions, European initiative : native reaction, European patron : native client. In this confident indigenous narrative of appropriation, the French soldiers were recomposed as Apitéèngen's political instruments, deployed against a local rival in the interests of his missionary protégé.

Ethnographically, Durand's denomination of "the accused Chiefs" as "brothers" and "uncles" of Apengou was probably an unwitting register of the varied statuses of their lineages in relation to the Waka clan: as Apacé-Pwöcâbin, rivals of the Amô for "absolute supremacy over the whole of the lineages of the Waka clan" (Bensa and Rivierre, n.d.), they would have been Apitéèngen's clan "brothers"; as Galaahî, relatively recent immigrant "subjects" of the Amô, they might have been classed as the latter's maternal uncles, since one strategy of integration used on the east coast by the highly mobile Galaahî was to assume the role of wife-givers to local "chiefly" lineages (Bensa and Rivierre, 1982: 130–3; 1988: 277–3; n.d.).[9] The designations "brothers" and "uncles" can thus be read as further instances of involuntary ethnographic inscription in a colonial text, identifiable and decipherable in correlation with insights derived from recent ethnographic investigation (see Table 2b).

Historically, the traces of "the Wagap affair" in colonial texts include faint impressions of an expansive indigenous politics as yet scarcely concerned by alien imperial presence, but soon to become its fierce and persistent competitor throughout the centre-north. For it was as participants in "the war made in January 1862 against the Christians" of Touho and Wagap that the renowned Kanak leaders known later to the French as Gondou and Poindi Patchili attained retrospective notoriety in colonial consciousness (*Moniteur*, 14 May 1865; Garnier, 1868: 6; Patouillet, 1873: 48). Durand's official report is inadvertently touched with the trail of their involvement: a mention of "Nendi" as one of several "weak tribes" allied to Kahoua (see Table 2a); a passing reference to "Ouendi-Poétili" as "chief" of the last settlement burned during the French expedition. Later colonial texts gave "Nendi" as the "tribal" name, or an alternative personal name, for Gondou (Guillain to Min., 3 Sep. 1865, ANM, BB4 847; *Moniteur*, 7–14 Feb. 1869). "Nendi" was a French rendering of the name of Gondou's clan *Nädù*, identified by Bensa and Rivierre as the dominant partner in an emerging, aggressive political formation called *Nädù bau Görötü* (1988). The activities of Gondou and his ally Poindi Patchili inflamed the centre-north of New Caledonia during the rest of the 1860s and embroiled the French in indigenous conflicts which they neither understood nor controlled.

After the Wagap expedition, so the colonial narrative ran, Gondou, "not wanting to submit", took refuge "with the Oumouha, the Ouali, etc.", over whom "he succeeded in imposing his will". These inland people, then scarcely known to the French, had been lumped with the "Nendi" in Durand's report as Kahoua's allies or dependents (see Table 2a). By 1865, the story continued, Gondou's "benefactors, driven from their territory", had "mostly taken refuge on lands formerly occupied by this Gondou", and joined the French in expeditions against him (*Moniteur*, 14 May, 1 Oct. 1865; Vincent to Poupinel, 25 July 1867, APO; Garnier, 1868: 48).

Missionary texts, as well as official, depicted Kahoua as "prime mover" of the attack on Touho (see Table 4a), but he apparently did not stay to share the weight of French repression with his Wagap allies. Durand disgustedly retailed a local rumour that, even before the expedition, "Kahoua had prudently retired... not scrupling to leave his savage allies in the lurch". Before long the French and the missionaries heard that he had been deserted by most of his former allies and supporters (Durand to Min, 25 Feb. 1862, ANM, BB3 730; Forestier to Poupinel, 4 Dec. 1862, APM). After this, Kahoua the terrible disappeared from colonial demonology, to be reinvented during 1865 as a newly minted ally of the colony. His change of camp was presumably encouraged by the growing threat of Gondou, whom he repeatedly denounced to the French. Kahoua personally led a contingent of allied warriors in support of a French campaign against Gondou in 1865. The *Moniteur* described his service as guide in a surprise night attack on the "village" of that "chief", who was said to have inspired in him such terror that he had to be forced at gunpoint to proceed (Guillain to Min., 3 Sep. 1865, AMN, BB4 847; *Moniteur*, 29 Jan., 14 May, 1 Oct. 1865). His trepidation was probably warranted, since Gondou had a formidable reputation for efficacy and brutality:[10] the missionary at Wagap reported that "hardly had the soldiers returned from the expedition than 4 of Cawa's men... fell to the blows [of Gondou]" (Roussel to ?, 14 Dec. 65, AAN 85.1).

That is the last trace of Kahoua I have found in colonial texts, bar a vivid description during the 1865 campaign by the geologist Garnier, who travelled extensively in New Caledonia during 1864–6.

PLATE 1   "Natives of the tribes of the chiefs Mango and Kaboua. Drawing by Emile Bayard from photographs of M. E. de Greslan" (Garnier, 1868: 41)

His superbly illustrated account owed more to its author's eye for a good story than to concern for historical accuracy, but it included clever pen pictures of individual Kanak, including Kahoua, with the bonus of a purported visual image, an engraving from a photograph attributed to Greslan (Table 5 and Plate 1). It is ironic that this "chief", seemingly so insignificant in the indigenous recollections heard by anthropologists, should be one of relatively few Kanak identified in colonial visual representations. Yet the near correspondence of the image with Garnier's words may be a cautionary reminder of the always problematic relationship between experience, "reality" and genres of representation: might a photograph, rather than a personal encounter, have directly inspired the written description?

POETICS AND RHETORICAL STRATEGIES

Reflecting on the enigma posed by *cèmuhî* oral poetry, Bensa and Rivierre remarked:

> The implicit reference of the poem to an event is at once so precise in its intention and so allusive in its form that informants themselves are sometimes at a loss. The symbols used... refer simultaneously to the most particular and the most general.... Thus are woven extremely diverse links between history and myth, myth and history. The poet juggles with symbols, he at once reveals, masks and interprets the event which supports the "ténô" (n.d.).

In such a narrative genre with such an agenda—locally acknowledged, if specifically contested—the relationships between form and event, storyteller and audience differ sharply from both Judaeo-Christian sacred history and post-Enlightenment varieties of narrative history. These, however unalike in some respects, share a conception of events as unique and chronological, while masking their present embeddedness in the distancing authority of the preterite, the third person, and the claim to truth, whether divine or objective. Anthropology, in yet another mix of time, tense and person, classically eschewed the event entirely, while exploiting the strategic conjunction of ethnographic present and third person: the third person neutralised the potential present bias of the tense, which paradoxically underwrote its trademark, essentialising "*allochronism* ['othertimism']" with the implied authority "I-Was-There" (Fabian, 1983: 2, 80–7; Guha, 1983b; White, 1987: 1–57).

Politics of language

With these differences in mind, I compare some of the ways in which language was deployed strategically to serve particular discursive agenda in texts sampled in the Tables, using as a general model Guha's brilliant dissection, drawing on Barthes and Benveniste, of colonial and national texts on subaltern insurgency in India (1983b). I see language choices as epistemological, discursive and therefore political, rather than as operating in a purely linguistic domain autonomous of praxis (Fabian, 1983: 86–7). Such choices need not be deliberate: unwitting ones reveal prevailing, taken-for-granted discursive conventions. Tropes—I reserve the term for images and concepts loosed from their metaphoric origins and taken as literally true—clustered in discourses provide shared vocabularies for conceiving and describing reality, and must be recognised and decoded by ethnohistorians seeking to exploit such descriptions for their own purposes. Choices of tense, voice, mood and terminology imply an author's subject position towards the objects of inquiry and intended audience.

Guha cautioned that, when using colonial (or, by extension, élite) texts with emancipatory historical intent, "we may not take any bias for granted...from the mere fact of its origin with authors committed to colonialism....Criticism must therefore start not by naming a bias but by examining the components of the discourse, vehicle of all ideology" (1983b: 9). He advocated close attention to the relative distribution in texts of indicative and interpretative segments, functions and indices, which serve respectively to report and explain, state and comment; he warned, though, that they were not mutually exclusive, that "they are often found embedded in each other" and "interpenetrate and sustain each other in order to give the documents their meaning, and...ambiguity" (1983b: 9–10). In the rest of this chapter, *inter alia*, I compare the distribution and the "co-ordination of the metonymic and metaphorical axes [functions and indices]" (Guha, 1983b: 12–13) in several categories of text sampled in the Tables, with indices italicised in Table 3.

Table 3's juxtaposition of Durand's contemporary narrative and Bensa and Rivierre's commentary on the modern oral histories displays resonances between colonial text and ethnography, though the anthropologists had not seen the commandant's report. Their mistaken assumption that Apengou still lived does not invalidate their reasoning, since the presumed intent to manipulate missionary and French presence for local political advantage could just as readily apply to his successors. Despite the gulf of time, culture, discourse, interest and poetics between the two sets of text and authors, each text nonetheless throws light on the other: the ethnographic text elaborates and systematises the other's deformed hints of inter-group relationships and spatial politics; the colonial text delineates and anchors the events and the historical actor, which the ethnography, and oral histories too, tend to telescope or symbolically conflate with the myth history of a group.

The tabular format is particularly apt for examining the interested deployment of tenses and epithets to particular discursive

TABLE 3 APENGOU/APITÉÈNGEN IN ADMINISTRATIVE AND ETHNOGRAPHIC TEXTS

(3a) Official representation	(3b) Ethnographic representation
"The deceased chief did not exercise authority by right of birth or adoption, but by *right of conquest*. When he seized power, three or four hundred inhabitants of Wagap *abandoned the tribe*... These *emigrants* can become a great *embarrassment*, should one of them claim the rights of the former dispossessed chief. However, Emmanuel Appengou, [who] died without offspring, has adopted to succeed him a young boy of twelve years... [who is] entirely *devoted to the mission*... At his final hour, Appengou, whose favourite was a *woman...devoted to the mission*, particularly *enjoined* his *subjects* to *obey* the missionaries and become *catholic*.... The will of a dying [chief] is *sacred* for these *savage populations*" Durand to Min., 31 Dec. 1861, ANM, BB3 725	"Apitéègèn... claims political supremacy over the entire [Waka] clan. He will try to take advantage of the missionaries to realise this stroke, and the '*Wagap massacre*'* comprises an essential episode in this *strategy* since it is intended to *eliminate opponents*, who also lay *claim to the chieftainship*... Apitéègèn Emmanuel gave his Wagap lands to the religious, and tradition has it that he *defended them* against those who contested the installation of the missionaries" Bensa and Rivierre, n.d.

*The execution of the four Wagap "chiefs" following the French expedition.

ends. The passage from the official colonial text (Table 3a) is a seemingly objective ethnohistorical description ratified by the implied claim of the local missionary (Durand's informant) to expertise in matters indigenous. It is written entirely in the third person. Though the sequence of tense and mood in the original French cannot be caught exactly in English, they are *imparfait* (past continuous) → *passé simple* (past historic) → present → subjunctive mood → *passé composé* (perfect) → *passé simple* → ethnographic present. There is nothing transparent or innocent in this: reiteration of the aorist underwrites the third person claim to objectivity; the shift mid-passage to the present tense and subjunctive mood is an aside denoting the pragmatic concern of the colonial administrator (and the missionary) for law and order over abstract principle; his concluding recourse to the ethnographic present invokes that tense's multiplex claim to scientific objectivity and personal expertise.[11] The aura of objectivity, though, is deceptive. The exigencies informing that single sentence in the present tense saturate the whole passage and are manifest in the author's selection of epithets: *right of conquest, emigrants, embarrassment, devoted, subjects* are by no means disinterested terms, but are indices which invest the text with meaning (Guha, 1983b: 9–15; Barthes, 1967: 71–2). They operate like "shifters": their "referent depends on the position of the speaker" (Carrard, 1992: 17), or, in this case, his missionary expert, with whose position the administrator starved of resources was happy enough to identify.[12]

A seemingly neutral description is thereby so constructed as to achieve three simultaneous ends:

- to ratify the (usurped?) authority of the "Christian chief" (polygyny minimised by his extenuating preference for a Christian favourite wife);
- to delegitimise the claims to the chieftainship (and by implication to land) of the (non-Christian) *emigrants* who *abandoned the tribe*
- to take for granted the unqualified power of the "chief" over his "subjects", appropriate it in the interests of conversion/(colonisation), and project it *post mortem* by invoking the timeless enslavement of savages to superstition, thereby ecumenically yoking militant rationalism and casual racism to received ethnographic wisdom.[13]

The passage by Bensa and Rivierre (Table 3b) is an ethnographic commentary on texted indigenous oral histories. It too is written in the third person and the authors also mobilise tenses to serve discursive agenda: the ethnographic present and the historic present convey scholarly authority and mask anticolonial sympathies, which I share, but a positivist historiography would deem illegitimate. The authors simultaneously, if ambiguously, celebrate indigenous agency and creative manipulation of colonial presence ("this strategy"), yet regret the "chief's" ruthless (unfair?) exploitation of (collaboration with?) foreigners to crush local rivals, whose descendants composed the oral histories. There is mild deception in the quotation marks put around the words "Wagap massacre" to camouflage an emotional response shared with the poet, and made explicit later in the commentary: "The *tragic* conclusion of the *ambush* is only evoked in the last verse: 'and he disappeared'…*vanquished* by the *coalition* of Apitéèngen and…the missionaries" (indices in italics) (n.d.).

Mutual complicities and the politics of representation

Moving from the specifics of linguistic strategies to more general questions of representation, Tables 3 and 4 instance the ethnocentric egoism of colonial authors and Table 4 its uncritical endorsement by an empiricist historian, as well as, indirectly, by ethnographers lacking significant indigenous historical input. Superficially the contemporary representations in Tables 4a and 4b look like straight reportage: they comprise mainly functions, metonymically related. It is tempting and convenient to read them literally, as mimetic reflections of reality. But a critical and sceptical eye will, as Guha put it, "detect chinks which have allowed 'comment' to worm its way through the plate armour of 'fact'" (1983b: 13). Such "chinks" account for important variations between the two categories of contemporary text: in Table 4a, missionaries consistently stressed Kahoua's hostility to themselves and their religion (with tacit certainty of Satanic inspiration); in Table 4b, colonial officials, more explicitly political, invoked possible external

TABLE 4　　KAHOUA OF POYES IN MISSIONARY AND OFFICIAL TEXTS, 1856–62, COMPARED TO MODERN ETHNOGRAPHIC TEXTS

(4a) Missionary representations	(4b) Administrative representations	(4c) Ethnographic representaions
"the chief of Puaie, the great Caua, the terrible enemy of the priests and of religion" Villiard to S-G, 30 Mar. 1856, APM	"the chiefs of Kaua and Tinpingué [Tipindjé] ... had defied our authority ... the Bayonnaise ... made an expedition into the interior ... , burned several villages and gave this tribe a lesson ... The chief punished [Kahoua] was one of the most feared in New Caledonia. He passed for the greatest warrior, but he dared defend none of his villages and lost much in public opinion" Gov. du Bouzet to Gov. Saisset, 25 Oct. 1858, ANOM, Carton 231	Kahoua was "the high chief of Poyes, clan Pwey, at Touho" Guiart, 1963: 103
"the too famous Kaua surnamed the Napoleon ... " Rougeyron to Poupinel, 7 Dec. 1859, APO	"Kaoua chief of the Pouaï, known as the Napoleon of the North, among the [Australian] biche la mare or sandalwood traders, and our declared enemy ... is the heart and soul of these projects [of which the acknowledged program is the destruction of the missions of the North and the expulsion of the French]" Saisset to Min., 1 Feb. 1860, ANM, BB4 723	"The title of **daame** (chief) [of the powerful Pwèi chiefdom] is held by the Bulièg" Bensa and Rivierre, 1982: 121
"the prime mover of the war, Kaua, had said [to the people of Touho:] we grant [you] peace, since we have achieved what we intended [,] to drive out the missionaries and destroy their houses and herds, but in addition you must throw away your loin cloths and rosaries, abandon prayer and resume our ancient customs" Thomassin to Poupinel, 4 Jan. 1862, APO	"Between Tuho and Hienghuen is the lair of a bandit called Kawa, who sets himself up as our sworn enemy; this man is only a very little chief. For some time, however, he has acquired a certain importance; he grows more so every day by attracting to him the malcontents and bad subjects of the other tribes. He was at [a punitive expedition at] Hienghuen with all his people, it was his influence which determined and organised the resistance" Lt Forget [former commander of the *Styx*] to Min., 15 June 1860, CM "Last October the men of Wagap and Hyenghen united to march against Kahoua, the former ally of the chief of the tribe of Hyenghen and our greatest enemy. ... Tired of his arrogance and pretensions the two tribes set off after him. They narrowly missed capturing him. His territory was completely sacked, his villages burned. He has now taken refuge in the bush" Durand to Min., 31 Dec. 1861, ANM, BB3 725 "Kahoua gave the signal for the movement. He had the people of Touo warned that they must return to their ancient customs ... on 16 January, the Touo Mission was attacked by Kahoua. The Catholic natives took up arms and repulsed him; there were two dead between them. Their victory was assured when the men of Wagap rushed in and took it from them. Beaten by much superior forces, the natives of Touo were obliged to call for peace and take refuge ... , after having seen their houses burned, as well as the Fathers' establishment" Durand to Min., 25 Feb. 1862, ANM, BB3 730	"Between 1850 and 1865, Pwèi is mentioned only through the person then identified as its chief, 'Kahoua ... '"; followed by a reference to Saussol 1979: 89, which cites and paraphrases *Moniteur* , 23 Feb. 1862 and 14 May 1865 Bensa and Rivierre, 1982: 122

manipulation—by perfidious Albion/Australia, a favourite trope—and gratuitously demeaned their opponent as an incompetent warrior or a low-ranking, opportunist product of colonial presence.

Like all representations, these are only historically informative when read in the light of their shaping discourses, interests, contexts and audiences. There were always tensions in the agenda of colonial reportage: primitivist tropes, both Catholic and secular, provided pliant, multivocal raw materials from which to fashion politically apt, useful, but not necessarily consistent images. On the one hand, there was a systemic colonial/Christian impulse to revile savages/pagans as disordered, cowardly and inept, in counterpoint to the discipline, fortitude and competence of the civilised and the converted. On the other hand, there was a pragmatic tendency in missionary and administrative texts alike to exaggerate dangers faced. The missionary Thomassin did so to justify his embarrassing flight from Touho, after which the Marists' richest mission and the Christians' settlements were sacked and burned. Whereas Durand's narrative remarked that Kahoua's attack on Touho was on the brink of defeat when he was saved by his Wagap allies (see Table 4b), Thomassin claimed that the Christians and catechumens "lost courage in seeing the number of their enemies, they judged all resistance useless and even harmful for fear of ... pushing them to a general massacre, they therefore gave up the ground without great opposition, there were dogged fights only near the mission, to give us time to flee" (Thomassin to Poupinel, 4 Feb. 1862, APO). On the official side, Durand's interests in inflating the numbers and ferocity of his opponents included the professional soldier's rhetorical stake in constructing an opponent worth of defeat, and the administrator's need to justify an arduous, expensive expedition—undertaken despite metropolitan reticence and parsimony (Min. to Durand, 15 Mar. 1860, ANOM, Carton 25)—yet still evince a firm grip on the reins of colonial government. Whereas in an earlier report Durand had stressed the innocuousness of Kanak alliances—"there effectively exists no federative link between the tribes" (Durand to Min., 26 May 1860, ANOM, Carton 42)—he now sketched a formidable coalition broad in scale and span.

Such disparities in colonial representations of the primitive do not denote mere inconsistency, contradiction or idiosyncrasy but are profoundly discursive, a reflex of ambivalences in the always demeaning and hierarchical civilised conceptions of the Other. Ambivalence is stark in the colonial constructions of Kahoua in Tables 4b and 5. Deemed hereditarily insignificant, his prominence attributed entirely to resistance to colonialism, he was nonetheless reckoned the mainspring of *all* indigenous conflicts, whether with Europeans or not. The tropes reinscribed Kanak in general as passive instruments of a single half-tame/half-wild savage, a negative product of colonialism, a native Satan. Because he is a savage/pagan, Kahoua always loses in confrontation with the civilised/Christian; because he is "wily" he knows when to change camps, but his natural savagery remains close to the surface. Gondou was similarly constructed as a minor "chief" of notable "energy and ... warlike and ferocious" (Garnier, 1868: 38), while he, Kahoua and Poindi Patchili—three arch-"rebels" in colonial demonology—were described as light-skinned and European of feature. Whether realist or not,

TABLE 5   KAHOUA OF POYES IN A PUBLISHED, RETROSPECTIVE, NON-OFFICIAL TEXT

"although his *tribe* was *not numerous*, this chief exercised great influence on the surrounding peoples because of his audacity and especially because of *the resistance he opposed to our invasion*, manifesting his hatred for us in cruel wars against the tribes which had given us their submission. Until recently we had always found Kahoua in the ranks of our enemies and considered him, with reason, as *the principal instigator of all the conflicts* which arose in these parts whether between the natives themselves or between them and the Europeans. However ... he had made his *submission*, pardoned by the governor of the colony, he was our *friend*. But if this *wily* chief had thus rallied to us, when he recognised the impossibility of a longer struggle, ... it is nonetheless beyond doubt that this sudden friendship was not deeply embedded in his heart beforehand and, to be certain of that, it sufficed to examine this man for an instant; to examine his observant eyes, which no detail escaped, and which followed each of our gestures and movements; to catch unawares finally the smile of disdain or hatred imprinted on his *sinister physiognomy*, when a young soldier passed heedlessly near him. It would especially be necessary to understand the mocking remarks he made about us to the warriors who surrounded him and which provoked them to peals of scornful laughter. Kahoua came before us dressed in sketchy *European dress*: a smock and a soft felt hat. He carried an umbrella in one hand and a long-barrelled gun in fairly good condition in the other. His face ... was nothing remarkable although it differed from those of his compatriots in that his *features* were more *regular*. *His skin was yellow* and not the colour of bronze; all those about him showed him the greatest deference I have ever seen accorded a Kanak chief"

Garnier, 1868: 58 (my emphasis)

such physical discriminations denote a profoundly systemic racism (*Moniteur*, 14 May 1865, 7–14 Feb. 1869; Garnier, 1868: 6, 38, 58).

Garnier's pen picture of Kahoua in Table 5, rich in colonialist tropes, makes the following classic narrative moves: "tribe not numerous" → "resistance...to our invasion" → "principal instigator of all the conflicts" → "submission" → "our friend" ["sinister physiognomy"/"European dress"/"regular features"/"skin...yellow"]. These unstable and ambivalent images may throw light on Kahoua's seeming absence from indigenous recollection. It was perhaps his iconic status as a monstrous offspring of colonialism, who underwent secular conversion from colonial demon to colonial hero, which made him at once integral to a colonial myth-history and less relevant to those of Kanak—especially his Christian descendants, embarrassed by his obstinate adherence to paganism.[14] Or perhaps he just provides bad material for a national hero—consistently unsuccessful as a resistor, and an eventual collaborator. Or, as Durand's missionary source put it (Table 4b), was it simply that other Kanak were/are sick of "his arrogance and pretensions" (Durand to Min., 31 Dec. 1861, ANM, BB3 725)?

I turn now to a final theme, which threads its elusive way through all genres of text: that of putative missionary involvement in the Wagap expedition and its brutal aftermath. There are three specific question marks: the enigma of Barriol's incitement of and participation in the reign of terror of the actual expedition; his encouragement of the subsequent military occupation of Wagap with the installation of a post; his complicity in the gruesome legal charade whereby four men who seemed to think they were voluntarily negotiating peace were summarily sentenced to death. Their conduct on the scaffold—"we had to use force to garrotte these wretches who defended themselves to the bitter end"—and the reported consternation of the numerous local witnesses suggest that their fate was unforeseen and that indigenous views of "justice" were not French (Durand to Min., 25 Feb. 1862, ANM, BB3 730). Durand's official report did not affirm missionary claims that Barriol pleaded for their lives, but the account of the mission superior, Rougeyron, has the plausibility of pragmatism: "R.P. Barriol implored for mercy for them, but in vain, they wanted justice to run its course; they were right, but it was our duty to show kindness and clemency" (Rougeyron to Poupinel, 23 Feb. 1862, APO). There is a certain ironic, deserved retribution in the rapid missionary change of heart on the question of the military post: from Rougeyron's "I am not opposed to it because only that can pacify the country and destroy the influence of this monster [Kahoua]" (Rougeyron to Poupinel, 5 Feb. 1862, APO), to his "it is desolating that they want to put the blockhouse at Uagap, below the mission… How to make a mission next to a camp? I am very embarrassed about that, and P. Barriol still more so" (Rougeyron to Poupinel, 23 Feb. 1862, APO).

Durand's official narrative and published order of the day were almost too insistent in reiterating public praise of Barriol as the inspiration for his punitive actions and as local expert and interpreter for the French during and after the expedition (see above): "I shall make it… my duty to bring to Your Excellency's attention the very praiseworthy conduct of R.P. Barriol"; the "chiefs" executed had been "signalled by Reverend Father Barriol as the main authors of the Tuho disaster" (Durand to Min., 25 Feb. 1862, ANM, BB3 730; *Moniteur*, 23 Feb. 1862). It was no doubt politic for the commandant to shift or at least share responsibility for actions which stretched his official brief to the limit. There is no hint of any such colonial division of liability in the Catholic Waka Amô lineage history, which depicted the missionary as the passive object of Apitééngen's "solicitude" and "protection" and the soldiers as the latter's tools (see Table 2c). However, an ambiguous image of Catholic missionary complicity in the execution of the "chiefs" was forged in their descendants' oral histories, as explained in Bensa and Rivierre's commentary: "This last episode of the poem makes the first direct allusions to the missionaries. According to the prose text, they provided the people of Tiunäo with tobacco. The poem seems to cast derision on these gifts which drew [the 'chiefs']… into the ambush" (n.d.). In other words, there is a strong insinuation that the capture of the "chiefs" followed their unsuspecting response to a French peace offer mediated by the missionary.[15]

Neither the matter nor the material lends itself to a single realist narrative. Any case made to condone, condemn or diminish

Barriol's complicity would depend on the tribunal: whether Western or indigenous, conservative or radical, religious or secular, Catholic or Protestant. My own radical, secular reading suggests that he probably was fairly heavily involved, for reasons of pragmatic missionary interest, and I do find offensive muscular Christian implication in the naked exercise of colonial power: Rougeyron's remark, that "it was our duty to show kindness and clemency", I take as acknowledgement that missionaries were meant to protect, not scourge their potential flock. Yet distribution of praise and blame to particular past actors does not feature largely on my historical agenda; I prefer to try to grasp the ephemera and the systematics of human interaction and experience. Accordingly, I am powerfully moved by the poignant history in the last verse of the modern *cèmuhî* poem (see above): the phrase "and he disappeared" is a long echo in the (near) present of the grief, shock and dislocation to local relationships between people and groups, and between people and places, occasioned by the Wagap expedition and its aftermath of execution and dispossession. Closer to the event, the trauma induced was attested to by Garnier (1867: 193–4; cf. Guiart, 1963: 101–7), who seems not actually to have met Poindi Patchili on his travels, but wrote of him with some sympathy: "He still remains in his savage mountains, far from the whites whom he hates because they killed chiefs, his relatives and friends, whose territories they took" (1868: 6).

EPILOGUE

Like the indigenous histories, I do not accord with contemporary colonial assumptions of necessary European centrality in indigenous thinking and experience, nor with orthodox History's thoughtless reinscription of this complacent Eurocentrism. Thus in his well-intentioned, anticolonial history of land matters in New Caledonia, largely based on transparent reading of published colonial texts, Saussol persistently categorised Melanesian violence during the colonial period as "reprisals", "rebellion", "revolt", "resistance", "insurrection"—mostly in reaction to land alienation

(1979). Such terms subsume a wide range of locally significant actions and relationships (including hostility to Europeans) as linear reflexes of European initiatives, in the context of a colonial sovereignty taken *a priori* to be both legitimate and effective. This presumption projects eventual colonial domination back to times and places when it was not part of indigenous experience, and takes for granted colonisers' claim to primacy in Kanak reckoning—as in the missionaries' Manichaean insistence that "this war ... is uniquely a war of religion; it is a true persecution", uncritically echoed by Durand: "[Kahoua's] grudge was really against our priests and not the Natives [of Touho]".[16] Saussol's assessment of the "Wagap affair" as more than "a simple revolt", as "a profound and coordinated movement" (1979: 93), was no doubt intended to compliment the scale, intensity, rationality and sophistication of Kanak "resistance", but anachronism and ethnocentrism made him largely oblivious to the intricate tracery of locally-motivated and constrained agency embedded in colonial, indigenous and ethnographic texts. My thesis by contrast is that missionaries were imagined, exploited and opposed by Kanak for their supposed local value; that the French were estimated in varied, labile ways—informed by uneven indigenous memories of the violent precedents of earlier, highly localised punitive expeditions—as a dangerous wildcard which leaders sought to circumvent or, hazardously, to deploy in support of their own and their group's agenda. This is a congruent interpretation to that of Bensa and Rivierre, who saw "the arrival of the Whites" as providing "a supplementary strategic possibility ... for clans in conflict" (n.d.).

The concept of indigenous agency which here enables a radical critique is not in itself radical: like any concept, its political valency depends on authors' intentions and discursive contexts of inscription and reading. From the venerable anticolonial perspective which represents the colonised as powerless victims of irresistible structural forces, arguments in favour of indigenous agency seem naïvely utopian, and suppose, moreover, that Kanak were too stupid or shortsighted to understand what was really happening to them. A postcolonial rejoinder would decry this classic position as ethnocentric, essentialist, hierarchical and teleological, pointing out that hindsight is the luxury (and the cross) of those who think they know the outcome, including historians, but that it was unavailable to actors, who had only culturally and strategically conceived experience to go on. Outcomes, anyway, like all discursive constructs, are always contested and unstable. On the other hand, arguments in favour of indigenous agency can be insidious when the concept is appropriated by reactionaries to deflect the shame of colonialism by invoking the responsibility of the colonised for their own oppression. This same motivation is sometimes imputed to postcolonial advocates of the concept of agency by anticolonial sceptics. A further postcolonial riposte would insist that postcolonial positions do not discount the always humiliating, sometimes tragic fact of colonialism, or the immorality of its drive for domination, but seek *as well* to contest the *a priori* assumption that colonialism always operated and signified locally in the ways its proponents intended.[17]

My own position is no more disinterested or politically neutral than those I critique, but its engagements are relatively knowing, admitted and reflexive. Its emancipatory intentions were outlined earlier: to liberate past indigenous actors from the stultifying representational tyranny of reified structures and colonial deformation by dislodging the metatrope—shared across the political spectrum—of monolithic colonialism. Rather than reinscribe colonial discursive hegemony by an oppositional strategy which nonetheless endorses colonial self-assessments of their own irresistibility, I aim to recolonise and exploit colonial texts by exposing the limits, internal fractures and vulnerability of colonial discourse/power. As in any emancipatory project, deconstruction and linguistic analysis of dominant texts and discourses is a key tool, because the relative historical absence/silence of natives, women and subalterns make ethnographic, feminist and social historians necessarily reliant on alien, hostile or indifferent texts which require creative critical reading, across the grain of their often repugnant politics and morality.

The fragments of narrative assembled in this chapter are not Kanak history. They are my history, which, whatever its idiosyncrasies and iconoclasm, is firmly lodged within a Western academic discourse. Hegel thought History and its typical form, the narrative, were both necessitated and enabled by the existence of the state, with its demand for "comprehensive and universally binding" judicial and political precedents (1952 [1857]: 181). If this is so, heuristic strategies such as those outlined in this chapter, complementing indigenous ways of conceiving, contesting and exploiting the past, might usefully be appropriated by Kanak seeking heroes, villains and exemplary events in the service of building a Kanak national identity and a Kanak nation.

NOTES

[1] Guha argued a parallel case, that peasant rebel consciousness in India was "a rival consciousness... firmly inscribed in elite discourse": "[colonial] documents do not get their content from that [colonial] will alone, for the latter is predicated on another will—that of the insurgent. It should be possible therefore to read the presence of a rebel consciousness as a necessary and pervasive element within that [colonial] body of evidence" (1983a: 17, 15).

[2] Guha showed how deconstruction of drastically partial, adversarial colonial discourses could enable the writing of a history of subaltern insurgency (1983b). See also Mani, 1991; Mills, 1993; Prakash, 1990; Stoler, 1992.

[3] My access to the two oral histories is via an undated typescript given to me by Bensa, comprising a detailed ethnographic commentary on the poem and a line-by-line translation by Rivierre of the prose story (Bensa and Rivierre, n.d.). The written text was published by Rivierre (1994: 39–70), who explained that it was "elaborated by representatives of the Waka-Amo lineage, and recorded in a notebook from which it was dictated to us". The Amô are the "chiefly" lineage of one of the three *mwo-daame*, "container-of-chiefs", which contest the chieftainship of the Waka clan; this clan corresponds roughly to the "Wagap tribe" of the colonial texts.

[4] For a congruent instance in recent Pacific Islands historiography see Neumann, 1992.

[5] I use the conventional translation "chief" for the dignitary called *daame* in *cèmuhî*, while endorsing Bensa's caveat on the inappropriateness of its implication of unquestioned political authority (Bensa, 1986; Douglas, 1994b).

[6] Despite the "Christian" name by which Europeans referred to Apengou, at least after a visit to the colony's headquarters in 1859, and his reputation as a "good catechumen" (Vigouroux to Poupinel, 6 Jan. 1858, APO), he seems not to have been baptised, since he remained polygynous at his death. His descendants' written official lineage history had him converted *in extremis* by Vigouroux, who was actually no longer serving at Wagap (Rivierre, 1994: 60).

[7] Of the dozen or so expeditions outside the pacified south, French reports claimed significant, unverified, loss of Kanak life in only four, ranging from 14 to 40. One senior administrator admitted: "our possession is more fictitious than real" (Chef du Génie et du Service des Ponts et Chaussées, "Mémoire militaire...", 20 Apr. 1863, ANOM, DFC, Carton 1).

[8] In letters written before his departure for Wagap, Durand had made it clear that he already intended to establish a post there (Durand to Rougeyron, 22 Jan. 1862, AAN, 83.1; Durand to Min., 25 Jan. 1862, ANM, BB3 730).

[9] Against this reading, contemporary official texts identified Ounine, the leading local Galaahî according to Bensa and Rivierre (n.d.), as "brother" of Apengou and the other "rebel chiefs" (Durand to Min., 25 Feb. 1862, ANM, BB3 730; Hardy, ["Rapport sur le champ de bataille à Wagap, 1862"], [1862], APM).

10 A colonial official reported Gondou's local reputation thus:

> "The house of his ancestors," said the natives trembling, "disappeared under the skulls of the victims he devoured; this ferocious Gondou," they added in their figurative language, "is not a man, he is a dog thirsty for blood; he does not speak, he barks; he bites those who come near him. He is so greedy he will devour us all, and end up eating himself, when he is alone in the land" (La Hautière, 1869: 171; see also Guiart, 1963: 109–10).

Garnier (1868: 48) gave a pidgin version of the same story: "'*Gondou he no allsame man he all same poika [dog]; he look one Kanak he houo-houo [barks]; he kai kai [eats] plenty man*'".

11 Durand's missionary informant, Montrouzier, was a respected naturalist.
12 Durand had received the formal instruction: "It is important from this double point of view [of religion and French colonisation] as by reason of the devotion towards us of the Christian tribes to second by every possible means the work of the missionaries such that it may draw to us the tribes which are still hostile" (Min. to Durand, Feb. 1861, ANOM, Carton 42).
13 The trope of a "high chief's" deathbed "profession of faith" and "sacred" instruction to his "subjects" to become Catholic was a familiar one, earlier rehearsed in the Isle of Pines (see Chapter Six). There was a more blatant instance of contemptuous civilised misreading of indigenous religiosity elsewhere in Durand's official report, when he wondered whether "the secret of the stubborn resistance with which they opposed us" during the expedition was to be found in "fanatised...minds; a renowned sorcerer, come amongst them from the North of the island, announced that our soldiers' arms will not kill them" (Durand to Min., 25 Feb. 1862, ANM, 3B3 730). This was a typical instance of a coloniser's opting for a demeaning civilised trope about primitive subjection to superstition, rather than acknowledge perseverance as a tactical option and ritual as a pragmatic necessity in indigenous fighting.
14 Rivierre now thinks that modern Christian attitudes towards an intransigent pagan ancestor probably explain Kahoua's virtual absence from the stories told to him and Bensa in the 1970s. In *cèmuhî*, "Kahoua" means *kauwöe*, "le cagou" (*Rhynochetos jubatus*, a local flightless bird) (Rivierre, 1994: 121). Rivierre says he is also recalled as "big balls", because of the way he was circumcised (pers. comm., 14 Dec. 1995).
15 Saussol referred to "the episode of the ambush that Melanesian oral traditions impute to the missionaries" and cited in support "a Melanesian version of the facts" of the Wagap affair given in a 1979 article by Bensa and Rivierre

(the "article" was never published and its authors say there is no extant manuscript):

> According to these sources, the Fathers ... agreed to set a trap for the protagonists of the "revolt" by inviting them to participate in a reconciliation feast in an enclosure encompassed in taut calico which hid the surroundings from sight. It is there, in the course of the feast, after their guard had been lowered by tobacco and alcohol, that the rebel chiefs were surrounded by the soldiers (1979: 81, 89–91, 478).

[16] Rougeyron to Poupinel, 5 Feb. 1862, APO; Durand to Min., 25 Feb. 1862, ANM, BB3 730. See Part Three on the multiplicity, complexity and instability of Kanak engagements with Christian missionaries and Christianity.

[17] In similar vein, Mani warned against the hegemonic tendency "to take at face value the self-aggrandizing claims of colonial or missionary texts", thereby granting colonialism "more power than it achieved" (1991: 394, 407); Fabian noted that "the factual outcome of colonization tends to overshadow the precariousness of the enterprise" (1991: 155). See also Guha, 1989; Prakash, 1995; Stoler, 1992: 182.

Chapter Five

Winning and Losing? Reflections on the War of 1878–79 in New Caledonia*

FOREWORD

*T*his chapter derives from a thus far unpublished narrative on the colonial wars of 1878–9 in New Caledonia. It originally appeared in 1991 in the Journal of Pacific History (26: 213–33), in a special issue of papers given at an Australian National University conference on "France in the Pacific". It was a companion piece to the 1990 ancestor of Chapter Three—ethnographic history to its historical ethnography, narrative to its abstractions. To conform to the journal's trademark empiricism I contrived to write in a fairly unreflective, realist style, qualified here with a dose of reflexivity. Even so, the editors, in unconscious parody of Barthes' "referential illusion"—the pretence that referents are speaking for themselves (1967: 69)—saw fit to purge my expository first paragraph of all explicit traces of authorial presence, leaching much of its intended meaning and predictably contorting its syntax. I have reinstated the original text. The chapter, as "actions-oriented" ethnographic history, calls into particular question the unwitting teleology of preordained historical outcomes and categorical polarities. It interweaves narrative and textual critique, with a leaning to story over text.

I had written the conference paper late in 1990 during a research/field trip to New Caledonia. I was actually incarcerated in an apartment in the heat of a Nouméa summer, unable for a series of minor but collectively compelling reasons either to work in the local Catholic archives or to get into the field. This was really my first experiencing of the self-indulgent, painful pleasure of undistracted solitary writing, to a rhythm entirely of one's own choice, ambivalently released from the diversions of offspring and students. In retrospect it was life-altering.

PROLOGUE

This chapter is a kind of social military history. In Chapter Three and elsewhere (1980a, 1992a) I argued that indigenous fighting in New Caledonia was pervaded by values of reciprocity, equivalence and restraint; that in colonial contexts, fighting included, Islanders acted in meaningful, creative ways which often contradicted European assumptions of external imposition and reflex reaction; that both contemporary texts and later histories tended to anticipate the colonial "conquest" of New Caledonia, overstate French military advantage, discount indigenous agency and generally denigrate Kanak performance. The question mark of the chapter title implies doubt about the categorical antithesis "winning"/"losing", typical of conventional, outcome-oriented military histories: "the 'outcome' approach to military history, like the time-honoured but outmoded 'causes and results' approach to general history", commented Keegan, "pre-judges the terms in which the narrative can be cast" (1976: 47).

In written histories of whatever political complexion, there is no doubt about the "outcome" of the wars of 1878–9 in New Caledonia: "the French" won; "the Melanesians" lost. Only the moral import of the agreed result varies: "the French" tended and tend to conceive it as the just and inevitable victory of civilisation over savagery;[1] modern Kanak and their sympathisers see it as nationalist martyrdom in an unequal encounter with rampant white imperialism (Anova-Ataba, 1969: 218; Dousset-Leenhardt, 1976: 23). Neither trope is mindful of grey areas and ambiguities, which belie *a priori* categories and ethnocentric or interested terminology. This chapter addresses the following questions, with particular reference to the Ouraïl theatre of the war.[2] How apt are absolute, ultimate categories to the contemporaneous intentions, actions and experience of protagonists? to contingencies of time and place? to the singularity of particular campaigns? Who were "winners" and "losers", when, how? What did "winning/losing" comprise in military, rather than post-war sociopolitical terms?[3]

BEFORE

The wars which galvanised New Caledonia from June 1878 until the early months of 1879, indelibly marking indigenous and colonial consciousness, were by far the largest of the nineteenth century colonial conflicts, in numbers involved, extent and intensity. Yet their onset stunned a complacent European populace, few of whom had recorded forebodings.[4] For much of the 1870s metropolitan parsimony had forced the colonial administration in Nouméa virtually to abandon permanent occupation of the area north of Bourail and Canala and rely on tours of inspection and occasional punitive expeditions to remind the natives of French presence. Rivière, senior officer on the local naval division, recalled that in May 1878 "there had been so little question of the Canaques" during his two years in the colony "that I could believe that they did not exist or no longer existed" (1881: 78–9). Governor Olry (6 July 1878), announcing the outbreak of war, marvelled that soldiers and settlers in the bush "regarded *canaques* as big children, sometimes sulky, but always inoffensive, they enjoyed a truly strange confidence, even intimacy".

What wishful thinking deemed quiescence might from the perspective of indigenous agency be labelled widespread readiness to pursue peaceful coexistence with Europeans to the limits of toleration; equally, some prepared to defend those limits with the club. In terms of permanent, effective colonial control, much of the main island outside the south remained unconquered in 1878.[5] Yet throughout the 1870s, penal and free colonisation had steadily expanded along the extensive plains of the mid-west coast, with little concern for indigenous livelihood and sensibilities. This book deals in categories and representations rather than causes, but it is noteworthy that the groups seemingly most active in covertly planning and initiating the 1878 war were among those most affected and outraged by their experiences at that time, though many had enjoyed good initial relations with European settlers. Groups in the La Foa region protested in vain about the insufficiency of reserves to which they were legally confined in 1877, while in areas of European pastoral settlement indigenous complaints about the devastation of

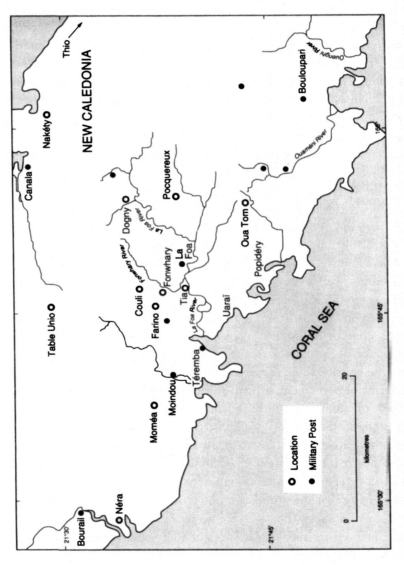

MAP 5   *The Ourail district, 1878–79*

gardens by unfenced stock often went unheard. In shocked retrospect in the aftermath of the "Great Revolt", Europeans redefined the mid-1870s as the deceptive calm before the storm, and rhetorically transformed simple savages into treacherous, inscrutable ones: "We must forever mistrust the natives who are not 'big children', but like all savages are secretive and vindictive", recommended a pamphlet published locally during the war (Anon, 1882: 130).

As with the nature of the outcome, most accounts, contemporary and later, concurred that the war of 1878 displayed an unusual degree of indigenous premeditation and detailed plotting, though European motives for advancing such a thesis could be racist, self-serving or romantically pro-Kanak. Yet substantial military alliances, lengthily orchestrated, were not unknown in fighting in New Caledonia, before or after contact with Europeans. From court martial evidence given by the "chief" known as Aréki, who alone amongst the leaders of the Kanak coalition avoided death in action or summary execution, it seems that the core of this alliance comprised the previously rival La Foa and Fonwhary "chiefs" Naïna and Ataï, together with other groups from Ouraïl, Pocquereux, the Ouaméni valley, Bouloupari, and the upper Thio valley. The war was probably long planned and coordinated, with diplomatic missions to most parts of the mainland, stockpiling of ordnance and elaborate ritual preparation.[6] The initial outbreaks were limited to the areas around La Foa and Bouloupari and might have occurred prematurely, before the organisers had succeeded in extracting firm commitments from groups elsewhere, pre-eminently the powerful east coast chiefdoms of Canala. It seems certain, though, that the Canala "chiefs" knew of the plan, if indeed they had not encouraged it with covert promise of support.[7]

OUTBREAK

War exploded on 25 and 26 June with successive series of coordinated surprise attacks on gendarmes, officials and settlers in the districts of Ouraïl and Bouloupari-Thio, during which some 125 men, women and children died (Anon. 1882: 54–8). The vast majority of the victims listed was European and about half were convicts, ex-convicts and their families. The actual assailants were often well known to their targets. The usual stratagem was to enter houses and offices casually or on plausible errands, take nonchalant position close to the intended victims and strike simultaneously with startling violence. Bodies were often mutilated. Subsequent parties, sometimes including women and children, looted and fired the properties and carried off the booty. The brutality, audacity, range and obvious synchronisation of the attacks were so incongruous with the "good-humoured, peaceful, cowardly beings" of most settlers' experience, as to seem entirely novel (Thomas, 1886: 48; *N-C*, 4 July 1878). Nearly a decade of apparent tranquillity, however, had dulled colonial memories. Sudden, drastic violence, using deception, was an honoured tactic in indigenous fighting, long familiar in attacks on Europeans (see Chapter Three), though employed in 1878 on a far wider scale than previously.

The tactic had, for example, been used in 1857 in the killing of 13 Europeans and 15 New Hebrideans (now ni-Vanuatu) at Mont-Dore, near Port-de-France (later Nouméa). The administrator Foucher retrospectively described this attack as a diversion planned by the Kabwa high "chief" Kuindo to cover a large-scale surprise assault on Port-de-France (1890: 28–36). The main drive, a complex pincers movement, was aborted when the defenders spied one of the concealed war parties: frontal attack on well-armed, vigilant troops holding sound defensive position was not normally part of indigenous military agenda. The putative diversion achieved total surprise and almost complete success, including seizure of a large quantity of firearms and ammunition. This attribution of considerable tactical sophistication to Kanak leaders might have been a victor's *post facto* transformation of the defeated into worthy opponents.[8] Yet other perceptive contemporary colonial observers discerned a capacity in indigenous fighting for coordination over a relatively wide area, tactical use of diversion and division of offensive forces to enhance the element of surprise (Rochas, 1862: 201–2; Mathieu, 1868; Rivière, 1881: 209–11). Foucher saw the intent of the stratagem used at Mont-Dore as "to murder without being exposed to combat" (1890: 14, 30), but this pragmatic dimension, unsurprisingly, did not impress contemporary Europeans, who were appalled by the savage propensity for unexpected and intensely violent action and righteously indignant at the methods used (Le Bris to Min., 23 Jan. 1857, ANOM, Carton 42). Even the surgeon-ethnographer Rochas, generally a sensitive interpreter of local military norms, implied dishonour in their stress on "guile...surprise, nay even...treachery" and labelled a typical subterfuge "a vile trap which they ornament with the name ruse of war" (1862: 202). Yet if Foucher's assessment of the Kanak tactical plan was correct, ruse of war is just what the Mont-Dore episode was, an important side show in a wider scenario. The failure of the latter to eventuate made these killings look like random slaughter—an interpretation congenial to most Europeans. A tactical evaluation, however, would note the careful preparation, implementation at the optimal time, and the discipline and efficiency of execution.

The initial Kanak onslaughts in 1878 displayed similar properties, with the addition of synchronisation over a much wider canvas— the attacks which scoured the Ouraïl district on the morning of 25 June spanned nearly 40 kilometres, radiating from La Foa: 12 kilometres south to Popidéry, 19 kilometres north-east to Dogny, 18 kilometres west to Moindou and the same distance south-west to Téremba, including the prison farms at Fonwhary and Tia and isolated settler households in between. Unlike the killings at Mont-Dore, the Ouraïl and Bouloupari attacks were the main act, presumably intended to be decisive, since subsistence economies could not indefinitely sustain campaigns conducted on their own soil. I read these attacks as a calculated use of terror by a few hundred, at most, outgunned warriors, who sought to eliminate European settlement at a single stroke, at least from the affected zone, to obtain vital firearms and ammunition, and to ignite the active support, there and elsewhere, of hesitant allies and neutrals. Belief in the emotional and political efficacy of sudden explosions of extreme violence looks like a perennial element in indigenous fighting. Enacted in the heat of anger, fanned by magic, dance and fervid oratory, such outbursts were short-lived; they were suited, militarily and psychologically, to part-time warrior cultures which also valued restraint, reciprocity, equivalence and equilibrium (see Chapter Three). Europeans, even if they admitted Kanak provocation, premeditation, careful planning and skilful use of dissimulation, saw such attacks above all as expressions of savagery, rather than as a tactic of war appropriate to indigenous culture, economic circumstances and particular strategic equations as read by local leaders. "The New Caledonians", moralised one metropolitan writer, "fight for their homes and their independence. Their fault and their crime is to have made on us a savage war, to have committed murder and cowardly surprises, to have butchered women and children" (Plauchut, 1878: 687).[9]

In calculating the military balance sheet, Europeans usually omitted the initial victims. Thus the *Sydney Morning Herald* reported (3 Sep. 1878): "Upon the side of the whites there has been one death... in an ambush, and... one horse killed.... Thus stands the list of killed... two months after the commencement of hostilities—of course exclusive of the victims which fell to the natives' treacherous axes and clubs, in number about 150". Saussol, generally a balanced commentator, also deprecated the major Kanak military achievement: "more than 80% of the effective total of victims [amongst Europeans and their dependents] succumbed to the initial massacres", where "the effect of surprise" was operative (1979: 212). Surprise and "stratagem", properly employed, rank highly as offensive tactics in European war (Clausewitz, 1968: 269–76); when used by "savages" they are at best discounted, at worst denigrated as "cowardly" and "treacherous".

CLIOMETRICS

Dousset-Leenhardt, consumed by romantic passion for an idealised and imaginary "Canaquie", described the "Insurrection" as a "total, irreversible revolt of the New Caledonian population against the society which was in a relationship of dominance with it" (1976: 23, 180). Saussol, more phlegmatic, more attuned to nuance and complexity in indigenous socio-political relations, properly challenged this image of "Canaque monolithism" and "the myth of a unitary and unanimous insurrection extending from the Ouenghi to the Koné". He also argued that, both technically and tactically, "Melanesians were badly adapted to this new war" (1979: 189, 228, 234). My reading bridges these extremes: on the one hand, the antecedents and conduct of the war of 1878–9 displayed a probably unusual degree of unanimity and coordination—by allies of the French as well as Kanak[10]—and significant innovation; on the other, there were evidently ambiguous or hesitant commitment, conflicting interests, rivalries and constraints on alliance formation. These were elements of a social landscape still comprising many more or less autonomous groups. They were divided by language and interests and linked by a whole range of relationships, both peaceful and antagonistic, which altered with time and circumstances and in which Europeans had come to figure in largely local terms.

It is unclear whether the initial outbreak on 25 June 1878 did occur prematurely, or whether it represented a desperate gamble by the main instigators to try to win over waverers. Despite the heavy European losses on the first two days of the war and a momentary panic in Nouméa, the administration was not unduly perturbed once the confinement of hostilities to the Ouraïl–Bouloupari region became apparent. The governor acknowledged, though, that the nature of the country and "the customs of the *canaques*" meant that "the work of repression and pacification ... will be long and arduous" (6 July 1878). Of critical significance was the decision taken at the outset by the "chiefs" of Canala to support the French, thereby reneging on any commitments made to Ataï and Naïna. By the third day of the war the Canala chiefdoms were firmly compromised: after a night march across the island to La Foa with as many as 400 warriors their war leader Nondo was wounded in a clash with Kanak. Other groups were less decisive, but their reticence was also costly to the Kanak in Ouraïl and gave breathing-space to the French after their initial disasters. The Kawa of Couli, on the margins of the Canala zone of influence, were said to have sought protection there. The "chiefs" of Moindou, Moméa and Farino, closely related to Ataï, refused to commit themselves at this stage—their "will to conserve their local autonomy, vis-à-vis the chiefs of the rebellion, being as strong as their hatred of the White", according to Guiart— while Aréki of Tom sought, without ultimate success, to remain unengaged (1968: 100, 113–14, 119; Caro, 1976; Rivière, 1881).

The pro-French, ambivalent or neutral stance adopted by so many groups meant that the initial warrior strength of those opposed to the French in the Ouraïl and Bouloupari districts was exiguous. Guiart roughly estimated their number at no more than 200 (1968: 118). I know of no convincing basis for gauging the number of participants at Bouloupari, the Ouaméni and the upper Thio valley, but reasonably precise information is available on the districts of Ouraïl, Canala-Nakéty and Houaïlou, which had been subject to delimitation of reserves in the previous two years. The report of the commission of delimitation which investigated Ouraïl from June to December 1877 listed the population, generally including gender distribution, of each "tribe" and "village" included administratively in the *arrondissement*.[11] It is therefore possible to make a plausible estimate of the likely number of warriors available in this region at various stages, on the assumption that about 60% of the males would have been of warrior age and capacity.[12] The report listed 141 persons (81 females) under the "tribe of Hattaï [Ataï]", 341 persons (153 females) under various fractions of the "tribe of La Foa[,] chief regent Naïna" and 48 persons (19 females) under the "tribe of Uaraï... chief Molaï [Moraï]": this gives a notional total of 167 warriors for those groups known to have been involved in the early stages of the war in Ouraïl. In addition, the warriors of Dogny (about 30) probably participated and those of Pocquereux (about 70) were involved at Bouloupari the next day and might have been active in Ouraïl. The grave numerical cost to the Kanak of the belated engagement of groups paying allegiance to Baptiste of Moindou and Aréki of Tom becomes apparent: the various elements of the "tribe of Moindou" included 182 males, while "the tribes of Méharé, Tom and Paraoué... under the domination of... Aliki [Aréki]" comprised 178 males. This means a notional 216 warriors who initially remained aloof. Thus the maximum number of warriors who might have been available in Ouraïl on 25 June was about 270, but the number actually involved was no doubt fewer, since it is unreasonable to assume 100% mobilisation.

On the same basis, the notional total of warriors at Canala alone was 633.[13] Their war leader Nondo was at times reported to have taken 300 to 500 warriors into the field. There was no consensus on the size of the party he led to La Foa on the night of 26–7 June, but it might have outnumbered the entire Kanak force in Ouraïl.[14] The French effective in the colony at the beginning of the war was nearly 2,500 men, including, fortuitously, the crew of the *Tage*, more than 400 strong, and 250 marine infantry whom that vessel was in the process of relieving. To officials on the spot this seemed few enough, but relative to their enemy they enjoyed the immense advantages of telegraphic communication, which the Kanak were unable consistently to interrupt, and high strategic mobility, thanks to steam-powered sea transport. They were reinforced by the end of November to about 3,000, irregulars apart. They were, however, thinly spread—there were convicts to worry about as well as Kanak—and many, particularly the young conscripts, might not have been of high quality nor suited to footslogging under tropical conditions.[15]

DURING

Within a few hours of the first attacks at La Foa, Kanak had surrounded the unfortified coastal post of Téremba, the sole French military foothold in Ouraïl. It was manned at the time by only 10–15 men, but was "easily defended", sited on high ground between the sea and a swamp (*SMH*, 25 Oct. 1878). A successful assault would have gravely compromised the French position in this district and perhaps resolved the hesitant to risk active participation on the Kanak side. The assailants, however, seemed halfhearted and withdrew in the face of "a few gunshots" (Rivière, 1881: 118). Their apparent pusillanimity struck Europeans as contemptible. "If the Kanaques had been more resolute", wrote a missionary eyewitness, "they [would have] annihilated Téremba" (Lecouteur to Fraysse, 3 July 1878, AAN, 16.1). Saussol reasoned similarly (1979: 217–18). Indeed they might, had they actually numbered the "four or five hundred" of European apprehension (Lecouteur to Poupinel, 1 Aug. 1878, APM). Moreover, most of those who invested Téremba must already have covered many kilometres that morning and engaged for some hours in the taxing tasks of ambush, killing and looting. The same missionary remarked that "the women walked in front and appeared very tired"; in the men's case, physical fatigue would have been compounded by emotional, with the dissipation of the ritually fuelled anger which had fed extreme violence. The issue was shortly placed beyond doubt by the opportune arrival of the naval vessel *Vire*, which landed a party of 33 sailors. With the debarkation the next day of troops from Nouméa, the Téremba garrison amounted to 120 soldiers, 32 sailors and 36 armed deportees. Newly palisaded, the post was impregnable against an enemy lacking artillery and was henceforth to serve the French as a secure base for supply and reinforcement (Olry, 6 July 1878; Rivière, 1881: 108–25).

Under the shock of the initial killings, the districts of Ouraïl and Bouloupari were virtually evacuated by Europeans, their settlements abandoned to arson and plunder (Vanauld to Olry, 26 June 1878, ANOM, Carton 43). But the Kanak in Ouraïl lacked the numbers and the resources to consolidate their advantage and prevent immediate French reoccupation of the centres of Moindou and Fonwhary. Fonwhary and Téremba, "seriously fortified" with wooden palisades, were the first in a network of "unassailable" military posts which were to dot the war zone and form the fulcrum of the French strategy of repression: by the end of 1878 there were 11 or 12 around La Foa and Bouloupari alone (Olry, 6 July, 2, 28 Aug., 28 Sep. 1878; Saussol, 1979: 238). For a while the posts were French islands in Kanak-controlled territory, but the bulk of the warriors withdrew to prepared positions in the thick bush of the lower La Foa valley. Rivière, the military commandant of the district, described the valley as "an inextricable tangle of vegetation...cut by ravines and little water courses and strewn with villages defended by barricades reinforced with wire taken from the telegraph" (1881: 187). They were, added Amouroux, "defended in the second line by *chevaux de frise* made from dry trees, branches to the fore" ([1881]: 57). Tactical withdrawal notwithstanding, the Kanak burned buildings previously overlooked, cut telegraph wires as fast as they could be repaired—though messages continued to get through—and targeted the enemy's war leaders, killing the military commandant of the colony in an ambush.

Kanak generally avoided face-to-face confrontation with armed troops: "they carefully avoid engagements and limit themselves to surprises", commented one missionary (Montrouzier to his brother, 26 Sep. 1878, AAN, 9.4). Little in either their military culture or particular strategic situation in Ouraïl—outnumbered, outgunned, their heartland already strewn with enemy strongpoints—inclined them to reckless offence against the odds; this was prudence rather than want of courage, as some of their opponents sometimes acknowledged.[16] From the outset this war differed from the wars of the 1860s in New Zealand in important respects, all detrimental to Kanak. The Maori, argued Belich (1986: 63, 102–7, 128–31, 177–88), were often able to screen their own heartland and force the British to attack on their terms by deploying *paa* lines on the fringes of Maori territory or in positions threatening the British line of supply. In New Caledonia the critical initial military action took place within Kanak territory, into which European settlement had already significantly penetrated. The vulnerable indigenous subsistence base was thereby exposed at once, the more so as it was the French who quickly established a network of fortified positions in the other's country.

Kanak disinclination to confront French firepower and their elusiveness in difficult, intimately-known terrain forced the latter to adopt an indiscriminate strategy of attrition, striking at the means of subsistence rather than enemy warriors directly: "fire and destruction had been applied to the native villages and plantations within easy distance [of the posts] ... . It was the Canaque system of warfare, which it was supposed they would feel most" (Thomas, 1886: 62). Olry complained that "everywhere the enemy is unattainable, dispersing in the woods when we advance and coming back close on our heels when we return to camp". The governor's tropes betokened his dilemma as well as his racism: Kanak were "ferocious beasts" whose "lairs" must be destroyed; the countryside must be "scoured" (*fouillé*), "cleaned out" (*nettoyé*), "purged" (6 July, 2 Aug., 28 Sep. 1878, 1 May 1879). Since the first days of the colony, similar complaints and imagery had punctuated colonial documentation like a refrain, rationalising recourse to attrition in both the earlier wars as well as in numerous smaller campaigns and expeditions.

Though promising eventual reduction of the enemy by hardship and starvation, it was not the preferred mode of the French military, since it was slow, costly, "exhausting and arduous", immensely frustrating and scarcely honourable: "without glory if not without danger and especially [not] without fatigue".[17] Saussol, whose assessment of Kanak military performance was not at all generous, saw the initial French adoption of a strategy of "total war" (that is, "attrition") in the 1850s as "an admission of weakness. It was, in the short term, the sole means by which the military authority might suppress guerrilla bands which its relatively weak forces did not permit it to control" (1979: 69). Arguably, though, it was an index of Kanak military *effectiveness*, despite inadequate armament, that they forced such an onerous and discreditable strategy on the French, even when the latter also enjoyed considerable numerical advantage.

Thus were the main elements of French strategy in 1878 defined: "to set up fortified posts amongst the insurgents around which mobile columns have been constantly in motion", thrusting "into rebel country, crossing it in every direction, burning villages and destroying plantations"; "to detach from the revolt as many tribes as possible by rallying them to our cause" (Olry, 2 Aug., 28 Sep. 1878). Success in the latter enterprise would not only deprive the Kanak of sorely-needed warrior numbers, but also provide the sole effective means—indigenous allies—by which the French could strike directly against them and hope to kill or capture suspected murderers. The *Sydney Morning Herald's* resident correspondent accurately if snidely predicted: "The troops will do well for destroying their camps and villages and protecting the different centres round which the 'colons' are rallying, but 'tis the native element that will give the best account in the pursuit of the murdering savages, as is well known to all old experienced colonists" (*SMH*, 12 July 1878).

For two months the French war effort consisted of haphazard mass expeditions to burn Kanak settlements, destroy food crops and trees and clear bush which might harbour lurking assassins. They hardly ever saw an enemy. This was stalemate, brittle product of the glancing encounter of elusive but ill-armed warriors with persistent but ill-adapted troops. In Nouméa colonists and officials chafed for vengeance and an end to this humiliatingly prolonged war; more to the point, it was widely feared that the tardiness of the repression might have "a disastrous effect in the tribes which have not yet taken part in the movement", that "prudence has been pushed to exaggeration" (Mauger, 1976: 12 July, 1 Aug. 1878, in Dousset-Leenhardt, 1976: 243, 245). These fears seemed to have been realised from mid-August when the killing of several settlers at Moindou apparently signalled the entry into the conflict of Baptiste and the groups within his sphere of influence; a month later war broke out further north, around Poya and Bourail. Yet according to a local tradition, Baptiste was deliberately compromised by other Kanak, who contrived the discovery of European human remains in his house (Guiart, 1968: 100, 113). In the Poya region there was a longstanding local conflict in which a settler had become embroiled. The mass killing of Europeans on 11 September, which provoked colonial intervention, was neither a reflex of previous French inaction nor a "revolt" against colonial authority, but pertained to local grievances and the lust for firearms of the contending parties. The inhabitants of coastal settlements at Bourail, previously allies of the French, had earlier rejected overtures from the Kanak in Ouraïl. Far from taking advantage of colonial inertia, their eventual entry into open hostilities with the French after 20 September was precipitated by the sack of their houses and gardens by nervous colonial authorities. Anticipating an attack, the latter probably sparked what they would have preferred to avoid.

By mid-August Rivière, frustrated by the stalemate in Ouraïl, had determined on less indiscriminate, more focussed tactics (1881: 186–201). He built a new post at La Foa, "the very centre of the insurrection" (1881: 199), and handpicked an élite column of 30 *francs-tireurs*, who adopted indigenous methods of bush-fighting. They were tough, older men, sailors and deportees, who, by moving fast and light, avoiding trails and using ambush and surprise, were sometimes able to come to grips with the Kanak and inflict personnel losses on them. They served Rivière as well aesthetically as militarily. His narrative of "the Canaque insurrection"—a distinguished novelist's overwrought, egocentred retrospection—primitivised and romanticised "the column" in ambiguous counterpoint to "the Canaques" (1881: 202–4, 213–219, 228):

> They have taken on the qualities of savages, patience and ruse, roughing it, complaining neither about privations, nor heat, nor cold. The nights... they pass less in sleeping than in keeping watch, lie in wait, prepare their [next] stroke. It is not that they always succeed; but always and more and more, they create a vacuum around them and spread terror (1881: 237).

"Resolutely" expedient, Rivière also armed twenty convicts as *éclaireurs de la brousse*, "bush scouts", and imaged them in a parallel amalgam of class and racial tropes: "another species of men, who would take on something of the qualities [of the *francs-tireurs*], but even better familiarised to the bush, wild beasts able to be hurled still more quickly at the Canaques in the scrub" (1881: 202). He thus made romantic virtue of necessity, rhetorically segregating "the column" from the grinding French strategy of attrition in which it participated, yet disclosing *malgré lui* how Kanak invulnerability forced him to fight the war their way. Henceforth, while the policy of destruction continued apace, much of the actual fighting in Ouraïl on the French side was done by *francs-tireurs* and by Canala warriors.

Two proximate events altered the character of the war in this theatre. Whether from slow decision-making or inability to muster a sufficient force in time, Kanak leaders delayed an all-out attack on the new post until 24 August, when its palisade was completed. The eventual offensive represented a massive investment of coordination and effort by most of the Kanak in Ouraïl, including Moindou and Tom, under the direction of Moraï of Uaraï and Naïna. Aréki, whose aloofness had not saved his settlements and gardens from the torch, was present, Ataï seemingly not. As represented by Rivière (1881: 209–11, 232) it comprised a noisy feint by a putative "two hundred" warriors, while from another direction the main body, "several hundred" strong, moved in silently under cover of a fold of ground. The French commander held his fire and was able to repel the main assault. The diversion's failure doomed the attack, since the assailants had few firearms, though they maintained a hail of slingstones for two hours, wounding three defenders. Bloodstains were the only traces of Kanak casualties, but prisoners later revealed that Moraï had been mortally wounded. This was the last reported instance of Kanak coordination for offensive purposes in the Ouraïl theatre. Its defeat permanently ceded the initiative in this region to the French and their allies, assuring them of eventual victory even before the entry into the war of groups further north (Olry, 28 Sep. 1878).

Henceforth the La Foa post was a major base for expeditions. Its elevated position enabled the French to monitor Kanak encampments in the nearby valleys through the traces of their fires. On 1 September it was the departure point for a coordinated thrust into the La Foa valley by three columns comprising 110 Frenchmen and about 200 Canala warriors. A further 100 or so troops were posted at key points on the margins of the valley to bar escape, while a separate column operated out of Moindou. This day saw a purported 16 or 17 Kanak killed to three of their opponents wounded; about 60 Kanak women and children were taken by the allies. Most of the dead were decapitated,[18] their heads doubly sacrificed: as grisly trophies presented in triumph to Rivière by Nondo and the convict scouts; as rhetorical tokens served up in Rivière's narrative of the victory of civilised savagery over natural (1881: 225–6, 228–30). The quality of the victims made it one of the most successful French actions of the war—they included Ataï, his priest and Baptiste of Moindou. Otherwise it was a partial failure, since Naïna and most of the Kanak warriors escaped. Not so from the French perspective at the time: that night at La Foa they sang, danced and fired a salvo from a small cannon, watched curiously by the men of Canala who had done most of the actual killing and celebrated their victory on the spot with what the French called a *pilou*, "ceremony". "This day", exulted Rivière, "was a real success", of "decisive importance" for the course of the repression in Ouraïl. According to his retrospective classification of the phases of the war: "[We had] at first to keep on the defensive, then take the offensive with sufficient forces and, after long and painful efforts while we dealt with Canaques *en masse*, reach the stage of the destruction of wandering, if still armed bands. That is where we are [now]... The real man chase is about to begin" (1881: 231–3).

Olry's reports—carefully crafted for his superiors' consumption—were equally confident (28 Sep., 22 Dec. 1878): by the end of September Ouraïl and Bouloupari had been "purged", 1,000 "rebels" were dead—a quite incredible figure—while those in Ouraïl had been "entirely dispersed"; all that remained was a "Canaque-hunt". With the outbreak of war further north, he deemed himself fortunate "not to have had to deal with all these people at once".

From this time, certainly, the Kanak in Ouraïl fragmented into small groups and generally abandoned the lower La Foa valley for more remote locations; yet roving bands prevented the reinstallation of colonists and forced the French to continue expeditions unabated for a further three months. The troops rarely saw a Kanak, but the expeditions were extraordinarily enervating, especially with the onset of the hot season.[19] By the end of October the prospect of interminable war and the total exhaustion of his *francs-tireurs* had forced Rivière to recommend that the drive for total victory be reconsidered and peace negotiations begun (1881: 257–60). Olry's reiterated protestations that the war was over in Ouraïl/Bouloupari rang hollow and not until the end of January 1879 could he credibly announce that "the repression is complete" (5 Feb., 7 Mar. 1879).

ALLIES

Official accounts only grudgingly divulge the resilience of the Kanak in 1878–9 and the extent of French dependence on their allies. Read against the grain with informed scepticism they do provide suggestive hints, which are amplified in the otherwise interested reports of missionaries, settlers and Australian journalists. The question of the nature, meanings and military significance of allied involvement is complex. The wars in which the French became involved in the Poya-Koné region and around Bourail from mid-September differed from that in Ouraïl and Bouloupari-Thio. The Poya-Koné conflict was mainly an indigenous affair, largely fought between Melanesians, for their own reasons, though Kanak warriors had several notable successes against French detachments (see Chapter Three). The allies eventually comprised a vast coalition, mainly from the interior and the east coast, and included some redoubtable former enemies of the French, who presumably saw a greater threat in Kanak rivals equipped with firearms and ammunition.

In the Bourail theatre, the Kanak displayed great desperation and military skill, keeping the foreign community in a virtual state of siege for more than two months: they picked off isolated settlers, regularly fired thatch roofs with slingstones trailing flaming bark and launched several attacks on French posts. A missionary based at Téremba was struck by the contrast with Ouraïl: the Kanak in Bourail, "who today show so much activity and ruse, far superior in that respect to the natives of Ouraïl", "are of unequalled audacity and unshakeable tenacity" (Hilléreau to Fraysse, 26 Nov. 1878; [Hilléreau] to ?, 5 Dec. 1878, AAN, 16.2). Missionary accounts tended to attribute the Kanak performance in Bourail to the tactical expertise of Naouno, whom fear had evidently induced to abandon his position as government interpreter and take to the bush. The warriors of Houaïlou, equivocal in June, played a major role as allies of the French in this theatre, as they did further north. An earlier political line-up in the Bourail region was reversed: previously defeated inland groups joined the French so as to balance accounts with coast-dwellers who, a decade earlier, had supported the French against them (Douglas, 1992a: 96–104). Patterns of allied motivation and engagement in the several theatres varied, but everywhere their contributions were critical.

The Canala chiefdoms were by far the most important allies during the initial phases of the war; they and the warriors of Nakéty were the major allies in the Ouraïl theatre, which was the main arena for their activities. The question of the motives of the Canala leaders is not at issue here, but it was perhaps significant that their *entente* with Ataï and Naïna, if it occurred, was newer than their long-standing, profitable alliance with the French; more recently they seem to have competed with these "chiefs" for influence over the high valleys above La Foa. They must have had a far more lively appreciation of French military potential than many other Melanesians, such as those in Ouraïl and Bouloupari who would rarely have seen European soldiers: warriors from Canala had participated in numerous French punitive expeditions, while in 1875 what the French took to be a "plan of revolt against the whites, organised by the chiefs of... Canala" was prematurely revealed and neutralised by brisk deployment of troops, which, reported the governor of the day, "astonished the Canaques" and "greatly impressed" the "chiefs". The affair was followed by some attention to local grievances (Pritzbuer to Min., 28 Jan. 1876, ANOM, Carton 32).

Colonial myth attributed the decision of the Canala "chiefs" to join the French in June 1878 to the courage and audacity of Servan, the French commandant at Canala, who accompanied Nondo and his warriors on their initial foray across the island and was assumed to control their actions: according to the Australian journalist James, "they obeyed like children" (Thomas, 1886: 99).[20] The logistic and political significance of Canala support was acknowledged to be profound (Maréchal to Olry, 10 July 1878, Carton 43). Militarily, they steadily expanded their role. By the middle of August Nondo's original war party had all gone home, but his warriors returned *en masse* to Ouraïl for the operation of 1 September. Colonial accounts gave most of the credit for this action to the energy and bravery of the French troops and their leaders. The Canala men seemed unusually "worried and hesitant" and Rivière wondered whether they were afraid of Ataï or ashamed of fighting him (1881: 227, 229). It was, however, the allies who actually attacked all those killed in the La Foa valley, including Ataï. Subsequently they made frequent incursions to Ouraïl, sometimes accompanied by Servan, but increasingly under Nondo's independent direction and control. There was no question about their responsibility for the death of Naïna in January 1879. Nondo was eventually admitted to French councils of war. James admired his sense of "strategy; for, with pieces of bread, he marked out on the dinner-table the mode of attack to be pursued on a large party of the rebels... Nondo was as good a general as any French officer in New Caledonia"—this from a man who derided the tactical sense of Ataï and the other Kanak leaders in Ouraïl and Bouloupari (Thomas, 1886: 103–9, cf. 59–60).

The French, rarely comfortable with the Canala alliance, were generally suspicious of the "chiefs'" motives, actions and reliability: "I have only mediocre trust in our allies", allowed Olry;

"while using them, I supervise them" (2 Aug. 1878). Their role in the death of Ataï was thought so compromising as to ensure their future loyalty, but their pride in their effectiveness and successes touched racist nerves and provoked the professional jealousy of the military.[21] Olry described the "emotion" inspired in settlers at Canala by "the attitude of...Nondo, whose arrogance was daily more pronounced. [He was] proud of the success he had obtained, and that he owes in large part to the inspiring manner in which he commands the natives". Amouroux, a deportee at Canala, instanced this "attitude": "he [Nondo] cries loudly that without him the rebel Kanak would have killed all the whites; that he is the Kanala high chief of the whites as well as the blacks". James was told by infantry officers that the Canala allies "were but a lot of vagabond pillagers, little better than the insurgents, whom it would be well, by-and-by, to exterminate", while a senior naval officer deplored their tendency "to want to monopolise devotion to our cause and to regard themselves as indispensable to our security".[22] Rivière (1881: 249) identified between the Canala warriors and the *francs-tireurs* "a rivalry of effort and of success...The column liked to assert itself without the Canaques, and Nondo, for his part, preferred to act alone with his warriors without anyone knowing too much about what he did".

The allies' propensity for independent action in pursuit of what they conceived as their own interests was galling for settlers and authorities alike: "much dissatisfaction is expressed against the conduct of the friendly natives", reported the *Sydney Morning Herald* (3 Sep. 1878). "They are accused of seeking more after the spoils of war and enriching themselves, without much care at whose expense, rather than killing the enemy". But cold-blooded obliteration of opponents was not a normal practice in indigenous fighting: killing occurred in heat and victors preferred to absorb the defeated, particularly women and children, or incorporate them within their sphere of influence. In 1878 it was agreed from the outset that the allies' legitimate booty should include captured women and children (Olry, 28 Sep. 1878): "I surrender to you in all propriety", went the governor's official pronouncement to the warriors of Canala, "the women of your enemies and all the plunder that you can make in their villages" (Olry to the warriors of Canala, 11 July 1878, MS copy, AAN, 16.1).[23] In October 1878 there were several puzzling encounters with Nondo's warriors in the disputed hinterland between Canala and La Foa. The commander of the *francs-tireurs* was convinced that "a great part of the revolted tribes...deprived of their chiefs, have taken refuge on the territory of Nondo" ("Récit détaillé", 24 Oct.–22 Nov. 1878). Rivière told how he came to the disquieting belief that Nondo "was engaging in pacification to his own profit", camouflaged by regular prestations to the French of the severed heads of warriors who refused his terms. Rivière wondered, chastened, whether energetic harassment by the *francs-tireurs* had served only to drive Kanak more readily into Nondo's arms (1881: 248–9, 255–8).[24] Guiart argued that "the principal war aim of the Canalas was attained, once the limit of their zone of influence was acknowledged to include the region of Table Unio and the back country of Couli and La Foa" (1968: 115). Missionary anecdotes suggest that the Canala "chiefs" aimed also to protect their dependents in these areas and to mitigate the impact of the repression on any Kanak who were prepared to accept their authority (Garnier to Fraysse, 24 Oct. 1878; Moris to Fraysse, 1 Jan. 1879, AAN, 16.2).

By late in 1878 the urgent need to bring the war to a close decided Rivière to take a leaf from Nondo's book, since on balance the "chief's" colonising activities seemed to have worked to French advantage. He accordingly recommended that the government adopt Nondo's strategy, by offering clemency to warriors who surrendered and agreed to accept exile (1881: 257–60). Servan and Olry concurred. Both French and Kanak were exhausted, but the Kanak in Ouraïl and Bouloupari, never numerous, were starving. Olry believed that "the rebels are weary of war;...they all seem very vexed with their chiefs who push them to fight to the bitter end" ("Récit détaillé", 24 Oct.–22 Nov. 1878). In their own wars and in earlier colonial confrontations, Melanesians had seen no virtue in continuing a struggle when human and material costs were liable to be too high: Tjibaou maintained in a newspaper interview that "the choice has always been to avoid massacres" (*Times on Sunday*, 22 Nov. 1987). The surrender process started at the end of December in Ouraïl and quickly snowballed, mediated by Nundo and Naouno, the former Bourail interpreter, who looked to Rivière like "a savage fitted for this role [of intermediary] and who, in contrast to Nondo, worked only for us".[25] A month later the remnants of "the tribes of Ataï and Naïna" capitulated to a "column of Canalans": they comprised 35 warriors and 28 women and children, with an arsenal of two sporting-guns and one revolver. By February 1879 only a handful of Kanak remained in Ouraïl. Many had been killed, though in nothing like the numbers claimed by the French, and those of the remainder who had not found refuge on allied territory were exiled, their lands sequestered and their "tribal" names struck from the colonial roll.[26]

AFTER

Who won this war in Ouraïl, militarily? Evidently, the French and their allies, notably the warriors of Canala. "Winning", however, meant different things to different victors and the French did not achieve the total obliteration of their enemies initially envisaged. Their eventual victory came, moreover, at the cost of far more time, expense and arduous effort than most Europeans had anticipated. Olry's confident pronouncements of the end of September remained unrealised until the new year. How was the war won? Preeminently through allied agency, the possibility of which stemmed from indigenous divisions; these, in turn, contributed to the paucity of Kanak personnel. The Kanak arsenal was also markedly inferior, though their lack of firearms, disastrous in offence, mattered far less defensively, because of the temperamental nature of the *chassepot*, the very poor marksmanship of French troops and indigenous agility and elusiveness (Rivière, 1881: 196; Thomas, 1886: 72, 75–6).

In sociopolitical terms, the allies achieved their immediate political goals while the French won handsomely, though colonists suffered considerable material loss and psychological trauma; virtually the entire Kanak population disappeared from Bouloupari, Ouraïl and much of Bourail, leaving vast tracts of land available for unencumbered European settlement. The costs to the vanquished Kanak and the dour persistence of the French seem to have intimidated many Melanesians for a long time; few, including allies, could have had illusions about the likely efficacy of wholesale recourse to force. The allies received no reliable guarantee of peaceful, inviolate enjoyment of their own country in the future; only a few months after the war ended Olry reported that "numerous disputes, on the subject of delimitation of land, had arisen between colonists and natives in the region between Canala and Tuo" (27 June 1879, SHM, BB4 1106). These were resolved at the time and the day of reckoning over land was at least postponed at Canala, until the onset of serious expropriation in the 1890s (Doumenge, 1974: 83–6; Saussol, 1979: 271–3, 281–304).

The question mark of the title and arguments developed here about indigenous agency apply with even more force to the campaigns in Bourail and Poya-Koné; from the Kanak perspective Ouraïl was very much a worst-case scenario. Further north, Kanak disadvantage in numbers and ordnance was less stark and they were able to maintain effective offensive modes for far longer, despite massive allied opposition. The allies' significance was patent and paramount, to the extent that in the Poya-Koné theatre French interests and involvement were often peripheral. Accordingly, outcomes were even more ambiguous in both military and political terms (see Chapter Three).

Malice and mistrust were pronounced in most contemporary assessments by the French military of the allied contribution in 1878–9. At best they acknowledged a key subordinate role, necessitated by the very nature of savagery, natural as well as human; thus the retrospective evaluation of an infantry officer who participated in the final stages of the repression:

> The Canalans... helped us, in this difficult country, to stamp out the rebels. Without them it would have been almost impossible for us to catch them in their mountains and ravines covered with inextricable forests, through which they run as nimble as cats. They burden themselves with nothing: no load, no clothes, they carry only their arms. We caught up with them by surprise, thanks to our *canaque* allies who, knowing the country well[,] guided us and helped us to surprise them (Kanappe, Note, 9 Jan. 1880, in Kanappe, 1984: 105).

The journalist James was sardonically contemptuous of the performance of both savages and Frenchmen, but I find his vitriol seductive enough to warrant the last word: "Almost everything which has been done, except the destruction of plantations, in which the French soldiers excel, has been by the Canaque auxiliaries" (*SMH*, 15 October 1878).

NOTES

* Narrative sections of this chapter are distilled from critical, across the grain reading and juxtaposition of mutually antagonistic categories of colonial texts. Official letters and reports, especially by Governor Olry, and including his "Récits détaillés des évènements de l'insurrection canaque", 28 Sep.–21 Feb. 1879, are archived mainly in ANOM, Carton 43 and SHM, BB4 1094, 1106 and 1604. Manuscript copies of reports telegraphed to Nouméa before, during and after the war by Servan, the French commandant at Canala, are held in ATNC, MI10. Official accounts were published in the official newspaper, *Le Moniteur*, and in Rivière's flamboyant literary work (1881). They are countered by a range of settler voices: in the newspaper *La Nouvelle-Calédonie*, an account by the deportee Amouroux (Amouroux and Place [1881]), and reports by the *Sydney Morning Herald*'s resident correspondent. The *SMH* special correspondent Stanley James, a noted travel writer, contrived sardonic, florid, self-important prose sketches of persons and events, and rehearsed his visit in a later book (Thomas, 1886); his very presence indexed the seriousness with which the war was regarded in the Australian colonies. Yet another perspective, usually critical of both government and settlers, is provided in the Catholic missionary letters, reports and journals archived in AAN, 16.1 and 16.2 and in APM.

1 Olry to Min., 6 July 1878. Except where otherwise indicated, all Olry's reports are deposited in ANOM, Carton 43, were addressed to the Ministre de la Marine et des Colonies, and are in this chapter identified by date alone.

2 There were four theatres, from both French and Kanak perspectives: Ouraï and Bouloupari-Thio from 25–6 June 1878; Poya-Koné from 11 September Bourail from 22 September. The Kanak campaigns overlapped markedly and indigenous movements and relationships owed nothing to the colonial administrative boundaries which provided a convenient grid for military reportage and for organising the repression. The war followed a similar pattern in Ouraïl and Bouloupari-Thio, but the antecedents, character and conduct of the two northern campaigns were significantly different. Considerations of space and interpretive coherence dictated a particular focus here. The Ouraïl theatre was better documented and offered more promise for reinterpretation along the lines proposed, since there the conventional "outcome" seemed most clear-cut. "Ouraïl" means the French administrative district of that name; the indigenous coastal settlement from which the name derived is referred to as "Uaraï".

3 Belich (1986: 298, 305–10) saw ultimate Maori defeat in the New Zealand wars of the 1860s as qualified by the "degree of their success along the way". The eventual decline in Maori power and autonomy owed most to land selling and depopulation during the subsequent peace and was mitigated by the self-confidence engendered and the respect earned by their "formidable resistance".

4 One who did was M.-J. Mauger, a public servant in Nouméa (1976: 22 June 1878, in Dousset-Leenhardt, 1976: 231).
5 This was ruefully acknowledged in the official soul-searching inspired by the war (Trentinian, "Rapport sur les causes de l'insurrection Canaque en 1878", 4 Feb. 1879, ANOM, Carton 43, reprinted in Dousset, 1970: 127–59; Petit-Thouars to Min., 24 Apr. 1879, ANOM, Carton 32). Guiart (1968: 109) referred to the Kanak in 1878 as "men who tried, in a desperate spasm, to drive back the conquering colonisation". Yet the French had *not* previously "conquered" the districts of Bouloupari, Ouraïl, Moindou or Poya—colonists and penal administration had simply moved in; the indigenous neighbours of the settlement at Bourail had fought *with* the French on the *winning* side in a war in 1868. Olry (22 Dec. 1878) admitted towards the end of the war that "the native population was not gradually driven back by colonisation;... [settlers] interpolated themselves among the *canaques*, impossible to trace a frontier between the two races; they are mixed and that in the most dangerous conditions for colonists; everywhere *canaques* grouped, everywhere isolated colonists".
6 For contemporary textual traces of such groundwork see Amouroux and Place, [1881]: 66, 75, 99–106; Mauger, 1976: 17 July 1878, in Dousset-Leenhardt, 1976: 244–5; Améline to Fraysse, 4 Aug. 1878, AAN, 16.1; see also Anova-Ataba, 1969: 204–5, 207, 214, 217; Guiart, 1968.
7 The Canala "chiefs" had been enthusiastic allies of the French since the earliest days of the colony and their warriors had participated in numerous expeditions against other indigenous groups. Yet by the mid-1870s there was considerable unrest there over the extent of European settlement (Pritzbuer to Min., 28 Jan. 1876, ANOM, Carton 32). For speculation about the prior knowledge and involvement of these "chiefs" in the antecedents of the 1878 war see Mauger, 1976: 17 July 1878, in Dousset-Leenhardt, 1976: 245; Améline to Fraysse, 4 Aug. 1878, AAN, 16.1; Petit-Thouars to Min., 24 Apr. 1879, ANOM, Carton 32; Rivière, 1881: 129–38; Anova-Ataba, 1969: 214; Dousset-Leenhardt, 1976: 99–100.
8 Another account written by a Marine Infantry officer closer to the event imputed no overall plan or coordination to these incidents (Malherbe, 1995: 154–7).
9 In hypocritical contrast, European use of summary mass execution, in panic, revenge or as calculated deterrent—often of persons innocent of involvement in the war—was widely justified as no more than savages deserved, though some decried the practice as unworthy of a civilised society: e.g., Mauger, 1976: 30 June 1878, in Dousset-Leenhardt, 1976: 236, cf. 238; *N-C*, 4 July, 21 Aug. 1878; *SMH*, 12 July, 3 Sep. 1878; Amouroux and Place [1881]: 26, 68–9, 104–14; Thomas, 1886: 89–93.
10 For my strategic differentiation of "Kanak" and "allies" see Chapter Three, n. 2.

11 Chef du Service des Domaines to Directeur de l'Intérieur, "Rapport...", Conseil d'administration, 19 Dec. 1877, ANOM, Carton 102.

12 I assume that 22% of males were too young to bear arms and 18% were too old or otherwise unable or unwilling to do so. According to a "table of the population" of the "Hienghène tribe", done "as exactly as possible" in 1880 by the local mayor and the rural policeman, 500 out of 681 men, in a total population of 1,521, were "able to bear arms" (Kanappe, 1984: 90, cf 100–1). 166 of the 298 "children" listed would have been male, assuming their gender distribution was the same as that of adults (55.7% men). This would mean a male population of 847, of whom 59% were "warriors", 20% were "children" and 21% were other non-combatants. By contrast, the report of the commission of delimitation on the Canala and Houaïlou districts in 1876 cited the number of "children" in five "tribes": they amounted to 23% of the total, compared with fewer than 20% at Hienghène. In no case is it clear what "children" comprised (Chef du Service des Domaines to Directeur de l'Intérieur, "Rapport", Conseil d'administration, 17 Nov. 1876, ANOM, Carton 99).

13 *Ibid.* A further 240 warriors, who also became allies of the French, were enumerated at nearby Nakéty.

14 The figure cited ranged from 100, to 150, to 250, to "more than 400" (Lecouteur to Fraysse, 3 July 1878, AAN, 16.1; Olry, 6 July 1878; Maréchal to Olry, 10 July 1878, ANOM, Carton 43; *SMH*, 15 Oct. 1878; Rivière 1881: 134).

15 My calculation of French numbers derives from interested official statistics cited in an anonymous draft "Note pour le Journal Officiel", 16–17 Oct. 1878 (ANOM, Carton 43); they are qualified by some creative arithmetic based on ship movements detailed by the governor in SHM, BB4 1094 and 1106. For varied, more or less negative commentary on the quality of French troops, see Montrouzier to his brother, 26 Sep. 1878, AAN, 9.4; *SMH*, 4, 9, 15 Oct. 1878; *L'Avenir militaire: journal des armées de terre et de mer et de l'armée territoriale*, 1 Jan. 1879; Rivière, 1881: 201, 258–9; Thomas, 1886: 64, 76. By contrast, the C-in-C, French Pacific naval division, praised "the little soldiers of the Marine Infantry" as being "everywhere... on a very military footing, animated with the best spirit" (Petit-Thouars to Ministre, 21 Mar. 1879, SHM, BB4 1110). This, though, was at the war's end, when they were buoyed by victory and many had had months of toughening in the field.

16 Olry referred to Kanak as "persistent", "tenacious and brave", while an English volunteer described their "boldness" as "astonishing" (Olry, 8 Aug., 28 Sep. 1878; *SMH*, 17 Aug., 3 Sep., 28 Nov. 1878; cf. Thomas, 1886: 58–60). See Chapter Three on the relationship of the tropes "fear" and "prudence".

17 Durand to Min., 4 Mar. 1861, ANM, BB3 725; Le Bris to Ministre, 3 Jan. 1857, ANOM, Carton 42.

18 Olry had announced a reward for Ataï's head and a subscription was opened at Canala to provide "bounties for the heads of the principal rebel

chiefs... and for each enemy Canack head" (Olry to the warriors of Canala, 11 July 1878; Servan to the colonists of Canala, 26 July 1878, MS copies, AAN, 16.1).

[19] During December, 42 men from the *Ségond* participated in two expeditions lasting a total of three weeks, during which they burned a few huts and devastated some gardens; all were "worn out with fatigue" and 28 fell by the wayside with dysentery and severe foot injuries; despite seeing "numerous traces" of Kanak, they encountered none, apart from four prisoners and two severed heads taken by Nondo (Sevène to Richier, 10 Dec. 1878, SHM, BB4 1604).

[20] Variations on the romance of Servan, James' flamboyant "hero of the war", were recounted in several categories of text: official (Olry, 2 Aug. 1878; *Moniteur*, 10 July 1878; Rivière, 1881: 129–37, 164, 176, 195); settler (Amouroux and Place, [1881]: 12–13); Australian (Thomas, 1886: 95–102; *SMH*, 15 Oct. 1878). Servan's own telegraphed reports are archived in ATNC, MI10. Catholic missionaries in Thio and Nakéty, near Canala, were less impressed with Servan and the Canala pagans, who were in competition with their neophytes for captured women and refugees and generally got a better colonial press than the Christians (Moris to Fraysse, 26 July 1878; Améline to Fraysse, 4 Aug. 1878, AAN, 16.1; Moris to Fraysse, 1 Jan. 1879, AAN, 16.2).

[21] *N-C*, 31 July, 21 Aug. 1878; *SMH*, 13 Sep., 9 Oct. 1878; Moris to Fraysse, 1 Jan. 1879, AAN, 16.2.

[22] The passages quoted are located as follows, in order of citation: "Récit détaillé", 24 Oct.–22 Nov. 1878; Amouroux and Place, [1881]: 83, 93; Thomas, 1886: 101; Essarts to Olry, 8 Dec. 1878–20 Jan. 1879, in "Récit détaillé", 16 Jan.–5 Feb. 1879.

[23] For a sample of variously interested contemporary opinion on the contentious question of allied booty, particularly women, see Servan to Antonio, 1 Aug. 1878; Moris to Fraysse, 6 Nov. 1878; Gilibert to Fraysse, 19 Dec. 1878, AAN, 16.1, 16.2; Olry, 28 Sep. 1878; *SMH*, 15 Oct. 1878; Rivière, 1881: 138, 157, 225–6, 277; Thomas, 1886: 109–10.

[24] For one missionary's assessment of Nondo's strategy see Hilléreau to Fraysse, 26 Nov. 1878, AAN, 16.2. As early as the end of July, indications had been received from prisoners that the "rebels... are discouraged and seek refuge with faithful tribes" (*Moniteur*, 31 July 1878).

[25] Rivière was "astonished and charmed" by Naouno's command of polite French, his literacy, manners and crispness of response (1881: 260–5); he had had, said Olry, "a dose of education" ("Récit détaillé", 22 Dec. 1878–16 Jan. 1879). The missionaries at Bourail and Téremba depicted him by contrast as an able opportunist, who serially manipulated allegiance to both sides to his own advantage (Lecouteur, "Bulletin militaire", 14 Sept., 19 Oct. 1878; Lecouteur, Hilléreau, various letters to Fraysse, Sep.–Dec. 1878).

[26] "Récits détaillés", 22 Dec. 1878–21 Feb. 1979; Olry, 28 Sep. 1878, 5 Feb. 1879; Rivière, 1881: 261–78; Saussol, 1979: 242–9.

PART THREE

Encountering Christianity

Part Three distils the essence of three essays written between 1987 and 1993 in which I explored tensions and contests between indigenous and missionary aetiologies of illness, dying and death, and related conceptions of power and the sacred. The theme was an extended detour from the ethnohistory of fighting, though it grew directly from the archival reading I was doing. Perhaps because, like most of my generation in the West, I lack direct experience of war, perhaps because until recently I saw it mainly as a male activity, or perhaps because these indigenous and colonial wars were—relatively— not very lethal, I had been able to maintain a certain distance and detachment in reading and writing about past fighting, though not about its renewal in my personal present (Douglas, 1985a). But disease is another matter in the colonial history of the Pacific islands, especially Aneityum, which arguably endured the worst post-contact demographic disaster of any of them. Mission texts are strewn with harrowing images of human agony and loss which can move me to tears. I found reflexivity—giving cautious rein to my own emotions and apprehensions as parent, spouse, child, friend—both a self-defence against the pain vicariously encountered, and, by relativising my own imaginings, a key to perceiving, if not necessarily understanding, the endless, baffling variety of human response and reasoning in the face of trauma.

It was in the ancestral version of Chapter Six that I first spelled out the central ethnohistorical implication of an antiobjectivist epistemology: that if knowledge is a contingent, present process of knowing, then contemporary colonial texts are rendered historically critical by virtue of contemporaneity. Whatever their blinkers and limitations, they are littered with more or less unwitting traces of past indigenous actions. I argued that missionary texts have particular ethnohistorical value, religious positivism notwithstanding, because they routinely contain detailed descriptions of what people did and said, written by authors with long field experience and vernacular expertise, who knew vocationally, like ethnographic historians, that actions and words are the only humanly accessible indicators of what people might think and feel. The Presbyterian missionary Geddie jubilantly remarked "a change in the conduct and habits of the natives" of Aneityum as signalling "signs of progress" for his mission, but did not "dare...speak with confidence yet of conversions"—of "a more deeply seated change—a change of heart" (Geddie to BFM, 2 Oct. 1850, *MR* 1851: 88). Unfortunately, missionaries' style, discourse and tropes are so alien and abhorrent to modern secular, rationalist readers that the latter may in consequence reject, neglect or devalue the writings of often acute and sensitive witnesses. The chapters in Part Three demonstrate the pertinence of such texts to ethnographically informed, critical reading, against and despite the grain of their generic ethnocentricity and their authors' religious, racial, gender and class prejudices. In that early version of Chapter Six the demonstration was mostly empirical. Here I interleave the practice of narrative construction with reflexive commentary on its poetics.

CHAPTER SIX

Autonomous and Controlled Spirits: Indigenous Rituals and Encounters with Christianity in Melanesia

FOREWORD

*T*his chapter is a fairly distant offspring to a long article of similar title published in the Journal of the Polynesian Society *(1989). The article came out of a paper I gave to a La Trobe University conference on Lawrence and Meggitt's differentiation of the relative religiosity of Highlands and Seaboard societies in Papua New Guinea. The paper developed their passing insight (1965: 22–3) that the kinds of ritual practised in different societies, and associated expectations, might have parallelled contrasting notions of proper relationships between human beings and spirits, and differing roles attributed to the latter in human affairs—hence "autonomous and controlled spirits". The paper likewise picked up well-matured themes in my teaching the history of indigenous encounters with Christianity in the Pacific Islands: that indigenous religious ideas were cardinal, and that Christian concepts and practices—like novelties generally—were always, if unevenly and idiosyncratically, domesticated by Islanders, not only in "conversion" but also in negative and ambivalent engagements with Christianity and its bearers.*

The chapter thus bears implicitly on the concepts of agency and appropriation which are leitmotifs in my slightly later work on Christianity in Melanesia, reworked here as Chapters Seven and Eight. Neither term figured in the original article. Its articulating concept was "actions" and proclaimed focus "actors as intending subjects". "Culture", still singular, holistic and undifferentiated, was projected on to entire "societies". In reconstituting the article as Chapter Six it seems apt to retain the hint of essentialism—which had been qualified in the

Conclusion by the concept of "actors' interests"—as a marker of where I then was intellectually. There was also in the original article an unrecognised tension between the antithetical demands of narrative realism, textualisation and reflexivity, manifested in a tendency for uncontrolled shifts between text and story. Here, too, I seek in this chapter to retain traces of the dilemma—inherent to any antipositivist history—while explicitly problematising it.

PROLOGUE

The starting point for this chapter is Lawrence and Meggitt's suggestion that in religions in the Papua New Guinea Highlands there is an "assumption that success in ritual is not automatic but depends on securing the goodwill of spirit-beings... [which] are accorded freedom of action", whereas on the Seaboard ritual is mainly coercive, there tends to be a "weaker association between religion and morality, and... man, convinced that spirit-beings are under his direction, regards ritual techniques as the most valuable knowledge in his possession" (1965: 8, 19). I argue that the differences identified—in the degree of control exercised over spirits by human ritual performers and in the relationships conceived to exist between spirits and human morality—may be discernible as broad emphases throughout Melanesia, not necessarily on a highlands/seaboard basis.[1] The distinction is useful in the interpretation and comparison of Islanders' engagements with Christian missionaries and Christianity, within as well as between Pacific cultures. I discuss the southern Vanuatu islands of Tanna and Aneityum and the Isle of Pines, in the south of New Caledonia, roughly between 1840 and 1861.

THREE ISLANDS

The places specifically referred to—Port Resolution on Tanna, Anelcauhat on Aneityum, and Vao on the Isle of Pines (see Map 2)—had equivalent early exposures to the outside world: mission contacts from around 1840, with the settlement of Polynesian teachers by the LMS; regular European trading visits from a little earlier. Anelcauhat was from 1844 the site for a large trading station which, some four years before the arrival of the first permanent European missionaries, provided varied opportunities for local people to travel and experience novelties. Trading stations were established somewhat later on Tanna and the Isle of Pines.

Creative ethnographic reading in early European texts of the scanty, fleeting, ambiguous traces of indigenous social relations on Tanna and Aneityum in the mid nineteenth century suggests marked variations on common social and political themes (Spriggs,

1981: 180–4). Tanna was considerably larger, lacked linguistic unity and was highly fragmented politically, with relationships patterned through exchange links and rituals, rather than permanent territorial entities. Groups were either very small (households clustered in settlements) or shifted with context and situation. Leadership was accordingly situational and contextual, diffused and dependent on acknowledged access to and control of ritual knowledge (Adams, 1984: 5–22). In this chapter, "Tanna" means the area around Port Resolution. Aneityum had a common language, *anejom*, and was divided into seven "chiefdoms", *nelcau natimarid* ("canoe of a chief"), each centred spatially on a permanent river system, each identified with an hereditary "high chief", *natimarid*, at the apex of a local hierarchy of lesser "chiefs", *natimi alupas*, of "districts", *nari-nelcau* ("half canoe").[2] "Chiefs" had acknowledged ritual powers. There was no overarching political hierarchy, but chiefdoms were linked by competitive reciprocal food exchanges and by alliances and enmities (Inglis, 1890: 188–92; Spriggs, 1981, 1985: 27–33; Tepahae, 1997: 16 Aug. 1997). The Isle of Pines (Kounié) also had a single language, *nââ kwênyii*, and was unified in a complex dual hierarchy. Authority was distributed between a group of immigrant clans, rulers of the people, and the clans of earlier settlers, who controlled agrarian rituals and much of the land and according to myth had invited the newcomers to be their "chiefs" (Lambert, 1900: 256–64). The European obsession, then and now, with what Keesing called "attributing... 'entitivity' to a world of relations and processes" (1985: 204)—in this case, with identifying fixed, territorially defined political units—was particularly distorting in relation to Tanna. Tanna struck most Europeans as anarchic, whereas Aneityum, with its hereditary "chief"/priests controlling apparently permanent territories, looked deceptively familiar.

CONVERSION, COSMOLOGIES AND MISSIONARY STRATEGIES

The traces of Aneityumese actions strewn through mission texts suggest a radical transformation by the mid 1850s: they had, claimed their missionary, "to a large extent embraced Christianity" (Geddie to BFM, 3 Oct. 1854, *MR* 1855: 125, 135–6). In comparison, Tannese engagements with Christian missionaries as registered by the latter were strikingly ambivalent. In the quarter century after 1840, periodic conditional admittance of European, Polynesian and Aneityumese missionaries, with some associated behavioural modifications, was regularly succeeded by violent attacks and selfconscious assertions of continuing adherence to Tannese ways. Yet Adams could argue convincingly that by 1854 some Tannese "incorporated [some Christian] rituals into their traditional belief structure" (1984: 75).

Like Adams, I conceive "conversion" dialectically, in terms of appropriation and transformation of new concepts and rituals in dynamic indigenous cosmological and strategic contexts. Melanesian cultures were and are religious: they routinely attribute significant worldly occurrences to the actions of extrahuman beings with whom certain human actors have relationships through ritual. In detail, this common religious orientation has myriad variants, within as well as between island worlds. Subtle discriminations in the nature and expectations of indigenous ritual relationships with spirits might significantly affect meanings made of Christian missionaries, concepts and behaviour. This chapter follows a trail through separate congeries of contemporary mission texts to identify different sets of differences: between the closely related, similar social worlds of Aneityum and Tanna; within and over time—internal variations and transformations—in the Isle of Pines. It was the socially and personally critical issue of disease which evoked the sharpest textual imprint of such differences.

Missionaries also patently had religious world views: providence was their ultimate explanatory metaphor. Gross doctrinal differences between Catholics and Protestants were often of less strategic moment than quirks of personality. The Nova Scotian Presbyterian Geddie on Aneityum and the French Catholic Goujon on the Isle of Pines both stressed the promise of salvation rather than the threat of punishment and damnation, both avoided confrontation and sought as far as possible not to give offence by challenging or deriding local customs. "Prudence and discretion", "patience and pity" (Goujon, 1848–54: 7 July 1850) were their watchwords. Both questioned the "propriety and prudence of denouncing temporal judgment" "in the shape of temporal punishment for ... [Islanders'] idolatrous and wicked practices" (Geddie to Bayne, 20 Aug. 1861, *HFR* 1862: 36). On Tanna in 1842–3, however, the LMS's young Scottish Presbyterians Turner and Nisbet, by their own accounts, displayed no such scruples or caution: "After they had been fighting for months among themselves, contrary to all our entreaties," wrote Turner, "God commenced to punish them with a deadly epidemic in the form of dysentery" (1861: 18). Few nineteenth century missionaries would have questioned the aetiology, but its practical implications varied. Nisbet and Turner "*told ... [Tannese] that they must look to God as inflicting ... [the epidemic], and regard their sins as the cause of their sufferings*" (Nisbet to Directors, Mar. 1843, LMS, SSL, Box 16, my emphasis). Geddie, by contrast, maintained that "the Gospel is a message of mercy and love, and should be addressed to the heathen in its most attractive form"; "our zeal in the cause of God must be tempered with prudence, or we are in danger of defeating our object in living among them" (1848–57: 1 Sep. 1848–1975: 36; Geddie to Bayne, 20 Aug. 1861, *HFR* 1862: 36). Goujon would have concurred, at least before the mission began to receive significant local support after the annexation of New Caledonia and the Isle of Pines by France in 1853, when he became more confrontationist towards pagan opponents.

Islanders made meanings of what missionaries said and did in their own cultural and strategic terms, independent of missionaries' intentions and aspirations. Pragmatists like Goujon and Geddie made allowances for this, while deploring the necessity. Turner, Nisbet and their successors on Tanna before 1865 would not make concessions to what they saw as the works of Satan. The LMS teacher Ta'unga implied that his Polynesian colleagues on the Isle of Pines were also unwisely ethnocentric. Distinctions in missionary strategies were as subtle as indigenous cultural variations. Yet the dynamic processes by which particular Islanders made sense of particular missionaries' actions and words in specific island contexts produced complexes of actions and meanings which observers interested in outcomes might label in dramatically 'opposed terms: as missionary "success" and

Islanders' "conversion", on the one hand; as missionary "failure" and Islanders' continued adherence to "paganism", on the other.

TANNA

Contemporary texts[3] suggest that on Tanna spirits were not thought to play a significant autonomous moral regulatory role,[4] but that spiritual intervention in human affairs assumed correct ritual performance by an expert, possessor of both appropriate ritual knowledge and a sacred stone, *navetimin*, which a spirit inhabited (Adams, 1984: 13–14, 18–22). According to Turner:

> ... the principal religious worship is paid to their Aremha. The word *aremha* ... signifies ... *"dead man"*: ... they pray to the spirits of their forefathers.... To these they present the first fruits of the yam—breadfruit &c naming them and using a prayer ... They say "we plant a banana and it grows—we plant a bread fruit and it grows—we plant a yam and it grows—our forefathers certainly cause all this" (1842–3: 19 Dec. 1842).

It seems, accordingly, that Tannese aetiology of disease required the ritual action of a human agent: "It seems... all but impossible," marvelled Nisbet, "for them to separate the idea of human agency from the cause of disease. Consequently in almost all cases of severe suffering the natural enquiry is, *who caused it*" (Nisbet to Directors, Mar. 1843, LMS, SSL, Box 16, orig. emphasis). That is, on Tanna, almost all disease was caused by sorcery;[5] furthermore, only the sorcerer who claimed responsibility for a particular affliction could, or would, stop it, upon receipt of a propitiatory gift. Turner recorded the procedure, as told by a Tannese man:

> The people here have strange notions as to the greater part of the disease that prevails among them. It is supposed to be caused by certain "sacred men". It is supposed that if these persons get hold of a few crumbs of food—a banana skin—a drop of blood, or saliva, or any such rubbish whatever that they have it in their power to sicken and put the party to death to whom it belonged.... They go to a large tree—scrape off some of the bark—mix it with the stuff—get a stone and besmear it all over. They now roll the rubbish in a leaf, in a thin elongated form, tye

> it tightly, and it is ready for burning.... Whenever the burning commences, it is supposed that the person to whom the rubbish, or "nahak"... belonged is thrown into great pain, and that if it is permitted to burn until all is consumed, the party shall certainly die. Whenever a person is attacked with severe pain, it is thought that someone is burning his *nahak*. He causes a shell to be blown—a sign that he is willing to give a present to the man who has got his nahak if he will but give over burning it (1842–3: 19 Dec. 1842).

Violence against the presumed *nahak* burner was always a likely response to illness or deaths. John Paton, Turner and Nisbet's eventual missionary successor on Tanna, wrote: "Every sickness or calamity that befalls them is ascribed to some person exercising the Nahak, and if they can fix that person, he is waylaid and killed... [It] was formerly the cause of their wars" (Paton to Kay, 11 Oct. 1861, *HFR* 1862: 100).

Turner further acknowledged Tannese belief that certain fatal diseases, especially influenza and dysentery, had ravaged the island since the arrival of foreigners (1961: 92):

> Some blame these disease makers for it [dysentery], but the majority think that we are causing it as a punishment to those who do not attend our religious services.... When you think of the superstitious dread with which *men* among themselves are regarded, you will not wonder at the Tanese investing *us* with superhuman power (1842–3: 19 Dec. 1842, orig. emphasis).

In January 1843, Turner and Nisbet refused a propitiatory gift of a pig, offered with the plea that they end the dysentery epidemic. Nisbet replied bluntly to a Tannese interrogator that "as we did not cause disease so we could not take a pig" (1842–3: 13 Jan. 1843). However, they must have put the lie to the disclaimer by insisting that "it was the displeasure of Jehovah they ought to fear and that *his* favor above everything else ought to be sought after" (Turner, 1842–3: Mar. 1843, orig. emphasis). This would have confirmed for Tannese the personal responsibility Turner and Nisbet had probably already claimed by offering medicine to sick persons, in seeming response to the signal made to alert the sorcerer responsible (Nisbet, 1842–3: 19, 21, 26 Nov. 1842).

Turner, Nisbet and their successors on Tanna saw no valid connection between their own belief that epidemics were "a judgment... of Jehovah" (Turner, 1845: 2) and what Nisbet called "the deeply superstitious notion that the missionaries and teachers possess and exercise the power of causing disease" (1847: 4). For more than twenty years, there was a discernible rhythm in Tannese engagements with Polynesian, European and Aneityumese missionaries: a call for teachers and missionaries by some Tannese during good times, followed by widespread accusations of sorcery and threatened or actual violence against them when disease or natural disaster struck. The equation of a vengeful god and indigenous aetiologies of disease and curing meant, in Tannese terms, malicious missionary sorcery. It helped make Tanna a notably alien and difficult mission field (Editorial, July 1862, *HFR* 1862: 169–71; Adams, 1984).

ANEITYUM

The situation on Aneityum, about 60 kilometres from Port Resolution, looks rather different. Here, mission texts seem to imply (and a modern indigenous account confirms),[6] spirits were accorded some freedom of action in human affairs, played a regulatory role in human morality and were approached ritually through prayers, sacrifices and bargaining, rather than coercion, as with Tannese sorcery. My distinction between autonomous and controlled spirits, though, is only one of degree. All Pacific cultures, even the most hierarchical, conceived relationships between human beings and spirits in terms of reciprocal dependence: ritual involved an exchange, not always between equals, and, as Valeri said of the ancient Hawai'ians (1985: 66), "usually ha[d] an aim" other than disinterested worship. Unresponsive or unsatisfactory spirits might be abandoned and made irrelevant by depriving them of ritual offerings.[7] Spirits were adopted or replaced, and perceived relative power was a key criterion of spiritual efficacy; this could be of critical significance for Islanders' engagement with Christianity's god.

Sorcery was certainly not unknown in Aneityum: according to Geddie, "chiefs are priests also. Those whom I know are either disease makers, or fruit makers, or thunder & lightening makers, or hurricane makers" (1848–57: 1 Mar. 1851–1975: 82; Inglis, 1887: 24). In 1852 he described what sorcerers did:

> When a disease maker wishes to cause sickness he endeavours to procure a portion of the person's hear ['hair'] or some fragment of his food or dress. He then chews up a quantity of sacred leaf, and puts the whole into his charming pot, which he sets on the fire. He then prays to his *natmasses*[8] to inflict disease on the person whom he wishes to charm. The process is called *naragess*,[9] and those who practise it are much feared by the people. It is not surprising that the disease makers have much influence when it is believed that the power of life and death is in their hands. This class however is hated as well as feared by the natives at large (1848–57: 4 Feb. 1852–1975: 118).

It seems clear, though, that *natmas* were also believed to intervene autonomously in human affairs to punish human actions.[10] According to Geddie's Scottish colleague Inglis, complacently negative about other people's spirits: "earth, and air, and ocean were filled with *natmasses*,... all malignant, who ruled over everything that affected the human race". "Benevolent deities they have none", he asserted. As on Tanna, stones "were the chief *fetishes*, or representatives of the *natmasses*" (1852: 529; 1887: 30, orig. emphasis).

Associated with the autonomous and moral regulatory roles of *natmas* was a taboo-like concept, "*itaup*" (Geddie, 1848–57: 1 Sep. 1848–1975: 35):[11] infringements were believed to make *natmas* angry and vindictive. Soon after Geddie's arrival, Samoan teachers were accused of offending the *natmas* by breaking a taboo on coconuts. "We of course", wrote Geddie, unusually relativist for his ilk, "pleaded ignorance of the restriction, but promised to observe it in time to come" (1848–57: 1 Sep. 1848–1975: 35). Before long some Aneityumese were extending the concept of *itap* to include Christian taboos, including Sabbath observance. This was general domestication of a new god and his taboos rather than reflex compliance with missionary injunctions, since obdurate opponents of the mission chose to act thus, as well as "the christian party", yet only in life-threatening cases—widow-strangling and fighting—did Geddie warn "that they would have to answer to God... at the last tribunal" (Geddie to BFM, 2, 3 Oct. 1850, *MR* 1851: 70, 101–2; 1848–57: 19 Feb 1849–1975: 46–7).

I contrast Tanna and Aneityum thus. On Tanna, where spirits were the equals of certain human actors, who controlled them through correct ritual performance, relationships with missionaries were seen as contests of rival sorcerers. Turner and Nisbet certainly thought so. On Aneityum, where "the sacred men...are the *servants* of the Natmasses" (my emphasis), the contest mainly engaged rival spirits. Opposition to Christianity was initially strongest amongst the "chiefs", who, because their authority was "priestly rather than...kingly", saw "that if Christianity succeeds, their craft is in danger" (Geddie, July 1849, in Patterson, 1882: 206; Inglis, 1887: 24). By early 1851, despite the risk that "if a chief embraces Christianity he must...give up his claim to supernatural powers and...lose much of his influence over the people", several "chiefs" and priests were already influential professors of Christianity; within six months Geddie reported that many had "renounced heathen worship" and sought Christian instruction (1848–57: 1 Mar., 25 Aug. 1851–1975: 82, 99).

Between 1848 and 1854, the actions and self-identification of a majority of Aneityumese underwent such radical transformation as to attract retrospectively the label "conversion" (Inglis, 1890: 105; McArthur, 1978: 281–2; Spriggs, 1985). Read literally, Geddie's "Journal" and published contemporary writings comprise a classic teleological Christian narrative of "the contest between the darkness and light", in which, thanks to "a vigorous agency and the divine blessing", "truth must and will triumph at last" (Geddie to BFM, 2, 3 Oct. 1850, *MR* 1851: 89, 100). Read critically against the grain, they suggest the inadequacy of purely impositional or simple replacement conceptions of conversion which fail to take account of the significance of indigenous agency and experience in transforming themselves. It is along these lines that I explore contemporary textual traces of Aneityumese aetiologies of disease.

Not long after his arrival, Geddie was reportedly accused of angering *natmas* by closing their route to the sea. Aneityumese "said that we would not suffer as their natmasses could not interfere with us, but that they would be visited by sickness and death by them" (1848–57: 1 Sep. 1848–1975: 36). In March 1849 some foreigners were evidently thought vulnerable to the wrath of the *natmas*: Aneityumese attributed "remittent and intermittent fevers" suffered by Samoan teachers and European traders to "a punishment inflicted... for breaking... [local] tabus". This was probably malaria, an endemic local sickness, rather than a recently introduced disease. Belief in the "existance and power" of *natmas*, which had begun to waver, was said to have been reinforced (1848–57: 1 Mar. 1849–1975: 47). All illness, Geddie learned, "is supposed by them to be caused by evil spirits who possess the sick person". He described the ritual ("wild ceremonies") by which a priest attempted to expel the spirit, adding: "We are blamed by many for causing the present sickness"—presumably malaria again, since it afflicted both Aneityumese and foreigners (1848–57: 1 Mar. 1850–1975: 67–8). This casual remark might be taken as an accusation of sorcery against the missionaries; however, it seems that blame attached not to the missionaries' rituals directly, but to the presumed offence taken by the *natmas* at the missionaries and the "indignities done to them, by those who profess to be christians... such as their eating sacred food, cutting down sacred groves, breaking and burning the alters of the *natmasses* &c." (Geddie, 1848–57: 20 Oct. 1850–1975: 77, 79).

Nohoat, the *natimarid* ("high chief") of Anelcauhat was depicted in Geddie's letters and journal as deeply ambivalent professing terror of the vengeance of the *natmas*, but wanting the missionaries to stay because their residence enhanced his prestige and he trusted Geddie's medicines: Geddie remarked that "a few of the natives place much confidence in our methods of treating disease" (1848–57: 1 Mar. 1850–1975: 67). Towards the end of 1850 he reported a sharp division between opponents and supporters of the mission. When several of the Christian party, including a "chief", died, the "heathen party" was triumphant and announced that the deaths were "a judgement inflicted by the natmasses on [the Christian party]... for embracing the new religion" (1848–57: 29 Mar. 1851–1975: 87). Nohoat seemed near panic. He charged Geddie and the Samoan teachers "with being the cause of sickness and death among them, and said that they had none of these things untill we came to their island.... He was evidently in great fear", saying he expected to die himself "on account of the offence we had given to the natmasses". Geddie replied that Christianity "did not save people from death, but taught them to be happy after death". Nohoat was "unconvinced and angry"; he praised the Tannese for bringing an end to sickness and death by driving away their missionaries and killing a teacher (1848–57: 4 Mar. 1851–1975: 84).

But in July 1851 accusations against Christianity as "the immediate cause of sickness and death" were silenced by an influenza epidemic which caused heavy mortality among the opponents of the mission. Most of the Christian party recovered, due, thought Geddie, to "time[ly] use of medicine", whereas the pagans "lie exposed in the open air, calling on their natmasses in vain to save them. The applications for medicine have been numerous of late" (1848–57: 10 July 1851–1975: 90). Charlotte Geddie added: "We dispense a great deal of medicine, the natives place a great deal of confidence in our *skill*,—their diseases are generally simple and easily removed if taken in time. Tea is in great demand... many think tea a cure for every disease".[12] In November 1851 an attempt was made to burn Geddie's house and church, apparently by "heathens". A non-violent confrontation between Christian and pagan parties followed, during which it emerged, to general surprise, that "the Christian party far outnumbered their enemies and contained most of the chiefs and leading men of the island". The "heathen" admitted "they were now only a handful, and it would be useless to contend longer against the new religion". Geddie, with a vocationally keen eye for God's "goodness" and "mercies" as well as the proper phasing of a conversion narrative, subsequently called the episode "a turning point in the history of the islands" and opined that it proved that "He that is for us is truly greater than those who are against us" (1848–57: 28 Nov. 1851–1975: 108–9).

Evidently most Aneityumese drew the same lesson, but in locally meaningful ways. They confirmed it by what I take to have been a deliberate program of breaking and testing taboos, which punctuated Geddie's journal from December 1851 to October 1852: widow strangling virtually ceased, sacred ground was planted, images of *natmas* were desecrated, sacred stones discarded, commoners were buried on land, like "chiefs", rather than at sea, sacrifices to *natmas* ceased or were conducted in secret, sorcery packages were publicly destroyed, prohibited food was eaten, all apparently without reaction from *natmas*. Geddie related how he helped Nohoat wrestle with and conquer his fears of offending the *natmas*, while simultaneously the missionary reinforced his own reputation as a curer:

> I saw a woman preparing the bark of a certain tree which ... was prohibited to the chiefs and sacred men, and eaten only by the common people. I asked the woman for a piece and began to eat it. Nohoat looked strangely at me, and then mustered courage to ask for a piece and began to eat also.... Nohoat appeared uneasy all the evening and at last retired to rest. He had not been long in his room ... when he sent for me, and told me that he was not sick, but he had a feeling which he could not describe, and which prevented sleep. I thought at once of the prohibited food which he had eaten. Knowing his confidence in medicine I told him not to be uneasy as I would soon cure him. I made up a pleasant and harmless draught for the old man which he drank. It had the desired effect on him for he soon sent me word that he was cured and all his strange sensations has [sic] passed away (1848–57: 1 Dec. 1851–1975: 110).

Repeated demonstrations of ineffectiveness presumably undermined the credit of the *natmas*, while, conversely, the Geddies' success as curers enhanced their god's prestige and their own ritual reputation in Aneityumese eyes. In 1854 Geddie claimed that "many now say that their *natmasses* are impotent, and that our God must be omnipotent, kind and true"; he attributed the weakening of "the prejudices of the heathen" to the fact that only one of 50 church members had died in more than two years (Geddie to BFM, 29 Nov. 1854, *MR* 1855: 167–8). Though mortality from endemic local diseases continued at times to be high, the ravages of introduced infectious diseases seem to have moderated temporarily. Medicines, better nursing, and the cessation of fighting, infanticide, widow-strangling and "chiefly" polygyny had, Geddie thought, stimulated some increase in the population, "to an extent that makes the natives wonder", and called in doubt the "general impression on the part of the natives [of these islands], that ... [Christianity] brings disease and death along with it" (Geddie to BFM, 3 Oct. 1854, *MR* 1855: 135–6).

There were obvious similarities between Tannese and Aneityumese religions, such that Aneityumese teachers were the most welcome and effective mission workers on Tanna (Stallworthy and Gill, 1859: 2; Adams, 1984: 73–6). No mission text that I have seen explicitly contrasted indigenous Aneityumese beliefs with Tannese.[13] Nonetheless, missionary narratives of particular episodes on each island consistently, if unwittingly inscribed veiled traces of differences along the lines proposed. To summarise: Aneityumese attributed disease to possession by *natmas*, supposed to have been offended by human infringements or to have chosen to respond to a sorcerer's ritual; Tannese tenaciously attributed disease to sorcery and gave the sorcerer primary responsibility. In this representation, Aneityumese aetiology was less determinist than Tannese and allowed for a wider variety and degree of contributory human actions. Geddie's tact, caution and attractive presentation of the gospel doubtless helped, but his credit and success as a curer on Aneityum apparently did not entail the automatic Tannese corollary of direct responsibility for the disease treated. Furthermore, the Christian notion of an omnipotent and inscrutable deity, towards whom propitiation was the only appropriate ritual mode, bore more resemblance to Aneityumese ideas of divinity and ritual than Tannese, making for readier mutual translatability and integration of concepts and ritual practices, as Inglis acknowledged: "The natives had a distinct belief in a future state, and in the efficacy of prayer and sacrifice to propitiate their offended deities...and although their beliefs were in many respects exceedingly erroneous, yet they were of great use to us in helping to lead them to understand and receive the Scriptural doctrines on these vital points" (1887: 31).

Through their practice of sacrifice to *natmas*, Aneityumese had an experiential familiarity with a principle of atonement. Possibly because they did conceive *natmas* as mainly vengeful and unpredictable—"selfish and malignant" Inglis put it (1887: 32)— many might have been attracted to a deity whom his priests successfully presented as both "omnipotent" *and* "kind", and whose responses to human behaviour, whether approved or disapproved, might have seemed more consistent and predictable.[14] The Christian promise of salvation—of hope in death—appears also to have struck a chord: the bereaved were consoled by "the prospects which christianity holds out beyond the grave" of again seeing dead relatives and friends (Geddie, 1848–57: 29 Mar. 1851–1975: 88), whereas in indigenous conception apparently only those who went simultaneously to the place of the spirits stayed together after death.[15] In at least one case, this worked to the mission's disadvantage:

> A heathen woman ... long opposed us on the ground that if her husband died she would not be strangled. Her husband did die, and her life was saved by force. She now holds out on the ground that if she embraces the gospel she will go to heaven after death and thus be seperated [sic] for ever from her husband who she supposes to be in hell (1848–57: 26 Aug. 1852–1975: 140).

To Geddie, the reasoning was wilfully "obstinate", the product of a "carnal mind"; another theoretical perspective might discern no inconsistency, but a common tendency for all Aneityumese, *whatever their religious allegiances*, to make similar meanings of the missionaries' message, derived from a common, flexible cultural logic (cf. Burt, 1982: 383; Keesing, 1989b: 209). Inglis later admitted that, while Christian Aneityumese had "completely lost" their belief in (the effectiveness of?) *natmas*, they retained for a long time "a partial belief that in the heathen islands around the power of witchcraft remained". Young men sometimes returned from Tanna or Erromango, islands renowned for the lethal power of their sorcerers, with "material for witchcraft", and threatened or attempted to perform sorcery, causing sickness or serious apprehensiveness in their proposed victim (1890: 22–5). Once a Tannese ritual expert working on Aneityum was called upon successfully to remove such an affliction. Aneityumese Christians continued to draw an aetiological equation between curing and ritual—not without reason, modern medical science might say ironically, given the missionaries' pharmacopoeia and contemporary medical logic:

> they ... thought that our cures, like those of their sacred men, were effected by incantation, and that one medicine must be able to cure every disease. ... It took years ... to make them all comprehend the difference between the charms and incantations of their sacred men, and the medicines and the medical treatment of the missionaries (Inglis, 1890: 183–4).

THE 1861 MEASLES EPIDEMIC

Differences between Tannese and Aneityumese aetiologies of disease and their implications for mission security and success were dramatically displayed in the contrasting interpretations of and responses to the epidemic of measles and dysentery which devastated the two islands and much of the southwest Pacific in 1860–1. Within "three or four months", Geddie mourned, "about one-third of the population [of Aneityum] were...swept into the grave" (Geddie to Bayne, 26 Aug. 1861, *HFR* 1862: 38),[16] demonstrating tragically the fragility of any earlier minor demographic recovery. In parts, at least, of Tanna mortality was probably as great (Adams, 1984: 116–33).

On Aneityum "an incendiary" fired the new church and schoolhouse. Within a week, a violent hurricane and tidal wave caused great damage and destroyed much food. "The natives", maintained Geddie, "regard it as a judgment on the island for that wicked deed [the arson]", "as indications of God's anger against the island"; more generally, many thought it "a judgment on them because they did not sufficiently value their privileges". He commented wryly that "the natives of this and other evangelised islands seem to view all calamities as the effects of sin...like the Jews of old". Ever the optimist in assessing divine intent, he preferred personally to regard "the visitations of God" as "needed...trials", more than punishment. The general Aneityumese response to "these sifting times" was said to be resignation, readiness "to submit to God's will in all things" and "more than usual attention to religion"; Geddie knew of no case of backsliding. Their wrath, once the epidemic had abated, was reserved for the suspected arsonist, who was "among the last of the Gospel opposers on Aneiteum". Most of the "chiefs" who tried the accused man wanted him put to death, but were persuaded that the evidence against him was only circumstantial. He was said to have been relieved to receive, for merely threatening to burn the church, a punishment of "thirty lashes, the confiscation of his land and trees, and banishment for life to a remote district of the island".[17] This was not the first time Geddie had found excessive the zeal of Christian Aneityumese. Yet their new god was not just a scourge of the unworthy: a year or two later Geddie noted, they received an unexpected breadfruit crop joyfully "as a direct interposition of divine goodness" (Geddie to Bayne 17 June 1863, *HFR* 1863: 313). Divine reward was a sadly rare occurrence on Aneityum. The missionaries estimated that in fewer than seven years the population had been halved by measles and subsequent epidemics of diphtheria and whooping cough (McArthur, 1974: 77–80).

The measles epidemic on Tanna was similarly followed by successive natural disasters.[18] The missionaries gathered that it was widely believed by Tannese that their troubles were caused either by Jehovah, in automatic response to ritual performed by Christian missionaries and teachers, or by *nahak* sorcerers anxious to drive out their rivals. Reported Tannese responses varied: some shunned the missionaries; others interrupted services to prevent effective ritual communication with Jehovah; some threatened violence; around Port Resolution, where for a time mortality was reasonably limited, attendance at services increased, apparently because the missionary Paton's rituals and medicine were presumed to have protected people in the immediate vicinity of the mission station. In early 1862, however, with sickness and death once more rife about the harbour, Tanna was again abandoned by its European missionaries.

Paton's colleague Matheson, based in the south of the island, undertook "a careful investigation of the motives, by which ... [Tannese] were individually actuated in attending public worship" (Matheson to Bayne, 1 Feb. 1861, *HFR* 1861: 301–2). His enquiry confirmed the missionaries' suspicion that in Tanna "we have all along had something of the form, ... [but] little or none of the real power of vital godliness". Beginning with "chiefs", Matheson probed Tannese expectations of Christianity. "Why were they so punctual in their attendance upon the house of God, and at the same time refuse to give up any of their heathenish practices?" A typical response came from a man deeply impressed by the wealth in European property Aneityumese had derived from their resident missionaries. He welcomed and protected Aneityumese teachers and thus received many material benefits. But when told that being a sincere Christian meant renunciation of all other gods and "heathen" practices, "he thought that I was requiring more of him and his people than God would require. To interfere with their long established manners, customs, &c., is in their estimation an unpardonable sin". This was a recurrent theme: on Tanna, far more than Aneityum, missionaries heard "the conduct of our fathers" objectified as characteristically Tannese, different from the ways of others, and proper (Paton to Kay, 24 May 1860, *RPM* 1860: 406). Particularly insistent were dignitaries called *yani en dete*, "master of the canoe", guardian of social well-being and local values and practices. "They consider", lamented Matheson:

> that if they suffer teachers and missionaries to live among them in order to supply them with temporal necessaries and in a measure to insure the security of foreigners trading with them, that they are a praiseworthy people. But so soon as you get a sufficient acquaintance with their language to recommend to them the gospel of Jesus, to interfere with their idolatry, ... so soon do they consider themselves justified in treating you as bad as they can..., provided you persist in speaking to them of Jesus. In short, they will let you live if you let them die in their sins (Matheson to Bayne, 1 Feb. 1861, *HFR* 1861: 302).

From the outset, Tannese seem to have engaged enthusiastically with modernity, but on their own assertive terms—what outsiders saw and see as intransigence. They were perhaps empowered by an indigenous cosmology which gave the assurance that men with appropriate ritual knowledge could control extrahuman beings for personal and collective benefit and to the detriment of rivals and enemies. Outsiders who challenged the propriety of Tannese ways and values were rebuffed by the confident invocation of "our conduct" as an indigenous political ideology (Paton to Kay, 10 June 1861, *RPM* 1862: 38). Presbyterian Christianity, widely adopted from the end of the nineteenth century, was converted into "Tanna law", only to be widely repudiated from the late 1930s in the name of *kastom* ("custom" in Bislama). In one or other guise—notably "cargo cult"—the theme of *kastom* pervades texts on Tanna by anthropologists and other twentieth century fieldworkers, as well as popular works and films:[19] *kastom* has clearly been central to the contested forging of Tannese identities, in opposition to external imposed authority of whatever persuasion, colonial or national.

A visiting LMS delegation in September 1861 commented:

> The contrast between the conduct of the Aneiteum people and those of the neighbouring islands is very striking. While the Tanese... ascribe their calamities to secondary sources, and vent their rage on those whom they suspect have had a hand in originating the evils from which they suffer, the Aneiteumese meekly and submissively look beyond man and secondary causes, to God; regarding their troubles as fatherly chastisements, and seeking to improve them to their own good and his glory (Murray, 1862: 2).

Read transparently, the passage is a literal description of how far Aneityumese had moved from indigenous assumptions. Read against the grain, its evangelical tropes and agenda camouflage the obscure textual imprint of differing aetiological emphases in the indigenous cosmologies. Apart from redefining the origins of and specific reasons for divine judgement, the Christian Aneityumese aetiology invoked was consistent with indigenous ideas, which might attribute disasters to the displeasure of *natmas* with human actions without requiring ritual intervention of a human agent. Since Geddie consistently "gave prominence to the fact that Christ came not to destroy men's lives, but to save them" (Inglis, 1887: 254), the intimate link drawn teleologically by Aneityumese between calamities and a wrathful Jehovah's judgement and punishment for human infringements cannot be seen as a mere reflex of European missionary teachings.[20] I argue, rather, that meanings made by Aneityumese of the latter and their application to the interpretation of experience were significantly informed by indigenous assumptions about the roles played by spirits in human affairs.

ISLE OF PINES

In November 1842, local people at Vao, on the Isle of Pines (Kounié), killed the crew and passengers of the trading brig *Star*. The passengers were three LMS teachers from Rarotonga and Samoa who had taken refuge on the brig when threatened by Touru, the "high chief", *vâ vörö*. In published mission and popular representations they were innocent victims of Touru's savage retaliation for unscrupulous assaults on his family by the traders (Turner, 1861: 412–16; Shineberg, 1967: 205–14). Another teacher, Ta'unga, then stationed at Touaourou, on the nearby mainland of New Caledonia, gave a different interpretation based on local information.[21] He depicted the teachers as the main objects of the attack on the *Star*.

There were plausible traces in contemporary mission texts of Touru's grievances against the teachers. A visiting LMS missionary described approvingly how "on the Sabbath they stand up in his presence to preach". This infringement of the customary protocol requiring "subjects" to crouch in the presence of the "high chief" spurred him to angry parody: "[he] throws himself down in a reclining posture in return" (Slatyer, 1842: 18 July 1842). Ta'unga's narrative (1968: 50–3) reads as a litany of failure by the teachers to meet exchange obligations incurred in their original admittance, probably conceived locally as adoption to the status of "subjects". One failed to help Touru's sons when they were assaulted by traders, provoking the "chief" to demand of the others: "'Why didn't he restrain the Europeans? My family was nearly killed by them. Why is it that he himself has fled? Why do you ill-treat me and my family? Why do you side with the Europeans? Aren't I your master?'". They, too, sought refuge on the *Star*, and repeatedly refused gifts Touru sent to encourage their return. Touru also sent a gift of food to the captain, "so that he would not detain the teachers", but when the Europeans saw the teachers' fear, they kept the gift and forcibly expelled the messengers, including the "chief's" son. Touru, enraged, decided to attack the ship, but it had sailed for Sydney. Some weeks later the *Star* reappeared at the Isle of Pines, and, wrote Ta'unga, "when the people found that it was the very ship which was carrying the teachers they reported it to the chief". The fatal attack was launched at once.

Imprinted in mission texts, particularly Ta'unga's, were traces of an even more serious local accusation against the teachers: that they were the "evil priests" of "a man-eating god" (1968: 46–9, 53; Buzacott to Tidman, 4 Jan. 1844, LMS, SSL, Box 16). Kounié people charged Ta'unga: "'[We] have died through you, for you prayed to your God to kill every one of us'". They claimed the traders said that Jehovah was not the Europeans' god, but the god of Samoa and Rarotonga. Touru advised the "chief" of Touaourou to "kill" the teachers "'or else just chase them away'". The teachers had already unwittingly proclaimed themselves as sorcerers by attributing numerous deaths from an epidemic of previously unknown sickness to the people's failure to receive the word of Jehovah: "the chief had been asking why they died. We said, 'It is because you have not received the word of God'" (Ta'unga, 1968: 37–8, 53, 63). Certainly the traders must have placed themselves in the local category of enemy by assaulting the "chief's" family and using violence in support of the teachers. But the teachers—self-proclaimed sorcerers, unreliable dependents, rejectors of "chiefly" prestations, deserters—probably threatened public well-being and hence the "high chief's" authority in ways that total outsiders did not. His responsibility to maintain community welfare and harmony demanded expulsion or execution of the causers of disease.

Ta'unga told how subsequently Touru arrived at Touaourou with a large party intending to kill the teachers resident there He demanded: "'Who are you to create all this trouble? Where did you find these things that have caused all our customs and our gods to disappear? Are you chiefs that you should start all these new sayings?'". Boldly confronted by Ta'unga, Touru relented, accepted a gift of yams from the teachers and made return gifts of "a manilla hat[,] ... a dark scarf[,] ... a coloured shirt and ... a huge quantity of food". "This", Ta'unga explained, "was similar to their customary way of behaving towards their own priests. That was the way they intended it". Anthropologically, Touru's prestation looks like an attempt to control the new god by encompassing him and his priests within a familiar paradigm of ritual exchange. In a later text Ta'unga said that Touru told him that "the power of the teachers' God" had stopped him killing them there and then (1968: 65–7). These enigmatic texted residues suggest that the "high chief" was in a quandary as to the appropriate strategy, exchange or rejection, to deal with the agents of a malevolent but powerful god.

When Goujon,[22] the French Marist, arrived at the Isle of Pines in 1848, after Touru's death, the Polynesians were vividly recalled as sorcerers. He described his first meeting with Touru's titular successor, his young grandson Vendegou. Asked "if we were missionaries", Goujon "answered yes: at once the word missionary was repeated softly by every mouth. He asked me then if we were Samoha or protest[ant] missionaries. I answered loudly, so that everyone heard it: no, we are French Catholic missionaries. Then we heard these words again repeated: French missionaries". Whatever the distinction meant, the word "missionary" was evidently significant. Goujon no doubt had a stake in denigrating his rival predecessors, but the story of their improprieties served him strategically, to justify extreme caution, rather than doctrinally. The "Samoans" were supposed to have used the threat of disease to force compliance with their customs and religious practices. When disease struck, killing many, the local people threatened the teachers. Islanders "recalled that at daybreak ... [the 'Samoans'] made signs and grimaced". That, explained Goujon, "made us judge it prudent to hide to say Holy Mass" and to eschew ritual gestures in public (1848–54: 15, 20 Aug., 10 Sep. 1848). The Marists did not proselytise for nearly two years and it was a further eighteen months before their first public ritual, a Sunday service held in a traditional round house before the "high chief" and assembled local dignitaries. Henceforth the Sabbath was generally observed as a local taboo.

The Catholics' reticence paid off in May 1852, when serious respiratory infections caused dozens of deaths and much sickness. At first in some places the missionaries were blamed and sick people were hidden from them or denied being ill. Innovations, especially Sunday observance and primers, were held responsible for the widespread suffering and abandoned by many. But when the "chiefs" and senior men debated the matter publicly they agreed that, although sickness had been "brought by the Europeans", no action should be taken against them, as the deaths were attributable to "their [own] *Dw* [*du*] or evil spirit", which, it was generally believed, "makes them die...before they reach extreme old age" (Goujon 1848–54: 10 June 1852).

Goujon had already written about belief in "the evil spirit (the du) which makes [people] ill, or die" and learned that it was an invisible presence recently brought from Maré in the Loyalty Islands (1848–54: 16 Sep. 1849). Early in 1850 one of his colleagues who attended a public debate on the *du* told him that it was attributed a moral regulatory role, inflicting illness on prominent men in punishment for general social transgressions: such as the deemed misbehaviour of local women, who, in return for tobacco, chose to have sexual relations with European sailors during the yam-growing season when local men were compelled to practise abstinence. A young woman was strangled "to expiate the common offences" and propitiate the offended *du* blamed for the illness of Touru's second son, Ouatchioumé, who served as "regent" for the young Vendegou (Goujon, 1848–54: 1 Jan. 1850). This was the only reference in Goujon's journal to the *du* as moral arbiter. The more consistent emphasis, thrashed out in public by "chiefs" and elders, was on its arbitrary vindictiveness, envy and *modus operandi* of possessing or being possessed by individuals who caused death by sorcery:

> This Dw keeps at a sometimes quite considerable distance from the sick person or from the chosen victim; he wears around his neck a mysterious bag containing nails from his former victims; he tempers the end of his dart in his bag and throws it at the sick person. If he hits, the blow is mortal. He deems that he has aimed straight when he sees blood run from his little bag (Goujon, 1848–54: 10 June 1852).

Goujon recalled that "the greatest obstacle we met on our arrival ... [was] a strong prejudice or a kind of superstition which caused the natives to regard us as maleficent beings bringing amongst them famine, illnesses and death". Fear of sorcery allegations led the Catholics, unlike Geddie, to be reticent in offering remedies: "because of their superstitions, that could sometimes bring troubles upon us and prejudice our ministry" (Goujon to Douarre, 1 Mar. 1850, AAN, 8.2; 1848–54: 5 Dec. 1849). Yet unlike the LMS teachers, the Marists heard no open accusations or threats. Perhaps because killing the teachers had not ended the deaths, alternative explanations were canvassed, centred on another recently-arrived spirit, the *du* from Maré, to which the Catholics might be an antidote. In a key juncture in Goujon's narrative, the Islanders gathered after Ouatchioumé's death early in 1850 for the post-harvest ritual presentation and distribution of first yams. In offering a formal share to Goujon, an invited guest, the presiding elder declaimed: "Drive out the Du... from the Isle of Pines, and stay with us".[23] During and after this gathering, three men were killed, "accused of being possessed or of possessing the Du which had made the... chief die". Straight after the first death, a warrior rushed threateningly into the crowd, but was pacified to near insensibility when approached by Vendegou, who gave him a feather "as a symbol of peace". At the first sign of trouble Goujon had taken refuge with the old men, one of whom, in a whispered running commentary, told him that the man was the killer, but that the *du* which had possessed his victim had switched to him and could only be exorcised by the "high chief" (1848–54: 28 Feb., 6 Mar. 1850).

According to Guiart (1963: 243), an engraving of a stone published in Lambert's mission ethnography (1900: 295) was identified at the Isle of Pines in the 1950s as the *du* referred to by Goujon. It was a piece of serpentine or jade, worked in the shape of a "grooved double cone" (Guiart), a "double marlinspike" (Lambert). Guiart thought it was the earliest form of the *doki*, or red god, which was imported from the Loyalty Islands or Vanuatu and inspired several virulent outbreaks of sorcery fears: most notably after 1920 in northern New Caledonia, amid widespread indigenous conviction of declining numbers due to high rates of disease and mortality (1959: 10–13). "Traditional sorcerers", Guiart claimed, had been "official personages, acting... the most often under the patronage of their group, and always to the cost of persons foreign to their clan". The "new" variety operated in secret, using novel, foreign techniques: anyone could cheaply obtain a *doki*, which might even be used against a kinsperson who had provoked anger or jealousy. The possessor of a *doki* was reciprocally possessed by the god: "it is a sanguinary and insatiable god; it must be fed regularly with human victims, otherwise it will strike the whole family of its possessor and finally the latter himself" (1959: 10, 12).

Logically, a belief in domesticated resident sorcerers, who attack external rivals and enemies, implies that one's own calamities are attributable to the latters' sorcerers. Ta'unga reported just such a pattern:

> When the people realised that a disease had become widespread they would fetch the priests and ask them, "Where does this sickness come from?" And the priests would tell them. It came from another district... Some group had fought against them, that was why it came. And when the people heard, they would make war on the people of that place.

Ta'unga saw clear implications of this aetiology for himself and his fellow teachers: "That was how many of our mission teachers died and that means were sought to kill us. Great was our affliction from this very cause, for many epidemics occurred while we were there and we were blamed for them. That was why many of us were killed" (1968: 59).

In these elusive textual traces of long past indigenous actions and words I discern a thread of pattern, which I was once tempted to represent as a shift between two kinds of sorcery. Ta'unga put an unequivocal case for unproblematic indigenous attribution of the 1842 epidemic to foreign sorcerers and their familiar—the mission teachers and their god Jehovah of Samoa and Rarotonga; it was an explanation encouraged by traders and unwittingly confirmed by the teachers themselves. By 1850, Catholic texts bore the imprint of another, equally indigenous logic: the *du* from Maré was also a foreign spirit, but its sorcerers were local people, reciprocally possessing and possessed by the *du*. Because they were within, their actions presumably threatened social well-being and integrity in ways that foreign sorcerers did not. Goujon recorded a ferment of public debate, which explored a variety of ritual explanations for the origins of new diseases and the causes of the deaths of important persons, and produced stern actions and radical strategies: killing suspected local sorcerers and mobilising the priests of another powerful alien god to drive out the spirit itself.

Writing in the 1950s about these matters, then still vividly recalled in the Isle of Pines, Guiart also differentiated two kinds of sorcery—"traditional" and "new"—but saw indigenous engagements with the *du* as a strategic response to Catholicism and its missionaries: "did they perhaps, faced by the authority of an imported religion, by the mystery of the power of its priests, need new techniques, lent a terrifying prestige by strangeness?" (1959: 10). Anchored in the anticolonial fieldworker's compelling ethnographic present, which tends to assume imposition of European hegemony from the earliest encounters, Guiart represented indigenous actions in reflex counterhegemonic terms. Different times make for different histories. Thirty years later, my postcolonial historian's eye for *contemporary* textual traces of indigenous agency displaced the image of automatic European centrality and discerned a reverse order of urgency: indigenous mobilisation of the French god to combat the *du*. A conscientious antipositivism would allow either and both as strategic possibilities, though I insist that compliance with the averred hegemony of the exotic is necessarily experienced in local cosmological terms.

Different times no doubt also do demand different strategies, but it is surely impossible, outside the artefact of narrative, to disentangle them and their settings from the authored texts which archive their residues. Whether sequenced as shift or pluralised as contrast, my narrative of differing indigenous ritual modes is clarified by some historical sociology, equally crafted. In 1842, the "high chief" Touru was an elder, long-established and with great authority. The known boundaries of Kounié's world had only recently been expanded. Touru's conventional explanation of the epidemics in terms of foreign sorcery was likely to have been convincing. Vendegou was of an age—about 18 in 1849—which in a gerontocratic society was unfit for the exercise of significant authority; he was sharply constrained by ritual experts and elders, especially his father's surviving brothers, Touru's other sons. Goujon commented:

> Close to Vacuma [Ouatchioumé] one saw only a few peaceable old men. Jimi [Vendegou, dubbed "Jimmy" by English traders and known thus until his death] has around him all kinds of people who dispute with him his house and the objects that he owns.... Jimi is feared but, it seems to me, little respected. Paca [Patchia, Ouatchioumé's brother] has for himself all the respect and all the confidence of the inhabitants of the island (1848–54: 28 Feb. 1850).

Furthermore, Touru's actions had failed to end the epidemics and much had happened in the intervening six years. Though Vendegou was personally well-disposed towards the Catholic missionaries—perhaps because they and their god offered support against those with whom he shared authority—he could not impose his opinions unilaterally and was said to have postponed abandoning polygyny in the hope of securing a male heir. "Kanak chiefs", wrote Goujon sympathetically, "have their difficulties, their politics" (1848–54: 12 May 1850). Explanations and decisions were negotiated by elders and "chiefs" in public assemblies, which at times could provide forums for expressions of displeasure with the "high chief" himself and which left their mark in Goujon's journal. In 1850 he told how Vendegou convoked a meeting of all the men of the island, to air grievances and confront rumours. The people of a district whose clans were reputedly among the most ancient and ritually powerful, and who had been much attached to Ouatchioumé, raised again the question of the *du* which had killed him. They implied that Vendegou had obtained it by exchange from Maré, opposed by Ouatchioumé, and that it was he who had had Ouatchioumé killed.[24] Vendegou took the floor in his own defence, arguing that, if the *du* had indeed come from Maré, it was because Maré people desired to kill the Pines' people in order to seize their newly acquired wealth. Patchia then harangued the gathering, claiming that the *du*, if it had ever come to the island, had already been killed. The assembly ended with an affirmation of ritual respect for the "high chief" by the malcontents, who made gifts and gestures of abasement to atone for their want of deference (Goujon, 1848–54: 31 Aug. 1850). The reciprocal dependence of "chiefly" and other clans, of "high chief" and elders, and of senior and junior generations had, however, been publicly displayed and ritually enacted.

Goujon, still presenting himself as a mediator, tried, like Geddie and Inglis, to turn indigenous ideas and ritual practices to the advantage of the mission by identifying the *du* with Satan and what he called the *vaiparé*, or good spirit, with Jehovah: "they use all kinds of sacrifices and religious formulae which approximate in form to our blessings, our ceremonies, and from which we can also profit, except for the difficulty of destroying their attachments to their customs, a difficulty which can only be overcome by grace" (1848–54: 5 Sep., 18 Oct. 1850, 10 June 1852). He doubted that the pragmatic, material indigenous attitude to ritual would fundamentally alter in the short term, but was ready to leave winning souls to grace and time:

> Here more than anywhere else perhaps, it seems to me advantageous to move from the material to the spiritual or to tend towards the spiritual through tangible things.... [Melanesians] understand that... [missionaries] can be useful to them from this point of view at least. Later when our reputation is well established, and we have perfectly won hearts, we can with the aid of grace, work fruitfully for souls (1848–54: 25 July 1850).

Geddie, another effective pragmatist, reasoned similarly: "The emancipation of any people from... heathenism is not the work of a few years, but of generations" (Geddie to Bayne, 8 Oct. 1860, *HFR* 1861: 129). Qualified ethnocentrism and guarded relativism notwithstanding, neither missionary questioned the eventual certainty that grace would remake Melanesians along conventional Christian lines. Yet the widespread persistence of instrumental notions of ritual throughout now mostly Christian Melanesia would seem to underwrite a radical conception of "conversion" as "indigenisation", and of Melanesian Christianities as varieties of indigenous religious experience.

The epidemic of 1852 and renewed agitation about the *du* were to the Catholic missionaries a major setback and a trial. Goujon later recalled that "the old men said: 'Missionary, your word is fine, and I believe your God [to be] powerful and good; but, you see, ours is jealous and pitiless: to abandon him, is to condemn ourselves to death'" (Goujon to Favre, Jan. 1857 [a], APM). Yet he demeaned the elders' evident commitment to defend and preserve "their customs" as the self-interest of unregenerate old polygynists. The "peaceable old men" of 1850 were rhetorically transformed into obstructive traditionalists deterring an equivocal high chief from making a more positive commitment to Christianity (1848–54: 28 Feb. 1850, cf. 15 Sep. 1854). Goujon's extant journal is at once diary—intimate, reflective and deeply personal—and generic missionary drama: a triumphal narrative of human resignation and perseverance in the face of malice and trials, subtext the age-old confrontation of Evil and Grace. Its final entry, a long passage recounting "a last assault on the obstinate malice of our natives", is evident theatre. It told how in 1854, with covert "high chiefly" approval, Goujon browbeat a refractory assembly of "chiefs" and elders into conceding "religious freedom": the right for local people to attend Sunday service and follow Christian teaching, especially on monogamous marriage (1848–54: 15 Sep. 1854). Subsequent letters related further benisons of grace: how several young people then attached themselves to the mission, and how Vendegou's deathbed "conversion" and public "profession of faith" in 1855 inspired a rapid increase in support, despite "the obdurate opposition of the elders" (Goujon to Favre, Jan. 1857 [a], APM). Grace is not my trope, nor Manichaeus my mentor. Rather I am struck by certain cross-cultural congruences of interests: between the mission and a young "high chief" anxious in life to consolidate his authority against the elders—and with a local reputation for enlisting powerful foreign spirits to that end—and intent in death on securing his succession; between the mission and young men generally, impatient with the constraints of seniors' authority, especially their control of marriage through polygyny.

By this time, grace's earthly agents had powerful secular allies, which they did not scruple to deploy against what Goujon called the "malice and...insubordination" of pagan opponents (Goujon to Favre, Jan. 1857 [b], APM). In September 1853 New Caledonia was annexed by France, aided in the Isle of Pines by the Catholic missionaries' intercession with Vendegou. Henceforth the mission journals and letters tell a story of ever more ruthless intervention in local politics, qualifying and eventually reversing the earlier strategy of reticence and non-confrontation. In 1856, by his own account, Goujon called in a French naval detachment to take violent summary action against the "enemies of religion", including Ouatchioumé's brother Patchia, once lauded as "the most peaceful man on the island...and the most interested in the welfare of his country" (Goujon to Favre, Jan. 1857 [b], APM; 1848–54: 28 Feb. 1850).

Within a year of the punitive action, Goujon reported that there were 200 baptised Christians and a complete Christian victory seemed assured: "we are rapidly approaching the total conversion of the island". This was due to "the grace of God alone", which presumably subsumed what he had earlier called the "energetic firmness [of the French] in intimidating the people" (Goujon to Mayet, June 1857; to Favre, Jan. 1857 [a], APM). By 1860 all reports suggested a transformation in Islanders' behaviour as radical as that which had occurred on Aneityum: fighting and cannibalism were abandoned and polygyny virtually so; everyone wore clothes and observed the Sabbath; the entire population gradually moved from households scattered on clan lands to form a large settlement around the new stone church which they had helped build at Vao, whence the men and women commuted to their gardens during the week.

Like Aneityum and Tanna, the Isle of Pines was ravaged by a measles epidemic in 1860–1, during which 170 out of a population of about 1,000 were said to have died (Poupinel to Nicollet, 30 Apr. 1861, *AMSM*, 2: 36). A mission sister sketched a stark image of suffering endured: "the ravaged population took itself now to one point, now to another, emigrating always, fleeing the infection which caught them everywhere and everywhere the plague claimed its victims" (Marie de la Croix to Marie de la Présentation, 1 July 1861, *AMSM*, 2: 62). Though the local people probably shared her belief that the epidemic was "God's anger", no sorcery accusations against the missionaries were reported there, unlike in two nearby places on the mainland where a missionary and a catechist were accused of "making people die through religion" and the catechist was killed (Rougeyron to Poupinel, 12 Jan. 1861, APO). As on Aneityum, the survivors on the Isle of Pines were said to have displayed a firmer commitment to Jehovah, his agents and their ritual and behavioural codes. A proselytising zeal inspired teams of young men to evangelise neighbouring peoples, against some of whom the Kounié had fought a decade earlier (Goujon to Lagniet, Sep. 1861, APM).

EPILOGUE

When I first wrote about these matters in the late 1980s, fitfully inclined to believe in the reality of representations—or at least in their theoretical potential to be complete—I concluded with a tentative taxonomy of indigenous aetiologies, ordered in terms of the relative autonomy attributed to spirits with respect to human ritual. Tanna and Aneityum furnished plausible extremes. Tannese emphasised the controlling causative role of a ritual performer, especially in natural disasters and mortality from disease, and the motif recurred in their reported cultural repertoires at least until the end of the nineteenth century. Aneityumese, Christian or not, attributed calamities primarily to divine retribution for disapproved human actions: that is, they gave spirits a pivotal role in policing human morality, though ritual allegiance to particular spirits depended on evaluations made of their relative power and responsiveness. Taxonomic symmetry would have the Isle of Pines slotted neatly in between, but the intimations of Kounié aetiology I had tracked through contemporary texts hardly lent themselves to tidiness and system: flux and versatility were persistent themes, at once impelling and approximated in a messy, indeterminate narrative. Mistrustful, like most historians, of systems and their timeless, reified categories, I was nonetheless tempted to retain the ordering advantages of taxonomy while subverting its essentialism with a dose of process, positing a shift in ritual emphasis at the Isle of Pines, from a closed, coercive pattern, reminiscent of Tanna, to a more open one.

Even then I knew it was artefact, that the images of successive ritual modes were doubly crafted and doubly ordered—by contemporary authors and by historian. Perhaps I did not quite remember that the seeming aetiological consistency and homogeneity of Tanna and Aneityum were equally texted contrivances. I still find it hard to juggle the entangled rival foci of actors, authors, text, representation and narrative: it is more elegant not to try too hard. I restate what I wrote then: that for an antipositivist the Isle of Pines texts give a vivid sense of the indeterminacies and negotiability of human experience, and a caution against deducing an *a priori* artifice of formal structures. It cannot be plausibly maintained, from a single, derivative trace in Goujon's journal, that on the Isle of Pines the *du* was thought to be a moral regulator with respect to human conduct, whereas mission texts on Aneityum are studded with the imprint of the moral policing role attributed to *natmas*.

Again, though several texted episodes on the Isle of Pines suggest a marked aetiological bias to sorcery, as on Tanna, especially in times of general crisis, yet the kind of sorcery could vary with the spirit deemed responsible, and that was subject to collective negotiation and competition. Public debates punctuated Goujon's journal, with men of high rank and status proffering alternative, sometimes novel explanations as tokens of disapproval or endorsement of each other's actions—especially those of the "high chief"—and as estimates of the relative power of different spirits and their human agents. Such assessments evidently shaped decisions about discarding and selecting explanations and gods. When on the Isle of Pines, as on Aneityum, Jehovah's power was generally acknowledged to be greater than that of vindictive local spirits, there were dramatic behavioural transformations. Catholic and Protestant missionaries alike believed that outcome to be divinely ordained and retrospectively acclaimed it as "conversion". Agnostic and postcolonial, I read their texts as stories of hedged human agency: of pragmatic choices and strategies, variously constrained, enabled and shaped by situation, contingency and personality, and by those contested, negotiated, shifting patterns of community ideas and values for which I know no better term than "cultures".

The original article had put a similar message, qualifying its own residual essentialism: that the Isle of Pines texts testify forcefully to the need—too often forgotten in formal ethnographies—for studies of cultures in action to take account of actors' interests; that cultures are enacted by persons, whose instrumental intentions, differentially potent, comprise part of the transformative potential of Sahlins' (1985) "structure of the conjuncture" of culture and action. As in the article, narrative economy here requires that I edit out the personal instrumental dimension with respect to Tanna. I rationalise the sleight of hand as fitting, given the image propounded of Tannese aetiological consistency, inflexibility and aplomb; but by my reading of texts on Tanna that image was both fitting and convincing, a position sustained by Adams' much more thorough and extensive textual expertise (1984). For Aneityum, I try to sidestep the interested artifice of the missionaries' texts by correlating traces of the actions of pagans and Christians, "chiefs" and "non-chiefs", men and women with a fairly consistent set of aetiological assumptions. Indigenous Polynesian aetiologies, too, seem generally to have emphasised relatively autonomous deities exercising moral regulatory functions, though they were expected to be efficacious and might be ritually abandoned if they proved unresponsive; these were also societies in which fairly rapid mass "conversions" to Christianity occurred. Melanesian aetiologies, like most things, look more mixed and repay multifaceted comparisons. Sifting texts for traces of subtle distinctions in indigenous ritual emphases, thickly contextualised in time and place and in terms of current discourses and agenda, is a worthwhile strategy for constructing narratives about how problematic encounters with Christian missionaries were also indigenous religious experiences, ultimately transformed into Islands Christianities.

NOTES

[1] The differences on which I seized were minor elements in the array identified by Lawrence and Meggitt. Lawrence later qualified their contentious Highlands/Seaboard dichotomy, maintaining "that the differences...do to some extent exist, although probably they are distributed randomly throughout Papua New Guinea as a whole instead of being confined to the highlands and seaboard respectively" (1982: 67; 1988).

[2] This an *anejom* version of the common Oceanic metaphor for a territory or social group as a container, commonly a canoe: cf. Maori *waka*, "canoe", "loose association of tribes"; *cèmuhî* (New Caledonia) *mwo-daame*, "container-of-chiefs" (Metge, 1976: 348; Rivierre, 1994: 251).

[3] Turner's "Journal" (1842–3) combined a general description of the island and its people with an historical overview of the failed mission (see also Turner 1861). Nisbet's "Diary" (1842–3) was a more immediate, quasi-daily account of personal experiences. Both also wrote long letters to the LMS on their arrival in Samoa after fleeing Tanna (in LMS, SSL). I thank Ron Adams for kindly providing transcripts of Turner's journal and Nisbet's diary.

[4] Turner identified a taboo-like concept, but gave no indication of the role attributed to spirits in its enforcement: "[breaking silence during the daily *kava* ritual] and a thousand other things are 'sacred'—strictly forbidden—and they fear that it would be the cause of some great evil, if not death, to transgress" (1842–3: 19 Dec. 1842).

[5] "Sorcery" technically refers to ritual performed—or supposed to have been performed—to persuade or coerce a spirit to inflict illness on or kill another human being. I limit the term to textual episodes where performance of such ritual was clearly imputed. Presbyterian missionaries commonly called such beliefs and practices "witchcraft": "Our natives are firm believers in witchcraft. Every sickness or calamity...is ascribed to some person exercising the Nahak" (Paton to Kay, 11 Oct. 1861, *HFR* 1862: 100; cf. n. 9). "Witchcraft" technically means innate, perhaps unwitting capacity to inflict harm, without need of formal ritual (Glick, 1973).

[6] The extant manuscript of Geddie's "Journal" (1848–57—published, overedited, but with no critical or ethnographic annotation, as Geddie, 1975) is an apparently abridged and reworked fair copy, written in his hand on paper watermarked "1864". Numerous of Geddie's letters and some contemporary journal "fragments" were printed, mainly in the *Missionary Register* and its successor the *Home and Foreign Record*. Many letters and reports by Geddie's colleague Inglis were published in the *Scottish Presbyterian* and its successor the *Reformed Presbyterian Magazine*, and he published several relevant books (1882, 1887, 1890).

[7] Valeri emphasised Hawai'ians' "awareness of the gods' dependence on man's recognition, on man's empowering of them...that gods who no

longer receive human recognition in the form of sacrifices and prayers die" (1985: 104).

[8] *natmas*, "spirit", "the name given to every deity, signifies literally a dead man" (Inglis, 1882: 97; 1887: 29). According to Tepahae, acknowledged expert on custom in Aneityum, *natmas* referred both to a dead body and the spirit which formerly inhabited it but did not denote "spirits" collectively, as became the missionaries' conventional usage and is adopted in this chapter (1997: 16 Aug. 1997).

[9] *naraces*, "witchcraft" (Inglis, 1882: 199).

[10] Tepahae confirmed that a "devil" ("pre-Christian spirit" in Bislama), might independently punish a person who offended it, for instance by the incorrect use of a sacred stone or the infringement of a taboo place (1997: 16 Aug. 1997).

[11] *itap*, "sacred, holy, forbidden" (Inglis 1882: 91).

[12] C. Geddie to Mrs J. Waddell, 16 Sep. 1851, in Geddie and Harrington [1908]: 25 (orig. emphasis). Goujon mentioned the reputed healing properties of tea in the Isle of Pines (1848–54: 15 Feb. 1850).

[13] That Inglis was not insensitive to such a contrast is suggested by a remark he made after he had visited, but not yet settled in Aneityum: "In Western Australia, death is always ascribed to witchcraft. In Aneiteum, it is always ascribed to the malignity of the *Natmasses*" (1852: 529).

[14] In terms strikingly similar to my case, Kwara'ae on Malaita, Solomon Islands, in the 1980s gave Burt to understand that "they regard conversion basically as a change of allegiance from their ancestors to a more benevolent deity who offers similar protective power and safeguards them from the wrath of their rejected ancestors. The issue is sometimes expressed as a contest of power" (1982: 383).

[15] Some mission texts and a modern indigenous account implied a link between this belief and the practice of strangling widows immediately following their husband's death (Geddie, 1848–57: 15 Jan. 1850–1975: 65; Murray, 1863: 47; Tepahae, 1997: 11 Aug. 1997).

[16] This amounted to "about 1200" people (Geddie to Bayne, 26 June 1861, *HFR* 1861: 298; 23 May 1862, *HFR* 1862: 292). See McArthur, 1974, 1978 and Spriggs, 1981: 70–94 for excellent demographic and epidemiological analyses.

[17] Geddie to Bayne, 3 Apr. 1861; Geddie to Turner, 4 May 1861, *HFR* 1861: 248–9, 276; Geddie to Bayne, 26 Aug., 12 Dec. 1861, 23 May 1862, *HFR* 1862: 39–40, 159, 293; Williamu to Napolos, 5 Sep. 1861 (trans.), in Inglis, 1890: 343.

[18] See Adams' detailed narrative of the epidemic, its aftermath and Tannese interpretations and responses (1984: 116–49).

[19] Attenborough, 1960; Bonnemaison, 1994; Brunton, 1981; Guiart, 1956a; Lindstrom, 1982; McKee, 1989.

[20] The question of likely Polynesian missionary input to the meanings made locally of Christianity was largely elided in European mission texts on

Aneityum and Tanna and is not broached in this chapter. Ta'unga's rich textual legacy on southern New Caledonia gives an inkling of the potential in such an enquiry.

[21] Ta'unga wrote about the *Star* killings and indigenous accusations against the LMS teachers in manuscripts written in 1842, 1846, 1847 and 1879 (1968: 37–8, 43–68). In 1845 he gave Turner a verbal account (Turner, 1861: 412).

[22] Goujon's "Journal" (1848–54) comprises often lengthy but irregular entries dating from his arrival at the Isle of Pines, with only a handful after the end of 1851. There is also a journal by his colleague Chapuy (1848–56) and manuscript letters by Goujon.

[23] Unusually, Goujon added a vernacular version of these purported words: "Go na pité ndu mo to aia ti Kuné,"—probably to underline the significance he placed on the statement.

[24] At the time and in traditions recorded a century later (Guiart, 1963: 243), some people associated Vendegou with the *du*'s malevolence. His premature death from tuberculosis, the same malady which had killed Ouatchioumé, might have been interpreted as the vengeance of a jealous *du*, which turned against its possessor as he increasingly inclined to the European god and neglected his reciprocal obligations to the *du*.

Chapter Seven

Dealing (with) Death in a Melanesian World: Indigenous Aetiologies and the "Sickness of the Christians"

FOREWORD

*C*hapter Seven *is descended from an essay written in 1992 as a tribute to Greg Dening (1994a). The festschrift in which it was published is a startling, eclectic, intensely personal collection—befitting Dening's catholic interests and influence, reflexive risk-taking and impatience with disciplinary fundamentalism. It was also so parochially published as to be little read outside its city of publication—befitting Dening's modesty and institutional loyalty. The essay, re-presented here in abridged and altered form, is the fulcrum for Part Three. At once historical ethnography and ethnographic history, it spans the comparative scope of Chapter Six and the detailed intimacy of Chapter Eight, helping to work an integrated narrative out of three related but discrete articles, and to reconcile the residual essentialism of the former with the qualified, textualised realism of the latter.*

PROLOGUE

This chapter re-presents a series of early encounters between Islanders and foreigners at Balade in northeastern New Caledonia. It extracts a story of one group's experiences of sickness, curing and death from enigmatic traces sedimented in several genres of contemporary texts, especially those written by Catholic missionaries. The texts' major virtues are relative contemporaneity and the expertise their authors gained from time in the field, familiarity with the vernacular, and professional interest in local beliefs and rituals. Their major drawback is their status as colonial discourse. There is nothing transparent about texted colonial images of indigenous actions and ideas, nor about the largely invisible translation processes which produced them: ethnographic abstraction and explication in French of indigenous practices and concepts; vernacular rendering of Christian concepts and values by missionaries; appropriation and reinterpretation of such translations by Islanders; translation by Islanders of Christian tropes for which missionaries were unable to find vernacular equivalents. To identify and decode the idiosyncratic and systemic distortions of such texts requires system, imagination, reflexivity and endless comparison. I build a sequential narrative from close critical reading, interspersed with ethnographic commentary bracketing contemporary anecdotes and ethnographic reflections. The period is from 1846, when a handful of Marists had maintained a toehold amongst the Puma of Balade for fewer than three years, to 1861, when New Caledonia had been nominally a French colony for close to a decade.[1]

"THIS PEOPLE HAVE NO SYSTEM OF RELIGION"[2]

In August 1846 an epidemic reached Balade from nearby Pouébo; it struck indiscriminately, with severe head, chest and stomach pains, tormenting coughs, earache and deafness, and often killed in a few days (Rougeyron, 1846–9: 1, 6–7; Leconte, 1847: 845). By December Rougeyron, the mission head during Douarre's temporary absence in France, gauged that more than a third of the population had already died in places known to the missionaries; no European was seriously afflicted and by February 1847 only one baptised Christian had succumbed. Rougeyron depicted local suffering in images no less terrible for a ghost of cliché:

> ...the plague...has struck so many victims that entire villages are deserted; in some huts clay vessels were found full of half-cooked taro, and the persons who were preparing the food were stretched out lifeless beside their fire. The dead can no longer be mourned according to the custom of the land nor even buried separately; they gather several in the same grave and still the cemeteries are full. Bodies remain for several days without interment, so tired they are from digging graves (Rougeyron to S-G, 14 Feb. 1847, APM).

During Douarre's initial sojourn, struggling to attain linguistic competence, he rarely mentioned Islanders' religious beliefs or rituals: "It is painful to contemplate a people without sacrifice, without altar, without worship, or at least, we have so far noticed none". He eventually acknowledged that "they do have some idea of the immortality of the soul" and remarked allegations of sorcery following deaths, and the killing of accused persons (Douarre, 1843–53: 4 Apr. 1844–25 Feb. 1846).[3]

Similar impressions were developed in an ethnography by Rougeyron on the "character, morals and customs of the islanders" (Rougeyron to S-G, 3 Sep. 1846, APM): the missionaries had encountered no trace of belief in an omnipotent creator god who punished and rewarded human behaviour, nor any sacrifice, priests or prayer; there was, however, belief in the immortality of the soul, an afterlife, generally malign ghosts, dreams and sorcery, and a newly evident fear of hell. This text was canonical in its rhythms, trappings and preconceptions: it interspersed the timeless generalising authority of the ethnographic present with anecdotal mooring in the preterite; it was larded with exemplary tales of quaint or horrific savages; it took a particular strand of Catholic dogma as absolute touchstone for discerning and evaluating other people's beliefs and practices. It married useful description and approval of native "wit", "intelligence" and "skill" to smug ethnocentrism, jeering condescension and moral obloquy: he admired the ability of local surgeons to perform procedures like trepanning and endorsed their use of bleeding, purging and poulticing—"you will agree that for savages, otherwise so backward, they are quite advanced in the science of the celebrated Hippocrates"; but he also mocked the crudity of shell instruments, their use of saliva as a salve, recourse to divination and general belief in sorcery.

Rougeyron's subsequent journal, more immediate and less contrived than the ethnography, referred often, especially during the epidemic, to the indigenous aetiology of death from disease. Pragmatically he noted Islanders' explanations because the missionaries were, or feared they would be, accused of making people die. Structurally this coincidence of event and inscription connotes a zone of cultural correlation between Melanesians and missionaries: although for the latter the normal signs of religion—in edifice, institution and ritual—were non-existent, banal or bizarre in New Caledonia,[4] nonetheless both peoples explained their worlds and their experiences in religious terms. For missionaries, local reasons for the epidemic were superstitious and misguided, but they derived from a familiar principle, presuming spiritual intervention in human affairs.

Marist and indigenous aetiologies, however, differed profoundly over the nature and source of spiritual intervention and potential human ritual roles in its direction. Throughout the epidemic the missionaries and their young catechists—baptised children who lived at the mission—spent their days visiting the sick in nearby settlements, seeking to baptise those *in extremis*, but often thwarted, since many, "imagining that we make them die by baptising them, and even by visiting them", hid or were hidden. In December Rougeyron commented: "We meet no one who does not beg us to spare them, and not to make them die". How was it that these folk did not therefore "rend us in a thousand pieces, both for revenge and to deliver themselves from death"? The answer was self-evident: "the Finger of God" (Rougeyron, 1846–9: 7–8, 11, 16; Montrouzier to Eymard, Jan. 1847; Rougeyron to S-G, 14 Feb. 1847, APM).

The interwoven strands of the missionaries' aetiology—providence, Satan and judgement—resonated in Rougeyron's writings during this trying period. "A particular Providence" explained their own immunity to the epidemic, their escape from attack, their "protection" from "accident", unexpected native generosity and support, and the devotion of the handful of Christians. "The domination of satan" produced "revolting" "crimes" such as cannibalism, suicide, killing of sorcery suspects and live burial of the dying, while, to eject the threatening missionary presence, he destroyed their flock of sheep with a fly plague and inspired local hostility against them, culminating in overt attacks. "The anger of the All-powerful" at the Islanders' unnatural and barbarous acts, their obdurate refusal to embrace Christianity, or, possibly, at "our [the missionaries'] sins" led him to inflict "the seven plagues of New Caledonia": drought, fleas, mosquitoes, famine, epidemic, flies and a burning sun. Secure in his conviction that "God is admirable in everything he does", Rougeyron found consolations in the setback to his cause and the suffering of others. The epidemic would in the end benefit the mission, since people had begun to believe in and fear God; moreover, several "chiefs" notorious for eating human flesh—"those old servants of the devil"—had been struck down by "the hand of the All-Powerful". The natives, he thought, also partly recognised "the hand of God" and some begged the missionaries to propitiate Jehovah on their behalf (1846–9; Rougeyron to S-G, 14 Feb. 1847, APM).[5]

TOWARDS AN ETHNOGRAPHY OF INDIGENOUS AETIOLOGIES

Contemporary European texts do not permit a systematic ethnography of local aetiologies of disease, death and calamity, nor the roles, if any, attributed to spirits in policing human morality, nor precise relationships conceived between spirits and human ritual performers (see Chapter Six). Mission texts, in particular, are nonetheless suggestive. The early journalists Douarre and Rougeyron derided local explanations and rituals as ignorant superstition. A decade later the missionary ethnographers Gagnière and Lambert acknowledged the import of rituals to Islanders and explored their practice and meanings from the engaged perspective of a strategy of proselytism emphasising precursors and analogies between old and new religions, transitions rather than abrupt cleavage.[6] Their ethnographies were phrased in a generalising idiom, though based on narrowly localised personal experience during the 1850s and 1860s ([Gagnière], 1905; Lambert, 1900). They were complemented by contemporary diaries and letters—analogous to field notes—which permit some unpacking of processes by which actions seen and words heard were reworked into ethnographic norms. Each category of text is partial, constructed and discursively embedded, but differently: the differences are instructive.

While premature death was always ascribed to spirits, these Islanders evidently conceived a range of possible avenues of spiritual attack on human beings and—unlike my image of the Tannese—did not insist on the necessary involvement of a human ritual performer, a sorcerer. Missionaries, therefore, need not be directly blamed for calamities attributed to their god. In October 1846 Rougeyron reported that the Mwelebeng of Pouébo attributed their afflictions during the epidemic to a host of malevolent spirits, some foreign, some local, all implied to act independently of human ritual stimulus: one man claimed that "Jehovah" wanted to make them die; some blamed "the spirit of... the [wrecked French warship] *Seine*"; others, hordes of whispering spirits of the dead, which thronged their houses, seeking to kill the living; still others spoke of a flame-spewing monster which they could not destroy (1846–9: 1–2). A senior naval officer, stranded at Balade for two months in 1846, reported that "the New Caledonians attribute everything unfortunate which happens to them to beings of a superior nature to their own, to sorcery and to evil spells" (Leconte, 1847: 824).

Lambert represented the world of the Belema of Belep as thronged with a variety of deities, nature spirits and monsters and countless spirits of the dead, addressed via several ritual modes (1900: 13–47). Deities, some benevolent, though more were malevolent, were usually approached through sacrifice and prayer. Nature spirits were capricious and could inflict sickness or madness on human victims, who might be cured by persons with appropriate magical knowledge. One hideous female divinity inflicted elephantiasis on those who crossed her traces and was in communion with a priest whose rituals protected against, caused and cured the disease. The spirits of dead "chiefs" received a specific cult; their anger at violation of its taboos produced violent, prolonged tempests which could be propitiated only through offerings of food and prayers.[7] A few spirits of the dead, believed to have great power from a divine source, were in communion with certain descendants, who used magic or prayer and sacrifice for divination, for preserving life in persons attacked by the spirit, or for sorcery.

Gagnière cited several explanations for affliction current at Balade and Pouébo in the 1850s, including direct vengeance by a spirit incensed, for example, by an error in a mourning ceremony: "the culprit will soon see his vision obscured, his reason troubled. Soon he will be afflicted by madness". Taboo-breaking could also have dire consequences: the priest who had imposed it would call down on violators "terrible anathemas which are always followed by the most frightful punishments, such as the loss of hair, of teeth, incurable ulcers, hideous illnesses and even death. By a virtue inherent in his person, he has moreover the special privilege of being able to raise... not only his own anathemas, but also those of others". Gagnière also mentioned nature spirits, which could inflict madness, and guardian spirits of particular localities, which punished persons under their protection with madness should they fail their ritual duties, but were normally generous and reserved their spleen for strangers (1905: 8–12, 21–2, 40).

Performance of ritual was thus seemingly not a prerequisite for spiritual attack on human beings, since spirits were deemed independent of human ritual. Belief in sorcery was nonetheless general, charges of sorcery were common and were likely to be fatal. Between August 1845 and June 1847 Rougeyron and Douarre mentioned ten separate instances of death attributed to sorcerers, and in eight cases, one or more accused persons were reported killed. Rougeyron claimed that acknowledged or supposed sorcerers were shown no mercy, while their killers were seen as public benefactors (Douarre, 1843–53: 27 Aug. 1845–25 Feb. 1846; Rougeyron, 1846–9; Rougeyron to S-G, 3 Sep. 1846, 14 Feb. 1847, APM). Gagnière implied that sorcery was a residual explanatory category, accounting for all otherwise inexplicable maladies: "they do not fail to attribute to ... [a sorcerer's] malefices any illness the cause of which is not clearly known to them" (1905: 37). Wallis, who must have met Gagnière, said the same (1994: 137). Lambert's journal referred to whole families "suspected of having the secret of making others die. When there is an unexpected death, their steps, words, their actions are scrutinised and interpreted, they must be found guilty, and the wretch on whom the anathema falls will shortly be pierced through with a spear or brained". He cited a single case to exemplify this purported norm—probably its source: after an unexpected death a young man whose parents had been the reputed cause of many deaths was accused of sorcery on the grounds of suspicious behaviour and only saved himself through flight (1855–75: 41).

Gagniere, in dispassionate, generalising ethnographic voice, described a sorcerer's ritual:

> Here is the most common method used ... to throw a spell. ... [The sorcerer] obtains secretly some remains or debris of the food of his enemy, or the enemy of he on whose behalf he will perform his sorcery; then he combines all this debris with any insect, makes it into a single package which he ties with the greatest care. When all these preparations are complete, he performs over the whole lot certain invocations or spells the secret of which he alone knows. This small package, he hides with the greatest precautions, either in the yard, or even inside the house of the prospective victim. If this package, or other similar ones, (for he sometimes makes several), are not discovered in time, the person against whom the malefices have been made, must fall ill and die, or at least, if he escapes, one of the members of his family will be victim in his place.

He added that a sorcerer, who could be of either sex, sometimes performed homoeopathic magic, using a lizard. He or she tightly tied the creature's neck or some other part of its body and the victim would suffer accordingly, until both lizard and victim died (1905: 37).[8]

Where specified, those reported to have been killed as sorcerers were strangers or marginal persons, often women. This suggests that the greater a sorcerer's reputed power, the greater his or her immunity from retaliation, and that persons executed were scapegoats. Rochas, the naval doctor with lengthy field experience in New Caledonia in the 1850s, argued:

> All [sorcerers] are not in possession of equal power: just as there is an aristocracy in this world here below there is also one in the invisible world, and those who deal only with some plebeian of that world enjoy slight power and thus slight respect. Far from being venerated and sacrosanct like the more powerful and clever, they must beware of a public calamity... [I]f they are suspected of having caused the death of some important person, they will be pitilessly massacred. There are sorcerers of both sexes, but old, ugly women are most likely to serve as scapegoats, as they are seen as the more terrible for hiding their art more carefully; and should a public calamity strike the tribe, they would protest their ignorance in vain, be declared *sorcerers despite themselves*, and massacred as such. In such a case, their murder is considered a public good, and its perpetrator has served the nation well (1862: 288, orig. emphasis).

His colleagues Vieillard and Deplanche reasoned similarly, adding that "when the missionaries arrived the natives considered them to be powerful sorcerers and imagined they could communicate their powers to all who followed their doctrine. But the latter[,] not enjoying the same impunity", were liable to be killed (1863: 25).

"BEINGS WHO WERE SUPERIOR TO THEM"[9]

Local notions of divinity, encompassing numerous potentially malevolent spirits, old and new, presumably provided a conceptual basis for interpreting the explicit missionary threat of "celestial anger", recorded by Rougeyron on three occasions in 1847 (1846–9: 16, 26, 32). What Islanders made of the intimate causal link drawn by the missionaries between the "heavenly thunderbolts" of a wrathful Jehovah and non-observance of a Christian moral code is unclear, given the implication in contemporary texts that spirits were not presumed to police human morality generally: while guardian spirits reproved derelictions in ritual duty committed by persons under their protection, others, especially nature spirits, inflicted madness or illness on human beings for selfish or capricious reasons. Rougeyron complained that, although "these wretched savages" acknowledged "the hand of God" in their suffering, they did not therefore cease committing "crimes revolting to humanity", suggesting that they did not share the missionaries moral teleology (Rougeyron to S-G, 14 Feb. 1847, APM; [Gagnière] 1905: 8–9; Lambert, 1900: 17–23; Montrouzier, 1860: 32).

Rougeyron heard Puma elders say they thought the first European vessels came from the sky and that Europeans were ancestral spirits "who...had become white and more beautiful in the other world"—a recurrent theme in the literature on early contacts in Oceania. European assumptions that Islanders regarded missionaries as "beings who were superior", "greater and more powerful" than their own most potent spirits (Leconte, 1847: 819), seemed confirmed in encounters such as the following, which Rougeyron deployed as ethnographic illustration of native ingenuousness:

> Recently several natives come to me and say: "Father, why are you mean with us?" "Me, mean with you, I who never stops giving to you." "Yes, but you do not arrange for us to be given rain, your compatriots, the whites, keep it all. Come and see our gardens, they are all dying for lack of rain. Call for rain." Everywhere I go they endlessly ask me for rain, as also to stop them dying, they believe they depend on us to satisfy their demand. They add when we are going to see the sick that we can recall them to life by giving them a certain water that we know of and which has many virtues.... They say that we know these things, as they know, for example, how to set a limb when it is dislocated (Rougeyron to S-G, 3 Sep. 1846, APM).

Ethnocentric and complacent, Europeans construed this exalted status in terms of a Christian hierarchical cosmology and dissociation of esoteric and practical knowledge. They were oblivious to or derided Islanders' insistence on reciprocities in human and ritual relationships, including hierarchical ones. For missionaries, native awe and fear of their presumed powers were at once a mirror of unquestioned European superiority, and, taken literally, an index of native credulity, superstitions and inherent inferiority. Rougeyron, though, showed that class prejudice could outface racial when it came to stereotyping primitives: "our savages...are not devoid of intelligence. It even seems to me that in general everywhere they are less narrow-minded than certain good folk we find in our mountain villages. They are simple, it is true, since they have never seen anything but what is in their island" (Douarre, 1843–53: 12 Apr. 1845; Rougeyron to S-G, 1 Oct. 1845, 3 Sep. 1846, APM).

In New Caledonia, as in all Pacific cultures, rituals were exchanges and human beings manipulated, coerced or bargained with spirits through prayers, spells and offerings (see Chapter Six). Human beings and spirits were reciprocally, though not necessarily equally, dependent. Douarre commented that "when someone is sick, they offer presents to the spirit of the chief; if the patient is cured, it is because the presents were pleasing; if they die, it is because the presents were not considerable enough and the persons who offered them had been miserly" (1843–53: 28 July 1845). Conversely, unresponsive or unsatisfactory spirits might be abandoned—deprived of ritual offerings—or even destroyed or killed, as arguably befell Cook in Hawai'i. By 1846 the Balade missionaries were convinced that their reputation as spirits or powerful priests insured them against violence. When subsequent experience shockingly belied this assumption, Europeans inevitably invoked their condensing trope of savagery, rather than seriously attempt to grasp the cultural significance of Islanders' actions. In quoting the purported comment "that we know these things, as they know... how to set a limb when it is dislocated", Rougeyron missed its point that missionary knowledge of weather and curing rituals was seen as equivalent and not necessarily superior to local knowledge of anatomy and manipulative techniques; that *all* knowledge of value was restricted, controlled and had both practical application and spiritual endorsement. Presumed missionary "superiority" did not mean they could not be brought to account for their actions, though it probably did allow them more leeway than less esteemed/feared beings.

Rougeyron reiterated that Islanders believed the missionaries to have the power to make people die, but discussed neither their supposed means nor the relationship conceived between their rituals and Jehovah's mortal anger. He sensed a paradox: "it is a mystery to us that these savages do not yet regard us as sorcerers, we to whom they attribute the epidemic which ravages them" (Rougeyron to S-G, 14 Feb. 1847, APM). Given the flexible indigenous aetiology of disease, a number of theories was probably current. Many believed baptismal water was lethal and Rougeyron claimed: "they fear my presence, my arrival at certain places. I am regarded as a bird of ill omen". Yet he recorded only one explicit charge of sorcery against a missionary: in June 1847, following the death of a Christian "chief", several persons accused Rougeyron "of being a sorcerer, of having made their chief die", but he was not molested (1846–9: 7, 11, 19). I conclude that, though Islanders knew and feared sorcery, though most believed the French priests made them die, and though many attributed the epidemic of 1846–7 to Jehovah's anger, as did the missionaries themselves, the causal role locally attributed to them was less clear-cut and invariable than they feared. Their own texts imply that their worsening relations with many Puma and Mwelebeng, culminating in open violence and abandonment of the New Caledonian mission in July and August 1847, owed more to local outrage at their perceived miserliness, denial of reciprocal obligations to hosts/allies and refusal to share their ample supplies during a severe famine, than to their reputation as sorcerers. This was also the missionaries' opinion, though they refuted the accusation (see Chapter Three).

Neither then nor later were Islanders unanimous as to the nature of the missionaries and the malevolence or otherwise of their undoubted powers. Apart from a handful of young Christians who were "of the greatest assistance" to the mission and who for Rougeyron were "consolations" contrived by God in the face of evil, one Christian "chief" also consistently defended the missionaries: Rougeyron reported his fierce public condemnation of the Puma high "chief" for having attacked "the sacred high chiefs that he had the good fortune to have in his tribe... [H]e struck more senior chiefs than he; moreover, those whom he struck were close to me, were my fathers" (1846–9: 30).

"THEY DIED BECAUSE THEY HAD LOIN-CLOTHS AMONG THEM"[10]

These reflections gleaned from the textual imprint of the 1846–7 epidemic can be set in temporal perspective by juxtaposing traces of indigenous actions and reactions during another epidemic, purportedly influenza, which broke out late in 1852 at Balade.[11] Mission stations at Balade and Pouébo, abandoned in 1847, had been restored and baptism of nearly 100 Puma inspired Douarre to cautious optimism. The new epidemic demonstrated the hollowness of any expectation of imminent general conversion and reminded missionaries that, as Forestier put it, "for a long time... [Islanders] will retain a certain belief in their superstitions even while abstaining from them; they will value practices which expose them to moral lapses". He thought that they suspected Christian rituals killed because baptism was most often offered to people *in extremis*, while the "sick and the lame" were among the first to convert: "Our Christians are incontestably inferior to the pagans in physical strength, they are mostly young or sick people". That Christian rituals and symbols "make them die" became general conviction when many converts succumbed, while mortality was much less amongst pagans and apostates: "it is an old conviction amongst them which is confirmed every day by a mortality which seems to choose our Christians for preference. Four times less numerous than the pagans, they have lost 3 or 4 times more people" (Forestier to S-G, 12 Mar., 20 Sep. 1853, APM).

Douarre recounted how pagans refused to attend church, while elders called for abandonment of Christian dress and resumption of former customs in order to avert death. In March 1853 the epidemic flared again, striking pagans as well as Christians: 47 Mwelebeng died in little more than a fortnight. Puma began to shun the missionaries and would not call them to attend the sick. Even converts began to murmur that "they died because they had loin-cloths [*ceintures*] among them or Christians" (Dourre, Journal, 20 Sep. 1852–20 Apr. 1853). Mission texts allowed that direct accusations against missionaries and/or their god were still muttered in 1852 and 1853, but it seems that major blame was now laid on the presence in a community of Christians and their rituals, represented metonymically in the symbol of their new commitment, the loin-cloth. This subtle shift in attribution of agency was perhaps a sign that Jehovah and his priests were now so thoroughly embedded in local consciousness that their manipulation by local players was more contentious than their acknowledged but unpredictable powers.

The significance of indigenous aetiology in shaping new concepts to account for unprecedented experiences was implied in Douarre's frustration over what were, to him, self-evident inconsistencies in local explanations. He complained that pagan deaths were interpreted differently from Christian. When converts told him that having loin-cloths and Christians in their settlement made them die he argued that pagans had died in the past and at other places when there were no loin-cloths or Christians, but they were unpersuaded. They applied a different logic to their own priests, such as an old diviner who had predicted no Puma would die: "I mentioned that without convincing anyone, too persuaded are they that if the sorcerer is wrong, it is because something has supervened which altered the prophecy" (Douarre, 1843–53: 28 Jan., 11 Apr. 1853).[12] It apparently did not occur to Douarre that unprecedented changes in behaviour and allegiances produced by numerous baptisms might have meant a significant supervention affecting divination.

In April 1853 Douarre himself died, agonisingly, from what colleagues diagnosed as the local malady complicated by myelitis, but his loss seemingly did not deflect indigenous accusations and fears. Forestier drew a harrowing image of how righteous missionaries forced their sacraments on people who believed they killed, but were too courteous, restrained or frightened to reject them forcibly:

> more often again when visiting the sick we have been received by threatening or terrified faces, and accused of bringing death in our train.... We had to search in the most obscure huts for the sick who were hidden from us; never, however, have we heard positive threats, they sought to trick us, [but] no one ever resisted us when we wanted to instruct or baptise the dying.

He, too, puzzled over the paradox that "we ought to have expected blows from spear or club, for the conviction that we made them die was universal amongst our poor savages"; he, too, saw "strong proof of the protection of God... that they confined themselves to muttering", as well as of "the ascendancy we have acquired". A colleague was consoled that the Balade Christians so feared hell that they did not want to die without confession (Forestier to S-G, 20 Sep. 1853; Montrouzier to his brother, 14 Oct. 1853, APM).

"THE SICKNESS OF THE CHRISTIANS"[13]

In September 1853 French annexation altered the formal context of Christian missionary work in New Caledonia, though its ongoing practical implications were for a long time limited to a slowly expanding zone of permanent French settlement in the far south.[14] By mid-1855 Rougeyron, now the mission superior, decided that continued pagan intransigence at Balade and Pouébo and the constant moral and physical danger to Christians and neophytes necessitated a new strategy: "that Babylon", Balade, was accordingly abandoned and about 120 Puma removed to a distant model settlement named Conception, established near the colony's headquarters on a large tract of land granted by the French military authorities (Rougeyron to S-G, 29 Oct. 1855, [1856], APM). Subsequent arrivals from the north brought the population to nearly 400.

Apart from enduring an onerous war in alliance with the French against the local inhabitants, to secure their occupation of this place, the migrants' bright new world was shadowed by strangely selective sickness and high mortality. By mid-1856 14 had died while pagans were largely spared, rehearsing the pre-existing nexus between Christianity and death. Eight months later the community had suffered 40 deaths, moving Rougeyron to despair: "We don't know what to attribute the sickness to, nor what remedy to bring to it. I do not see that it is our fault; they are trials to which we must submit.... [We must] resign ourselves to God's will". Pagans, though, knew one reason why so many Christians died: admittance into churches of menstruating women, contact with whom was thought to cause "all sorts of ills" (Rougeyron to Poupinel, 4 Oct. 1858, APO). In little more than five years Conception lost well over a third of its residents, including 60 who succumbed to the measles epidemic which swept the islands from

October 1860. A naval doctor reported that in 1856 they were dying "rapidly and in fairly large numbers" from several diseases particularly tuberculosis (Vinson, 1975: 32). A visiting Marist blamed chest problems on the climate and the victims—chilly mornings, faulty hygiene, bad blood and the childlike fecklessness of natives, even converted ones. Returning three years later, he described the "ravages" of tuberculosis as "constant...especially against the Christian tribes". It was called "*christiano*, the sickness of the Christians"; many Islanders who converted did so in the belief that this disease was a consequence of baptism and would kill them (Poupinel to Colin, 2 Dec. 1857; to Nicollet, 30 Apr. 1861, *AMSM* 1: 109–10; 2: 36–7). Their empirical reasoning probably had sound epidemiological grounding, given the mission's ideologically-inspired preference for large, close-settled communities, and the favourable conditions for droplet infection provided by regular church and school attendance.

Rougeyron's story of Louis Tadinan, a young Puma "chief" who as a child had been the first indigenous convert in New Caledonia, bears retelling. Phrased as a parable, it personalised the highly stylised tropology of conventional missionary discourse, while registering traces of the resilience of early converts facing extreme suffering and loss:

> The Good God certainly loves Louis, for he has tested him too much. In the past year, death has snatched away his small child, his mother, his father-in-law, his two brothers, his two cousins and his two closest friends. At each death, his heart broke with sorrow, and despite the wounds which tore this so loving heart, he always showed himself totally resigned to the will of God (Rougeyron to Poupinel, 30 Jan. 1857, *AMSM* 1: 72).

Near death, apparently from a virulent form of tuberculosis to which young males were especially susceptible, Louis was allowed to return to Balade from Conception to catechise his kinspeople before dying in his own place.[15] Poor Louis would seem to have cast his evangelical seed on stony ground. Not so perhaps the germs of the affliction which killed him. Rougeyron later found Balade almost deserted—"most are dead"—while visiting colonial officials reported that the few Puma still there, obdurately opposed to the mission, "were disappearing visibly from consumption" (Rougeyron to S-G, 15 Mar. 1858, *AMSM* 1: 162; Testard to Min., 23 Apr. 1858, ANOM, Carton 42; Broglie to ?, 28 Dec. 1859, APM).

POWER, DEATH, LIFE

My liberal bourgeois agnosticism finds the pragmatics of Melanesian ritual more congenial than the mysteries of Catholic resignation. I can scarcely imagine how Islanders bore the agony of suffering and torment of loss resulting from awful diseases which defied ritual remedies known and novel. Perhaps unprecedented morbidity and mortality required the doubtful efficacy of instrumental ritual to be complemented by the paradox of an omnipotent deity who, while purportedly "doing all things well", scourged the innocent with the guilty and counterpoised the promise of salvation with the fearful threat of damnation—all construed in locally meaningful ways for indigenous ends.

Hell featured more often than salvation in early missionary evaluations of indigenous understandings of their message. Two years after their arrival, Rougeyron claimed that people at Balade trembled when the missionaries spoke of hell: "Everyone wants to pray for no one wants to go to hell". His ethnography elaborated: "There is now not a single person who does not fear hell; its very name makes the most libertine or the most hardened shudder.... Today no one refuses to pray and almost everyone would like to be baptised" (Rougeyron to Girard, 2 Jan. 1846; Rougeyron to S-G, 3 Sep. 1846, APM). I do not know what words he used to convey his frightening image, nor what they signified to his hearers, but I read an implication, consistent with my understanding of indigenous ideas on the matter, that rituals and taboos, sometimes embracing "moral" behaviour in the Christian sense, continued to be seen as keys to controlling the present and averting catastrophe in the afterlife. When Christians were "not at all discouraged or frightened" of death and accepted it "in peaceful and saintly fashion", when people continued to convert, despite certainty that it would kill them, missionaries admired but did not wonder: they knew resignation and martyrdom when they saw it, and Rougeyron admitted he could scarcely resign himself as well (Rougeyron to Poupinel, 14 Nov. 1860, 1 Jan. 1861, APO; Anon. [1861]). Though puzzled that pagans stayed their hand against those whom most believed made people die, missionaries always had as ultimate explanation their final cause of divine protection.

Since neither martyrdom nor providence is my metaphor—and nor, presumably, were they indigenous metaphors—I remain perplexed. In Chapter Three I argued that there was and is in New Caledonia a widely held and often practised indigenous ethos of restraint: withdrawal, as in hiding the sick from the lethal presence of death-dealing priests, was consistently preferred to confrontation. These Islanders seem to have met calamity with a flexible aetology and eclectic readiness to weave in novel elements. Since no one appeared to doubt the new god's presence or potency, or the vivid reality of eternal fire and eternal pleasure, strategies were needed to handle him and his confident, overbearing priests; the reverse of this dangerous coin was learning ritual means to appropriate and channel that power to local or subversive ends. By this reasoning, everyone with an interest in the matter—committed Christians, apprehensive converts, lukewarm supporters and all shades of opponent—engaged with the Christian god, his priests and rituals, ambiguously motivated by desire for power/salvation and fear of death/damnation. It was, paradoxically, only with the measles epidemic in 1860–1 that the ghastly reputation of Catholic Christianity began to fade: in the north fewer Christians than pagans died, while Belep escaped entirely, thanks, claimed Gagnière, to a "fervent novena" offered by the Christians to the Virgin (Gagnière to Visiteur-Général, 12 June 1861, APO). It had already proved its political efficacy earlier in 1860, when the Mweleberg, armed by the colonial government, drilled by their missionary and led by their Christian "chief", repulsed a pagan offensive before embarking on a war of conquest which established Mwelebeng and Christian political and spiritual hegemony through the northeast (see Chapter Eight).

EPILOGUE

A more powerful god, more efficacious rituals, better management of death, fear of hellfire, a promise of life: a mix of such elements was implied or invoked in conversion studies elsewhere. This chapter is not a study of conversion *per se*, though it touches on it often. I see "conversion" as one of several empowering strategies and discourses contrived and appropriated by Islanders to cope with, control, exploit or subvert novel persons, spirits, rituals, ideas, things; it might also have served to evade, undermine or displace the efficacy of malevolent or punitive local spirits, as looks likely to have been the case in Aneityum (see Chapter Six). The theme of agency is thus foregrounded, with Islanders conceived as actively engaged in constructing and manipulating alien encounters; so too is that of change as "vernacularization" (Rafael, 1988: 15)—locally enacted and meaningful. My more general intent is to display and exploit the ethnographic potential of contemporary colonial texts to throw light on particular indigenous strategies for handling problematic pan-human experiences: deflecting, appropriating and exercising power in cross-cultural encounters; translating and domesticating the esoteric and the exotic; tackling calamity and death.

NOTES

1. The Société de Marie was given papal ratification in Lyon in 1836 for the express purpose of evangelising the western Pacific. A resurgent Catholicism (Gibson, 1989: 199–201, 227–30), in tacit partnership with rekindled post-Napoleonic French colonial designs, aimed to stake its claims in a part of the world thus far largely untouched by Protestant missionary enterprise or British imperialism.
2. As late as 1852 Mary Wallis heard this from the missionaries at Balade. She opined otherwise: "I think that they have [a religion], and that it will be found out upon a better acquaintance". A month later Father Forestier conceded grudgingly: "'they do acknowledge that there are superior spirits, but no good ones. They are all bad'" (1994: 136, 143).
3. See Chapter Six, n. 5 for my use of the technical term "sorcery"; it matches neither colonial usage nor any discrete contemporary indigenous category that I know of—the power to inflict harm via ritual was one of several attributed to a variety of ritual practitioners (Lambert, 1900: 19–23, 28–9; Leenhardt, 1930: 235; Vieillard and Deplanche, 1863: 25–30, 57–8).
4. Wallis the Protestant was far less ethnocentric about what constituted religion: "The Caledonians have no temples dedicated to their gods, but they have their sacred places, generally about the graves of their departed friends [and relatives]... [whose] spirits... they worship. They think that some of them control the elements and the events and occurrences of their lives" (1994: 132). By contrast, she was shocked by some of the rituals performed by her "kind friends" the Catholic missionaries: genuflection on entering the church "appeared like worship to images, and the Bible forbids such worship" (1994: 112, 139).
5. Inglis pontificated similarly in the aftermath of the 1861 measles epidemic on Aneityum. Tragically for Aneityumese his self-serving prognostications did not eventuate, and they died in droves during epidemics in 1866 and 1867 (Inglis to Bayne, 9 Oct. 1861, *HFR* 1861: 329; McArthur, 1974: 77–9).
6. Gagnière to Poupinel, 1 May, 3 Dec. 1859, 12 May 1860, 25 Feb, 12 May 1861, APO; Lambert, 1855–75: 24; 1900: 27. Most of their colleagues—though not Goujon (1848–54: 5 Dec. 1849)—recoiled from the whiff of heterodoxy in their strategy, and insisted that conversion depended on God's authority alone and required an absolute break with the past.
7. Wallis encountered just this belief at Balade in 1852: "We have had rather a hard gale for the last two days, which the Caledonians have been prophesying, because Fijians have walked over their *tabu* grounds and disturbed the spirits of the dead.... The fury of the disturbed spirits being appeased, the weather is again becoming pleasant" (1994: 145).
8. For anthropologists' descriptions of sorcery rituals in New Caledonia see Guiart, 1959; Leenhardt, 1930: 235–40; Métais, 1967.

[9] Leconte, 1847: 819.
[10] Douarre, 1843–53: 11 Apr. 1853.
[11] Wallis gathered from Forestier that local people regarded this particular sickness as pre-European: he "informs us that the natives have told them that influenza would visit the islands, this year, it being the fifth year since its last visit. They say that it comes every five years, and great numbers often die with the disease". Her husband was extremely ill, as were most of their associates and their Fijian labourers, while the missionaries had all been afflicted, but recovered (1994: 139–40).
[12] Contemporary ethnographers routinely, if contemptuously, reported similar indigenous rationalisations when a ritual failed to effect a nominated result (Lambert, 1900: 197–203; Rochas, 1862: 292–3; Vieillard and Deplanche, 1863: 30).
[13] Poupinel to Nicollet, 30 Apr. 1861, *AMSM* 2: 36.
[14] The historical context also altered, since the archived official mission journal ended with annexation. I know of only one journal extant from the late 1850s (Lambert, 1855–75). Much surviving missionary correspondence from this period comprises pious, overwrought reports to headquarters and eminent Marists. However, conserved in APO there is an invaluable stash of more immediate and personal letters dating from 1858.
[15] For contemporary medical opinions on indigenous susceptibility to tuberculosis see Rochas, 1862: 132; Vieillard and Deplanche, 1863: 57.

CHAPTER EIGHT

Power, Ritual and the Appropriation of God: Christianity and Subversion in Melanesia

FOREWORD

The much longer original of this chapter was published in History and Anthropology *(1995) and elaborated the nuanced concept of agency I had begun to theorise in 1992 (1992b). It also marked my first explicit deployment of the notion of strategic appropriation as a way of conceptualising indigenous encounters with novelties—people, ideas and things—and Islanders' engagements in their own personal and collective transformations. The dual stress on actors/actions and change which had long threaded through my work thus came together in the linked concepts of agency and appropriation. These concepts were at once woven into the fabric of the narrative and reflexively interrogated in terms of a shifting politics of reading and representations: particularly my academic's tendency to ethnocentric universalisation of liberal secular values. The chapter retains elements of theoretical reflection, but these themes are developed more fully in the Prelude.*

PROLOGUE

Historians and historical anthropologists have lately explored creative appropriations of Christianity by colonised peoples as an ideology of resistance to the Euro-American colonial hegemony of which it was a primary vehicle.[1] With respect to New Caledonia, Guiart cast early twentieth century conversions to a Protestant Christianity brought by Loyalty Island pastors in oppositional terms, as "a subtle, in many ways efficient, and at times overt, form of resistance to the worst aspects of colonial rule" (1962: 132–3). Most such formulations do acknowledge a dialectic of the known and the novel in subaltern appropriations of elements of dominant discourses, but estimations of the significance and likely efficacy of subaltern agency range in tone from pessimistic to celebratory. Anthropologists of the radically threatened or dispossessed tend to stress "the colonization of consciousness" and invoke a reflex counterhegemony (Comaroff and Comaroff, 1991: 312; Keesing, 1994); less gloomy commentators recognise subaltern irony and stress "the creative invention that lies at the very heart of the reception process" (Chartier, 1989: 171–4; Prakash, 1990). Such moral and aesthetic choices always have their politics, no more nor less than the indigenous strategies and choices they categorise. Though not denying that colonialism was often tragic and always dehumanising for the colonised, I am inclined to read resilience, irony and creativity in their endurance of tragedy and assertions of their humanity, and to see non-activism as a culturally and strategically informed and constrained choice, just like activism.

This chapter echoes the two preceding in its focus on the initial phases of indigenous engagements with Christianity in New Caledonia. I deploy a crossgrained ethnographic reading of early (1846–66) Catholic mission texts in order to chart fleeting traces, lodged in narratives contrived for other purposes, of inventive, politically charged indigenous appropriation and subversion of Christian ideas about the afterlife in contexts of recurrent epidemics and intractable new diseases. I locate several episodes within wider contests to dictate terms of discourse, particularly over perceived outcomes and causation. Islanders of varying shades of commitment, support and opposition to the mission can be seen to have engaged in struggles for discursive power with each other and with missionaries, mobilising known and novel strategies in efforts to control, exploit, evade or dislodge the efficacy of spirits, including the Christian god.

DEADLY ENCOUNTERS

The first reliably recorded epidemic of novel sickness in New Caledonia was at the Isle of Pines in 1842, and occasioned the revenge killing of three Polynesian evangelists of the London Missionary Society (LMS).[2] In Chapter Six this and later epidemics at the Isle of Pines after the Marist installation there in 1848 are correlated with textual traces of local aetiologies and ritual praxis. Chapter Seven tracks the imprint in contemporary texts of a devastating sequence of new epidemic and endemic diseases endured by the Puma of Balade from August 1846, not only in their northern homeland but at the Catholic settlement of Conception, near Nouméa, where most of the Christian converts and neophytes among them relocated after French annexation in 1853. Epidemics—mainly respiratory and intestinal complaints and measles—were typically reported first in areas frequented by Europeans. During the 1850s Christian communities seemed the worst afflicted, reinforcing indigenous belief that "Christianity makes [people] die" (Forestier to S-G, 12 Mar. 1853, APM). The recurrent trauma of epidemic was aggravated by the permanent scourge of tuberculosis, or "*christiano*, the sickness of the Christians". A touring Marist dignitary lamented: "Many Caledonians, when they convert, are convinced that this terrible malady will be a consequence of their baptism. To embrace the [Christian] faith, is for them to sacrifice themselves to death". Missionaries told how Conception lost well over a third of its residents between 1855 and 1861, and how "consumption and scrofula" appeared to have made mostly Christian Touho "their chosen domicile" (Poupinel to Nicollet, 30 Apr. 1861, *AMSM* 2: 36–7; Forestier to Rocher, 7 Aug. 1861, APO).

In mission narratives, epidemics were typically constructed as divine dispensations, whether trials of the devout, or punishment of the ungodly. A Manichaean cosmology and teleology left no discursive space for indigenous agency in my sense (see Prelude): even violence was satanically inspired, a preordained step toward an inevitable outcome. Their texts, nonetheless, provide grist for ethnohistorical mills because they are fleetingly imprinted with the cryptic stamp of different narratives. In the wake of the missionaries' flight from Balade in July 1847, mission children told them how Puma mimicked Christian rituals; smashed, discarded or profaned sacred objects; donned vestments; taunted and desecrated the icon of a saint identified as Jehovah: "They made a game of jeering at the statue. They attached a cord to its neck; they dragged and overturned it several times. Then they told him to get up, if he was al-powerful, as we had told them; after that they tatooed the face of the statue, cut off its arm and nose". The body of the lay brother slain in the retreat was mutilated, mocked and insulted and his head later suspended outside the high "chief's" house, as were the captured skulls of fallen enemies. Missionaries, appalled, but confident of the centrality of their own presence, cast such acts in negative or oppositional terms, as "infamy", "impiety" and "contempt for whites". Reconfigured according to what I take to be indigenous notions of the pervasiveness, ambiguity and mundanity of the sacred, the purported actions might have been deliberate ritual inversions, aimed to neutralise or control sacred power. I read the parody as intentional, rather than unselfconscious emulation or mere angry reflex. The innuendo of appropriation with subversive intent, deployed in a field of power relations, not only suits my inclination for a discourse of indigenous agency, but tallies with the missionaries' own fugitive apprehensions: "they put on priestly ornaments and simulate our most holy ceremonies, and feign, mockingly, to celebrate our fearful mysteries" (Rougeyron, 1846–9: 25; Collomb, 1847: 35–9, 45–50).[3]

By 1860 the sparsely peopled far south of the island had been conquered by the French, but elsewhere the bulk of the indigenous population remained oblivious to the implications of annexation and indifferent or hostile to the mission. There were isolated, if at times highly destructive, French punitive expeditions, but before 1862, insofar as the colony meant much at all to people outside the south, it was as an occasional ally of the Catholic mission. Balade was described as an "almost deserted" backwater, its remnant population dramatically reduced by disease and emigration and resolutely hostile to the Marists (Laurent to Min., 13 Jan. 1857; Broglie to ?, 28 Dec. 1859, APM).[4] Yet at nearby Pouébo and in the Belep Islands, northwest of the mainland, mission texts told a success story of mass conversions, spearheaded by the "double authority" of powerful Christian "chiefs" and charismatic missionaries (Rougeyron to Poupinel, [Oct. 1859], APO), whose evangelical strategies sought to sanitise—rather than proscribe—selected local beliefs and ceremonies so as to render them fit vehicles for the operation of grace. As one of them put it: "[the missionary] examines the [local] customs in order to leave be those which have nothing bad about them and destroy later those which are reprehensible, he studies the language" (Lambert, 1855–75: 24).

This summary signals my themes and anticipates a puzzle, foreshadowed in Chapter Seven. Early missionary efforts in New Caledonia coincided with novel epidemic and endemic diseases which many Islanders, Christian and pagan alike, were said variously to attribute to "Christianity"—the presence of its envoys, their god, their symbols and rituals, its local adherents and their actions. Yet there were few apostasies among the baptised, others continued to attend services and to seek baptism, while even the missionaries' harshest opponents did not deny their potency, repudiate all their ideas or deploy effective violence against them. What was it about Christianity that attracted and repelled Islanders? What can plausibly be inferred about the complex and varied ways in which indigenous ideas about the human/divine interface reciprocally informed and were shaped by experience of missionary discourse and actions?

THE POETICS AND POLITICS OF BEING HIPPOLYTE BONOU

In mission hagiography Bonou, the Christian "first chief in fact, but the second in title" of the Mwelebeng chiefdom of Pouébo, was represented as a worthy recipient of grace, whose agent he became in the successful evangelism of his people (Gagnière to his brother, 2 May 1866, APM; Rougeyron, n.d., 1928). Sedimented in these and other texts, however, were more complex traces of his actions, including hints of how he and they were locally construed. Though Bonou was said to have berated the missionaries for desertion when they quit the island in 1847 (Rougeyron, 1846-9: 35), he later abandoned Pouébo in his turn, accompanying the Marists to a model Catholic community in Polynesian Futuna, whence he returned in 1852, baptised as Hippolyte, to resume control of the chiefdom as "regent" for the younger *teama*, "first chief". He "astonishes us all", enthused one missionary, "by his disinterestedness, his ability and his energy" (Forestier to S-G, 20 Sep. 1853, APM).

Despite Bonou's reputedly formidable personality and "great authority and influence", the Mwelebeng chiefdom was evidently neither united nor homogeneous in the 1850s. Missionary metanarratives predictably invoked satanically induced religious schism: "the pagan party...is furious against Religion and Civilisation which come to destroy their customs and their alleged happiness... The devil tries in vain to destroy religion" (Rougeyron to S-G, [1856]). But their more prosaic texts hinted at existing divisions along generational and geographical lines, sharpened by the linked vexations of Christian worship and Bonou's autocracy. As at the Isle of Pines (see Chapter Six), many elders—unregenerate pagans, cannibals and polygynists to missionary pens—were suspicious of innovations, feared Christian missionaries, rituals and symbols, and resented their code of behaviour. Their aversion flared into open hostility in times of public calamity, particularly epidemics, which they took as confirmation of their trepidations: "The old men of Pouépo", complained Douarre, "recommended casting off the loin cloth [symbol of Christian identification] and following their former customs, in order not to die" (1843-53: 8 Jan. 1853).[5] There were also hints of fissure between the Mwelebeng "chiefs'" immediate dependents, who almost all lived northwest of the Pouébo river and supported or tolerated the mission, and pagan settlements to the southeast over which they exercised tenuous and contested authority.

The novel symbiosis of Christian "chief" and missionary had significant transformative potential for local attitudes, as well as actions and relationships. The mission wanted to bolster the temporal authority of well-disposed "chiefs" and instil a Christian work ethic: one way to do both was to encourage commercial production and trade of local products for approved projects, such as church-building, all centralised under "chiefly" control. Casual official observations suggest that Pouébo provided a fertile medium for such initiatives. One visitor remarked "a beginning of commerce and spontaneous civilisation [by Bonou], without the intervention of Europeans", apart from missionary recommendations (Broglie to ?, 28 Dec. 1859, APM; Mathieu to Durand, 22 Jul. 1861, ANOM, Carton 42). I surmise that "chiefs" like Bonou embraced such projects in support of centralising agenda of their own, to bring outlying or contested places under their authority and to subvert, or at least qualify indigenous arrangements which diffused authority between the "chief" and some of his "subjects": genealogically "junior", "subjects" also included masters of the soil and other ritually potent dignitaries whose authority sanctioned and checked that of the "chief", to whom they were "elder" in generational terms (Douglas, 1994b: 179–81).[6]

There were textual traces of the "chief"-mission partnership in action at Pouébo as early as 1853 when Gagnière explained how Bonou policed thefts from the mission and killing with cannibal intent: "at the first theft we had our chief burn all the culprit's houses; at the second, four yam gardens paid [the price]; as for the killer[,] his legs saved his life, and he only returned after several months' exile" (Gagnière to S-G, 18 Sep. 1853, APM). There were recurrent allusions to this episode in mission texts, showing neatly how an "historical event" can serve multiple discursive ends, depending on genre of text and author's agenda. In a later panegyric of Bonou as Christian hero and martyr Rougeyron stressed his deft manipulation of the *teama* and prudent deference to customary principles of rank and authority, rather than his ruthless suppression of savagery under missionary direction—Gagnière's more contemporary theme. In a contemporary letter of his own Rougeyron used the story to illustrate Bonou's *lack* of sufficient "influence... to put a stop to disorderliness", as exemplar of unaided confrontation of savagery by intrepid missionaries. Montrouzier, the missionary at Balade, praised Bonou's tact, prudence and "talent for controlling everything without insulting the first chief" (Rougeyron, n.d.; Rougeyron to ?, 20 Mar. 1853, AAN, 74.1; Montrouzier to his brother, 14 Oct. 1853, APM). By my reading, Gagnière's intent was to dramatise the progress of the Pouébo mission at a time when it had but a tenuous foothold. Montrouzier was an interested bystander ruefully contrasting Bonou's effectiveness with the debilitating disharmony of the Puma "chiefs". Rougeyron's letter was classic mission propaganda, replete with slavering savages and civilised hair standing on end: "There you have it; reverend Father, a sketch which must let you see what a people we have to deal with". His later biography sought to vindicate a Christian martyr.

Another textual episode dramatised the west/east rift in the Mwelebeng chiefdom as an assault by the emergent diarchy on a "custom" accorded high emotional value, though of recent innovation. For some years numerous dogs had roamed the settlements, scavenging in the cemeteries. Some were adopted into families, their pups suckled by women and their deaths publicly mourned. Aghast at "this strange abuse", the missionaries encouraged Bonou to enforce a canine extermination program. The partly Christianised western settlements complied, but those to the east "resisted... the orders of their two first chiefs". The ensuing armed clash was a "revolt" in the missionaries' lexicon and according to the code of laws they and the "chiefs" had recently solicited from the colonial authorities: "Any disobedience to the tribal chief, or to persons designated by him to watch over public safety will be punished".[7] From the perspective of the thus constituted periphery, however, "revolt" was no doubt a false epithet. The fighting lasted some days, occasioned several serious wounds and necessitated a compromise resolution (Rougeyron, n.d.; Poupinel to S-G, 2 Dec. 1857, *AMSM* 1: 118).

To missionary chagrin the eastern settlements remained unreconciled to Bonou's authority. By mid-1855 the *teama* had openly sided with the pagans, ordered the Christians to quit their loin cloths and rosaries and underwritten a degree of persecution when most refused. For missionaries, religion as they conceived it had to be the main point at issue, but their own subtext of local hostility to Bonou's pretensions is at least equally compelling. Mwelebeng pagans were evidently not alone in their disquiet about his subversion of established patterns of authority and behaviour, as Rougeyron acknowledged: "It is he who has the greatest authority and influence in the region, although second chief, and that is what has just leagued against him all those tribes which want at all costs to maintain their pagan customs and banish from the island the religion and civilisation of the whites" (Rougeyron to abbé de Meydat, 28 June 1855, *AMSM* 1: 13; to S-G, [1856], APM).

To missionaries, Bonou's political manoeuvres were justified by Christian religious intent, befitting his perceived role as secular arm of the church militant, but their stories hinted at the persistence of an indigenous ritual-politics receptive to innovation. There is something of this in one of the few extant contemporary indigenous texts, an allegory entitled "The first and the second chief of the Aobats", which the missionary Lambert—an accomplished linguist and ethnographer—transcribed at Belep and translated "as literally as possible" as a specimen of local literature. A rare echo of contemporary native voices, this story apparently had wide currency in the north, as an abridged variant was also published by Rochas, who had a stint at the Balade post in the 1850s (1862: 220–3).[8] In cadence, tone, agenda and tropes it differs sharply not only from the mission texts, but from my own. I try to summarise it as faithfully as possible to Lambert's translation, allowing that it challenges my interpretive focus on actors' strategies and agency.

The "second chief", *mweau* ("second son"), of the Aobats was "good for nothing, so the men of the tribe did not consider him a chief". His brother the "first chief", *teama* ("eldest son", "high chief"), convoked his "subjects" for the arduous communal labour of a major fishing expedition. The canoes returned laden with seaweed, which the men shared as fish, and which only the despised *mweau* was prepared to identify truly. He and his pathetic following of two men set off to fish in their turn, mocked by the *teama* for going alone.

> The Mouaéou is quick to spot a bank of large fish. Then shouting to his two men, "Quick, quick, fish!" The Mouaéou vigorously pushes the fish into the net, tirelessly stabs them with his

spear and loads the canoe, he fills one side, the other is quickly full, he then loads the platform. "Let's go", says the Mouéaou then; they set sail and return to the village.

Their reappearance with such a huge catch was taken as a bad omen and the other men encouraged the *teama* to kill the *mweau* before he killed them. The *teama* refused and instead distributed the fish. Incited by the men, he sought to humiliate his brother by setting him an impossible task, but the *mweau* encountered two female deities who accomplished it for him while he slept. Thoroughly alarmed, the men responded: "Let us get rid of him without delay, or before long he will reign over us". In a further effort to discredit, they challenged him to present the sun to the *teama* at a forthcoming *phiilu*, "ceremony". The *mweau* diffidently sought out the two deities, who captured the rising sun and completed his offering to the *teama* with a vast array of valuables. When the box containing the sun was opened at the *phiilu*, everyone fell dead, but the *mweau* revived them with water. In a further ploy, the men abandoned him on a battlefield, but he routed the enemy unaided, killing many. Sent for by the *teama*, he remarked: "I understand, they want to kill me". He prepared himself carefully, "adjusts his hat, blackens his body [like a warrior or a mourner], puts on his bracelet and leaves". As he bent to enter the "chief's" enclosure, awaited by the *teama* and the elders, his head was chopped off.

Both mission and official commentators thought the allegory marked their own centrality in local politics. In separate exegeses, Lambert saw it as a call to assassinate Bonou by "the pagan party grouped around the first chief of Pouébo" (1900: 335), whom "he eclipses ... by his power and riches; ... only because he is helped by the missionaries[,] ... represented as two powerful divinities, who make him succeed in everything; but in the end their protégé has to fall to the axe" (Lambert to Poupinel, [1860], APM). Rochas added that the jealousy provoked in Bonou's neighbours and rivals by his missionary-inspired prosperity and success had been exacerbated by his "frank and loyal" cooperation with the French; the dénouement of the fable—in this version the fatal blow was struck by two children—was especially appreciated by listeners (1862: 220, 223).

I remark several themes, all enigmatic. The allegory vaunted the propriety of cooperative effort over individual, yet collective agency was less successful, with or without esoteric aid, until the very last act. In what might have been ironic repudiation of the proclaimed missionary value of hard work, those who did so persistently lost out to the mostly passive *mweau*, whose polite inertia before the windfall of divine assistance was matched by fatalism when confronted with his own imminent murder. His use of water to resuscitate those struck dead by the liberated sun recalls one pole of the wildly variant local beliefs reported about the qualities of the missionaries' holy water: "that we can recall [the sick] ... to life by giving them a certain water that we know of and which has many virtues"; that its touch was widely deemed to be lethal (Rougeyron to S-G, 3 Sep. 1846, APM; Rougeyron, 1846–9: 7; Anon. [1861]). The *teama*, initially depicted as the motor of group action, latterly ceded initiative to his "subjects", whose consternation at the *mweau*'s undeserved achievements eventually necessitated his elimination. As morality tale, the story denied any causal link between human behaviour and divine actions: the deities were benevolent to the *mweau*, but in arbitrary and autonomous fashion, in keeping with what one can detect about indigenous expectations of the more powerful varieties of spirits (see Chapter Seven). As myth, it inscribed a version of the widespread motif of conflict between elder and younger brothers, embodying different kinds of authority, differently sanctioned, with potential for normative inversion should clever, opportunistic juniors upstage their more hidebound seniors, for example by taking creative advantage of novelties (Douglas, 1994b).[9]

This indigenous allegory of Bonou as the inert creature of powerful alien esoteric agents challenges my interested image of him as the Marists' active partner, or even the initiator, in a radical program to fashion an expansive, more centralised—but also less responsive—mode of authority in the Mwelebeng chiefdom. Certainly, the allegorical representation—his enemies'—was also evidently partial and political. But what does one make of intention and ambition when confronted by an aetiology which, subsuming personal agency in spiritual, seemingly disjoined intention, action and outcome (Strathern, 1987: 21–5)? I do not, of course, shrink from appropriating missionary texts to my own interpretive agenda, though they, too, did not believe in individual agency unmediated by spiritual: their two-tiered aetiology blended a metanarrative of providence and Satan with a mundane narrative of bounded, morally responsible individuals exercising free will—"the struggle between grace and nature" (Rougeyron to Abbé de Meydat, 23 Oct. 1855, *AMSM* 1: 15). There is a whiff of critical double standard on my part here, a certain squeamishness about subjecting indigenous texts to the same sceptical radical critique and ruthless historical exploitation as colonial. I take such scrupulosity as morally appropriate given the discursive power asymmetries and dependent relationship between the two broad categories of text (the published indigenous text was stagemanaged by missionaries), but it ought to be acknowledged. A pluralist epistemology ought to give credence, if not equal salience, to multiple interpretative frames; one's own is one such.

Years ago I put a case for endemic tension in New Caledonia, before and after the arrival of Europeans, between the ritual-political aspirations of centralising, perhaps individualistically-inclined "chiefs", especially young ones, and the collectively-oriented restraining influence of elders, complementary dignitaries who controlled important ritual domains (1982): I thought then, and still do, that Bonou was one such instance.[10] Equally, though, this reading might also be in part my retrospective projection of an outcome on to an actor's prior intentions. Contemporary texts concurred that by 1861 Bonou had consolidated his authority within the Mwelebeng chiefdom, particularly over the recalcitrant eastern settlements, and that he had also acquired significant influence in neighbouring groups. Moreover, many Mwelebeng pagans had professed Christianity, which was attracting keen interest elsewhere in the region. This politico-religious transformation happened in the wake of spectacular Mwelebeng military victories achieved over a numerous pagan coalition. The Mwelebeng warriors were aided by 30 or so Christians from Conception, armed with firearms by the colonial government (which could spare no troops), and a small local Christian militia drilled by a missionary under the command of Bonou, who "wore a sabre at his side, sash and general's hat, topped by a 3 coloured plume". They claimed 45 enemy dead, an exceptionally large number for an indigenous war in New Caledonia (see Chapter Three). On the morrow of the last battle the missionary held a military mass for "our soldiers", who attended in fighting regalia (Villard to Poupinel, 13 May 1860, APO). There are unmistakable signals, permeating the hyperbole and braggadocio of the missionary narratives, that the temporal power of the Christian "chief" and the religious credit of his missionary allies and advisers had been notably and mutually enhanced: "all the enemies are trembling, begging for peace. And all the friends or allies are trembling also and ask for missionaries. The demands were made *not to us but to Hypollité [Bonou], which signifies [their] seriousness*" (Villard to Poupinel, 16 Aug. 1860, APO; my emphasis). In both Islanders' and missionaries' worlds, religion and politics were reciprocally, though not identically, dependent: "this war", went one pious summation:

> served to show the devotion and the affection of the Poébos for their missionaries, their religious spirit, and their attachment to religion... It raised the Poébos in the eyes of their still pagan allies,... [who] saw them in a better light and recognised that religion had made them much greater (Anon. [1861]; Rougeyron to Rocher, 23 Oct. 1862, APO).

Further exploration of traces of indigenous conceptions and experience of the pragmatic interplay of power, spirits and rituals requires some backtracking.

APPROPRIATION OF HELL

Throughout the 1850s and beyond, death from disease evidently remained a sticking point in Islanders' relationships with Christian missionaries and inspired marked ambivalence in indigenous evaluations of their acknowledged power, and the virtues or otherwise of their presence. Mission texts reiterated familiar themes that missionaries, their god, rituals, symbols or supporters were held responsible for the persistent high mortality and regular epidemics which challenged local aetiologies and defied available curing techniques. These texts did not just record native perceptions of a simple linear sequence of effect/cause/blame/reaction, but hinted at creative engagement with novelties—experiences, ideas, objects and persons—which Islanders deployed in action to construct and reconstruct themselves and their worlds, such as by appropriation, and at times subversion, of Christian ideas about the afterlife.

At the end of 1855 Rougeyron reported "great trials" at Pouébo, which he depicted as an epic Manichaean struggle: "the devil seems to be disputing desperately the prey which we have snatched from him":

> several persons [having] fainted and been taken for dead, having returned to life, recounted with an air of truthfulness which was entirely sincere, that they had seen Monseigneur [Douarre] and all our Christians,[11] some, very miserable on trees and the others burning in heavenly fire near the furnace of the sun; while in the entrails of the earth they had seen all the pagans' souls happy in the highest degree. That was confirmed by an old woman 20 leagues from the mission who had never seen Mgr. She depicted him burning in heavenly fire.
>
> You could not believe... how much evil this diabolical story has done, even among our Christians; the pagans who have Christian children snatched their children back, saying that we were among them only to make them die and render them unhappier still in the other world (most of our [original] Balade Christians... are dead, while the pagans are shining with health). Others urged their Christian relatives to offend God, to commit sins in order not to go to Heaven above where we said that those go who had no sin; but rather to go to hell below, where everyone was happy; they added that we should not be believed that we deceived them and that they were to do entirely the opposite of what we prescribed (Rougeyron to S-G, 28 Dec. 1855, APM).[12]

Ultimately the Christians of Pouébo maintained their commitment: during the next few months Rougeyron reported that they numbered 400 odd in a generally well-disposed population of about 3,000, the number of catechumens had increased and the "spirit of the tribe" was markedly better. His explanatory trope was the inevitable repulse of Satan's agents by providence (Rougeyron to S-G, [1856]; 10 Oct. 1856, APM). More prosaic, I see a rehearsal for the dramatic victories of 1860, a first instance of military success weighting general indigenous ambivalence in favour of the missionaries, their god and their rituals. For in early 1856 a pagan coalition attacked Pouébo, in defence, thought Rougeyron, of "pagan customs" against Bonou's authority and the "religion and civilisation of the whites". Whereas the *teama*, "pagan and polygamous,... supported the foreign tribes against his own", the Christians were said to have fought with courage and hardihood, backed—morally if not materially—by a decrepit swivel gun manned by a mission lay brother (Rougeyron to S-G, [1856]; Villard to S-G, 30 Mar. 1856, APM; Laurent to Ministre, 13 Jan. 1857, ANOM, Carton 42).

Rougeyron's account of the Pouébo visions is ethnographically of most interest for its subtext, with its hint of a complex imbrication of indigenous and novel concepts and experience: through the medium of visions, attributed literal, though differential authority in both religious cultures, there unfolded a contest to control the terms of discourse. While a counterhegemonic element might be discerned in pagans' transposition of heaven : happy :: hell : unhappy and their inversion of missionary injunctions, they also creatively appropriated notions of salvation and damnation, with revaluation and scrambling of the key metonyms, above/heaven/sun (fire) : below/hell/earth, which they used to subvert missionaries' authority and indict them as dealers in death and deception. In a slightly later letter—a remarkably ethnocentric reduction of indigenous beliefs and rituals to Catholic ontology—Rougeyron stressed native invention and revealed more clearly the political stakes in this discursive contest:

> All Caledonians believe in a future life, but equal for everyone. There is neither <u>punishment</u> for the wicked, nor any <u>reward</u> for the good. They are all indifferently underground in a delightful place where they give themselves over to amusements. For there are many dances, so they have little fear of death. But those who are Christians are not admitted, they float aimlessly amongst the trees of the forests, where they are unhappy, more unhappy still [are] those who rise higher for they [are] burned by the sun. *This is a recent invention of the pagans to prevent religion taking root in their island.* Finally seeing that despite this infernal trick

many were becoming Christians anyway and very sincerely they said that god called to him by death those who were faithful to Religion, who were without sin; consequently if one wanted not to die, it was necessary to commit sins (Rougeyron to Poupinel, 4 Oct. 1858, APO; underlined in original; my emphasis).

Similar reasoning was reported by Villard, the missionary at Touho. In 1856 the high "chief's" brother, who had encouraged the missionaries to settle at Touho but was now dying, "accused the [Christian] religion of making him sick and making him die". He begged a fellow catechumen on a fast day to "'<u>eat with me then so that I might have a companion in this fire</u> (hell) <u>which they tell us about</u>'".[13] "Sorcerers" called in for professional consultation by the high "chief" declared that the dying man would only recover if he cast off his loin cloth and ceased going to services, because they were attended by menstruating women: that is, discard a Christian key symbol and restore a local taboo.[14] To Villard the sick man was a "hypocrite, liar" because on the one hand he told the missionaries that "he did not believe in these things", while on the other he "changed completely and openly": he and his brother the high "chief" continued to attend catechism and claimed to be "good friends" to the missonaries, but at the same time they sought "by every possible means to seduce the catechumens into reviving their superstitions". This crisis provoked the missionaries to invite the remaining Touho neophytes to emigrate to Conception, where they would be free "to live in a Christian fashion"; 88 persons—40 men, 44 women and four infants—were duly spirited away (Villard to S-G, 30 Mar. 1856; Lagardelle to Morcel, 25 Mar. 1857, APM).

At both Pouébo and Touho the struggle for discursive power was actualised in battles to control people's bodies: the dying and the neophyte Christians, particularly "chiefs" and young people. The missionaries' political agenda were explicit. Rougeyron threatened that, should the Pouébo Christians "be too exposed in this infernal battle", he would repeat the Balade experiment of physical displacement by removing them to a separate settlement, "where we shall dominate [them] as fathers and masters"; during 1856 a substantial contingent did indeed follow him to Conception. It was a telling bottom line, given what had happened at Balade since the

Christians left. Villard claimed the exodus from Touho as "a *coup d'état*, we put ourselves directly in opposition to the high chief, for a chief is only as powerful as the number of his subjects". However, a tug of war between foreign and local priests for spiritual control of the dying Touho "chief" was won by the locals when he opted to die "with all the honours, all the superstitions of a pagan chief" (Rougeyron to S-G, 28 Dec. 1855, 10 Oct. 1856; Villard to S-G, 30 Mar. 1856, APM). Villard later heard that Touho elders had decreed his own death in revenge for the young man's: "it is religion which made him die; we must kill the missionary". Thomassin, a more experienced missionary, better versed in the vernacular, made explicit reference to sorcery: "the missionaries were accused of having made ... [the 'chief'] die by a spell, or rather religion had killed him, therefore religion was no longer needed" (Villard to S-G, 30 Mar. 1856; Thomassin to S-G, 10 May 1857, APM). The high "chief" was supposed to have backed down in the face of opposition from his mother, a catechumen, and from Apengou, the powerful high "chief" at nearby Wagap, who thought well of missionaries (see Chapter Four).

I see sedimented in Villard's and Thomassin's remarks the shadowy imprint of indigenous conceptions of causation in terms of concrete human or spiritual actions or symbols, in contrast to the nomothetic Christian trope of good and evil in collision. Islanders' existential experience of "religion" as instrumental rituals encouraged eclectic sampling and appropriation of foreign ideas, objects and practices, which they refashioned to suit their own interests and cultural logics. This pragmatic relativism was vexedly admitted by a few of the more percipient missionaries, such as Lambert writing of the Belema of Belep in 1858: "when one stays [amongst them] and enters into the detail of their life, one easily sees that in saying yes to what we teach them, they do not say no to their ancient beliefs" (1855–75: 47).[15] It is unlikely that at this stage Islanders encountered Christianity/civilisation systemically or holistically, as antithetical to their own objectified religion/culture, though they no doubt had a lively sense of differences and variety.[16] In their pluralism and tolerance of distinctions they were unlike missionaries who, engrossed in Manichaean antinomies, ultimately saw antagonism to themselves, their rituals and their supporters in starkly oppositional, cosmic terms, as in the following, typically hyperbolic sample:

> Poébo was the pearl of the New Caledonian missions. Civilisation and religion for some time were making such progress there as to irritate the Devil. He in fact proved that he was furious; for he assembled four pagan tribes against Poébo... [T]heir loudly declared motive was hatred of religion. They had said that they would make peace only when Poébo ceased to sing [mass] morning and evening. It was clearly therefore a Caledonian persecution: either die or abandon the faith (Anon. [1861]).

Inclined to the mundane by principle and preference, I see indigenous hostility as strategic and directed not at the missionaries' religion in an abstract, esoteric sense, but at particular signs and symbols experienced as baneful—Christian rituals, dress and devotional objects. From this perspective, neither opposition nor support need be total or mutually exclusive: seeming inconsistencies in behaviour, such as continuing to attend catechism while consulting local "sorcerers" and attempting to subvert the commitment of converts, need not be rated the "hypocrisy" of the missionary lexicon, but might be better classified as eclectically pragmatic.

At Touho in 1856, as at Pouébo, local hostility to missionaries as purveyors of illness and death was evidently deflected by external attack and quelled by active missionary alliance in the ensuing war. Not four months later, several members of the high "chief's" family expressed the wish to be Christian and the future of the mission seemed assured. By 1860 most of the 700 or so residents of Touho were at least nominally Christian, but missionaries complained that the splendid brick church was never full because the Christians, "terrified" by the high mortality to which they seemed particularly susceptible, were intimidated by neighbouring pagans' threats and warnings that "religion kills" (Rougeyron to Poupinel, 15 June 1860; Thomassin to Poupinel, 18 May 1860, APO; Anon. [1861]).

"SOURCE OF LIFE ... CAUSE OF DEATH"[17]

I conclude this excursion through early textual traces of indigenous experiences of disease and epidemic in New Caledonia by sampling contemporary descriptions of the epidemic of measles, complicated by dysentery and pneumonia, which swept the colony from October 1860 to early 1861, shortly before it devastated Tanna and Aneityum (see Chapter Six). Missionaries estimated that up to a third of the population died in some places, while in those where accurate counting was possible between one-tenth and a quarter perished: 60 out of 300 at Conception and 170 out of fewer than 1,100 at the Isle of Pines (Forestier to Rocher, 7 Aug. 1861, APO; Poupinel to Nicollet, 30 Apr. 1861, *AMSM* 2: 36). These Catholic communities suffered badly, but others in the north had relatively few fatalities, while the Belema of Belep escaped entirely.

At Conception the Christians were said to have awaited death fearlessly: they were, said an anonymous report, true martyrs, for their "superstitions" convinced them "that, in becoming Christian,... they were embracing a religion which would make them die" (Anon. [1861]). Rougeyron was astonished at their resignation, which outstripped his own: "If heaven is being peopled", he lamented, the settlement was diminishing, "and soon will be nothing but a veritable cemetery" (Rougeyron to Poupinel, 14 Nov. 1860, APO). At the colony's administrative headquarters of Port-de-France, where the epidemic actually began among the native residents, many soldiers were ill with "typhoidal fevers and dysentery" and some died (Frémont to Poupinel, 15 Nov., 31 Dec. 1860, APO). On the Loyalty Island of Ouvéa, where there was a rival LMS mission, the epidemic had its compensations from a Catholic viewpoint. One-fifth of the supporters of an apostate "chief" died, while the Protestants fared even worse, provoking some to accuse the Catholic missionary of sorcery. When Catholics also fell ill, the epidemic was attributed to Europeans in general, and when persons baptised *in extremis* died, the Catholic priest was refused access to the sick, "because it was, they said, his gaze and baptism which made them die" (Anon. [1861]).

At Yaté a catechist was killed, probably in revenge for the epidemic—"which in their superstitious beliefs they impute to us"—since many people died in the settlement where he was based and almost none in those nearby; missionary aetiology supplied what presumably was to them a more rational explanation: "it is an implacable and particular persecution of the devil against our missions". The missionary at Canala was accused of "making people die and of being the author of their ills" (Rougeyron to Poupinel, 1, 12, 29 Jan. 1861, APO). An Islander who carried the mail between Port-de-France and Canala was killed by an inland group which had had few contacts with Europeans. Three of its members told the French that they had acted on their "chief's" belief "that the whites were the authors of the sickness... and that the box borne by the courier contained spells capable of inflicting death" (Durand to Ministre, 1, 26 Feb. 1861, ANM, BB4 797). The box and its contents were subsequently returned, apparently after ritual fumigation. At Arama, where the epidemic raged and Gagnière was himself afflicted, it was said no one wanted baptism as they feared its deadly influence, and the sick were hidden from the missionaries (Anon. [1861]). At Touho, which also suffered heavily, Thomassin cloaked harrowing images of respiratory complications in a sardonic rhetoric:

> [Here is] a thing you have never suspected and that certainly you will not believe, but which is believed here thanks to the spirit of calumny: it is that I am a sorcerer. I make the rain and the fine weather; I spread death everywhere, I kill souls and bodies... Every Sunday, during the sprinkling of holy water, I kill as many spirits as I give shakes of the aspergillum. If by chance, there are a few curious or new listeners, they can be seen moving to avoid my blow. What they fear especially, is holy water. They regard themselves as dead, when a drop falls on them: this water penetrates their insides, and eats away their lungs and their heart (quoted in Anon. [1861]).

But in the north the novel incidence of the epidemic struck missionaries as "miraculously" providential, while from an indigenous perspective it was apparently a dramatic demonstration of Christian ritual efficacy:

> No tribe has been spared; catholics,... pagans, all have been severely hit. However, it is said that this time, in mixed tribes, ours have had fewer losses to mourn, and in the North the Christians have lost fewer people than the pagans. On reaching these remote parts, it seemed to have lost its violence. At Poébo, as at Conception and the Isle of Pines, no one was spared, but the number of victims was relatively much less (Poupinel to Nicollet, 30 Apr. 1861, *AMSM* 2: 36).

Most wonderful of all, Belep, which had been ravaged by an epidemic in the first half of 1860, was "entirely spared" the measles, thanks, exulted Lambert and Gagnière, to a "fervent novena", a "great outburst of prayer", which the Christians offered to the Virgin. Modern oral histories represented early Belema engagements with Christianity as uninflected by fears, so potent elsewhere, about its presumed lethal impact, attributing the epidemics which did afflict them to a vengeful local spirit (see below).[18] Belief joined experience at Belep to confirm Christianity as "a source of life, instead of being feared there as a cause of death" (Gagnière to Poupinel, 12 June 1861, APO; Lambert 1855–75: 51–3; 1900: 228–30).

At Pouébo, too, according to Gagnière, Christianity now looked like salvation for a dying populace, vindicating his theory and method of proselytism, which Lambert also applied at Belep, and which made Christianity meaningful by correlating it with indigenous beliefs and rituals, conceived symbolically as Judaic remnants. Beginning with Genesis, Gagnière explained, he had represented the Bible publicly as the sole repository of divinely instituted belief and practice:

> As words turned up which relate to their observances or beliefs, I insisted that this [pagan] practice is divine that its author is the same god as Christianity's; then comes the motive, the time when it was obligatory, the abrogation, the prohibition, the substitution by this or that other Christian practice of which it was the symbol (Gagnière to Poupinel, 12 June 1861, APO).

Since Gagnière, like all his fellows, conceived human strategies as more or less feeble means to facilitate the mysterious workings of grace, he need not contemplate the likely dialectics of reverse conversion, of vernacularisation of Christianity. The risk that his method might camouflage satanic subversion of eternal verities did, however, exercise his more authoritarian confreres.[19]

EXEGESIS

How is one to decipher this congeries of particular evaluations of complex dialectics of experience, context, personality and circumstance, these random and varied impressions inscribed long ago by men whose world was as opaque to me as those of the men and women of whom they wrote? My reading and writing are fed by the following assumptions. One is that indigenous cultures in New Caledonia, pervasively hierarchical, were infused with expectations of reciprocity and equivalence in social and ritual relationships and were able to accommodate novelties, whether persons, objects, actions or ideas. Another is that missionaries and Islanders both had religious epistemes, which they acknowledged in each other but did not share. A third is that missionary discourses, always hierarchical, paternalist and assured of European racial and cultural superiority, were rendered profoundly ambivalent by the Christian premise of the spiritual equality of all humanity: though at times complicit with the harshly racist, scientific evolutionism which underwrote European settler colonialism,[20] mission discourses in general were humanised by a vision of the *pagan* (as distinct from the *savage* of secular evolutionary discourse) as equal in the sight of God, apt for salvation and susceptible of improvement through education.[21]

Power and the relative malevolence/benevolence of spirits were common denominators in the dynamic, often ambivalent range of Islanders' actions and statements traced in this chapter, but power was a multifaceted, multivalent, slippery quality. Indigenous aetiologies of disease, death and disaster were varied, flexible and open to innovation: so far as one can tell, they embraced a variety of spiritual agencies, jealous of their spaces, taboos and ritual dues, often capriciously malevolent and more or less responsive to prayers, offerings or magic performed by living human beings; they included widespread belief in the lethal possibility of sorcery (see Chapter Seven). Christian missionaries, their god, rituals, symbols and codes, were readily encompassed, in widely varied, mutable ways, positive, negative and neutral.

From the outset, missionaries were in no doubt as to their elevated status and potency in indigenous conception, as "superior" beings, "greater and more powerful" than the most awesome local spirits (Leconte, 1847: 819). Because they conflated indigenous notions of the divine with their own, they were taken aback by violence in 1847: superior beings ought to be invulnerable to mundane passions, but were not in islands' logic, in which the ritual relationship between human beings and spirits was one of reciprocal, though usually not equal, dependence. A decade later, Rougeyron showed that experience could teach perspective, if not cultural relativism:

> As we were the first Europeans they had seen, they took our ship for a house of celestial dwellers... the sun, the rain, the thunder etc. being in the neighbourhood of our celestial residence, these things were of our making... Disabused shortly of this gross error, the pagans have continued to believe, at least in part, that the sorcerers of the country had power over the sun and the rain (Rougeyron to S-G, 4 Oct. 1858, APO).

Power—*ujet*, "power, efficacy", in *yâlayu*—was not a fixed commodity, but could take many guises and required constant pragmatic ratification. Jehovah and his priests were evidently quickly naturalised and competitively mobilised as formidable elements in local consciousness, contests and contexts. Lambert's allegory about Bonou is eloquent on the varied powers attributed to missionaries. Native eclecticism meant that local spirits might withdraw or be relegated to insignificance, but they were not obliterated by Jehovah; his most effective agents were those like Gagnière and Lambert, whose ideology, however coercive, allowed some space for pluralism, in rituals and beliefs as well as spirits. The texts implied a range of indigenous conceptions of encounters between Jehovah and local rivals, glossed by missionaries as satanic manifestations, with predictable celebration of contests depicting their rebuff or discouragement. In the later of two stories from Belep, a well-known diviner, challenged publicly to invoke the spirits with whom he was in communion, stated that since the missionaries' arrival "the spirits have gone away; they are hiding, I don't know where they are any more". Lambert claimed notable tactical success at Belep in engineering such confrontations and contriving demonstrations of Jehovah's supreme power, especially over the elements: he challenged his listeners, "Why fear or invoke spirits who are not to be feared and who cannot answer your prayers?" (Lambert to Dumont, 25 May 1859, *AMSM* 1: 330–2; Lambert 1900: 27, 197–202). Islanders no doubt conducted their own tests of relative divine efficacy, like the Aneityumese described by Geddie (see Chapter Six).[22]

It is also likely, given the frightful retribution believed to follow derelictions in ritual duties and taboo-breaking, that domestic spirits were supposed to have inflicted illness in retaliation for the Christians' defection, symbolised in the wearing of loin cloths, their non-performance of ritual obligations and their flouting of taboos and ritual restrictions. Mission texts did not often entertain the possibility, though there was fleeting mention of Islanders' disquiet about the presence in church of menstruating women and a tantalising snippet from the Isle of Pines: "the old men said: 'Missionary, your word is fine, and I believe your God [to be] powerful and good; but, you see, ours is jealous and pitiless: to abandon him, is to condemn oneself to death'" (Goujon to Favre, Jan. 1857 [a], APM).[23] Correlatively, becoming a Christian might also have served to evade, undermine or displace the efficacy of malevolent or punitive local spirits, as was reported on Aneityum and Malaita (see Chapter Six; Burt, 1982: 383; Keesing, 1989b: 199–206, 211). The theme of Christianity as source of protection against local esoteric power recurred in Belep oral tradition. Guiart bracketed the 1855 conversion of Ouaoulo, *teama*, "high chief", of Belep and renowned as a sorcerer and weather magician (Lambert, 1855–75: 18; Mathieu to Durand, 22 July 1861, ANOM, Carton 42), with a myth cycle he recorded in the field in the 1950s. It recounted how Ouaoulo had ordered the death of a rival "chief", also a famous magician, whose vengeful spirit inflicted a devastating epidemic: "It is not surprising", speculated Guiart, "in the face of the fear provoked by the epidemic...that Hwaulo later thought to seek refuge in conversion" (1966: 30). The modern Marist ethnographer Dubois was told that Belema blamed the murdered "chief's" vengeance for all the epidemics which scourged them from the 1840s to the 1860s, rather than Europeans or their Christian god. Ouaoulo was said to have feared his rival more dead than alive, since he had become a *jawa*, "deified ancestor"; thus beset, the *teama* was responsive to missionary assurances that their god was strongest of all, a *jawa ec*, "male god", "the name the Belema give him still" (1985: 506). Local conviction that Jehovah and his priests exceeded their rivals in both power *and* benevolence could be a heady mixture. Nonetheless, such evidence did not necessarily retain authority in the face of conflicting experience: by the mid 1870s Montrouzier admitted that high mortality and Marist neglect had provoked disillusionment with Christianity at Belep, "which at one time gave us so much consolation":

> Our people retain the external forms for the most part. However,...there are several young people who openly profess themselves tired of being Christians.... They have at the same time, retaken their former customs and...do nothing to show they do not want to keep them. One would call them birds escaped from the cage, who enjoy the freedom and are afraid of being recaptured.... One would say that they believe themselves to have been deceived (Montrouzier to Fraysse, 15 Apr. 1876, AAN, 30.1).

I conclude this chapter by rehearsing its major theme: indigenous appropriation of Christian notions of the afterlife in novel contexts of high mortality. Early European observers, missionary and secular alike, were all but unanimous that these people had no indigenous concept of reward and punishment after death, though missionaries sought anxiously for traces of such belief (Rougeyron to Poupinel, 4 Oct. 1858, APO; see also Rochas, 1862: 280). In his 1846 ethnography Rougeyron, sublimely persuaded of "the great truths of [his own] Religion", lamented that the Islanders "have forgotten almost everything [since the Fall] and so confuse things that we can see little difference in their thought between the good and the evil in the underground kingdom of the[ir] deity. An all powerful God creator of all things avenger and rewarder seems totally unknown to them at least in the part of the island in which we live". Yet he had already discerned a transformation in this regard: "There is now not a single person who does not fear hell; its very name makes the most libertine or the most hardened shudder". For Rougeyron this was plain good sense: "One must effectively be mad and raving mad to remain indifferent to the prospect of this endless road of a miserable eternity. Today no one refuses to pray and almost everyone would like to be baptised" (Rougeyron to S-G, 3 Sep. 1846, APM). Years later, on Ouvéa during the measles epidemic, when many claimed the Catholic priest killed by "his gaze and baptism", an old man was reported to have said to the missionary: "Father and sacred chief, I believe in God and in you; I fear hellfire. I have resolved to convert". As gage of good faith, he had sent away one of his wives and returned her brideprice (Anon. [1861]). I cannot say how missionaries framed their horrifying message,[24] nor what their hearers might have made of it, since there seems to have been no indigenous notion of extreme suffering after death. The Pouébo and Touho cases argue, however, that Islanders did not just passively accept and react to the missionary threat of damnation, but made the concept of hell their own.

By contrast, the Christian notion of heaven, which Islanders appropriated enthusiastically, struck a familiar chord. Rougeyron maintained, seconded by Lambert, that they believed in an indiscriminately pleasant existence after death (Rougeyron to Poupinel, 4 Oct. 1858, APO; Lambert, 1900: 13–16). Rochas, too, claimed: "they have a paradise, but no hell" (1862: 280). The attraction of the prospect of heaven—construed in literal local terms?—for committed Christians was palpable in the reported words of Ouaoulo of Belep, Lambert's partner in the project to convert those islands:

> "I no longer believe the word of our old men. You are right, you others; your belief and your way of doing things are good. I believe that there is only one God, who does everything; I believe strongly that our souls do not die and that we are in our country as on a visit. We shall leave it soon to go to heaven, if we are good. I should very much like to die... in order to see what you tell us" (Lambert to Dumont, 25 May 1859, *AMSM* 1: 329).

It might have been this promise, fortified perhaps by the relative indifference to death of Islanders and their experiential imbrication of human and extrahuman worlds, the living and the dead, which inspired the extraordinary resignation of Christians and prospective converts. Rougeyron marvelled during the measles epidemic that:

> our poor pagan natives, when they consent to embrace the [Christian] religion, make the sacrifice of their life. When they are Christian, they die in a peaceful and holy fashion, because they expect to die from the death <u>of the Christianos</u>. They call by this name the disease of consumption which leads them to the tomb. Are they not martyrs? (Rougeyron to Poupinel, 1 Jan. 1861, APO; underlined in original).

At least for Christians, both avoidance of eternal fire and attainment of heaven after death seem to have been corollaries of observance of the missionaries' general behavioural code. This might have implied an aetiological transformation, an elaboration on the local concept of taboo, since indigenous spirits were apparently not presumed to play a general social role in policing human morality. Ouaoulo's heartfelt testimony included the phrase "if we are good", while Lambert mentioned "those who want to be good" in the same letter. A somewhat earlier text explained that the idiom "to make their country good", as a synonym for "making it Christian, putting a stop to wars and libertinism", had become "the rallying cry of the friends of progress" at Balade—those who would shortly form the nucleus of the new mission settlement at Conception (Forestier to S-G, 12 Mar. 1853, APM). Yet the story of the Pouébo visions also indicates that the concept of heaven, like hell, was inflected by pagans in original and contestatory fashion. Thus heaven and hell, like the missionaries themselves and their god, were naturalised in varied ways across a whole dynamic spectrum of engagement, from radical opposition, to neutrality, to fervent support.[25]

There is much about all this which continues to puzzle and appall me, none more so than Thomassin's tale of the holy water. What could possibly have inspired "curious or new listeners" to attend services if they already knew the need to duck its deadly drops (Anon. [1861])? It must come back to power, *ujet*, construed ambiguously in local experience as lethal but efficacious: the power to kill, the power to cure, to damn and to save, to be successful and to earn prestige, to discountenance rivals and defeat enemies. By this reading the "wildly variant" indigenous beliefs about holy water, referred to earlier, do not betoken contradiction or confusion, but are reflexes of the multifaceted and equivocal nature of power. There is no gainsaying the commitment of the handful of dedicated Christians, though they readily acknowledged the likely costs. Many Islanders in 1861 must still have been oblivious or indifferent to missionaries, but many others were ambivalent, desiring access to the missionaries' power and to heaven but fearing death/damnation and irked by many of their proscriptions and affiliations. Even their most bitter opponents readily embraced an idea of their god, his potency and the vivid reality of both eternal pain and eternal pleasure. In various ways, those who knew of them contrived strategies to appropriate and channel that power to local ends, while some sought to thwart or subvert it. Rougeyron acknowledged as much in 1858, though he largely missed the import of his insight: "this [denial of the native paradise to Christians] is a recent invention of the pagans to prevent religion taking root in their island" (Rougeyron to Poupinel, 4 Oct. 1858, APO).

EPILOGUE

Pagan coalitions in the north in the 1850s and early 1860s conjoined resentment and fear of missionaries, their god and their rituals with hostility to Bonou: the early alignment of Mwelebeng and mission must have looked like a project to enforce a new politico-religious hegemony, trailing France—with its tendency to spasmodic, unpredictable, sometimes brutal interventions—in its wake. Bonou chose to register his commitment to innovation and modernity in symbols of sartorial elegance and military status, commissioning his missionary allies to acquire on his behalf "a complete costume" at a cost of 109 francs: it should include "a reasonably elegant black overcoat", "well made white trousers", "a gentleman's vest" and scarf, "a pleated white shirt" and "especially a naval officer's peaked cap with pure or fake gold braid", depending on cost (Forestier to Rocher, 7 Aug. 1861, APO).

After 1862 the pagans, briefly cowed or subdued by Christian victories, found an unlikely ally in the newly-appointed colonial governor, Guillain, an anticlerical who recruited them to an energetic campaign against Marist and Mwelebeng dominance in the north. During an official visit to Pouébo in 1863, the Mwelebeng entertained Guillain with a *phiilu*, "dance", in the course of which he was formally addressed by Bonou, "dressed as a perfect *gentleman*" and wearing a thickly braided old style naval officer's cap. An aide, apparently oblivious to the Christian affiliations of most of the seemingly savage performers, his own civilised sensibilities piqued, described Bonou's "European costume, amongst completely naked savages, and worn by one of the actors in an entirely savage scene" as "shockingly incongruous". The governor was likely more offended by the prominent role played by a missionary interpreter, unappreciated mediator between the colonial state and its subjects (La Hautière, 1869: 116, orig. emphasis). In the event, Bonou was to be a notable victim of the anticlerical, antiMwelebeng project: in April 1866 the "chief" was accused of abuse of authority and missionary-inspired insubordination to the colonial administration, suspended "from his functions as second chief of Pouébo" and exiled to the Isle of Pines, where he died a few months later during an epidemic of respiratory sickness ("Décisions du gouverneur", 24 Apr., 1 May 1866, *Moniteur*, 6 May 1866). The prophetic allegory of his demise by virtue of acquisition of unnatural power through alien esoteric associations was thus curiously fulfilled, as missionaries acknowledged (Gagnière to his brother, 2 May 1866, APM; Lambert, 1900: 319). Unfortunately for Islanders, pagan as well as Christian, the agency by which this outcome was achieved—newly energised, heavyhanded colonial intervention—was equally as alien as the mission and far less disinterested so far as native welfare was concerned.

On numerous occasions, especially in the 1860s, in 1878–9 and in the 1890s, the Marist mission defended Melanesians—or at least the Catholics among them—against abuse and injustice by secular authorities. In the 1860s the contest between state and church was locally phrased as one between *"soldatisme* and *missionarisme"*

(Roussel to Poupinel, Aug. 1875, APM), between "the soldiers' religion" and the missionaries': the former was defined by Rougeyron as "not having any [religion]", as atheism, but other missionaries specified that it involved officially-sanctioned abandonment of Christian dress and "retaking all their pagan customs", "conserving their idolatrous and sorcerous ways, save for human and cannibal sacrifices" (Rougeyron to ?, 30 Nov. 1867; Poupinel to ?, n.d.; Guitta to Bailly, 30 Sep. 1865, APM). Missionaries saw in all this a cosmic drama of irreligion and religious persecution, in which natives featured as instruments of Satan or passive victims. I, by contrast, am drawn as a moth to flame to a vision of local agency: a complex dialectic of indigenous appropriation and refashioning of competing alien ideologies for domestic ends and to subvert unappreciated aspects of the practical agenda of colonisers and missionaries. It was a dialectic anticipated in earlier indigenous engagements with Christian missionaries outlined in Part Three of this book. I surmise—though at this stage the theme remains a mote in my interpretive eye—that these early narratives might clarify later phases of indigenous colonial and postcolonial experience in New Caledonia and elsewhere, when Christian ideas, rituals and ministers were appropriated and recast as anticolonial or anti-élitist ideologies, strategies and agents: such as the supplanting of Catholicism in some areas of New Caledonia from the 1890s by an alternative, Protestant ideology, purveyed by native pastors and construed as the "word of life" (Guiart, 1962: 131–2).

In the 1970s and 1980s evangelical Christianity was in the van of the Kanak independence movement, while the Catholic church was seen by independentists as alien, authoritarian and colonialist. Several moderate leaders of the FLNKS were former Catholic priests, including the FLNKS leader Jean-Marie Tjibaou, who was killed by the radical Djubelly Wea, a former student for the Protestant ministry, outraged by what he considered to be Tjibaou's betrayal of the Kanak cause. Thus might traces of past discourses resonate in present ironies.

NOTES

[1] E.g., Ileto, 1979; Kaplan, 1990; Rafael, 1988; Taussig,, 1980; see also Mbembe, 1988.
[2] Protestant missionary settlement in mainland New Caledonia in the mid-nineteenth century was confined to the extreme south and lasted only five years (1840–5); all the resident missionaries were Polynesian converts brought by the LMS from Samoa or Rarotonga (Ta'unga 1968: 25–76).
[3] These intimations of the parodic in ritual inversion recall Taussig's account of how runaway slave leaders in seventeenth century Columbia "initiated their converts in a ritual that mocked Christian baptism and denied God, the saints, and the Virgin Mary in order to achieve salvation in the afterlife and wealth and power in the here and now" (1980: 42).
[4] An official head count in 1857 listed 538 persons remaining at Balade (du Bouzet to Min., 25 Nov. 1857, ANOM, Carton 42).
[5] Equivalent apprehensions were reported on the part of elders at Belep and Wagap. In these two of the most powerful east coast chiefdoms, high "chiefs" well disposed to Christian missionaries and their worship were said to have faced popular contumacy and even the threat of abandonment from "subjects" who "wanted absolutely nothing to do with missionaries" (Lambert to Dumont, 25 May 1859, *AMSM* 1: 330; Vigouroux to Poupinel, May 1859, APO; Montrouzier, 1860: 9).
[6] In the east coast *cèmuhî* language, "subjects" are semantically "elder" in relation to the "chief", conceived as "the eldest son of his subjects". "Chief" is an inadequate translation of the *yâlayu* (Balade) and *caac* (Pouébo) term *teama* and its cognates in other Kanak languages, since its connotation of acknowledged authority to rule and command elides the contextual, invertible quality of New Caledonian hierarchies (Bensa and Rivierre, 1982: 74–5, 91, 108–11; Bensa, 1986; Douglas, 1994b).
[7] "Code pénal de la tribu de Muélébé", Article 14, 15 Feb. 1854, ANOM, Carton 67.
[8] "Le Téama et le Muau des Aobats", in Lambert to Poupinel, [1860], APM. Labelled "Literature in New Caledonia", the letter was published in *AMSM* 1: 437–9, while the text was reproduced in Lambert's published ethnography under the rubric "War Chants" (1900: 326–35). Rochas also classed it as "Literature". The "Aobats", vehicle for the allegory, were the Aovaac of Arama, west of Balade.
[9] Wallis differentiated the spheres of action and authority of first and second born males of "chiefly" rank (1994: 147, quoted Chapter Three, n. 17). Smith (1974: 61–9) outlined variants of the elder: younger relationship in New Zealand Maori myths and politics, as did Kaplan with respect to Fiji and Sahlins to Hawai'i (Kaplan, 1990: 8–9; Sahlins, 1981a: 56–64). Jackson (1978) explored inversions in normative and fictional representations of the

status and personal qualities of elder and younger brothers by Kuranko (Sierra Leone) and Maori.
10. See Chapter Six for the case in point of Vendegou at the Isle of Pines in the 1850s.
11. "Our Christians" here meant about 70 young people from Balade and Pouébo who had gone with the missionaries to Futuna and mostly died since their return to New Caledonia in 1852.
12. See Owens (1970) for a detailed interpretation of creative appropriation and contestation by Maori of Wesleyan concepts, including heaven and hell.
13. Villard to S-G, 30 Mar. 1856, APM (underlined in original). Chapter Six cites a passage from Geddie's Journal recounting a contemporaneous instance of subversive appropriation of Christian notions about the afterlife by an Aneityumese woman (1848–57: 26 Aug. 1852–1975: 140). Forty years before, the LMS missionary Davies described how a Tahitian priest prayed and sacrificed to Satan to cure a sick woman whose "crime" had been to attend the mission school; he accused the missionaries of deceiving Tahitians. Davies added that the term "Satani is commonly now applied to the [Tahitian] gods" (1961: 168).
14. Rougeyron explained that "women who have their periods remain isolated, in a house apart, until their infirmity has passed. All sorts of harm must befall those who cross the threshold where they are. One of the causes of the great mortality of our Christians results from our making these women enter the Church" (Rougeyron to Poupinel, 4 Oct. 1858, APO; Patouillet, 1873: 81–2).
15. The Comaroffs put a parallel case with reference to the Tswana of southern Africa, arguing that during their early, mid-nineteenth century encounters with evangelical missionaries, their "tolerant relativism encouraged them to try to adopt piecemeal into *setswana* [Tswana ways] those elements of *sekgoa* [European ways] that might enhance their lives", on "the presumption that peoples of different worlds might learn, and might incorporate, one another's ways and means without repudiating their own" (1991: 210–11, 225, 243–8). Bensa argued in general, somewhat essentialist terms for Kanak receptiveness to innovation as an enduring reflex of the pragmatic interplay of ideas, rituals, horticultural techniques and politics (1990: 130, 15*).
16. Guiart argued otherwise, on the purported "evidence" of "early mission reports": "from the beginning the people [of Oceania] tended to view everything new that was offered them by the missionaries as a whole, as a 'package deal'.... Melanesians and Polynesians discovered functionalism and structuralism for themselves through being confronted with the white man's culture and society" (1962: 122–3). This impression of instant objectification requires deconstruction as an artefact of missionary Manichaeism. See also Jolly's discussion of the politically fraught theme of relationships between indigenous "self-consciousness of difference[,] ... the internalization

of... [a] Western concept of culture and its externalization as a symbol in political struggles with European others" (1992: 57-60). The Comaroffs provide a detailed South African case study of such transformations (1991).

[17] Gagnière to Poupinel, 12 June 1861, APO.

[18] It is an index of European presumption of their own centrality in postcontact native reckoning that Europeans, then and later, usually took for granted indigenous assumption of a causal link between whites and recently introduced diseases. That such connections need to be explored in context is suggested by Reynolds' argument that Aboriginal Australians, convinced of the superior powers of their own "clever men", long attributed novel epidemics, including smallpox but not venereal disease, to sorcery performed by enemy groups (1982: 56-8; for a twentieth century case in point in the Kimberleys, see Widlok, 1992: 120).

[19] The volume and preoccupations of his correspondence during 1859-61 suggest that Gagnière was in regular conflict with his colleagues and superiors over his insistence on the need to differentiate "Caledonian superstitions" into the "diabolic" and the "revealed", and to mobilise the latter to the mission cause (Gagnière to Poupinel, 1 May, 3 Dec. 1859, 12 May 1860, 25 Feb., 12 June 1861; Villard to Poupinel, 16 May 1859, APO).

[20] The well-known stereotyped contrast between French assimilationist and British segregationist colonialism was scarcely borne out in New Caledonia, despite periodic official claims to the contrary—particularly during the governorship of Guillain (1862-70), an anticlerical, self-professed utopian socialist who espoused a secular program of civilisation and assimilation for Melanesians analogous to and in direct competition with the Marists' project of religious conversion (e.g., Guillain to Ministre, 30 Apr. 1863, ANOM, Carton 26; *Moniteur*, 14 Feb. 1869). Yet it was Guillain who initiated the segregationist, evolutionist policy whereby Melanesians were eventually incarcerated in reserves preliminary to their presumed inevitable racial demise. However "cultural" their racism with respect to certain Africans and Asians, French observers tended to classify "Melanesians"/"Kanaks" as racially primitive in "scientific", evolutionary terms (e.g., Bourgarel, 1862: 251-91; Deplanche, 1868-9; Dumont d'Urville, 1832; Garnier, 1873: 214-15; Vinson, 1975: 11-18). In France the tide of scientific racism flowed freely from the end of the eighteenth century, whereas in Britain it was for decades challenged and partly diverted by evangelical obduracy (Stocking, 1968: 13-14; Hall, 1991). In New Caledonia the racism of settlers terrified of savages and avid for land occupied by indigenous people lost little in virulence compared with that of their counterparts in Australia (e.g., *N-C*, 4 July, 21 Aug. 1878; on French settler racism and evolutionary assumptions in Algeria, see Prochaska, 1990; on Australia, see Morris, 1992; Reynolds, 1987).

[21] For echoes of the profound ambivalence and tortuous reasoning of Catholic thinking on human similarities and difference, see Douarre's commentary

on an episode of cannibalism: "What a people, great God! and yet, I am their father", and his reference to Balade people as "these unfortunate savages today become my children" (1843–53: 25 Feb., 11 June 1846). Equally convoluted, Inglis provided a sample of his preaching to Aneityumese "of the privileges and of the birth of God's children... because they had Abraham for their father" (1887: 123–6). He found "great satisfaction" that they were able to made "good their claim to be considered a part of our common humanity; their voices mastered the difficulties of the minor key as of the major". Yet his humanism was qualified by racial stereotyping of "those sable children of Ethiopia": "here, as in all other things, in the case of a people sunk so low, very moderate attainments must satisfy us" (1887: 141, 147). On the general theme, see Comaroff and Comaroff, 1991; Fabian, 1983: 26–7; Hall, 1991; Thomas, 1992a.

22 Ta'unga described how the younger brother of a "chief" prayed to Jehovah for success in a forthcoming battle. When victory ensued, "he brought his idols and threw them into the fire. His faith in Jehovah increased greatly" (1968: 74).

23 Aneityumese belief that disease was inflicted by vengeful ancestors insulted or spurned by Christian missionaries and converts was a persistent theme in Geddie's early journal (see Chapter Six). Similar beliefs were reported from widely disparate settings: amongst sixteenth century Andean Indians (Taussig, 1980: 171–2) and modern Kwaio pagans on Malaita, Solomon Islands (Keesing, 1989b: 200).

24 On the stress on hellfire and damnation in Tridentine Catholicism in France and its persistence into the mid-nineteenth century, see Gibson, 1989: 15–29, 241–67.

25 Keesing cited an analogous example of domestication of the concept of heaven by a pagan Kwaio woman who stated: "It's all right for you [her children] to go up [to heaven]. I'm just going to stay here" (1989b: 202).

FINALE

Whig in the Closet:
Past Continuous, Future Perfect?

Re-encountering these Disciplined inscriptions by earlier selves, I strain to recall the sub-texts and the dead ends, recuperate elisions and allusions, and hear the echoes in the silences—a sobering reminder of the leaps of inference and faith which underwrite any textual exegesis. "Knowing there are gaps in one's thoughts", warns Marilyn Strathern, "becomes at once a pointer to and a cover for what is to be no longer recalled... [P]eople in general know where they are because they know that they (their ideas) have come from somewhere else now necessarily 'forgotten'" (1991: 55). The "journey" metaphor for a life or a career or a mind appeals as a strategy for selective recuperation of "forgotten" ideas which have left textual sediments. It is how I think about and experience my own life, work and intellectual history. A journey, of course, is usually not endlessly linear—one may return to the starting point or to points along the way. But even then journeys are always recursive: a start or a waypoint revisited is never the same time and place. Indeed, recursion permeates this book, as both autobiographic and analytic motif:[1] its subterranean theme, which surfaces in Chapter Four and Part Three, is the ways in which ideas, interests and practices recur in new guise and new circumstances, and are deployed to novel ends and to encompass the novel. The ideas and imperatives which first moved me were not systematically conceptualised, but some later re-emerged, along with new ones, under a variety of theoretical umbrellas or in different methodological settings.

"Journey" is not only a useful trope for reimagining where one has been; it can also anticipate that the going will continue, since I resist the notion of arrival or closure as other than an inevitable textual strategy. Most physical journeys follow known itineraries or maps to anticipated destinations, but the teleology of that image is at odds with all the past selves re-met in the writing of this book. My trajectory is retrospectively envisaged and open-ended: in most respects—respectably antiWhig, antimodernist and secular—I reject the trope of "progress", or at least decry millenarian aspects of its secular and religious eschatologies. Yet there is an irony embedded in the recourse to images of journey and trajectory, because I do furtively imagine my intellectual autobiography as a kind of academic pilgrim's progress, a sometimes painful, recursive movement towards—if nothing as final as enlightenment—then cumulative, enhanced clarity of understanding, however contingent and threatened. In academic mid-life, I ache for the mathematician or physicist of whom I have heard it said that if they do not make an original mark by their thirties, they never shall. This book, this present retrospective on an intellectual practice, politics, ethics and aesthetics, is product of a longish pause for reflection, not an end in itself. There is much more reading, thinking, arguing, comprehending and writing to do.

NOTES

[1] Stoler identified recursion—the tendency for discursive elements to resurface in new guise and new relationship in altered (or different) discursive settings—as a basic technique in Foucault's strategic and heuristic armoury: "While many of the components of his analysis remain, they appear with different conceptual weight in different projects and with a function that is never quite the same. ... [T]his tension between rupture and recuperation ... is at the very basis of *how* Foucault worked and understood the nature of discursive transformations" (1995:xi, 72, orig. emphasis). See also Strathern's substitution of Tyler's conception of the ethnographer as traveller with that of the anthropologist as a cyborg whose "writings form a kind of integrated circuit between parts that work as extensions of another" (1991:14–16, 54–5).

Abbreviations

AAN	Archives de l'Archevêché, Nouméa
AMSM	*Annales des Missions de la Société de Marie*
ANM	Archives nationales, section marine
ANOM	Archives nationales, section outre-mer
APM	Archivio dei Padri Maristi
APO	Archives of the Province of Oceania
ATNC	Archives territoriales de la Nouvelle-Calédonie
BFM	Board of Foreign Missions
BO	*Le Bulletin officiel de la Nouvelle-Calédonie*
CM	Collection Margry
DFC	Dépôt des Fortifications des Colonies
FLNKS	Front de Libération nationale kanak et socialiste
HFR	*Home and Foreign Record*
JO	*Le Journal officiel de la Nouvelle-Calédonie*
LMS	London Missionary Society
Min.	Ministre de la Marine et des Colonies
Moniteur	*Le Moniteur de la Nouvelle-Calédonie.*
MR	*Missionary Register*
N-C	*La Nouvelle-Calédonie*
Nouvelles	*Les Nouvelles calédoniennes*
RPM	*Reformed Presbyterian Magazine*
S-G	Supérieur-Général de la Société de Marie
SHM	Service historique de la Marine
SMH	*Sydney Morning Herald*
SSL	South Seas Letters

Bibliography

Abramson, A. (1989) Comment on Thomas 1989 *Current Anthropology*, 30, 34.

Adams, R. (1984) *In the Land of Strangers: a Century of European Contact with Tanna, 1774–1874*, Canberra: Development Studies Centre, Australian National University.

Allen, M. (1981) Rethinking Old Problems: Matriliny, Secret Societies and Political Evolution, in *Vanuatu: Politics, Economics and Ritual in Island Melanesia*, ed. M. Allen, 9–34, Sydney: Academic Press.

Allen, M. (1984) Elders, Chiefs and Big Men: Authority Legitimation and Political Evolution in Melanesia *American Ethnologist*, 11, 20–41.

Amouroux, [C.] and H. Place ([1881]) *L'administration et les Maristes en Nouvelle-Calédonie: insurrection des Kanaks en 1878–79*, Paris: Périnet.

Annales des Missions de la Société de Marie, Lyon.

Anon. (1847) Extrait d'un journal de bord de la corvette la Brillante, adressé en souvenir au Révérend Père Rougeyron, chef de la mission française en Calédonie, TS copy, Nouméa: Archives de l'Archevêché.

Anon. ([1861]) Rapport sur la Nouvelle-Calédonie en 1860 et 1861, MS draft, Rome: Archivio dei Padri Maristi.

Anon. (1882) *Nouvelle-Calédonie: insurrection des tribus canaques des circonscriptions de Bouloupari à Koné: massacres des 26 et 27 juin et 11 septembre 1878: listes nominatives des victimes*, Nouméa: Imprimerie civile.

Anon. (ed.) (1995) Mélanésia 2000—Dossiers—Documents et témoinages *Journal de la Société des Océanistes*, 100–1, 57–164.

Anova-Ataba, A. (1969) L'insurrection des Néo-Calédoniens en 1878 et la personnalité du grand chef Ataï *Journal de la Société des Océanistes*, 25, 201–19.

Anova-Ataba, A. (1984) *D'Ataï à l'indépendance*, Nouméa: Edipop.
Archives de l'Archevêché, Nouméa.
Archives nationales, section marine, Paris.
Archives nationales, section outre-mer, série Nouvelle-Calédonie Aix-en-Provence.
Archives of the Province of Oceania, Rome.
Archives territoriales de la Nouvelle-Calédonie, Nouméa.
Archivio dei Padri Maristi, section Oceania, Nova Caledonia, Rome.
Attenborough, D. (1960) *Cargo Cult*, London: BBC Television.
Babadzan, A. (1988) Kastom and Nation-Building in the South Pacific, in *Ethnicities and Nations: Processes of Interethnic Relations in Latin America, Southeast Asia, and the Pacific*, ed. R. Guidieri, F. Pellizzi and S. Tambiah, 199–228, Houston: Rothko Chapel.
Barker, J. and D. Jorgensen (ed.) (1996) *Regional Histories in the Western Pacific*, special issue, *Oceania*, 66: 3.
Barth, F. (1966) *Models of Social Organization*, Occasional Paper 23, London: Royal Anthropological Institute of Great Britain and Ireland.
Barthes, R. (1967) Le discours de l'histoire *Informations sur les Sciences sociales*, 6, 65–75.
Bateson, G. (1958 [1936]) *Naven: a Survey of the Problems Suggested by a Composite Picture of the Culture of a New Guinea Tribe Drawn from Three Points of View*, Stanford: Stanford University Press.
Bateson, G. (1972) *Steps to an Ecology of Mind*, New York: Ballantine Books.
Belich, J. (1986) *The New Zealand Wars and the Victorian Interpretation of Racial Conflict*, Auckland: Auckland University Press.
Bensa, A. (1981) Références spatiales et organisation spatiale dans le centre-nord de la Grande Terre, in *Atlas de la Nouvelle-Calédonie et dépendances*, planche 18, Paris: ORSTOM.
Bensa, A. (1986) L'emprise comme institution: un cas d'organisation politique canaque (Nouvelle-Calédonie) *Bulletin de Psychologie*, 39, 253–57.
Bensa, A. (1990) Des ancêtres et des hommes: introduction aux théories kanak de la nature, de l'action et de l'histoire, in *De jade et de nacre: patrimoine artistique kanak*, ed. R. Boulay, 130–60, Paris: Réunion des Musées Nationaux.
Bensa, A. (1995) *Chroniques kanak: l'ethnologie en marche*, Paris: Peuples autochtones et développement.
Bensa, A. (1996) De la micro-histoire vers une anthropologie critique, in *Jeux d'échelles: la micro-analyse à l'expérience*, ed. J. Revel, 37–70, Paris: Gallimard-Le Seuil.

Bensa, A. and P. Bourdieu (1985) Quand les Canaques prennent la parole: entretien avec Alban Bensa *Actes de la Recherche en Sciences sociales*, 56, 69–83.
Bensa, A. and A. Goromido (in press) The Political Order and Corporal Coercion in Kanak Societies of the Past (New Caledonia) *Oceania*.
Bensa, A. and J.-C. Rivierre (1982) *Les chemins de l'alliance: l'organisation social et ses représentations en Nouvelle-Calédonie (région de Touho—aire linguistique cèmuhî)*, Paris: SELAF.
Bensa, A. and J.-C. Rivierre (1988) De l'histoire des mythes: narrations et polémiques autour du rocher Até (Nouvelle-Calédonie) *L'Homme*, 28, 263–95.
Bensa, A. and J.-C. Rivierre (n.d.) Papiers inédits, TS, in author's possession.
Bérard, [L.-T.] (1854) *Campagne de la corvette l'Alcmène en Océanie pendant les années 1850 et 1851: journal de M. Bérard, officier d'administration du bâtiment*, Paris: Imprimerie Paul Dupont.
Berndt, R. (1964) Warfare in the New Guinea Highlands, in *New Guinea: the Central Highlands*, ed. J. Watson, special issue, *American Anthropologist*, 66(4), part 2, 183–203.
Bernstein, R. (1983) *Beyond Objectivism and Relativism: Science, Hermeneutics, and Praxis*, Oxford: Basil Blackwell.
Biersack, A. (ed.) (1991) *Clio in Oceania: Toward a Historical Anthropology*, Washington, DC: Smithsonian Institution Press.
Bonnemaison, J. (1994) *The Tree and the Canoe: History and Ethnogeography of Tanna*, tr. J. Pénot-Demetry, Honolulu: University of Hawaii Press.
Boon, J. (1982) *Other Tribes, Other Scribes: Symbolic Anthropology in the Comparative Study of Cultures, Histories, Religions, and Texts*, Cambridge: Cambridge University Press.
Bott, E. (1981) Power and Rank in Tonga *Journal of the Polynesian Society*, 90, 7–81.
Bourdieu, P. (1977 [1972]) *Outline of a Theory of Practice*, tr. R. Nice, Cambridge: Cambridge University Press.
Bourgarel, A. (1860) Armes des néo-calédoniens *Revue algérienne et coloniale*, 3, 283–86.
Bourgarel, A. (1862) *Des races de l'Océanie française: de celles de la Nouvelle-Calédonie en particulier*, Paris: Victor Masson et fils.
Bowden, R. (1979) *Tapu* and *Mana*: Ritual Authority and Political Power in Traditional Maori Society *Journal of Pacific History*, 14, 50–61.
Brown, P. (1963) From Anarchy to Satrapy *American Anthropologist*, 65, 1–15.

Brunton, R. (1975) Why Do the Trobriands Have Chiefs? *Man*, 10, 544–58.
Brunton, R. (1981) The Origins of the John Frum Movement: a Sociological Explanation, in *Vanuatu: Politics, Economics and Ritual in Island Melanesia*, ed. M. Allen, 357–77, Sydney Academic Press.
Le Bulletin officiel de la Nouvelle-Calédonie, Nouméa.
Burt, B. (1982) Kastom, Christianity and the First Ancestor of the Kwara'ae of Malaita *Mankind*, 13, 374–99.
Bwenando, Nouméa.
Campbell, I.C. (1989) *A History of the Pacific Islands*, St Lucia: University of Queensland Press.
Carell, V. (1985) Tahiti Carries it off with a Successful Culturefest *Pacific Islands Monthly*, 56 (9), 30.
Caro, J. [M. Leenhardt] (1976 [1930]) Le mémorial de Poindi *Dépêche coloniale et maritime* 23 July 1930, in R. Dousset-Leenhardt, *Terre natale, terre d'exil*, 203–6, Paris: G.-P. Maisonneuve & Larose.
Carrard, P. (1992) *Poetics of the New History: French Historical Discourse from Braudel to Chartier*, Baltimore: Johns Hopkins University Press.
Carrier, J. (ed.). (1992) *History and Tradition in Melanesian Anthropology*, Berkeley: University of California Press.
Chakrabarty, D. (1992) Postcoloniality and the Artifice of History: Who Speaks for "Indian" Pasts? *Representations*, 37, 1–26.
Chapuy, A. (1848–56) Journal, 25 May 1848–4 July 1856, MS, Nouméa: Archives de l'Archevêché.
Chartier, R. (1989) Texts, Printing, Readings, in *The New Cultural History*, ed. L. Hunt, 154–75, Berkeley: University of California Press.
Chowning, A. (1979) Leadership in Melanesia *Journal of Pacific History*, 14, 66–84.
Clark, J. and J. Terrell (1978) Archaeology in Oceania *Annual Review of Anthropology*, 7, 293–319.
Clausewitz, C. von (1968 [1832]) *On War*, abridged, ed. Anatol Rapoport, tr. J.J. Graham, Harmondsworth, Middlesex: Penguin.
Clay, B. (1992) Other Times, Other Places: Agency and the Big Man in Central New Ireland *Man*, 27, 719–33.
Clifford, J. (1982) *Person and Myth: Maurice Leenhardt in the Melanesian World*, Berkeley: University of California Press.
Clifford, J. (1983) On ethnographic authority, *Representations*, 1, 118–46.
Codrington, R.H. (1891) *The Melanesians: Studies in their Anthropology and Folk-lore*, Oxford: Clarendon Press.

Collection Margry, MS copies, Paris: Bibliothèque nationale.
Collingwood, R.G. (1961 [1946]) *The Idea of History*, London: Oxford University Press.
Collomb, J.-G. (1847) Journal, 7 Apr.–22 July 1847, MS, Rome: Archivio dei Padri Maristi.
Comaroff, J. and J. (1991) *Of Revelation and Revolution: Christianity, Colonialism and Consciousness in South Africa*, vol. 1, Chicago and London: University of Chicago Press.
Cook, J. (1961) *The Voyage of the* Resolution *and* Adventure *1772–1775*, ed. J.C. Beaglehole, Cambridge: Hakluyt Society.
Crick, M. (1982) Anthropological Field Research, Meaning Creation and Knowledge Construction, in *Semantic Anthropology*, ed. D. Parkin, 15–37, London: Academic Press.
Cummins, H.G. (1977) Tongan Society at the Time of European Contact, in *Friendly Islands: a History of Tonga*, ed. N. Rutherford, 63–89, Melbourne: Oxford University Press.
Danielsson, M.-T. and B. (1985) Flosse's French Festival *Pacific Islands Monthly*, 56 (9), 22, 25, 56.
Davidson, J.W. (1966) Problems of Pacific History *Journal of Pacific History*, 1, 5–21.
Davies, B. (1991) The Concept of Agency: a Feminist Poststructuralist Analysis *Social Analysis*, 30, 42–53.
Davies, J. (1961) *The History of the Tahitian Mission 1799–1830*, ed. C.W. Newbury, Cambridge: Hakluyt Society.
Dening, G. (1980) *Islands and Beaches: Discourse on a Silent Land, Marquesas 1774–1880*, Carlton, Vic.: Melbourne University Press.
Dening, G. (1991) A Poetic for Histories: Transformations that Present the Past, in *Clio in Oceania: Toward a Historical Anthropology*, ed. A. Biersack, 347–80, Washington, DC: Smithsonian Institution Press.
Dening, G. (1992) *Mr Bligh's Bad Language: Passion, Power and Theatre on the Bounty*, Cambridge: Cambridge University Press.
Dening, G. (1995) *The Death of William Gooch: a History's Anthropology*, Carlton South, Vic.: Melbourne University Press.
Deplanche, E. (1868–9) Ethnologie calédonienne *Bulletin de la Société linnéenne de Normandie* 2ᵉ série, 4, 185–210.
Diaz, V. (1994) Simply Chamorro: Telling Tales of Demise and Survival in Guam *Contemporary Pacific*, 6, 29–58.
Dornoy, M. (1984) *Politics in New Caledonia, 1945–77*, Sydney: Sydney University Press.
Douarre, G. (1843–53) Journal, 21 Dec. 1843–20 Apr. 1853, MS copy, Nouméa: Archives de l'Archevêché.

Douglas, B. (1970) A Contact History of the Balad People of New Caledonia 1774–1845 *Journal of the Polynesian Society*, 79, 180–200.
Douglas, B. (1972) A History of Culture Contact in North-Eastern New Caledonia, 1774–1870, PhD thesis, Canberra: Australian National University.
Douglas, B. (1979) Bouarate of Hienghène: Great Chief in New Caledonia, in *More Pacific Islands Portraits*, ed. D. Scarr, 35–47, Canberra: Australian National University Press.
Douglas, B. (1980a) Conflict and Alliance in a Colonial Context: Case Studies in New Caledonia, 1853–1870, *Journal of Pacific History*, 15, 21–51.
Douglas, B. (1980b) The Role of Theory: Reflections of a Repentant Empiricist, TS, paper given to Pacific History Conference, Clare, South Australia, 10 May 1980.
Douglas, B. (1982) "Written on the Ground": Spatial Symbolism, Cultural Categories and Historical Process in New Caledonia *Journal of the Polynesian Society*, 91, 383–415.
Douglas, B. (1984) Ethnography and Ethnographic History: some Recent Trends *Pacific History Bibliography and Comment*, 19, 36–42.
Douglas, B. (1985a) Reflections on Political Murder: New Caledonia 1984 *Arena*, 70, 21–6.
Douglas, B. (1985b) Ritual and Politics in the Inaugural Meeting of High Chiefs from New Caledonia and the Loyalty Islands *Social Analysis*, 18, 60–84.
Douglas, B. (1989) Autonomous and Controlled Spirits: Traditional Ritual and Early Interpretations of Christianity on Tanna, Aneityum and the Isle of Pines in Comparative Perspective *Journal of the Polynesian Society*, 98, 7–48.
Douglas, B. (1990) "Almost Constantly at War"? An Ethnographic Perspective on Fighting in New Caledonia *Journal of Pacific History*, 25, 22–46.
Douglas, B. (1992a) Doing Ethnographic History: the Case of Fighting in New Caledonia, in *History and Tradition in Melanesian Anthropology*, ed. J. Carrier, 86–115, Berkeley: University of California Press.
Douglas, B. (1992b) Doing Ethnographic History: Reflections on Practices and Practising, in *Pacific Islands History: Journeys and Transformations*, ed. B. Lal, 92–196, Canberra: *Journal of Pacific History*.
Douglas, B. (1993) Pre-European Societies in the Pacific Islands, in *Culture Contact in the Pacific: Essays on Contact, Encounter and*

Response, ed. M. Quanchi and R. Adams, 15–30, Cambridge: Cambridge University Press.
Douglas, B. (1994a) Discourses on Death in a Melanesian World, in *Dangerous Liaisons: Essays in Honour of Greg Dening*, ed. D. Merwick, 353–78, Parkville, Vic.: History Department, University of Melbourne.
Douglas, B. (1994b) Hierarchy and Reciprocity in New Caledonia: an Historical Ethnography *History and Anthropology*, 7, 169–93.
Douglas, B. (1995) Power, Discourse and the Appropriation of God: Christianity and Subversion in a Melanesian Context *History and Anthropology*, 9, 57–92.
Douglas, B. (1996a) L'histoire face à l'anthropologie: le passé colonial indigène revisité *Genèses*, 23, 125–44.
Douglas, B. (1996b) Introduction: Fracturing Boundaries of Time and Place in Melanesian Anthropology *Oceania*, 66, 177–88.
Douglas, B. (in press a) Inventing Natives/Negotiating Local Identities: Postcolonial Readings of Colonial Texts on Island Melanesia, in *Pacific Answers to Western Hegemony: Cultural Practices of Identity Construction*, ed. Jürg Wassmann, Oxford: Berg Publishers.
Douglas, B. (in press b) Art as Ethnohistorical Text: Science, Representation and Indigenous Presence in Eighteenth and Nineteenth Century Oceanic Voyage Literature, in *Double Vision: Re-imagining Art and Colonialism in the Pacific*, ed. N. Thomas and D. Losche, Cambridge: Cambridge University Press.
Douglas, B. (forthcoming) Recuperating Indigenous Women: Female Sexuality and Missionary Textuality in "Disciplined" Perspectives, in *Governing Bodies: Race, Person and Gender Beyond Europe*, ed. M. Jolly and N. Thomas.
Doumenge, J.-P. (1974) *Paysans mélanésiens en pays Canala—Nlle Calédonie*, Talence, France: Centre d'Etudes de Géographie Tropicale.
Dousset, R. (1970) *Colonialisme et contradictions: étude sur les causes socio-historiques de l'insurrection de 1878 en Nouvelle-Calédonie*, Paris: Mouton & Co.
Dousset-Leenhardt, R. (1976) *Terre natale, terre d'exil*, Paris: G.-P. Maisonneuve & Larose.
Dubinskas, F. and S. Traweek (1984) Closer to the Ground: a Reinterpretation of Walbiri Iconography *Man*, 19, 15–30.
Dubois, M.J. (1985) *Histoire résumée de Belep (Nouvelle-Calédonie)*, Nouméa: Imprimerie Graphoprint.
Dumont d'Urville, J.-S.-C. (1832) Sur les îles du Grand Océan *Bulletin de la Société de Géographie*, 17, 1–21.

d'Entrecasteaux, A.-R.-J. de Bruni (1808) *Voyage de Dentrecasteaux envoyé à la recherche de La Pérouse... rédigé par M. de Rossel*, 2 vols, Paris: Imprimerie impériale.
Fabian, J. (1983) *Time and the Other: How Anthropology Makes its Object*, New York: Columbia University Press.
Fabian, J. (1991) *Time and the Work of Anthropology: Critical Essay 1971–1991*, Chur: Harwood Academic Publishers.
Feil, D.K. (1987) *The Evolution of Highland Papua New Guinea Societies*, Cambridge: Cambridge University Press.
Feinberg, R. and K. Watson-Gegeo (ed.) (1996) *Leadership and Change in the Western Pacific*, London: Athlone Press.
Firth, R. (1936) *We, the Tikopia: a Sociological Study of Kinship in Primitive Polynesia*, London: George Allen & Unwin.
Firth, R. (1968 [1957]) A Note on Descent Groups in Polynesia, in *Peoples and Cultures of the Pacific: an Anthropological Reader*, ed. A. Vayda, 207–17, Garden City, NY: Natural History Press.
Firth, R. (1970) *Rank and Religion in Tikopia: a Study in Polynesian Paganism and Conversion to Christianity*, London: George Allen & Unwin.
Ford, E. (ed.) (1974) *Papua New Guinea Resource Atlas*, Milton, Qld.: Jacaranda Press.
Forster, G. (1777) *A voyage round the world... during the years 1772, 3, 4, and 5*, 2 vols, London: B. White, J. Robson, P. Elmsly and G. Robinson.
[Foucher, E.] (1890) *Coup d'oeil rétrospectif sur les premières années de l'occupation de la Nouvelle-Calédonie: souvenirs d'un des trois moineaux, sur les épisodes et expéditions qui ont eu lieu pendant les années 1855, 1856 et 1857*, Nouméa: Imprimerie nouméenne.
Fraser, H. (1984) The Fourth South Pacific Festival of Arts *Pacific Islands Monthly*, 55 (11), 20–2.
[Gagnière, M.] (1905 [1859]), *Etude ethnologique sur la religion des Néo-Calédoniens*, Saint-Louis: Imprimerie catholique.
Garnier, J. (1867) Voyage à la Nouvelle-Calédonie *Tour du Monde*, 16, 155–208.
Garnier, J. (1868) Voyage à la Nouvelle-Calédonie *Tour du Monde*, 18, 1–64.
Garnier, J. (1870) Les migrations polynésiennes, leur origine, leur itinéraire, leur étendue, leur influence sur les Australasiens de la Nouvelle-Calédonie *Bulletin de la Société de Géographie* 5 série, 19, 5–50, 423–68.
Garnier, J. (1873) *Voyage autour du monde: la Nouvelle-Calédonie (côte orientale)*, Paris: Henri Plon.

Geddie, C. and C. Harrington (1908) *Letters of Charlotte Geddie and Charlotte Geddie Harrington*, Truro, Nova Scotia: News Publishing Co.
Geddie, J. (1848–57) Journal, 29 July 1848–11 Dec. 1857, MS copy, Canberra: National Library of Australia.
Geddie, J. (1852) The Inhabitants of Aneityum *Missionary Register of the Presbyterian Church of Nova Scotia*, 3, 7–9, 19–22, 36–7, 83–4.
Geddie, J. (1975) *Misi Gete: John Geddie, Pioneer Missionary to the New Hebrides*, ed. R.S. Miller, Launceston: Presbyterian Church of Australia.
Geertz, C. (1975 [1973]) *The Interpretation of Cultures*, London: Hutchinson.
Geertz, C. (1990) History and Anthropology *New Literary History*, 21, 325–9.
Gewertz, D. and E. Schieffelin (ed.) (1985) *History and Ethnohistory in Papua New Guinea*, Sydney: University of Sydney.
Gibson, R. (1989) *A Social History of French Catholicism 1789–1914*, London: Routledge.
Gilson, R.P. (1970) *Samoa 1830 to 1900: the Politics of a Multi-Cultural Community*, ed. J.W. Davidson, Melbourne: Oxford University Press.
Glick, L. (1973) Sorcery and Witchcraft, in *Anthropology in Papua New Guinea: Readings from the Encyclopaedia of Papua and New Guinea*, ed. I. Hogbin, 182–6, Carlton, Vic.: Melbourne University Press.
Godelier, M. (1982) *La production des grands hommes: pouvoir et domination masculine chez les Baruya de Nouvelle-Guinée*, Paris: Fayard.
Godelier, M. and M. Strathern (ed.) (1991) *Big Men and Great Men: Personifications of Power in Melanesia*, Cambridge: Cambridge University Press.
Goldman, I. (1970) *Ancient Polynesian Society*, Chicago: University of Chicago Press.
Goujon, P. (1848–54) Journal, 23 July 1848–15 Sep. 1854, TS copy, Nouméa: Archives de l'Archevêché.
Grace, G. (1968) Classification of the Languages of the Pacific, in *Peoples and Cultures of the Pacific: an Anthropological Reader*, ed. A. Vayda, 63–79, Garden City, NY: Natural History Press.
Green, R.C. (1967) The Immediate Origins of the Polynesians, in *Polynesian Culture History: Essays in Honour of Kenneth P. Emory*, ed. G.A. Highland et al., 215–40, Honolulu: Bishop Museum Press.

Green, R.C. (1989) Comment on Thomas 1989 *Current Anthropology*, 30, 35–6.
Greenblatt, S. (1991) *Marvelous Possessions: The Wonder of the New World*, Oxford: Clarendon Press.
Groves, M. (1963) Western Motu Descent Groups *Ethnology*, 2, 15–30.
Groube, L.M. (1971) Tonga, Lapita Pottery, and Polynesian Origins *Journal of the Polynesian Society*, 80, 278–316.
Guha, R. (1983a) *Elementary Aspects of Peasant Insurgency in Colonial India*, Delhi: Oxford University Press.
Guha, R. (1983b) The Prose of Counter-Insurgency *Subaltern Studies*, 2, 1–42.
Guha, R. (1989) Dominance Without Hegemony and its Historiography *Subaltern Studies*, 6, 210–309.
Guiart, J. (1956a) Culture Contact and the "John Frum" Movement on Tanna, New Hebrides *Southwestern Journal of Anthropology*, 12, 105–16.
Guiart, J. (1956b) L'organisation sociale et coutumière de la population autochtone, in J. Barrau, *L'agriculture vivrière autochtone de la Nouvelle-Calédonie*, 15–43, Nouméa: Commission du Pacifique Sud.
Guiart, J. (1957) Les modalités de l'organisation dualiste et le système matrimonial en Nouvelle-Calédonie *Cahiers Internationaux de Sociologie*, 22, 21–39.
Guiart, J. (1959) Naissance et avortement d'un messianisme: colonisation et décolonisation en Nouvelle-Calédonie *Archives de Sociologie des Religions*, 7, 3–44.
Guiart, J. (1962) The Millenarian Aspect of Conversion to Christianity in the South Pacific, in *Millennial Dreams in Action: Essays in Comparative Study*, ed. S. Thrupp, 122–38, The Hague: Mouton and Co.
Guiart, J. (1963) *Structure de la chefferie en Mélanésie du sud*, Paris: Institut d'Ethnologie.
Guiart, J. (1966) *Mythologie du masque en Nouvelle-Calédonie*, Paris: Musée le l'Homme.
Guiart, J. (1968) Le cadre social traditionnel et la rébellion de 1878 dans le pays de la Foa, Nouvelle-Calédonie *Journal de la Société des Océanistes*, 24, 97–119.
Guiart, J. and A. Bensa (1981) Clans autochtones: situation pré-coloniale, in *Atlas de la Nouvelle-Calédonie et dépendances*, plate 18, Paris: ORSTOM.
Gunson, N. (1962) An Account of the *Mamaia* or Visionary Heresy of Tahiti, 1826–1841 *Journal of the Polynesian Society*, 71, 209–42.

Gunson, N. (1964) Great Women and Friendship Contract Rites in Pre-Christian Tahiti *Journal of the Polynesian Society*, 73, 53–69.
Gunson, N. (1979) The *hau* Concept of Leadership in Western Polynesia *Journal of Pacific History*, 14, 28–49.
Gunson, N. (1987) Sacred Women Chiefs and Female "Headmen" in Polynesian History *Journal of Pacific History*, 22, 139–71.
Gunson, N. (1992a) An Introduction to Pacific History, in *Pacific Islands History: Journeys and Transformations*, ed. B. Lal, 1–13, Canberra: *Journal of Pacific History*.
Gunson, N. (1992b) Unity and Diversity in Polynesia: the Historiographical Perspective, in *Pacific History: Papers from the 8th Pacific History Association Conference*, ed. D. Rubinstein, 225–34, Mangilao, Guam: University of Guam Press & Micronesian Area Research Center.
Hall, C. (1991) Missionary Stories: Gender and Ethnicity in England in the 1830s and 1840s, in *Cultural Studies*, ed. L. Grossberg, C. Nelson and P.A. Treichler, 240–76, New York: Routledge.
Hallpike, C.R. (1977) *Bloodshed and Vengeance in the Papuan Mountains: the Generation of Conflict in Tauade Society*, Oxford: Clarendon Press.
Hau'ofa, E. (1971) Mekeo Chieftainship *Journal of the Polynesian Society*, 1971, 152–69.
Hau'ofa, E. (1975) Anthropology and Pacific Islanders *Oceania*, 45, 282–9.
Hau'ofa, E. (1981) *Mekeo: Inequality and Ambivalence in a Village Society*, Canberra: Australian National University Press.
Hegel, G. (1952 [1857]) *The Philosophy of History*, tr. J. Sibree, Chicago: Encyclopædia Britannica, Inc.
Heider, K. (1970) *The Dugum Dani: a Papuan Culture in the Highlands of West New Guinea*, Chicago: Aldine Publishing Company.
Heider, K. (1979) *Grand Valley Dani: Peaceful Warriors*, New York: Holt, Rinehart and Winston.
Helliwell, C. (1994) "A Just Precedency": the Notion of Equality in Anthropological Discourse *History and Anthropology*, 7, 363–75.
Hobsbawm, E. (1983) Introduction: Inventing Traditions, in *The Invention of Tradition*, ed. E. Hobsbawm and T. Ranger, 1–14, Cambridge: Cambridge University Press.
Hobsbawm, E. and T. Ranger (ed.) (1983) *The Invention of Tradition*, Cambridge: Cambridge University Press.
Hogbin, I. (1931) The Social Organization of Ontong Java *Oceania*, 1, 399–425.
Hogbin, I. (1946) Local Government for New Guinea *Oceania*, 17, 38–65.

Hogbin, I. (1963) Government Chiefs in New Guinea, in *Social Structure; Studies Presented to A.R. Radcliffe-Brown*, ed. M. Fortes 189–206, New York: Russell & Russell Inc.

Home and Foreign Record of the Presbyterian Church of the Lower Provinces of British North America, Halifax, Nova Scotia.

Hooper, A. and J. Huntsman (ed.) (1985) *Transformations of Polynesian Culture*, Auckland: Polynesian Society.

Howe, K.R. (1977) *The Loyalty Islands: a History of Culture Contacts 1840–1900*, Canberra: Australian National University Press.

Huntsman, J. (1971) Concepts of Kinship and Categories of Kinsmen in the Tokelau Islands *Journal of the Polynesian Society*, 80, 317–54.

Ileto, R. (1979) *Pasyon and Revolution: Popular Movements in the Philippines, 1840–1910*, Quezon City: Ateneo de Manila University Press.

Inglis, J. (1852) Extracts from Report of a Missionary Tour in the New Hebrides &c., on Board H.M.S. *Havannah*, in 1850 *Scottish Presbyterian*, 61–5, 425–32, 461–4, 486–91, 522–9, 556–63.

Inglis, J. (1882) *A Dictionary of the Aneityumese Language*, London: Williams and Norgate.

Inglis, J. (1887) *In the New Hebrides: Reminiscences of Missionary Life and Work, Especially on the Island of Aneityum from 1850 till 1877*, London: T. Nelson and Sons.

Inglis, J. (1890) *Bible Illustrations from the New Hebrides, with Notices of the Progress of the Mission*, London: Thomas Nelson and Sons.

Jackson, M. (1978) Ambivalence and the Last-Born: Birth-Order Position in Convention and Myth *Man*, 13, 341–61.

Jackson, M. (1989) *Paths Toward a Clearing: Radical Empiricism and Ethnographic Enquiry*, Bloomington: Indiana University Press.

Jinks, B., P. Biskup and H. Nelson (ed.) (1973) *Readings in New Guinea History*, Sydney: Angus and Robertson.

Jolly, M. (1987) The Chimera of Equality in Melanesia *Mankind*, 17, 168–83.

Jolly, M. (1992) Specters of Inauthenticity *Contemporary Pacific*, 4, 49–72.

Jolly, M. (1994) Epilogue: Hierarchical Horizons *History and Anthropology*, 7, 377–409.

Jolly, M. and M. Mosko (ed.) (1994) *Transformations of Hierarchy: Structure, History and Horizon in the Austronesian World*, special issue, *History and Anthropology*, 7(1–4).

Le Journal officiel de la Nouvelle-Calédonie et dépendances, Nouméa.

Joyce, R.B. (1971) *Sir William MacGregor*, Melbourne: Oxford University Press.

Kanappe, G. (1984) *Après 1878: les souvenirs du capitaine Kanappe: la fondation de Hienghène*, ed. C. Courtis, Nouméa: Imprimerie Graphoprint.
Kapferer, B. (1977) First Class to Maradana: Secular Drama in Sinhalese Healing Rites, in *Secular Ritual*, ed. S. Falk Moore and B. Myerhoff, 91–123, Assen: van Gorcum.
Kapferer, B. (1979) Introduction: Ritual Process and the Transformation of Context *Social Analysis*, 1, 3–19.
Kaplan, M. (1990) Meaning, Agency and Colonial History: Navosavakadua and the *Tuka* Movement in Fiji *American Ethnologist*, 17, 3–22.
Kawa, B. (ed.) (1996) *Revue du Conseil Coutumier du Territoire de la Nouvelle-Calédonie—novembre 1996*, Nouméa: Espace Pub.
Keegan, J. (1976) *The Face of Battle*, London: Jonathan Cape.
Keesing, R. (1982) Kastom in Melanesia: An Overview *Mankind*, 13, 297–301.
Keesing, R. (1985) Conventional Metaphors and Anthropological Metaphysics: the Problematic of Cultural Translation *Journal of Anthropological Research*, 41, 201–17.
Keesing, R. (1987) Anthropology as Interpretive Quest *Current Anthropology*, 28, 161–76.
Keesing, R. (1989a) Creating the Past: Custom and Identity in the Contemporary Pacific *Contemporary Pacific*, 1, 19–42.
Keesing, R. (1989b) Sins of a Mission: Christian Life as Kwaio Traditionalist Ideology, in *Family and Gender in the Pacific: Domestic Contradictions and the Colonial Impact*, ed. M. Jolly and M. Macintyre, 193–212, Cambridge: Cambridge University Press.
Keesing, R. (1994) Colonial and Counter-Colonial Discourse in Melanesia *Critique of Anthropology*, 14, 41–58.
Keesing, R. and R. Tonkinson (ed.) (1982) *Reinventing Traditional Culture: the Politics of Kastom in Island Melanesia*, special issue, *Mankind*, 13(4).
Knauft, B. (1990) Melanesian Warfare: a Theoretical History *Oceania*, 60, 250–311.
Kurtovitch, I. ([1997]) La naissance d'une nouvelle société calédonienne, TS, in author's possession.
La Billardière, J. de (1800) *Relation du voyage à la recherche de La Pérouse...pendant les années 1791, 1792, et pendant la 1ère. et la 2e. année de la République Françoise*, 2 vols, Paris: H.J. Jansen.
La Ferrière, J. (1845) *Voyage aux îles Tonga-tabou, Wallis et Foutouna, à la Nouvelle-Calédonie et à la Nouvelle-Zélande, exécuté du 1er novembre 1843 au 1er avril 1844*, Paris: Imprimerie royale.

La Hautière, U. de (1869) *Souvenirs de la Nouvelle Calédonie: voyage sur la côte orientale; un coup de main chez les kanacks; pilou-pilou à Naniouni*, Paris: Challamel ainé.
Lambert, P. (1855–75) Petit journal, TS copy, Nouméa: Archives de l'Archevêché.
Lambert, P. (1900 [1879–80]) *Mœurs et superstitions des Néo-Calédoniens*, Nouméa: Nouvelle Imprimerie nouméenne.
Langer, S. (1957 [1942]) *Philosophy in a New Key: a Study in the Symbolism of Reason, Rite, and Art*, 3rd ed., Cambridge: Harvard University Press.
Latham, L. (1978) *La révolte de 1878: étude critique des causes de la rebellion de 1878, en Nouvelle-Calédonie*, tr. Edouard Terzian, Nouméa: Société d'Etudes Historiques de la Nouvelle-Calédonie.
Lawrence, P. (1982) Madang and Beyond, in *Melanesia: Beyond Diversity*, vol. 1, ed. R.J. May and H. Nelson, 57–72, Canberra: Research School of Pacific Studies, Australian National University.
Lawrence, P. (1988) Twenty Years After: a Reconsideration of Papua New Guinea Seaboard and Highlands Religions *Oceania*, 59, 7–27.
Lawrence, P. and M.J. Meggitt (1965) Introduction, in *Gods, Ghosts and Men in Melanesia: Some Religions of Australian New Guinea and the New Hebrides*, ed. P. Lawrence and M.J. Meggitt, 1–26, Melbourne: Oxford University Press.
Leconte, F. (1847) Notice sur la Nouvelle-Calédonie, les mœurs et les usages de ses habitants *Annales maritimes et coloniales* 3ᵉ série, 2, 811–69.
Leenhardt, M. (1930) *Notes d'ethnologie néo-calédonienne*, Paris: Institut d'Ethnologie.
Leenhardt, M. (1935) *Vocabulaire et grammaire de la langue Houaïlou*, Paris: Institut d'Ethnologie.
Leenhardt, M. (1947) *Do kamo: la personne et le mythe dans le monde mélanésien*, Paris: Gallimard.
Leenhardt, M. (1979 [1947]) *Do kamo: Person and Myth in the Melanesian World*, tr. B. Miller Gulati, Chicago: University of Chicago Press.
Legorjus, P. (1990) *La morale et l'action*, Paris: Fixot.
Lepervanche, M. de (1967–8) Descent, Residence and Leadership in the New Guinea Highlands *Oceania*, 38, 134–58, 163–89.
Lindstrom, L. (1982) Leftamap Kastom: the Political History of Tradition on Tanna (Vanuatu) *Mankind*, 13, 316–29.
Lindstrom, L. and G. White (1997) Introduction: Chiefs Today, in *Chiefs Today: Traditional Pacific Leadership and the Postcolonial State*, ed. G. White and L. Lindstrom, Stanford: Stanford University Press.

Lini, W. (1982) Keynote Address Presented to the "Australia and the South Pacific" Conference, Canberra, February, 18–19, 1982 *Pacific Islands Monthly*, 53(4), 25–8.
Linnekin, J. (1985) *Children of the Land: Exchange and Status in a Hawaiian Community*, New Brunswick, NJ: Rutgers University Press.
Linnekin, J. (1992) On the Theory and Politics of Cultural Construction in the Pacific *Oceania*, 62, 249–63.
London Missionary Society, South Seas Letters, Congregational Council for World Mission, London.
Luders, D. (1996) Legend and History: Did the Vanuatu-Tonga Kava Trade Cease in A.D. 1447? *Journal of the Polynesian Society*, 105, 287–310.
Lutkehaus, N. (1990) Hierarchy and "Heroic Society": Manam Variations in Sepik Social Structure *Oceania*, 60, 179–97.
McArthur, N. (1974) Population and Prehistory: the Late Phase on Aneityum, PhD thesis, Canberra: Australian National University.
McArthur, N. (1978) "And, behold, the plague was begun among the people", in *The Changing Pacific: Essays in Honour of H.E. Maude*, ed. N. Gunson, 273–84, Melbourne: Oxford University Press.
Macintyre, M. (1994) Too Many Chiefs? Leadership in the Massim in the Colonial Era *History and Anthropology*, 7, 241–62.
McKee, M. (1989) Waiting for the Skies to Open *Pacific Islands Monthly*, 59(15), 26–7, 30.
Malherbe, V. de (1995 [1859]) Mémoire sur la Nouvelle-Calédonie de 1856, 3 octobre au 5 octobre 1859, in J. Dauphiné, *Les débuts d'une colonisation laborieuse: le sud calédonien (1853–1860)*, 107–69, Paris: Editions l'Harmattan & Nouméa: Agence de Développement de la Culture Kanak.
Mani, L. (1991) Cultural Theory, Colonial Texts: Reading Eyewitness Accounts of Widow Burning, in *Cultural Studies*, ed. L. Grossberg, C. Nelson and P.A. Treichler, 392–408, New York: Routledge.
Marcus, G. (1978) *The Nobility and the Chiefly Tradition in the Modern Kingdom of Tonga*, Memoir 42, Wellington: Polynesian Society.
Marcus, G. (1989) Chieftainship, in *Developments in Polynesian Ethnology*, ed. A. Howard and R. Borofsky, 175–209, Honolulu: University of Hawaii Press.
Martin, J. (1827 [1817]) *An Account of the Natives of the Tonga Islands with an Original Grammar and Vocabulary of their Language Compiled and Arranged from the Extensive Communications of Mr William Mariner, Several Years Resident in those Islands*, 3rd ed., 2 vols, Edinburgh: Constable and Co. and Hurst, Chance and Co.

Mathieu, A. (1868) Aperçu historique sur la tribu des Houassios ou des Manongôés *Le Moniteur de la Nouvelle-Calédonie*, 433, 9–11.
Maude, H.E. (1971) Pacific History—Past, Present and Future *Journal of Pacific History*, 6, 3–24.
Mauger, M.-J. (1976 [1878]) Journal, extracts, 5–6 June–1 Aug. 1878, in R. Dousset-Leenhardt, *Terre natale, terre d'exil*, 231–45, Paris: G.-P. Maisonneuve & Larose.
Mbembe, A. (1988) *Afriques indociles: Christianisme, pouvoir et état en société postcoloniale*, Paris: Editions Karthala.
Mead, M. (1956) *New Lives for Old: Cultural Transformation—Manus, 1928–1953*, London: Victor Gollancz Ltd.
Meggitt, M. (1971) The Pattern of Leadership Among the Mae-Enga of New Guinea, in *Politics in New Guinea*, ed. R. Berndt and P. Lawrence, 191–206, Nedlands: University of Western Australia Press.
Meggitt, M. (1977) *Blood is their Argument: Warfare among the Mae Enga Tribesmen of the New Guinea Highlands*, Palo Alto, CA: Mayfield Publishing Co.
van Meijl, T. (1994) Maori Hierarchy Transformed: the Secularization of Tainui Patterns of Leadership *History and Anthropology* 7, 279–305.
Meillassoux, C. (1978) The "Economy" in Agricultural Self-Sustaining Societies: a Preliminary Analysis, in *Relations of Production: Marxist Approaches to Economic Anthropology*, ed. D. Seddon, tr. H. Lackner, 127–57, London: Frank Cass.
Métais, E. (1967) *La sorcellerie canaque actuelle: les "tueurs d'âmes" dans une tribu de la Nouvelle-Calédonie*, Paris: Musée de l'Homme.
Metge, J. (1976) *The Maoris of New Zealand: Rautahi*, revised ed., London: Routledge and Kegan Paul.
Mills, S. (1993 [1991]) *Discourses of Difference: an Analysis of Women's Travel Writing and Colonialism*, London: Routledge.
Missionary Register of the Presbyterian Church of Nova Scotia, Pictou, Nova Scotia.
Mitchell, W. (1978) On Keeping Equal: Polity and Reciprocity Among the New Guinea Wape *Anthropological Quarterly*, 51, 5–15.
Mohanty, C. (1991) Introduction: Cartographies of Struggle: Third World Women and the Politics of Feminism, in *Third World Women and the Politics of Feminism*, ed. C. Mohanty, A. Russo, L. Torres, 1–47, Bloomington: Indiana University Press.
Mohanty, C. (1992) Feminist Encounters: Locating the Politics of Experience, in *Destabilizing Theory: Contemporary Feminist Debates*, ed. M. Barrett and A. Phillips, 74–92, Cambridge: Polity Press.

Le Monde, Paris.
Le Moniteur impérial de la Nouvelle-Calédonie et dépendances, 1859–61; thereafter *Le Moniteur de la Nouvelle-Calédonie: journal officiel de la colonie*, 1862–21 Aug. 1870. Thereafter *Le Moniteur de la Nouvelle-Calédonie: journal officiel paraissant tous les dimanches*, 28 Aug. 1870 et seq, Nouméa.
Montrouzier, X. (1860) *Notice historique, ethnographique et physique sur la Nouvelle-Calédonie*, Paris: Lahure.
Moore, H. (1994) *A Passion for Difference: Essays in Anthropology and Gender*, Cambridge: Polity Press.
Moore, S. Falk (1975) Epilogue: Uncertainties in Situations, Indeterminacies in Culture, in *Symbol and Politics in Communal Ideology: Cases and Questions*, ed. S. Falk Moore and B. Myerhoff, 210–39, Ithaca, NY: Cornell University Press.
Moore, S. Falk (1977) Political Meetings and the Simulation of Unanimity: Kilimanjaro 1973, in *Secular Ritual*, ed. S. Falk Moore and B. Myerhoff, 151–7, Assen: van Gorcum.
Moore, S. Falk and B. Myerhoff (1977) Introduction: Secular Ritual: Forms and Meanings, in *Secular Ritual*, ed. S. Falk Moore and B. Myerhoff, 3–24, Assen: van Gorcum.
Morris, B. (1992) Frontier Colonialism as a Culture of Terror *Journal of Australian Studies*, 35, 72–87.
Morrison, J. (1935) *The Journal of James Morrison Boatswain's Mate of the Bounty Describing the Mutiny and Subsequent Misfortunes of the Mutineers together with an Account of the Island of Tahiti*, ed. Owen Rutter, London: Golden Cockerel Press.
Mosko, M. (1992) Motherless Sons: "Divine Kings" and "Partible Persons" in Melanesia and Polynesia *Man*, 27, 697–717.
Murray, A.W. (1862) The Fifteenth Missionary Voyage of the "John Williams" among the Islands of Western Polynesia *Samoan Reporter*, 23, 2–4.
Murray, A.W. (1863) *Missions in Western Polynesia: Being Historical Sketches of these Missions, from their Commencement in 1839 to the Present Time*, London: John Snow.
Myerhoff, B. (1977) We Don't Wrap Herring in a Printed Page: Fusion, Fictions and Continuity in Secular Ritual, in *Secular Ritual*, ed. S. Falk Moore and B. Myerhoff, 199–224, Assen: van Gorcum.
Narokobi, B. (1980) *The Melanesian Way: Total Cosmic Vision of Life (and his Critics and Supporters)*, Port Moresby: Institute of Papua New Guinea Studies.
Nayacakalou, R.R. (1975) *Leadership in Fiji*, Melbourne: Oxford University Press.

Neumann, K. (1992) *Not the Way it Really Was: Constructing the Tolai Past*, Honolulu: University of Hawaii Press.
Newbury, C.W. (1967) *Te hau pahu rahi*: Pomare II and the Concept of Inter-Island Government in Eastern Polynesia *Journal of the Polynesian Society*, 76, 477–514.
Nisbet, H. (1842–3) Diary, 25 June 1842–31 Jan. 1843, Pacific Manuscripts Bureau microfilm, Melbourne: State Library of Victoria.
Nisbet, H. (1847) Voyage of the "John Williams" to the New Hebrides and New Caledonia Groups under the Superintendence of Messrs. Gill and Nesbit *Samoan Reporter*, 5, 3–4.
La Nouvelle-Calédonie: journal d'annonces légales et judiciaires, Nouméa.
Les Nouvelles Calédoniennes, Nouméa.
Oliver, D. (1955) *A Solomon Island Society: Kinship and Leadership Among the Siuai of Bougainville*, Cambridge: Harvard University Press.
Oliver, D. (1971) Southern Bougainville, in *Politics in New Guinea*, ed. R. Berndt and P. Lawrence, 276–97, Nedlands: University of Western Australia Press.
Oliver, D. (1974) *Ancient Tahitian Society*, 3 vols, Canberra: Australian National University Press.
Oppenheim, R.S. (1973) *Maori Death Customs*, Wellington: Reed.
Ortner, S. (1973) On Key Symbols *American Anthropologist*, 75, 1338–1346.
Ortner, S. (1984) Theory in Anthropology since the Sixties *Comparative Studies in Society and History*, 26, 126–66.
Otto, T. (1994) Feasting and Fighting: Rank and Power in Pre-Colonial Baluan *History and Anthropology*, 7, 223–39.
Owens, J. (1970) Religious Disputation at Whangaroa, 1823–7 *Journal of the Polynesian Society*, 79, 288–304.
Pacific Islands Monthly, Sydney to 1988, thereafter Suva.
Paini, A. (1996) Boundaries of Difference: Geographical and Social Mobility by Lifuan Women, PhD thesis, Canberra: Australian National University.
Patouillet, J. (1873) *Voyage autour du monde: trois ans en Nouvelle-Calédonie*, Paris: E. Dentu.
Patterson, G. (1882) *Missionary Life among the Cannibals, Being the Life of the Rev. John Geddie, D.D., First Missionary to the New Hebrides*, Toronto: James Campbell & Son, James Bain & Son, and Hart & Co.
Pawley, A. (1982) Rubbish-Man Commoner, Big Man Chief? Linguistic Evidence for Hereditary Chieftainship in Proto-Oceanic Society,

in *Oceanic Studies: Essays in Honour of Aarne A. Koskinen*, ed. J. Siikala, 33–52, Helsinki: Finnish Anthropological Society.
Pénard, L. (1857 [1856]) Mémoire de M. le docteur Pénard, chirugien principal de la marine, in *Documents relatifs à la Nouvelle-Calédonie*, Paris: Imprimerie impériale.
Philipp, J. (1983) Traditional historical narrative and action-oriented (or ethnographic) history *Historical Studies*, 20, 339–52.
Pigeard, C. (1846) *Voyage dans l'Océanie centrale, sur la corvette française le Bucéphale*, Paris: Arthus Bertrand.
Plauchut, E. (1878) La révolte des canaques *Revue des Deux Mondes*, 30, 672–89.
Powell, H.A. (1960) Competitive Leadership in Trobriand Political Organization *Journal of the Royal Anthropological Institute*, 90, 118–45.
Prakash, G. (1990) Writing Post-Orientalist Histories of the Third World: Perspectives from Indian Historiography *Comparative Studies in Society and History*, 32, 383–408.
Prakash, G. (1995) Introduction: After Colonialism, in *After Colonialism: Imperial Histories and Postcolonial Displacements*, ed. G. Prakash, 3–17, Princeton, NJ: Princeton University Press.
La Presse calédonienne, Nouméa.
Prochaska, D. (1990) Making Algeria French and Unmaking French Algeria *Journal of Historical Sociology* 3, 305–28.
Rafael, V. (1988) *Contracting Colonialism: Translation and Christian Conversion in Tagalog Society under Early Spanish Rule*, Ithaca, NY: Cornell University Press.
Ram, K. (1993) Too "Traditional" Once Again: some Post-Structuralists on the Aspirations of the Immigrant/Third World Female Subject *Australian Feminist Studies* 17, 5–28.
Ralston, C. (1989) Changes in the lives of ordinary women in early post-contact Hawaii, in *Family and Gender in the Pacific: Domestic Contradictions and the Colonial Impact*, ed. M. Jolly and M. Macintyre, 45–64, Cambridge: Cambridge University Press.
Ralston, C. and N. Thomas (ed.) (1987) *Sanctity and Power: Gender in Polynesian History*, special issue *Journal of Pacific History* 22(3–4).
Read, K.E. (1959) Leadership and Consensus in a New Guinea Society *American Anthropologist*, 61, 425–36.
Reformed Presbyterian Magazine, Edinburgh and Glasgow.
Reid, A.C. (1977) The Fruit of the Rewa: Oral Traditions and the Growth of the Pre-Christian Lakeba State *Journal of Pacific History* 12, 2–24.

Reynolds, H. (1982) *The Other Side of the Frontier: Aboriginal Resistance to the European Invasion of Australia*, Ringwood, Vic.: Penguin.
Reynolds, H. (1987) *Frontier: Aborigines, Settlers and Land*, Sydney: Allen & Unwin.
Rivière, H. (1881) *Souvenirs de la Nouvelle-Calédonie: l'insurrection canaque*, Paris: Calmann-Lévy.
Rivierre, J.-C. (1994) *Dictionnaire cèmuhî-français*, Paris: Peeters.
Robarts, E. (1974) *The Marquesan Journal of Edward Robarts, 1797–1824*, ed. G. Dening, Canberra: Australian National University Press.
Rochas, V. de (1860) Lecture sur les Néo-Calédoniens *Bulletin de la Société d'Anthropologie*, 1, 389–416.
Rochas, V. de (1862) *La Nouvelle-Calédonie et ses habitants: productions, mœurs, cannibalisme*, Paris: Ferdinand Sartorius.
Rogers, G. (1977) "The Father's Sister is Black": a Consideration of Female Rank and Power in Tonga *Journal of the Polynesian Society*, 86, 157–82.
Rosaldo, R. (1993 [1989]) *Culture and Truth: the Remaking of Social Analysis*, London: Routledge.
Rougeyron, P. (1846–9), Journal, 7 Sep. 1846–30 Oct. 1849, TS copy, Nouméa: Archives de l'Archevêché.
Rougeyron, P. (1928 [1874]) Du paganisme au christianisme: le chef calédonien Hippolyte Bonou (1830–1867) *Annales de Marie*, 4, 106–17, 172–86, 208–20.
Rougeyron, P. (n.d.) Abrégé de la vie de Hippolyte Bonou, chef de la tribu de Pouébo en Nouvelle-Calédonie, MS copy, Nouméa: Archives de l'Archevêché.
Routledge, D. (1985) *Matanitu: the Struggle for Power in Early Fiji*, Suva, Fiji: University of the South Pacific.
Sahlins, M. (1958) *Social Stratification in Polynesia*. Seattle: University of Washington Press.
Sahlins, M. (1963) Poor Man, Rich Man, Big Man, Chief: Political Types in Melanesia and Polynesia *Comparative Studies in Society and History*, 5, 285–303.
Sahlins, M. (1976) *Culture and Practical Reason*, Chicago: University of Chicago Press.
Sahlins, M. (1981a) *Historical Metaphors and Mythical Realities: Structure in the Early History of the Sandwich Islands Kingdom*, Ann Arbor: University of Michigan Press.
Sahlins, M. (1981b) The Stranger-King: or Dumézil Among the Fijians *Journal of Pacific History*, 16, 107–32.
Sahlins, M. (1985) *Islands of History*, Chicago: University of Chicago Press.

Sahlins, M. (1991) The return of the event, again; with reflections on the beginnings of the great Fijian war of 1843 to 1855 between the kingdoms of Bau and Rewa, in *Clio in Oceania: Toward a Historical Anthropology*, ed. A. Biersack, 37–99, Washington, DC: Smithsonian Institution Press.
Said, E. (1993) *Culture and Imperialism*, London: Chatto and Windus.
Salisbury, R.F. (1964) Despotism and Australian Administration in the New Guinea Highlands, in *New Guinea: the Central Highlands*, ed. J. Watson, special issue, *American Anthropologist*, 66(4), part 2, 225–39.
Saussol, A. (1979) *L'héritage: essai sur le problème foncier mélanésien en Nouvelle-Calédonie*, Paris: Musée de l'Homme.
Scaglion, R. (1996) Chiefly Models in Papua New Guinea *Contemporary Pacific*, 8, 1–31.
Scarr, D. (1970) Cakobau and Ma'afu: Contenders for Pre-eminence in Fiji, in *Pacific Islands Portraits*, ed. J.W. Davidson and D. Scarr, 95–126, Canberra: Australian National University Press.
Scheffler, H. (1965) *Choiseul Island Social Structure*, Berkeley: University of California Press.
Schieffelin, E. (1980) Reciprocity and the Construction of Reality *Man*, 15, 502–17.
Schneider, D. (1976) Notes Toward a Theory of Culture, in *Meaning in Anthropology*, ed. K. Basso and H. Selby, 197–220, Albuquerque: University of New Mexico Press.
Scott, J. (1991) The Evidence of Experience *Critical Enquiry*, 17, 773–97.
Seligmann, C.G. (1910) *The Melanesians of British New Guinea*. Cambridge: Cambridge University Press.
Service historique de la Marine, Paris.
Shineberg, D. (1967) *They Came for Sandalwood: a Study of the Sandalwood Trade in the South-West Pacific 1830–1865*, Carlton, Vic.: Melbourne University Press.
Slatyer, T. (1842) Journal of a voyage in the Camden from Samoa among the New Hebrides, etc. June 6th 1842, MS, Sydney: Mitchell Library.
Smith, B. (1960) *European Vision and the South Pacific 1768–1850: a Study in the History of Art and Ideas*, Oxford: Oxford University Press.
Smith, J. (1974) *Tapu Removal in Maori Religion*, Memoir 40, Wellington: Polynesian Society.
Spear, T. (1981) Oral Traditions: Whose History? *Journal of Pacific History*, 16, 133–48.

Spivak, G. (1988) Can the Subaltern Speak? in *Marxism and the Interpretation of Culture*, ed. C. Nelson and L. Grossberg, 271–313, Urbana: University of Illinois Press.

Spriggs, M. (1981) Vegetable Kingdoms: Taro Irrigation and Pacific Prehistory, PhD thesis, Canberra: Australian National University

Spriggs, M. (1984) The Lapita Cultural Complex: Origins, Distribution, Contemporaries and Successors *Journal of Pacific History*, 19, 202–23.

Spriggs, M. (1985) "A School in Every District": the Cultural Geography of Conversion on Aneityum, Southern Vanuatu *Journal of Pacific History*, 20, 23–41.

Stallworthy, G. and G. Gill (1859) Thirteenth Missionary Voyage to Western Polynesia and Savage Island *Samoan Reporter*, 20, 2–5

Standish, B. (1978) *The "Big-Man" Model Reconsidered: Power and Stratification in Chimbu*, IASER Discussion Paper 22, Boroko, PNG: Institute of Applied Social and Economic Research.

Stephen, M. (1977) *Cargo Cult Hysteria: Symptom of Despair or Technique of Ecstasy?* Occasional Paper 1, Melbourne: Research Centre for Southwest Pacific Studies, La Trobe University.

Stocking, G. (1968) *Race, Culture and Evolution: Essays in the History of Anthropology*, New York: The Free Press.

Stocking, G. (1987) *Victorian Anthropology*, New York: The Free Press.

Stoler, A. (1992) "In Cold Blood": Hierarchies of Credibility and the Politics of Colonial Narratives *Representations*, 37, 151–89.

Stoler, A. (1995) *Race and the Education of Desire: Foucault's History of Sexuality and the Colonial Order of Things*, Durham, NC: Duke University Press.

Strathern, A. (1966) Despots and Directors in the New Guinea Highlands *Man*, 1, 356–67.

Strathern, A. (1971) *The Rope of Moka: Big-Men and Ceremonial Exchange in Mount Hagen, New Guinea*, Cambridge: Cambridge University Press.

Strathern, A. (ed.) (1982) *Inequality in New Guinea Highlands Societies*, Cambridge: Cambridge University Press.

Strathern, M. (1987) Introduction, in *Dealing with Inequality: Analysing Gender Relations in Melanesia and Beyond*, ed. M. Strathern, 1–32, Cambridge: Cambridge University Press.

Strathern, M. (1988) *The Gender of the Gift: Problems with Women and Problems with Society in Melanesia*, Berkeley: University of California Press.

Strathern, M. (1991) *Partial Connections*, Savage, MD: Rowman & Littlefield.

Stuart, M. (1803) *De mensch, zoo als hij voorkomt op den bekenden aardbol*, vol. 2, Amsterdam: Johannes Allart.
Sydney Morning Herald, Sydney.
Ta'unga (1968) *The Works of Ta'unga: Records of a Polynesian Traveller in the South Seas, 1833–1896*, ed. R.G. and M. Crocombe, Canberra: Australian National University Press.
Taussig, M. (1980) *The Devil and Commodity Fetishism in South America*, Chapel Hill: University of North Carolina Press.
Taussig, M. (1993) *Mimesis and Alterity: a Particular History of the Senses*, New York: Routledge.
Tepahae, P. (1997) Interviews, 11–20 August 1997, tapes, in author's possession.
Terrell, J. (1978) Archaeology and the Origins of Social Stratification in Southern Bougainville, in *Rank and Status in Polynesia and Melanesia: Essays in Honor of Professor Douglas Oliver*, 23–43, Publications de la Société des Océanistes 39, Paris: Musée de l'Homme.
Thomas, J. [S. James] (1886) *Cannibals and Convicts: Notes of Personal Experiences in the Western Pacific*, London: Cassell.
Thomas, N. (1986) *Planets Around the Sun: Dynamics and Contradictions of the Fijian* matanitu, Sydney: Oceania Monographs.
Thomas, N. (1989a) Domestic Structures and Polyandry in the Marquesas Islands, in *Family and Gender in the Pacific: Domestic Contradictions and the Colonial Impact*, ed. M. Jolly and M. Macintyre, 65–83, Cambridge: Cambridge University Press.
Thomas, N. (1989b) The Force of Ethnology: Origins and Significance of the Melanesia/Polynesia Division *Current Anthropology*, 30, 27–41.
Thomas, N. (1990a) *Marquesan Societies: Inequality and Political Transformation in Eastern Polynesia*, Oxford: Clarendon Press.
Thomas, N. (1990b) Partial Texts: Representation, Colonialism and Agency in Pacific History *Journal of Pacific History*, 25, 139–58.
Thomas, N. (1992a) Colonial Conversions: Difference, Hierarchy, and History in Early Twentieth-Century Evangelical Propaganda *Comparative Studies in Society and History*, 34, 366–89.
Thomas, N. (1992b) The Inversion of Tradition *American Ethnologist*, 19, 213–32.
Thomas, N. (1992c) Review of G. White (1991) *Identity Through History: Living Stories in a Solomon Islands Society*, Cambridge: Cambridge University Press, *Man*, 27, 925–6.
Thomas, N. (1994a) *Colonialism's Culture: Anthropology, Travel and Government*, Cambridge: Polity Press.

Thomas, N. (1994b) Kingship and Hierarchy: Transformations of Politics and Ritual in Eastern Oceania *History and Anthropology*, 7, 109–31.

Thurnwald, R. (1934) Pigs and Currency in Buin: Observations About Primitive Standards of Value and Economics *Oceania*, 5, 119–41.

Tjibaou, J.-M. (1976) Recherche d'identité mélanésienne et société traditionnelle *Journal de la Société des Océanistes*, 53, 281–92.

Tjibaou, J.-M. (1981) Etre Mélanésien aujourd'hui *Esprit*, 57, 81–93.

Tjibaou, J.-M. (1996a [1977]) Interview with M. Degorce-Dumas, in J.-M. Tjibaou, *La présence kanak*, ed. A. Bensa and E. Wittersheim, 35–45, Paris: Editions Odile Jacob.

Tjibaou, J.-M. (1996b [1981]) Interview with J. Chesneaux, in J.-M. Tjibaou, *La présence kanak*, ed. A. Bensa and E. Wittersheim, 117–22, Paris: Editions Odile Jacob.

Tjibaou, J.-M., P. Missotte, M. Folco and C. Rives (1976) *Kanaké, Mélanésien de Nouvelle-Calédonie*, Papeete, Tahiti: Editions du Pacifique.

Tonkinson, R. (1981) Church and *Kastom* in Southeast Ambrym, in *Vanuatu: Politics, Economics and Ritual in Island Melanesia*, ed. M. Allen, 237–67, Sydney: Academic Press.

Tonkinson, R. (1982) Kastom in Melanesia: Introduction *Mankind*, 13, 302–305.

Torgovnick, M. (1990) *Gone Primitive: Savage Intellects, Modern Lives*, Chicago: University of Chicago Press.

Trolue, F. and J. Caihe (1995) Vers l'éveil d'un peuple *Journal de la Société des Océanistes*, 100–1, 153–64.

Turner, G. (1842–3) Journal, 19 Dec. 1842–Mar. 1843, MS, London Missionary Society, South Seas Journals 134, London: Congregational Council for World Mission.

Turner, G. (1845) First Missionary Voyage of the "John Williams" to the New Hebrides and New Caledonia Groups under the Superintendance [sic] of Mess. Murray and Turner *Samoan Reporter*, 2, 2–4.

Turner, G. (1861) *Nineteen Years in Polynesia: Missionary Life, Travels, and Researches in the Islands of the Pacific*, London: John Snow.

Turner, V. (1967) *The Forest of Symbols: Aspects of Ndembu Ritual*, Ithaca, NY: Cornell University Press.

Turner, V. (1974a [1969]) *The Ritual Process: Structure and Anti-Structure*, Harmondsworth, Middlesex: Penguin.

Turner, V. (1974b) *Dramas, Fields and Metaphors: Symbolic Action in Human Society*, Ithaca, NY: Cornell University Press.

Turner, V. (1975) *Revelation and Divination in Ndembu Ritual*, Ithaca, NY: Cornell University Press.
Turner, V. (1977) Variations on a Theme of Liminality, in *Secular Ritual*, ed. S. Falk Moore and B. Myerhoff, 36–52, Assen: van Gorcum.
Union Calédonienne (1980) *Travaux du XIe Congrès, Nouméa, 29–30–31 août 1980*, Nouméa: Imprimerie Graphoprint.
Valentine, C.A. (1963) Social Status, Political Power, and Native Responses to European Influence in Oceania *Anthropological Forum*, 1, 3–55.
Valeri, V. (1985) *Kingship and Sacrifice: Ritual and Society in Ancient Hawaii*, tr. Paula Wissing, Chicago and London: University of Chicago Press.
Ve'ehala and Tupou Posesi Fanua (1977) Oral Tradition and Prehistory, in *Friendly Islands: a History of Tonga*, ed. N. Rutherford, 27–39, Melbourne: Oxford University Press.
Verguet, C. (1854) *Histoire de la première mission catholique au vicariat de Mélanésie*, Carcassonne: P. Labau.
Vicedom, G. and H. Tischner (1943–48) *Die Mwowamb*, 3 vols, Hamburg: Cram, de Gruyter & Co.
Vieillard, E. and E. Deplanche (1863) *Essais sur la Nouvelle-Calédonie*, Paris: Librairie Challamel aîné.
Vigors, P. (1850) Private Journal of a Four Month's Cruise Through Some of the "South Seas Islands", and New Zealand in H.M.S. "Havannah", TS copy, Auckland: Library of the Auckland Institute and Museum.
Vincent, J.-B. (1895) *Les canaques de la Nouvelle-Calédonie: esquisse ethnographique*, Paris: A. Challamel.
Vinson, L.-P.-E. (1975 [1858]) Eléments d'une topographie médicale de la Nouvelle-Calédonie et de l'Ile des Pins *Bulletin de la Société d'Etudes Historiques de la Nouvelle-Calédonie* 22, 7–32; 23, 5–26.
Wallis, M. (1994) *The Fiji and New Caledonia Journals of Mary Wallis, 1851–1853*, ed. D. Routledge, Suva, Fiji: Institute of Pacific Studies and Salem, MA.: Peabody Essex Museum.
Ward, A. (1982) *Land and Politics in New Caledonia*, Canberra: Department of Political and Social Change, Australian National University.
Warry, W. (1987) *Chuave Politics: Changing Patterns of Leadership in the Papua New Guinea Highlands*, Canberra: Department of Political and Social Change, Australian National University.
Watson, J. (1971) Tairora: the Politics of Despotism in a Small Society, in *Politics in New Guinea*, ed. R. Berndt and P. Lawrence, 224–75, Nedlands: University of Western Australia Press.

White, G. and J. Kirkpatrick (ed.) (1985) *Person, Self, and Experience: Exploring Pacific Ethnopsychologies*, Berkeley: University of California Press.

White, G. and L. Lindstrom (ed.) (1997) *Chiefs Today: Traditional Pacific Leadership and the Postcolonial State*, Stanford: Stanford University Press.

White, H. (1978) *Tropics of Discourse: Essays in Cultural Criticism* Baltimore: Johns Hopkins University Press.

White, H. (1987) *The Content of the Form: Narrative Discourse and Historical Representation*, Baltimore: Johns Hopkins University Press.

Widlok, T. (1992) Practice, Politics and Ideology of the "Travelling Business" in Aboriginal Religion *Oceania*, 63, 114–36.

Williams, F.E. (1936) *Papuans of the Trans-Fly*, Oxford: Clarendon Press.

Williams, F.E. (1940) *Drama of Orokolo: the Social and Ceremonial Life of the Elema*, Oxford: Clarendon Press.

Winiata, M. (1956) Leadership in Pre-European Maori Society *Journal of the Polynesian Society*, 65, 212–31.

Young, M. (1971) *Fighting With Food: Leadership, Values and Social Control in a Massim Society*, Cambridge: Cambridge University Press.

Young, M. (1983a) *Magicians of Manumanua: Living Myth in Kalauna*, Berkeley: University of California Press.

Young, M. (1983b) The Massim: an Introduction *Journal of Pacific History*, 18, 4–10.

Young, M. (1994) From Riches to Rags: Dismantling Hierarchy in Kalauna *History and Anthropology*, 7, 263–78.

Index

Adams, Ron 229, 257, 259
Agency
  concept of 19–21, 72–3, 161, 168, 186–7, 225, 286, 293, 295–6
  indigenous 3, 14, 20–1, 135, 150–2, 167–8, 170–1, 185–7, 195, 206–7, 210–17, 235, 257, 281, 288, 314, 317
  indigenous women 114–120
Allen, Michael 65
Aneityum (Vanuatu) 227–31, 233–44
  "conversion" to Christianity 235–40
  epidemics 237, 242, 282
    measles, 1861 241–2
  indigenous aetiology 233, 235–9
    and Christianity 238–42, 244, 256
  indigenous political systems 228
  itap ("taboo") 234, 260
  natmas ("dead body", "spirit") 234–40, 260
  relationships with spirits
    autonomous spirits 233, 256
    sorcery 233–4, 240
  religion cf. Tanna 233, 235, 239, 241, 244, 256
Anthropology
  and history 8, 11–14
  and reflexivity 11
  colonial ethnography 124

culture concept, critique of 10, 13
ethnographic present 4, 8, 20, 161, 265
ethnographic voice 170
ethnography as dialogue 10, 12, 82
feminist 18
French 11–13
historical ethnography 123–5, 135
missionary ethnography 265–8
politics of language 175–6
structural-functionalist 3, 4
teleology 8, 20
Antipositivism 15–19
  and pluralism 19, 165–8, 251, 296
Apitéèngen/Apengou of Wagap 164, 165–72, 189, 301
Appropriation, indigenous 21, 161, 171, 225, 285
  of Christianity 229, 246, 250–1, 254, 281, 286, 288, 298–300, 307–12, 314, 316, 318
Aréki of Tom 197, 201, 208
Ataï of La Foa 197, 201, 208, 209, 212–13

Barriol, Father Eugène 169–70, 183–5
Barthes, Roland 16–17, 21, 176
Belich, James 158, 205, 218
Bensa, Alban 11–13, 163, 165, 170, 175, 177–9, 186, 189
"Big man" leadership 41–5

351

heredity in 44
Bonou, Hippolyte, of Pouébo 289–97, 312–13
Boula, Henri Wahemuneme 70, 79–82, 86–8, 94, 96
Boon, James 10
Bott, Elizabeth 64
Bougainville (PNG), indigenous leadership 42, 45
Brunton, Ron 66

Chartier, Roger 16, 161
"Chieftainship"
  colonial impact on 39
  complex Polynesian hierarchies 58–61
  correlation with Austronesian language 5, 24, 46
  in New Caledonia, Fiji and Polynesia 49–61
  in western and central Melanesia 45–9
  Polynesian 32
  postcolonial, in Melanesia 31
  postcolonial, in western Polynesia and Fiji 31
  precolonial, in Melanesia 39–40
  sacred 49–50
Christianity
  "conversion" as indigenisation 229, 244, 253, 309–11, 314
  and power 237–9, 257, 260, 280–1, 296, 307–9, 311, 318
  indigenous encounters with 225–314
Class, in complex Polynesian hierarchies 58–60
Clifford, James 10, 25
Collingwood, R.G. 11
  anti-objectivist philosophy of history 2, 16
Colonial categories, critique of 114–20, 135, 148–50, 156, 164, 178, 182–7, 190, 195–200, 207, 230–1, 257
Comaroff, Jean and John 316, 317
Cosmologies and aetiologies
  indigenous 229, 244, 258, 266–74, 301, 303–5
  missionary 229–30, 239, 241, 266–7, 279–80, 287–8, 290, 296, 298, 304–6
Custom
  definition 110
  New Caledonia (la coutume) 73–109
  Tanna (Vanuatu, kastom) 243–4

Dani (Irian Jaya), indigenous leadership 44
Deductive reasoning, critique of 35–9
Dening, Greg 11, 14, 23, 31, 263
Douarre, Bishop Guillaume 115–17, 132–4, 137, 139, 265, 275–6
Dousset-Leenhardt, Roselène 148, 200
Durand, Lt-Colonel Jean 168–73, 181, 183–4

Empiricism
  radical/critical 16, 22
  unreflective 2–8
Essentialism, critique of 7–8, 10–14, 29–30, 89, 161
Ethnohistory 15

Fabian, Johannes 191
"Fatal impact", critique of concept 19
Festival of Pacific Arts, 4th 75, 81, 96, 102–3
Fighting, indigenous Kanak 124–44
  against Europeans 140–4, 245
  alliances 129–30, 138–40, 171, 197
  alliances with French 143–4, 171

and gender 114–21
cf. European 130–4
cf. New Guinea 127
colonial representations of 125–44
innovations in 143, 296–7
norms and values 127–40, 153–4
reciprocity 136–40, 141–2
   vengeance 132–3, 137–40, 245
restraint in 134–6, 141–2, 280
and women 118–19, 121
rhetoric in 135, 153–4
rhythm in 126, 131, 139–40
ritual in 131, 135, 138, 140, 297
tactics 130, 133, 140–4, 157
violence in 131, 139, 199
women in 114–17, 120–1
Firth, Raymond 48

Gagnière, Father Matthieu 267–70, 291–2, 305, 317
Garnier, Jules 173–5, 182–3, 185
Geddie, Rev. John 224, 229–30, 233–44, 253, 259
Geertz, Clifford 4, 23
Gender
elision of 29, 113–20
"traditional" relations romanticised 120
Godelier, Maurice 32
Goldman, Irving 38
Gondou 172–3, 182, 190
Goujon, Father Prosper 229–30, 246–57
Guha, Ranajit 16, 21, 163, 176–9, 189
Guiart, Jean 249–51, 308–9, 316
Guillain, Governor Charles 313, 317
Gunson, Niel 31–2

Heider, Karl 44
Historical realism
conventional 16, 17
qualified 17
tension with textualisation

and reflexivity 18, 226, 256
History
and anthropology 8, 11–14, 163
and fiction 16
and texts 14–21, 124, 161–3, 223–4
and the present 2, 8, 11, 124, 161, 175, 223
and the state 187–8
antipositivist 11, 15–19, 161–3, 223
colonial, Europe decentred 15, 148, 161–3, 165–8, 185–7, 191, 251, 294–6
ethnographic 193
"Melbourne Group" 3–4, 11, 23
indigenous 161–3
inductive method 3, 17
"Island-centred" 14, 19
and Anthropology 3
Canberra school 2–3
military 27, 194
narrative 17
oral 15, 165, 175
outcomes and causation 8, 14, 19–20, 151, 186–7, 194
positivist/objectivist 2, 5, 163, 165–8
"postcolonial" 17–21
cf. anticolonial 185–7, 251
theoretical eclecticism 13

Ideology
and ritual 72
as strategy 70, 82–3
Inequality in Melanesia
anthropological interest in 32–3, 37
precolonial social stratification 45, 65
Inglis, Rev. John 259, 260, 282, 318
Isle of Pines (New Caledonia) 227–31, 244–55
"conversion" to Christianity 254–5
du ("evil spirit") 247–53, 261
epidemics 247

measles, 1860–1 255
indigenous aetiology 247–51, 256–7
and Christianity 255, 261
indigenous political systems 228
missionaries (Polynesian) as sorcerers 245–7, 250
"our customs" 246, 252–3
relationships with spirits
sorcery 245–52
Star massacre 244–6

Jackson, Michael 5, 16, 315–16
James, Stanley 149, 150, 212, 217

Kahoua of Poyes 165, 168–75, 179–83, 190
"Kanak", as term of reference 24, 70, 155
Kapferer, Bruce 104–5
Keesing, Roger 10, 228, 318
Knauft, Bruce 135
Kuindo of Kabwa 198

Lambert, Father Pierre 134, 138, 140, 267–70, 293, 305
Langer, Susanne 104–5
Language
and radical critique 176–9
politics of 21–2, 175–9
tropes 176
use of tenses 11, 164, 175–6, 178–9, 265
Lawrence, Peter 225, 227, 259
Leadership, indigenous Pacific 29–67
age as criterion in 43–4
big men 41–5
changing interpretations of 29–33
hereditary 45–61
ideology and practice 47–8, 51–3, 61–2
New Caledonia 76–9
New Caledonia, Fiji and Polynesia 49–61
Polynesian/Melanesian dichotomy 5, 29–39, 50, 56–7
popular sanctions on 32, 44, 47–8, 52, 56, 315
power as relative attribute of 49, 53
rank and power 55–6, 57–61
western and central Melanesia 39–49
Leenhardt, Maurice 9, 11–13, 24–5

Macintyre, Martha 18, 66
Mani, Lata 191
Manus (PNG), indigenous leadership 43, 66
Maohi (Society Islands), indigenous leadership 59–60
Maori (New Zealand/Aotearoa), indigenous leadership 53–6, 67
Marcus, George 23, 32, 64
Marquesas, indigenous leadership 58
Matheson, Rev. John 242–3
Meggitt, Mervyn 66, 225, 227
Meijl, Toon van 67
Mekeo (PNG) indigenous leadership 33, 48–9
"Melanesian", as term of reference 70
Melpa (Western Highlands, PNG), indigenous leadership 43, 65
Missionary strategies
alliance with chiefs 167, 291, 302
analogy with indigenous beliefs and rituals 239, 252, 268, 289, 305–6, 282, 317
force 254–5, 296–7, 299
humanism, paternalism cf. race 317–18
promise of salvation 229–30, 237, 239–40, 244
prudence 229–30, 247

separation of Christians 277, 300–1
threat of damnation 229–30, 232–3, 234–5, 246–7, 318
Myerhoff, Barbara 73, 99

Naïna of Fonwhary 119, 197, 201, 208, 209, 212
Naouno of Bourail 211, 214–15, 221
Narrative 17
  colonial cf. ethnographic cf. indigenous 167–8, 170–1, 175, 177–9, 293–6
New Caledonia (see also Fighting, indigenous Kanak; Isle of Pines)
  Catholic missionaries 125, 164, 264, 282
    complicity with colonial agenda 169–70, 183–5, 190–1, 254–5, 296–7, 314
    humanism, paternalism cf. race 317–18
    Kanak subversion of 288, 298–301, 314
    opposition to colonial agenda 313
    regarded as sorcerers 273–4, 301, 303–4
  chiefs 70–109
    alliance with missionaries 167–8, 254, 289–97
  colonial control, limitations to 148, 164, 189, 195, 219, 288
  colonial fighting 144–221
    ambiguous outcomes 152, 215–17
    arduousness for French 152, 201, 206, 210, 215, 221
    attrition as French strategy 147–8, 152, 205–10
    cf. New Zealand/Aotearoa 158, 205, 218
    comparative military arithmetic 150, 200–3, 209–10, 220
    French dependence on indigenous allies 149, 152, 206, 210, 215
    French military values 147, 156
    French strategy and tactics 147–9, 204–15
    indigenous allies (of the French) 144–5, 148–9, 173, 201–3, 206, 210–17, 313
    Kanak coalitions 146, 164–5, 171–2, 197, 299, 312
    Kanak disadvantages 144, 150, 199, 202–5, 215
    Kanak innovations 145–6
    Kanak strategy and tactics 144–7, 150–4, 157–9, 197–211
    magic as Kanak tactic 154
    modern fighting 152–4
    reciprocity as Kanak value in 146
    representations of Kanak in 150–2, 156, 181–3, 197–217
    restraint as Kanak value and tactic 150, 153–4, 158, 214
    violence as Kanak tactic 150, 198–200
  "Wagap affair" 165–86
  wars of 1878–9 118–19, 145–52, 194–221
  women in 118–19, 213
colonialism 74
  and Catholic missionaries 169–70, 183–4, 190, 313, 317
  and racism 317
  cf. British 317
  complacency re Kanak 195
  executions 170, 183–5
  expropriations 169, 185, 195, 215–16
  internal fractures 207, 313
  Kanak strategies 195

military posts 169, 183–4, 204, 207–9
"conversion" to Christianity 277–81, 289, 296–7, 302, 305, 308–11
Council of High Chiefs 91–5, 102, 107
custom (*la coutume*) 73–109
custom and class 107
custom and development 109
custom and politics 76, 79–80, 92, 98, 100–1, 107, 109
Custom Councils 109, 110, 114
endemic diseases 277
   tuberculosis 278–9, 283, 287
epidemics 264–7, 275–7, 283, 287
   measles, 1860–1 277, 280, 303–6
festivals, customary 75–6, 100–2
gender 113–20
independence movement 74–5, 107
indigenous aetiology 267–74, 293–5
   and Christianity 271–80, 287, 289, 297–312
   cf. missionary 266–7, 301–5
indigenous ambivalence re Christianity 273–80, 290–314
indigenous cf. colonial values 76–80
indigenous histories 165, 190–1, 293–6
indigenous leadership 35, 51–3, 76–9
   constraints on chiefly authority 52–3, 168, 251–4, 291–6, 315
indigenous leadership cf. Maori 53–6
indigenous marriage
   colonial representations of 116–20
   female agency in 116–20
indigenous political systems 77, 128–9

indigenous politics 126–40, 165–83, 251–2, 289–97
indigenous relationships with spirits 268–312
   and missionaries 271–80, 289, 294–5
   autonomous spirits 268–73, 293–5, 306–9
   "power" as "efficacy" 306–9, 311
   sorcery 265, 269–71, 282, 303–6
   taboo 269
indigenous religion 265–76, 282
   appropriation of heaven 310–11
   appropriation of hell 265, 279, 298–300, 309–10
indigenous women 113–20, 316
Lifou (Loyalty Islands) 74–6, 81–108
Loyalty Islands 74
modern political parties 111
punitive expeditions, French 142–3, 169–73
women's movement 114
Nisbet, Rev. Henry 230–3, 259
Nohoat of Anelcauhat 236
Nondo of Canala 201, 202–3, 205, 212–15

Oliver, Douglas
   leadership in south Bougainville 42–3, 44, 45, 63–5, 66
   rank and power in ancient Tahiti 58–60
Olry, Governor Jean 195
Oppositional reasoning, critique of 69
   ascribed/achieved leadership 35, 54–5, 61–4
   chief/big man 29–49
   ideology/practice 5, 10, 12, 62–3, 72
   Manichaean antinomies 290 301–2, 316

Polynesian/Melanesian 5, 7–8, 24, 29–39, 50
resistance/collaboration 24, 154, 158
structure/action 5, 257
structure/communitas 72, 97
violence/non-violence 154
winning/losing 194, 215–17
Otto, Ton 66

Paton, Rev. John 232, 242
Patouillet, Jules 6, 115, 119–20
Personhood, theories of 32–3
Poindi Patchili 172, 182, 185
Polynesian missionaries 115, 244–7, 260, 315
Postcolonial
critique 17, 161–3, 186–7
definition 18–19
Primitivism
critique of 19, 190, 200–1
trope of "savage" 126, 127–8, 134, 150, 157, 190, 200, 205, 207–9, 216–17, 273
and class 272–3

Race
assumption of Polynesian superiority, critique of 5–6, 24
central tenet of colonialism 317
concept naturalised 29, 37
decentred as critical strategy 5–6
missionary ambivalence about 306
Reciprocity
concept of 136–7
indigenous expectation of Europeans 141–2, 146, 272–4
indigenous relationships with spirits 233, 246, 249, 272–3, 307
Recursion 319–21
Reflexivity 6–7, 13, 17–18, 114, 187, 285, 295–6, 306

Relativism
indigenous cf. missionaries 301, 316
spectre of for positivists 18
Representations
politics of 13, 17–22, 179–83, 291–2, 296
visual cf. written 175
Reynolds, Henry 317
Ritual
and fighting 131
customary performances in 88–90
exchanges in 83–8, 90
form and performance 69, 83–90, 99–107
humour in 105–6
ideology and emotion 89–90, 103
indigenous 225, 227, 268–71, 301
"nonce" 99–100
relationships with spirits 225, 227, 229–312
secular 73, 99
sorcery 259
structure and communitas 72–73, 97, 101–7
Rivière, Commander Henri 195, 207–15, 221
Rivierre, Jean-Claude 163, 165, 170, 175, 177–9, 186, 189, 190
Rochas, Victor de 24, 121, 133–4, 157, 271
Rougeyron, Father Pierre 183–4, 264–74, 277–80, 291–3, 298–300

Sahlins, Marshall 5, 65
Pacific leadership 35–39, 62
structural history 9–10, 31–3
the "Melanesian big-man" 37, 41
the "Polynesian chief" 37
Saussol, Alain 148, 151, 185–6, 190–1, 200, 206
Servan, Lt-Commander Adéa 212, 221

Social and cultural change
  agency, appropriation and
    indigenisation 14, 281, 285
  and ritual 10, 69, 103–7
  in New Caledonia 9
  need to theorise 4
  theories of
    Bensa, Alban cf. Leenhardt,
      Maurice 11–12
    Geertz, Clifford 4
    practice-oriented 5, 23
    Sahlins, Marshall 9–10
Stoler, Ann 321
Strathern, Andrew 43–5, 65
Strathern, Marilyn 32–3, 319, 321

Ta'unga 115, 126, 131, 132, 230,
  245–6, 250, 260–1
Tadinan, Louis, of Balade 278
Tanna (Vanuatu) 227–33
  ambivalence re Christianity 233,
    242–4
  epidemics 230, 232–3
    measles, 1861 242
  indigenous aetiology 231–2, 239, 256
  indigenous political systems 228
  missionaries as sorcerers 232–3
  "our conduct"/*kastom* 243–4
  relationships with spirits
    controlled spirits 231, 256
    sorcery 231–3, 242
  religion cf. Aneityum 235, 239,
    241, 244, 256
  taboo 259
Taussig, Michael 315
Teleology, critique of 19–20, 151,
  193–4
Tepahae, Philip 121, 260
Terrell, John 66
Texts, colonial
  critique of 6, 18, 124–5, 162,
    178–83, 264
  definition 23

ethnohistorical exploitation
  of 6, 14–17, 21, 124–5, 132, 162,
  187, 189, 281
indigenous presence in
  14–15, 126, 162, 168, 172, 186, 189,
  286–8, 293
Texts, missionary 283
  critique of 265
  ethnohistorical value 223–4, 264
  rationalist prejudices against 224
Thomas, Nicholas 31–2, 58
Thurnwald, Richard 45, 66
Tikopia (Solomon Islands),
  indigenous leadership 48–9
Tjibaou, Jean-Marie 85–6, 89, 91–4,
  98–9, 106, 110, 111
Tonga, indigenous leadership 60–6
Touru of Kounié (Isle of Pines)
  244–6, 251–2
Tradition
  definition 110
  "invention" of 10, 89
  politics of 12
Trobriands (PNG), indigenous
  leadership 46–7, 66
Turner, Rev. George 230–3, 259
Turner, Victor 5, 72, 89, 97

Valentine, Charles 38, 43
Valeri, Valerio 233, 259
Vendegou of Kounié (Isle of Pines)
  247, 249, 251–4, 261
Vicedom, Georg 45, 63, 66

Wahuzue, Franck 76, 79–80, 91–2,
  94, 102, 110–11
Wahuzue, Noël 79–80, 81, 86–8, 98,
  102
Wallis, Mary 134–5, 155, 282, 283
White, Hayden 16, 17

Young, Michael 47–8, 66